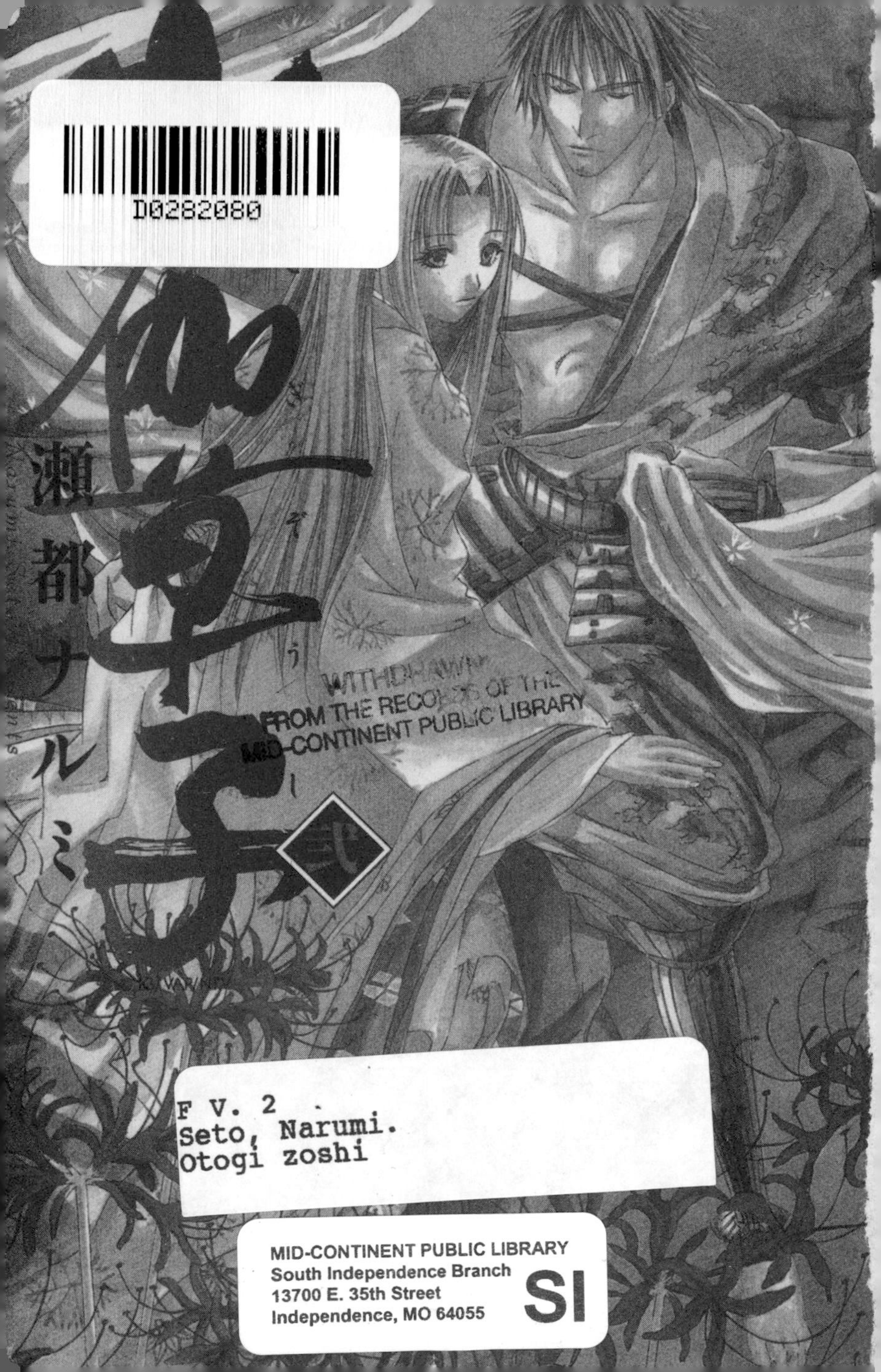

瀬都ナルミ
弐

Otogi Zoshi Vol. 2
created by Narumi Seto

Translation - Adrienne Beck
English Adaptation - Jim Alexander
Copy Editor - Sarah Morgan
Retouch and Lettering - Gloria Wu
Production Artist - Bowen Park
Cover Design - John Lo

Editor - Carol Fox
Digital Imaging Manager - Chris Buford
Pre-press Supervisor - Erika Terriquez
Art Director - Anne Marie Horne
Managing Editor - Vy Nguyen
Production Manager - Elisabeth Brizzi
Editor-in-Chief - Rob Tokar
VP of Production - Ron Klamert
Publisher - Mike Kiley
President and C.O.O. - John Parker
C.E.O. and Chief Creative Officer - Stuart Levy

A **TOKYOPOP** Manga

TOKYOPOP Inc.
5900 Wilshire Blvd. Suite 2000
Los Angeles, CA 90036

E-mail: info@TOKYOPOP.com
Come visit us online at www.TOKYOPOP.com

ISBN: 1-59816-504-6

First TOKYOPOP printing: November 2006
10 9 8 7 6 5 4 3 2 1
Printed in the USA

VOLUME 2

BY NARUMI SETO

HAMBURG // LONDON // LOS ANGELES // TOKYO

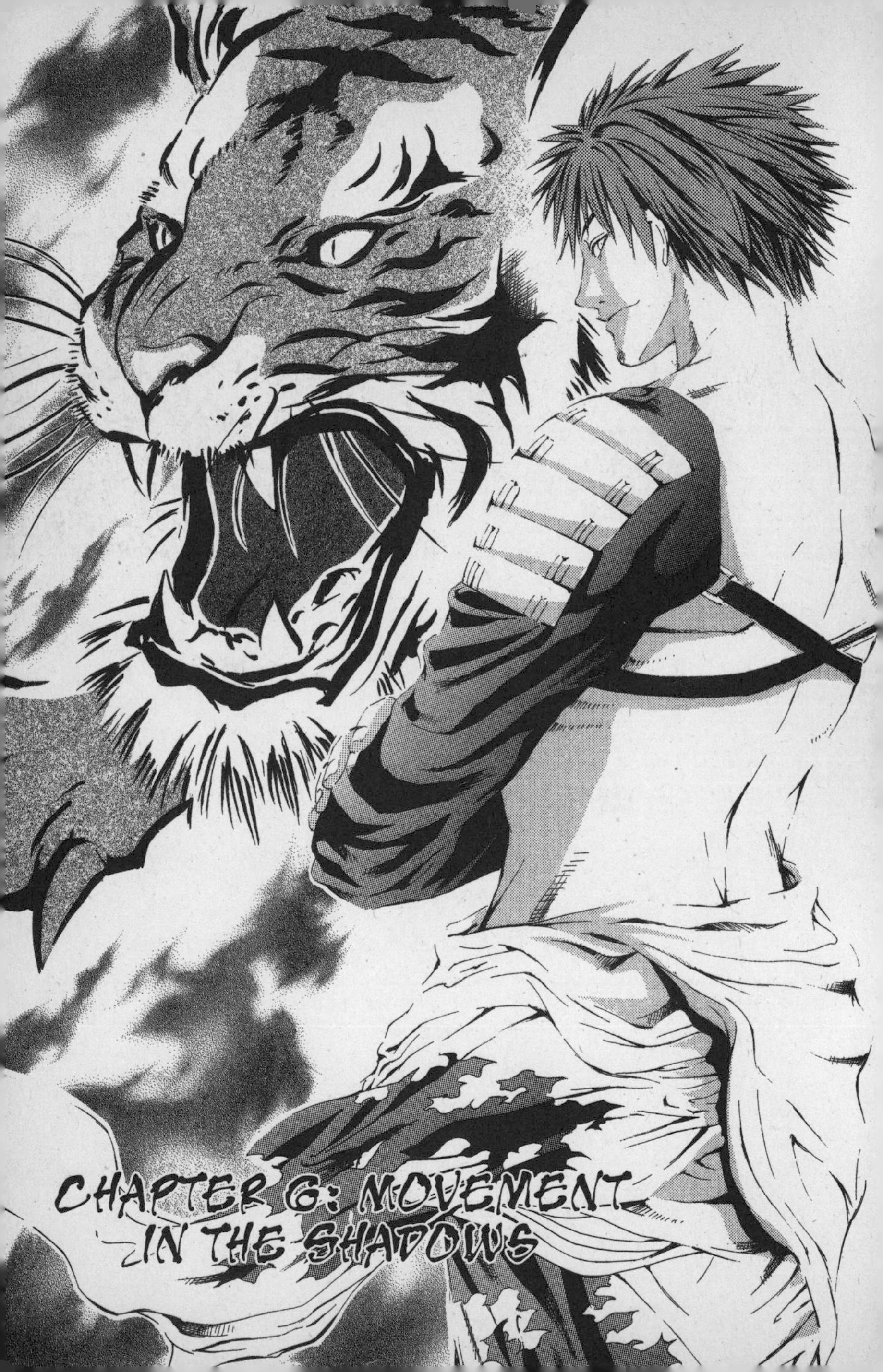
CHAPTER 6: MOVEMENT
IN THE SHADOWS

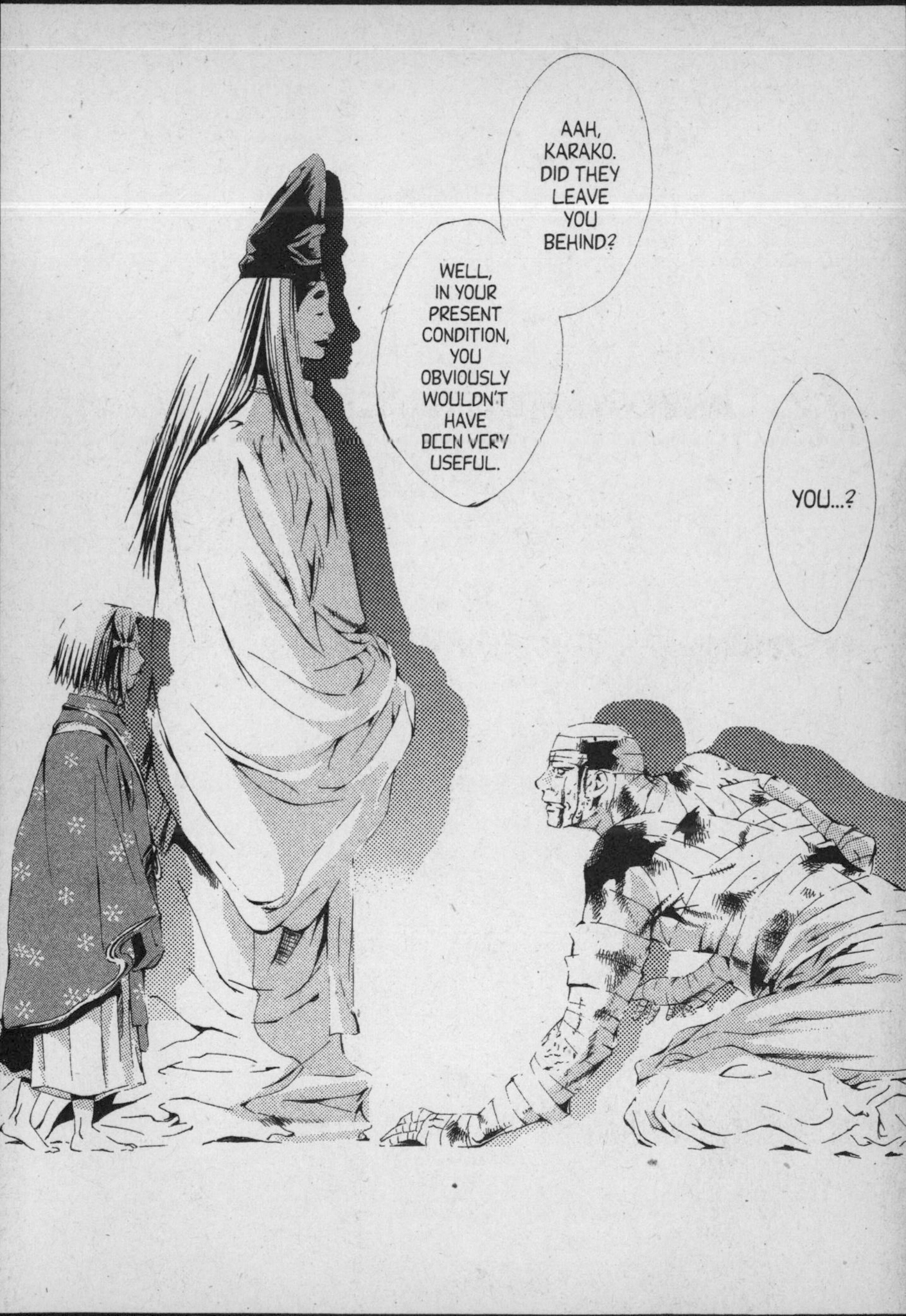
AAH, KARAKO. DID THEY LEAVE YOU BEHIND?
WELL, IN YOUR PRESENT CONDITION, YOU OBVIOUSLY WOULDN'T HAVE BEEN VERY USEFUL.
YOU...?

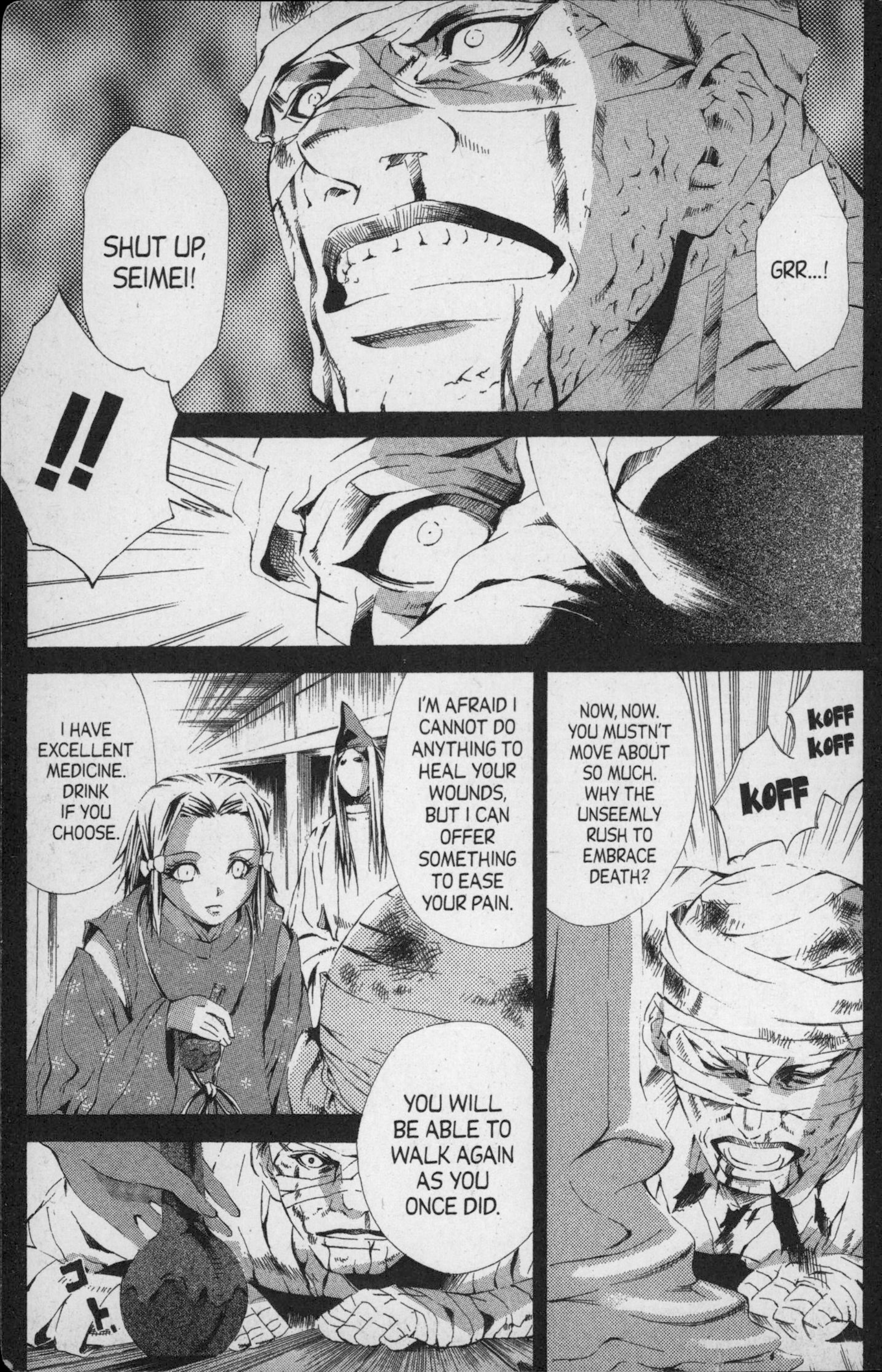
GRR...!
SHUT UP, SEIMEI!
!!
KOFF KOFF
KOFF
NOW, NOW. YOU MUSTN'T MOVE ABOUT SO MUCH. WHY THE UNSEEMLY RUSH TO EMBRACE DEATH?
I'M AFRAID I CANNOT DO ANYTHING TO HEAL YOUR WOUNDS, BUT I CAN OFFER SOMETHING TO EASE YOUR PAIN.
I HAVE EXCELLENT MEDICINE. DRINK IF YOU CHOOSE.
YOU WILL BE ABLE TO WALK AGAIN AS YOU ONCE DID.
コト

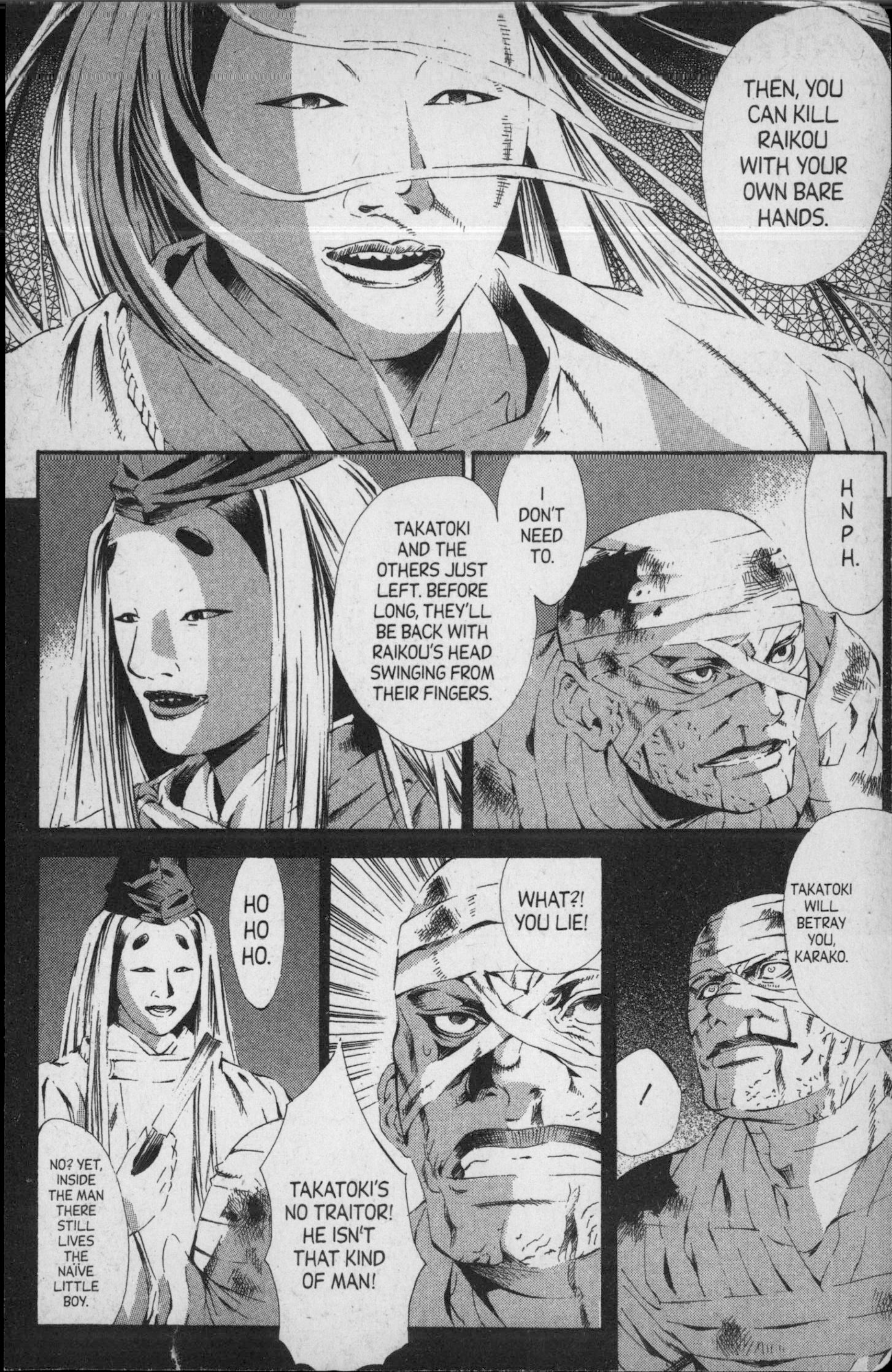
THEN, YOU CAN KILL RAIKOU WITH YOUR OWN BARE HANDS.
HNPH.
I DON'T NEED TO.
TAKATOKI AND THE OTHERS JUST LEFT. BEFORE LONG, THEY'LL BE BACK WITH RAIKOU'S HEAD SWINGING FROM THEIR FINGERS.
TAKATOKI WILL BETRAY YOU, KARAKO.
!
WHAT?! YOU LIE!
TAKATOKI'S NO TRAITOR! HE ISN'T THAT KIND OF MAN!
HO HO HO.
NO? YET, INSIDE THE MAN THERE STILL LIVES THE NAÏVE LITTLE BOY.

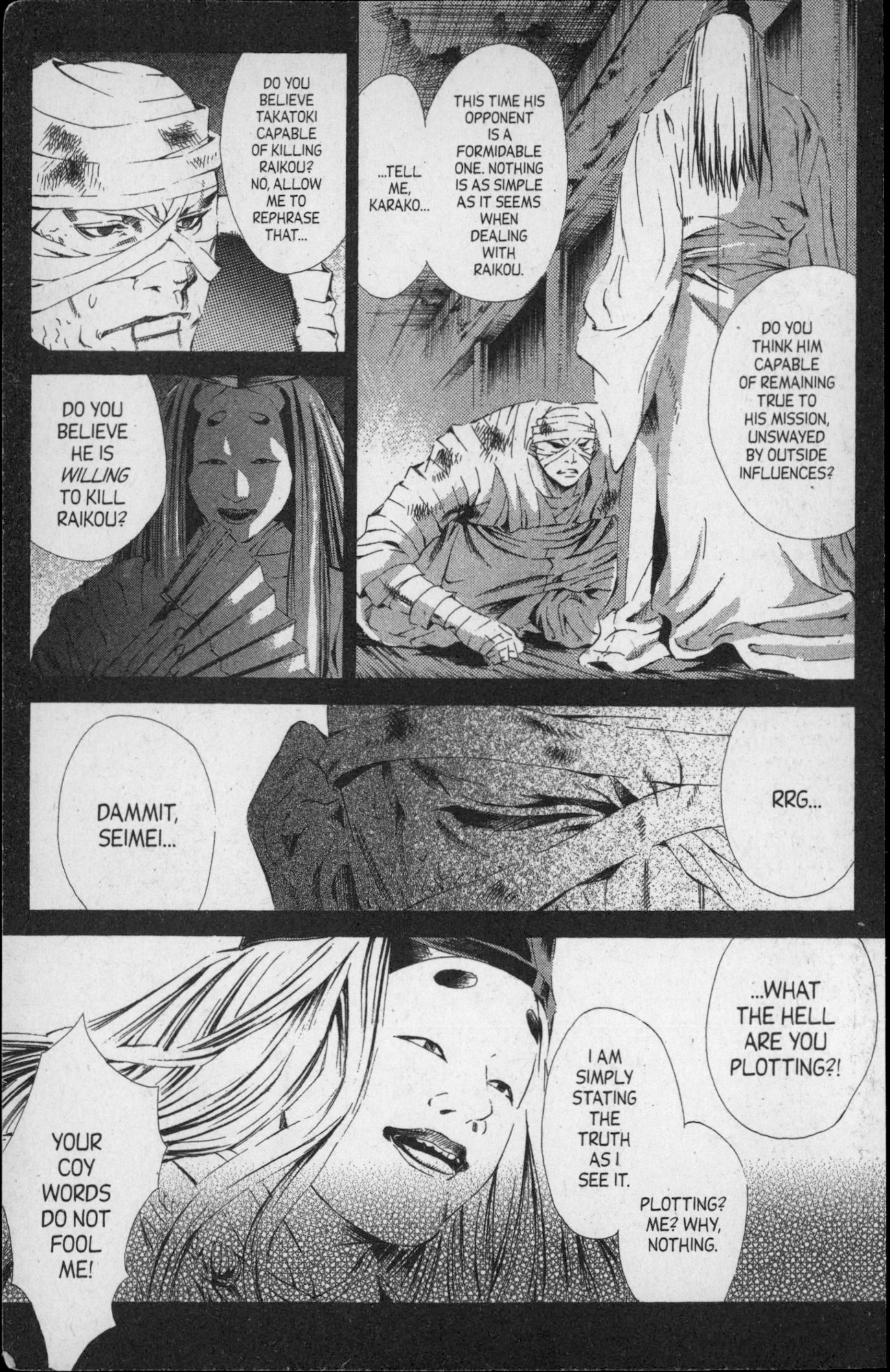
THIS TIME HIS OPPONENT IS A FORMIDABLE ONE. NOTHING IS AS SIMPLE AS IT SEEMS WHEN DEALING WITH RAIKOU.
...TELL ME, KARAKO...
DO YOU BELIEVE TAKATOKI CAPABLE OF KILLING RAIKOU? NO, ALLOW ME TO REPHRASE THAT...
DO YOU BELIEVE HE IS *WILLING* TO KILL RAIKOU?
DO YOU THINK HIM CAPABLE OF REMAINING TRUE TO HIS MISSION, UNSWAYED BY OUTSIDE INFLUENCES?
RRG...
DAMMIT, SEIMEI...
...WHAT THE HELL ARE YOU PLOTTING?!
I AM SIMPLY STATING THE TRUTH AS I SEE IT.
PLOTTING? ME? WHY, NOTHING.
YOUR COY WORDS DO NOT FOOL ME!

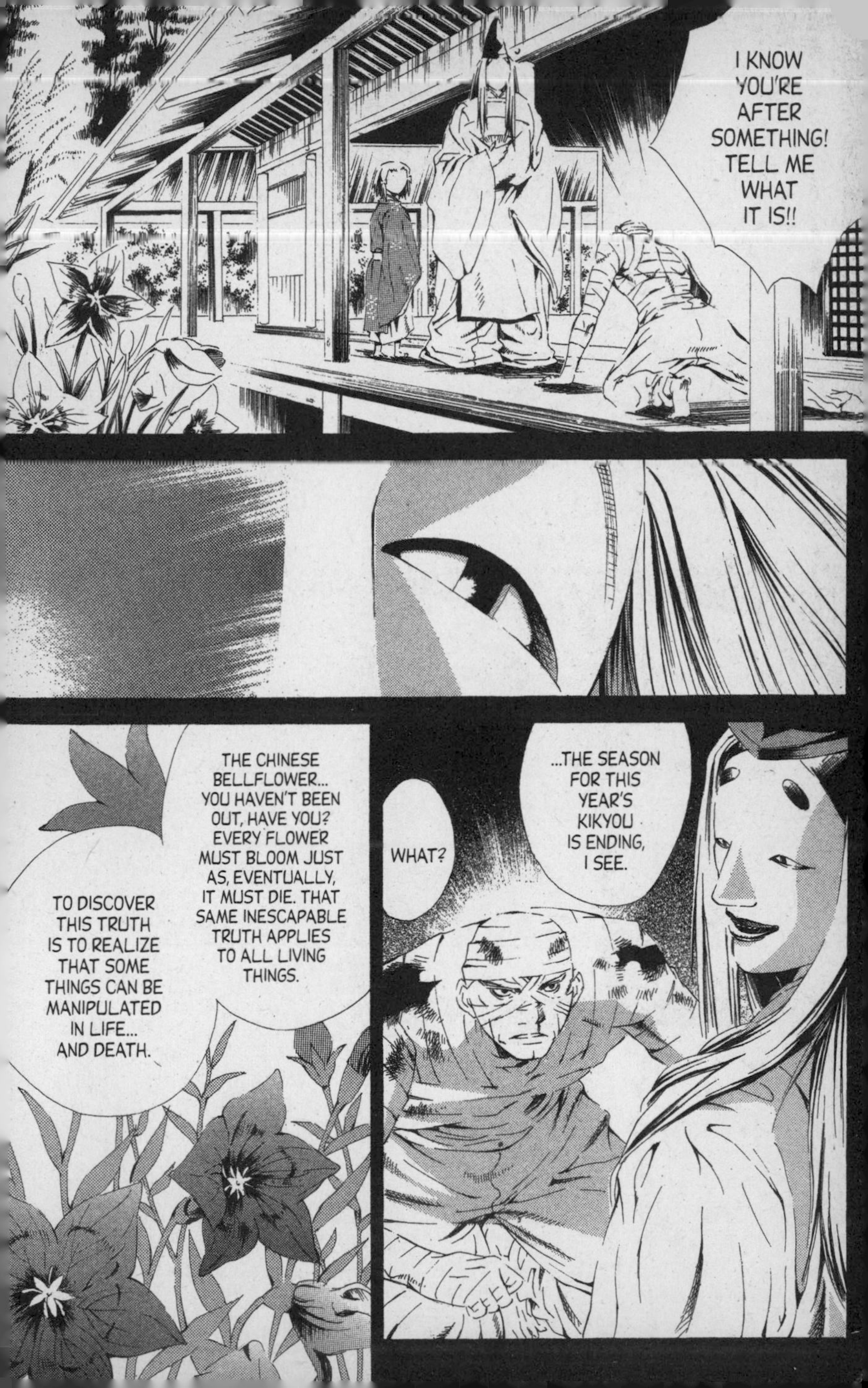
I KNOW YOU'RE AFTER SOMETHING! TELL ME WHAT IT IS!!
...THE SEASON FOR THIS YEAR'S KIKYOU IS ENDING, I SEE.
WHAT?
THE CHINESE BELLFLOWER... YOU HAVEN'T BEEN OUT, HAVE YOU? EVERY FLOWER MUST BLOOM JUST AS, EVENTUALLY, IT MUST DIE. THAT SAME INESCAPABLE TRUTH APPLIES TO ALL LIVING THINGS.
TO DISCOVER THIS TRUTH IS TO REALIZE THAT SOME THINGS CAN BE MANIPULATED IN LIFE... AND DEATH.

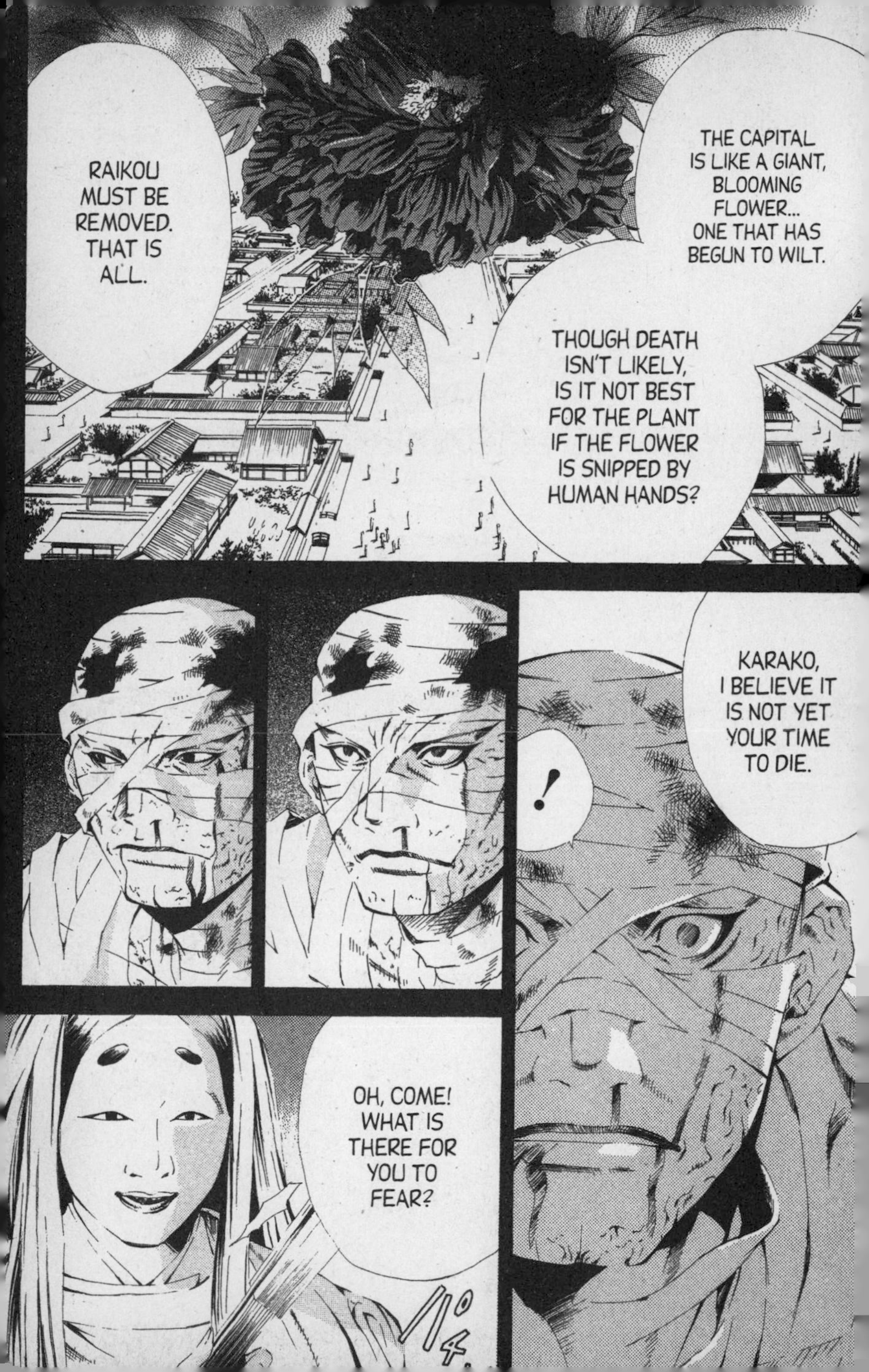
THE CAPITAL IS LIKE A GIANT, BLOOMING FLOWER... ONE THAT HAS BEGUN TO WILT.
THOUGH DEATH ISN'T LIKELY, IS IT NOT BEST FOR THE PLANT IF THE FLOWER IS SNIPPED BY HUMAN HANDS?
RAIKOU MUST BE REMOVED. THAT IS ALL.
KARAKO, I BELIEVE IT IS NOT YET YOUR TIME TO DIE.
!
OH, COME! WHAT IS THERE FOR YOU TO FEAR?

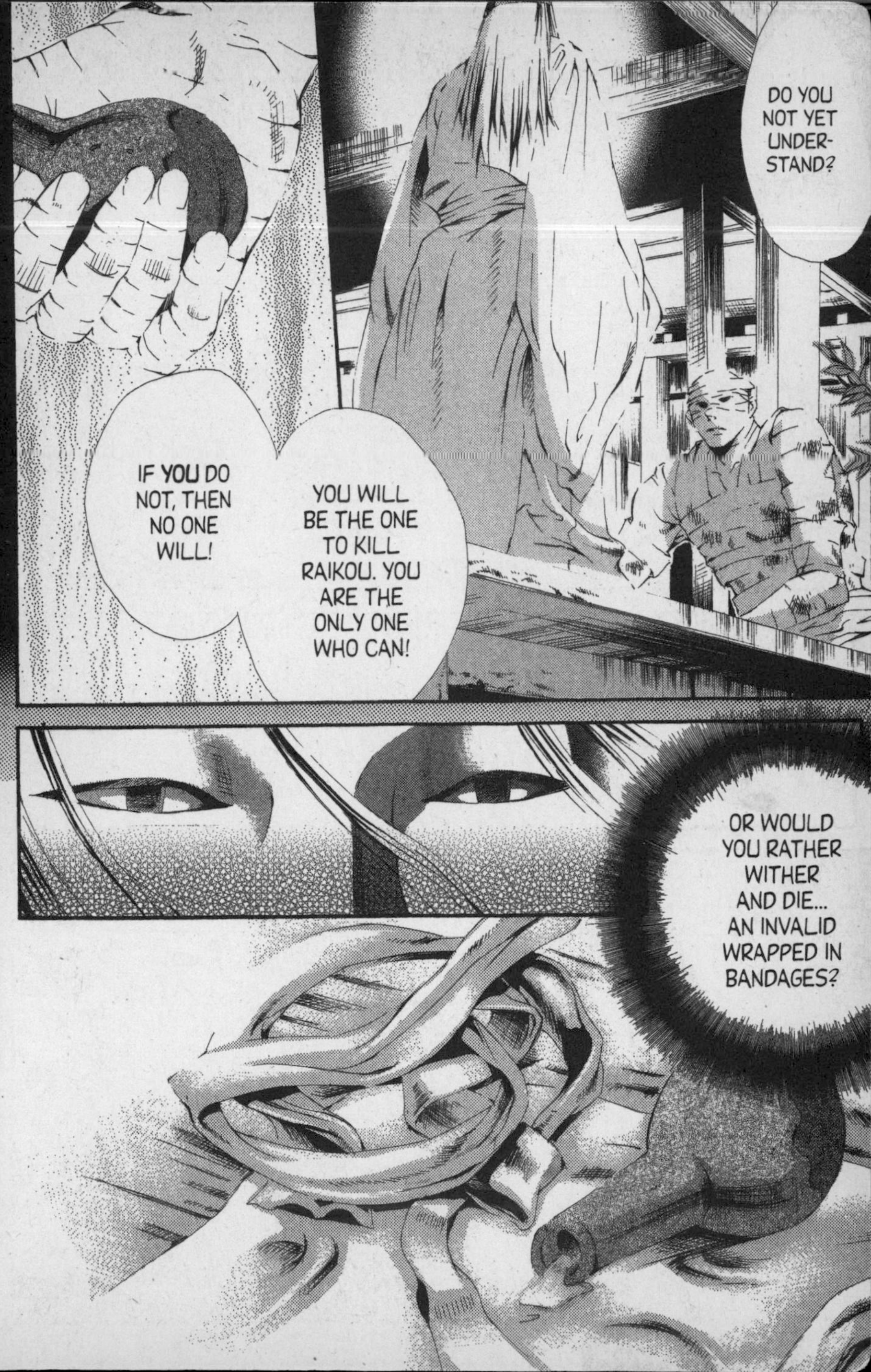
DO YOU NOT YET UNDER-STAND?
YOU WILL BE THE ONE TO KILL RAIKOU. YOU ARE THE ONLY ONE WHO CAN!
IF YOU DO NOT, THEN NO ONE WILL!
OR WOULD YOU RATHER WITHER AND DIE... AN INVALID WRAPPED IN BANDAGES?

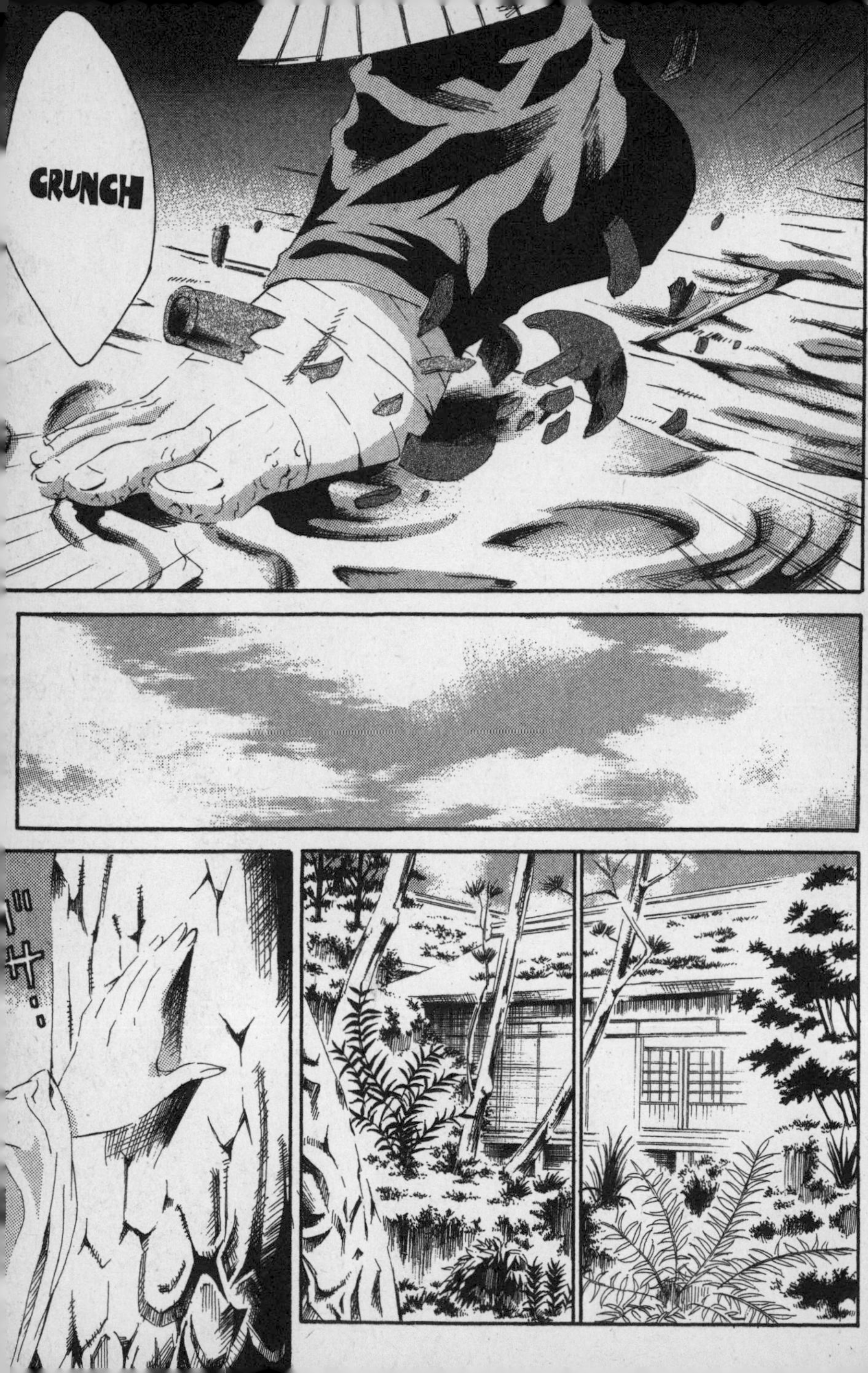
CRUNCH

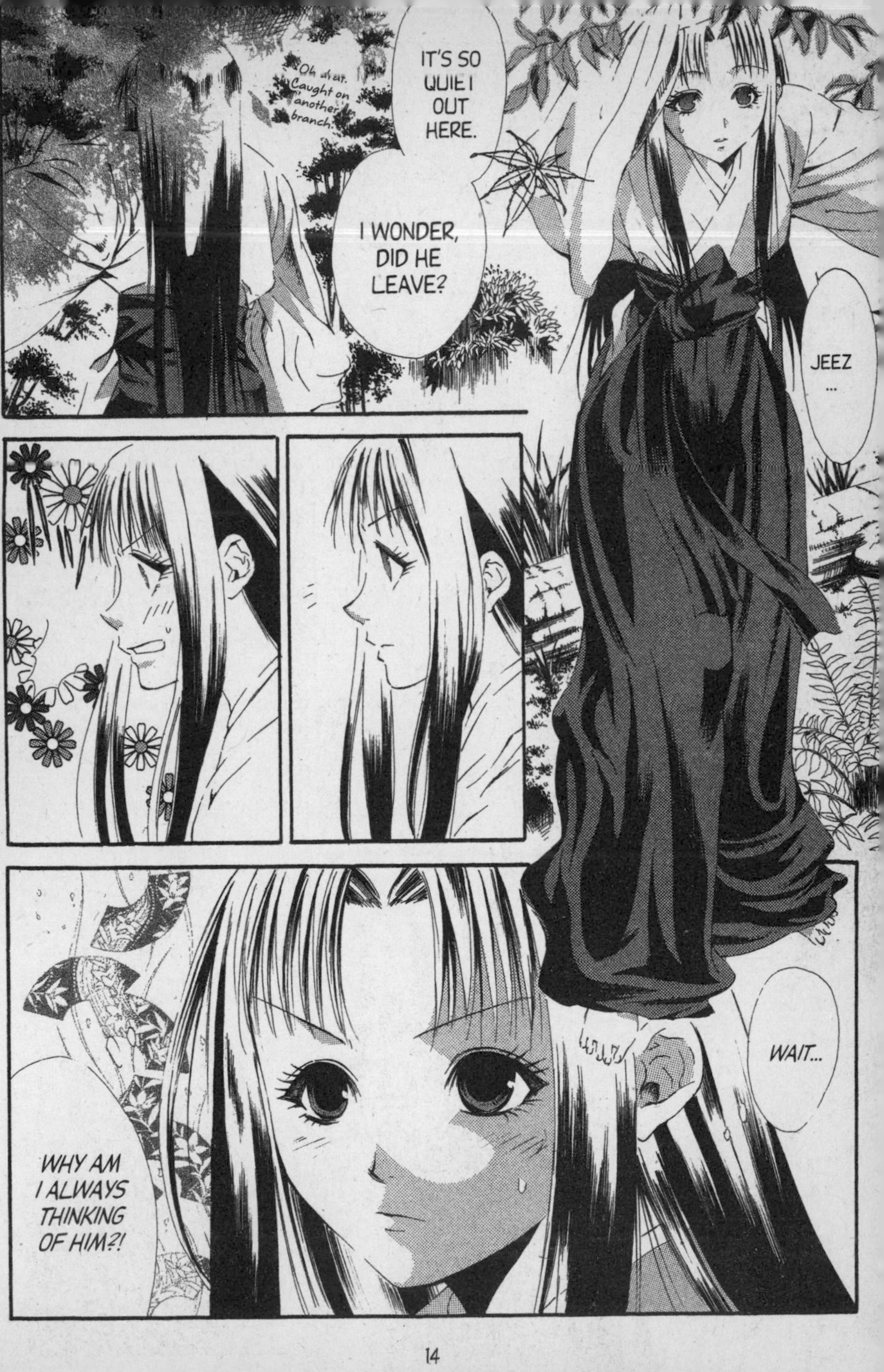
Caught on another branch.
IT'S SO QUIET OUT HERE.
I WONDER, DID HE LEAVE?
JEEZ ...
WAIT...
WHY AM I ALWAYS THINKING OF HIM?!

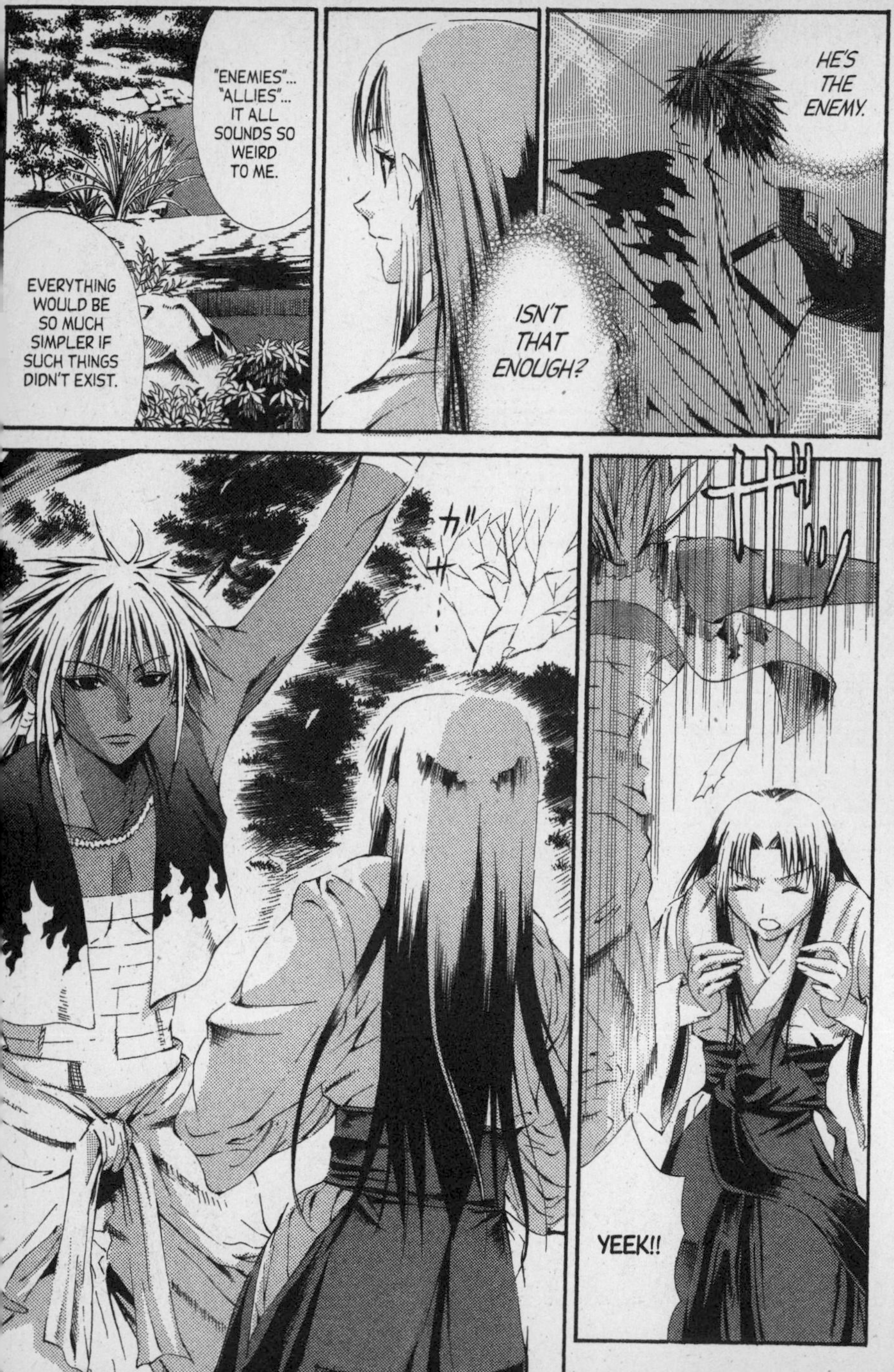
HE'S THE ENEMY.
ISN'T THAT ENOUGH?
"ENEMIES"... "ALLIES"... IT ALL SOUNDS SO WEIRD TO ME.
EVERYTHING WOULD BE SO MUCH SIMPLER IF SUCH THINGS DIDN'T EXIST.
YEEK!!

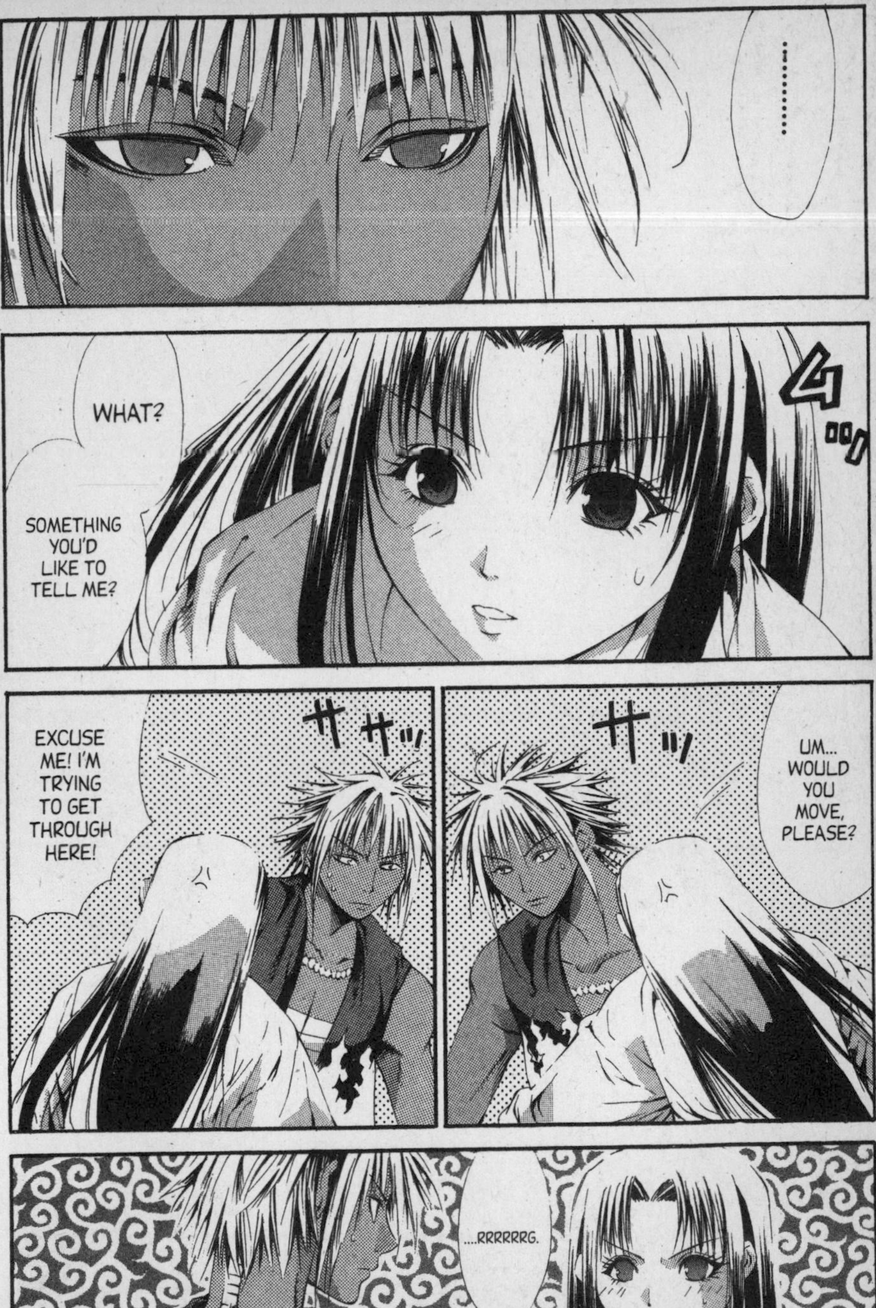
......
WHAT?
SOMETHING YOU'D LIKE TO TELL ME?
UM... WOULD YOU MOVE, PLEASE?
EXCUSE ME! I'M TRYING TO GET THROUGH HERE!
....RRRRRRG.

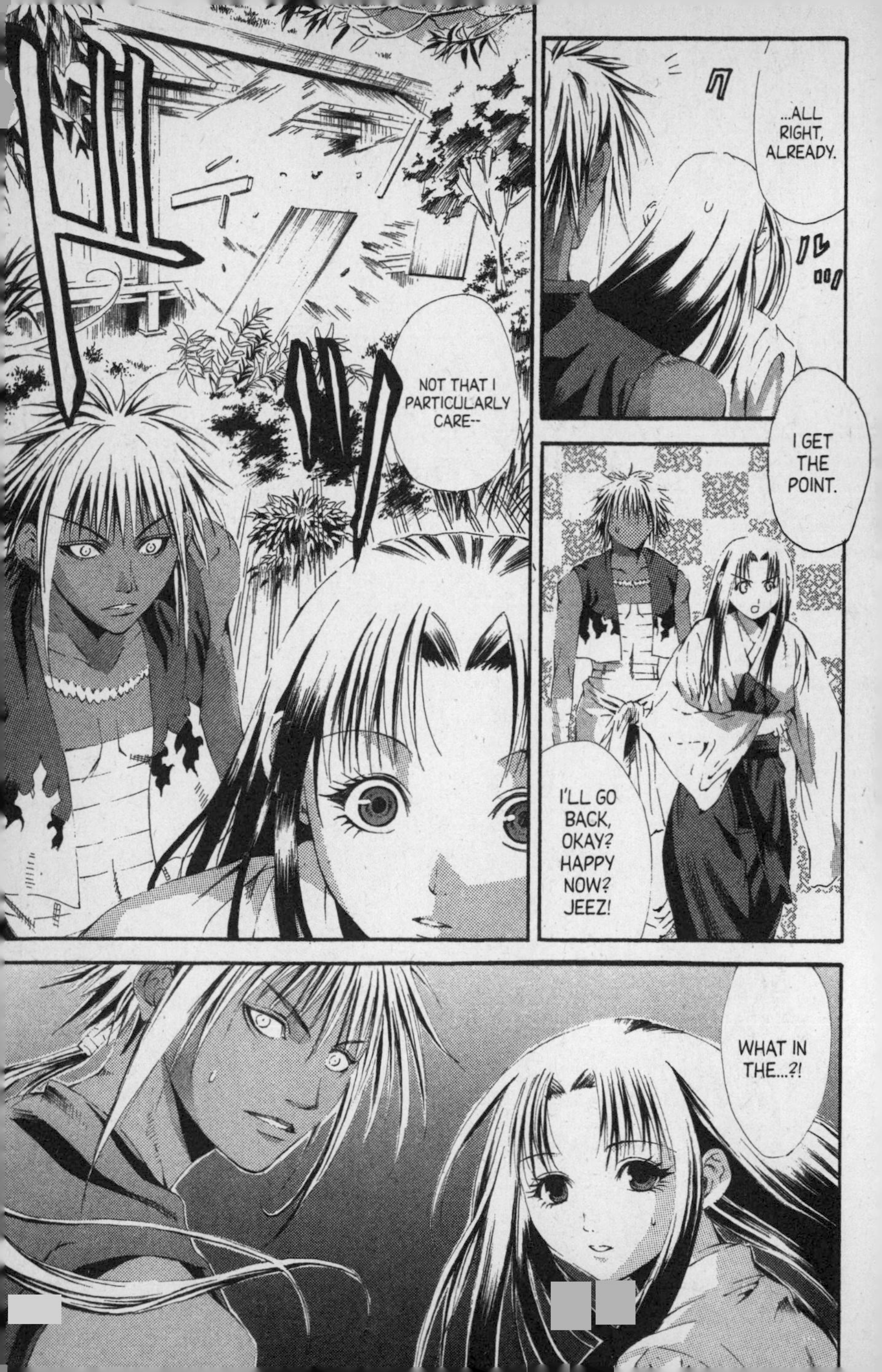
...ALL RIGHT, ALREADY.
I GET THE POINT.
I'LL GO BACK, OKAY? HAPPY NOW? JEEZ!
NOT THAT I PARTICULARLY CARE--
WHAT IN THE...?!

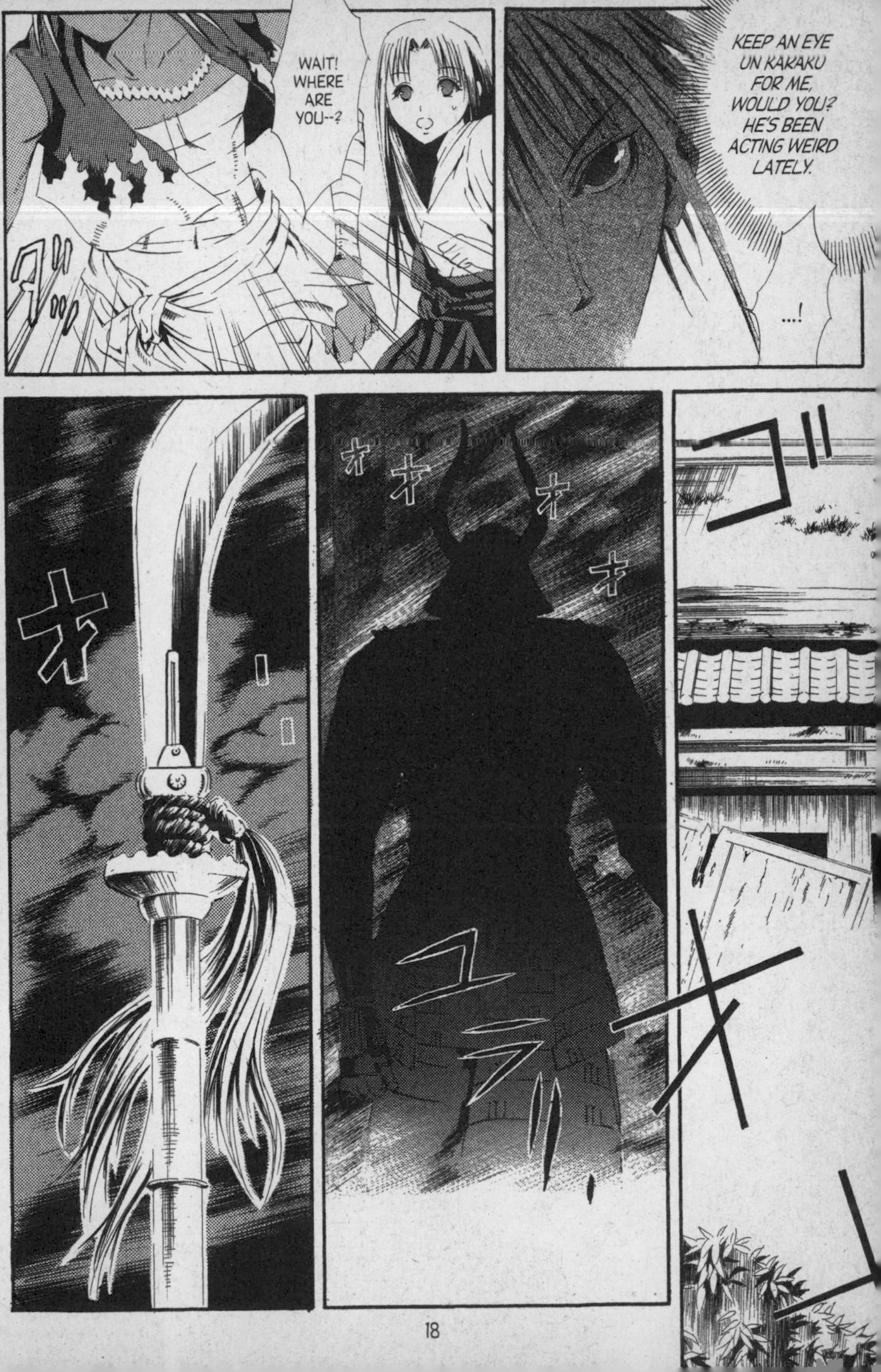
KEEP AN EYE UN KAKAKU FOR ME, WOULD YOU? HE'S BEEN ACTING WEIRD LATELY.
...!
WAIT! WHERE ARE YOU--?

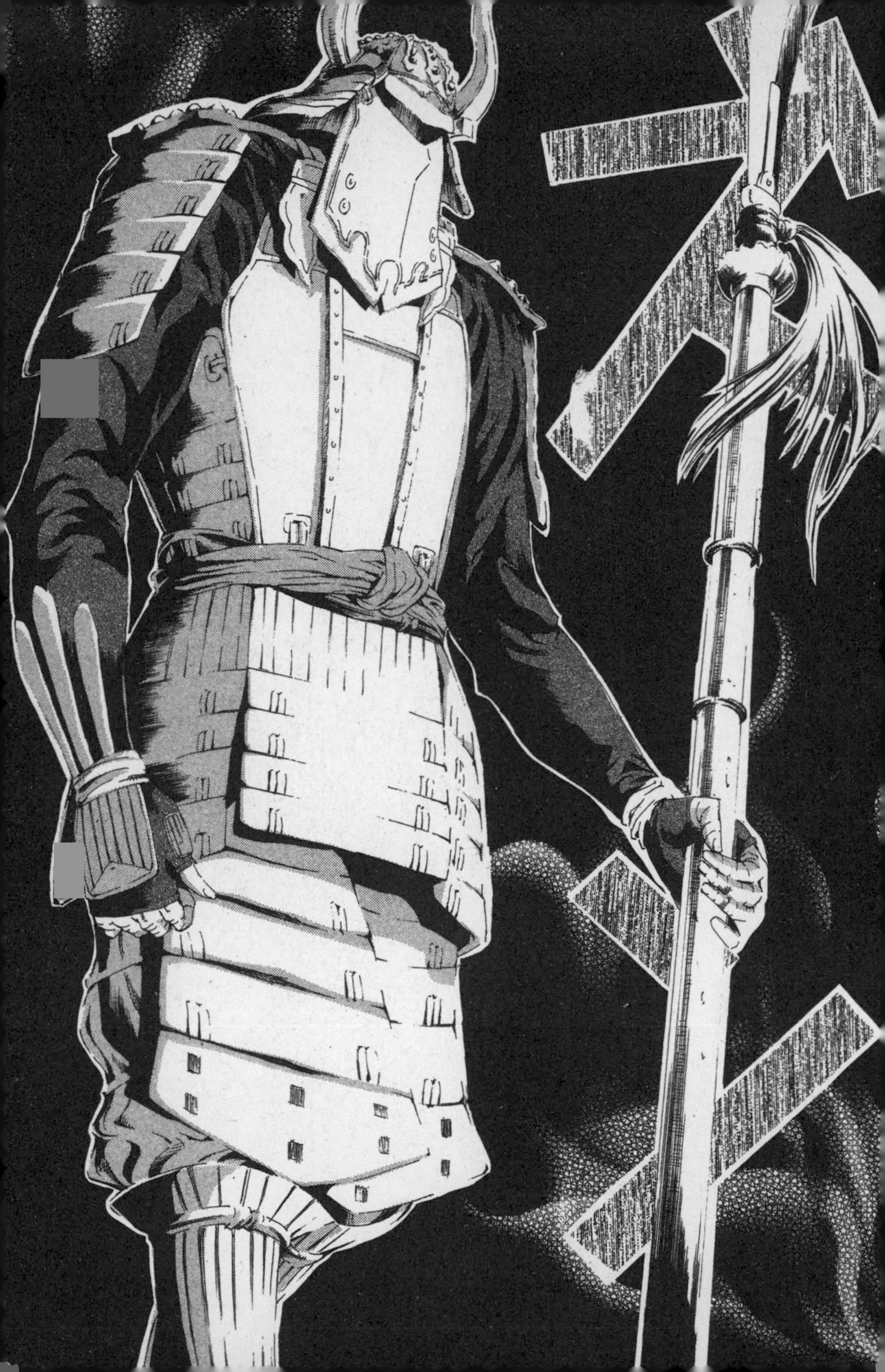

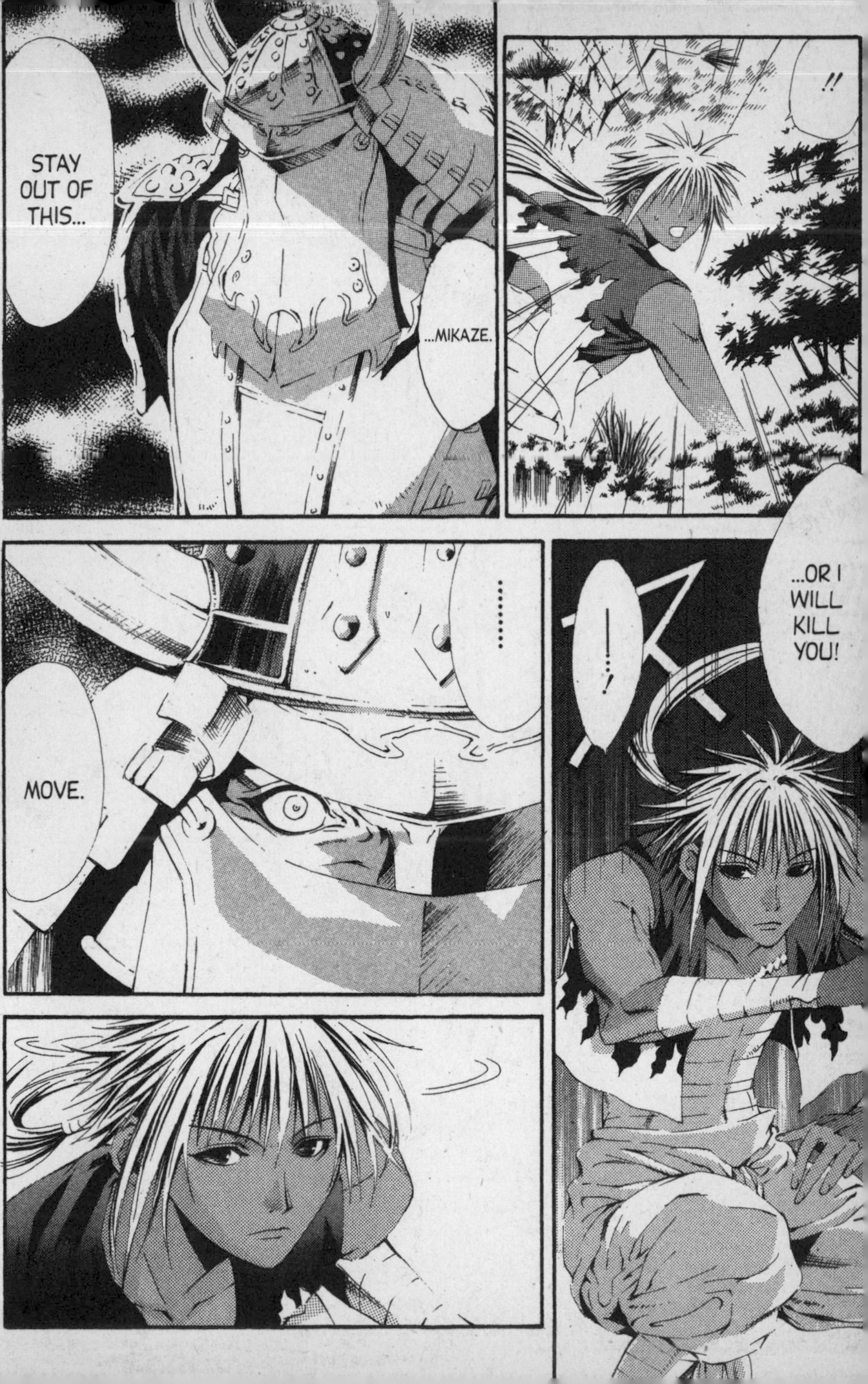
!!
STAY OUT OF THIS...
...MIKAZE.
...OR I WILL KILL YOU!
......
—...!
MOVE.

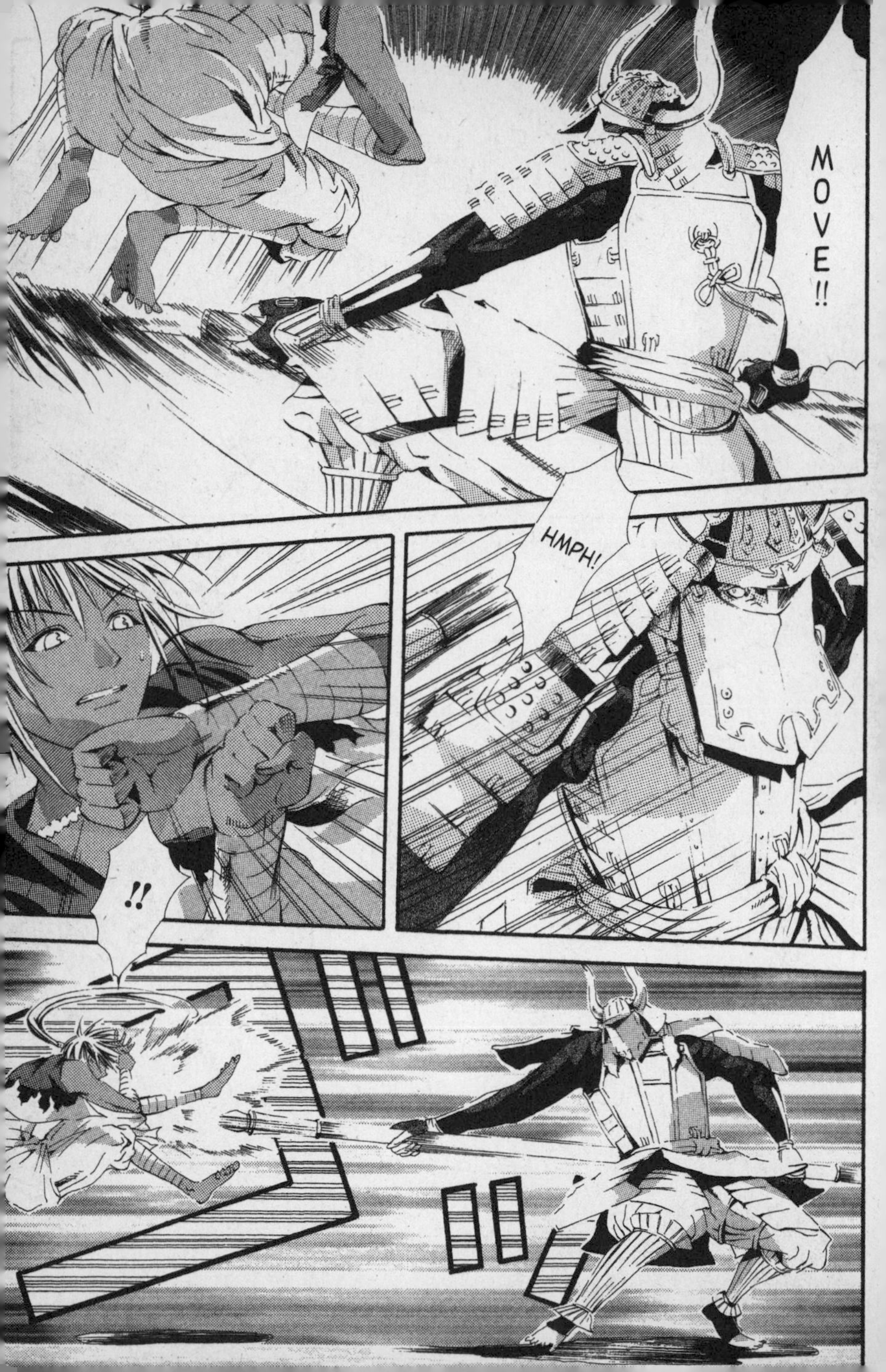
MOVE!!
HMPH!
!!

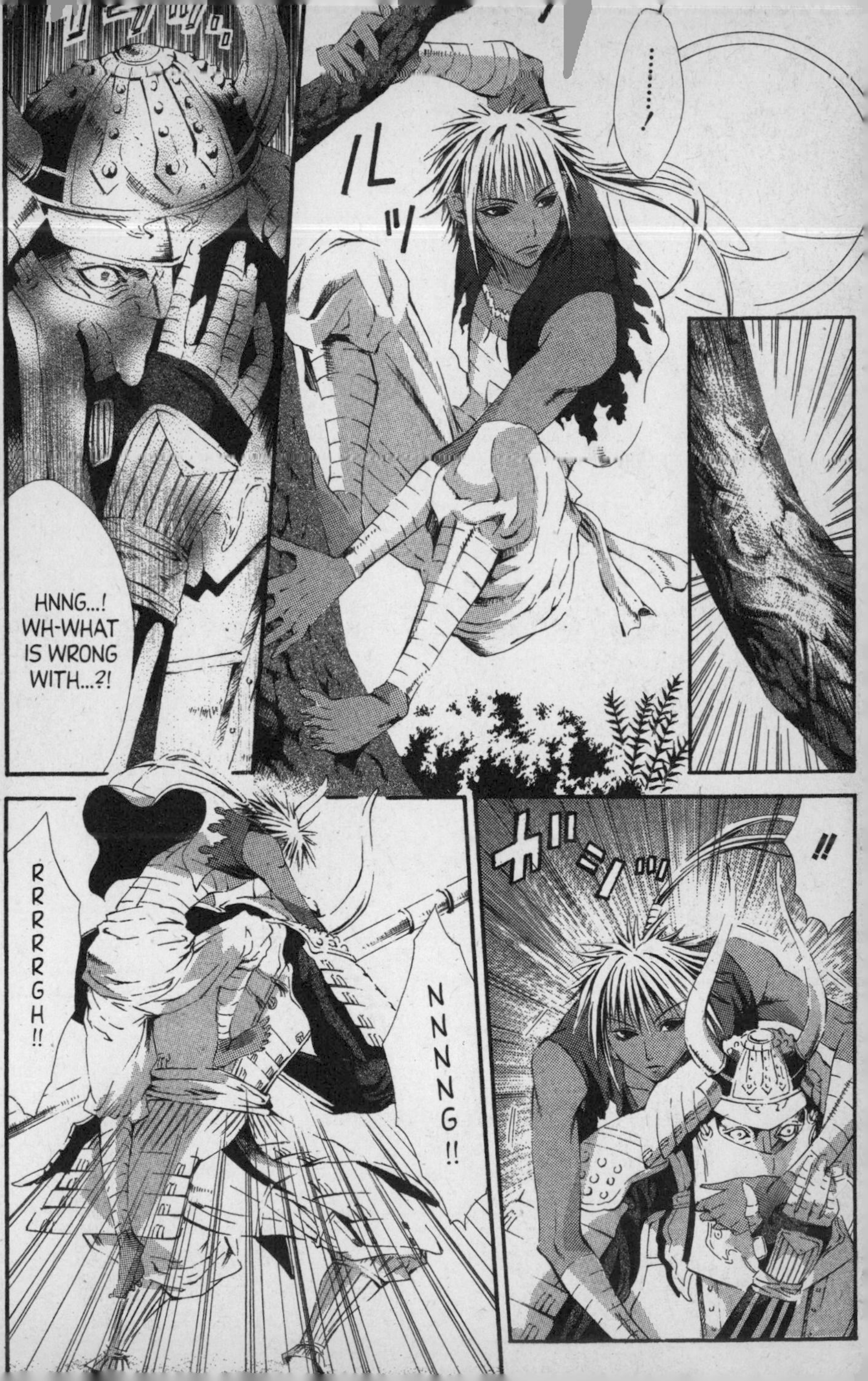
......!
HNNG...! WH-WHAT IS WRONG WITH...?!
!!
NNNNG!!
RRRRRRGH!!

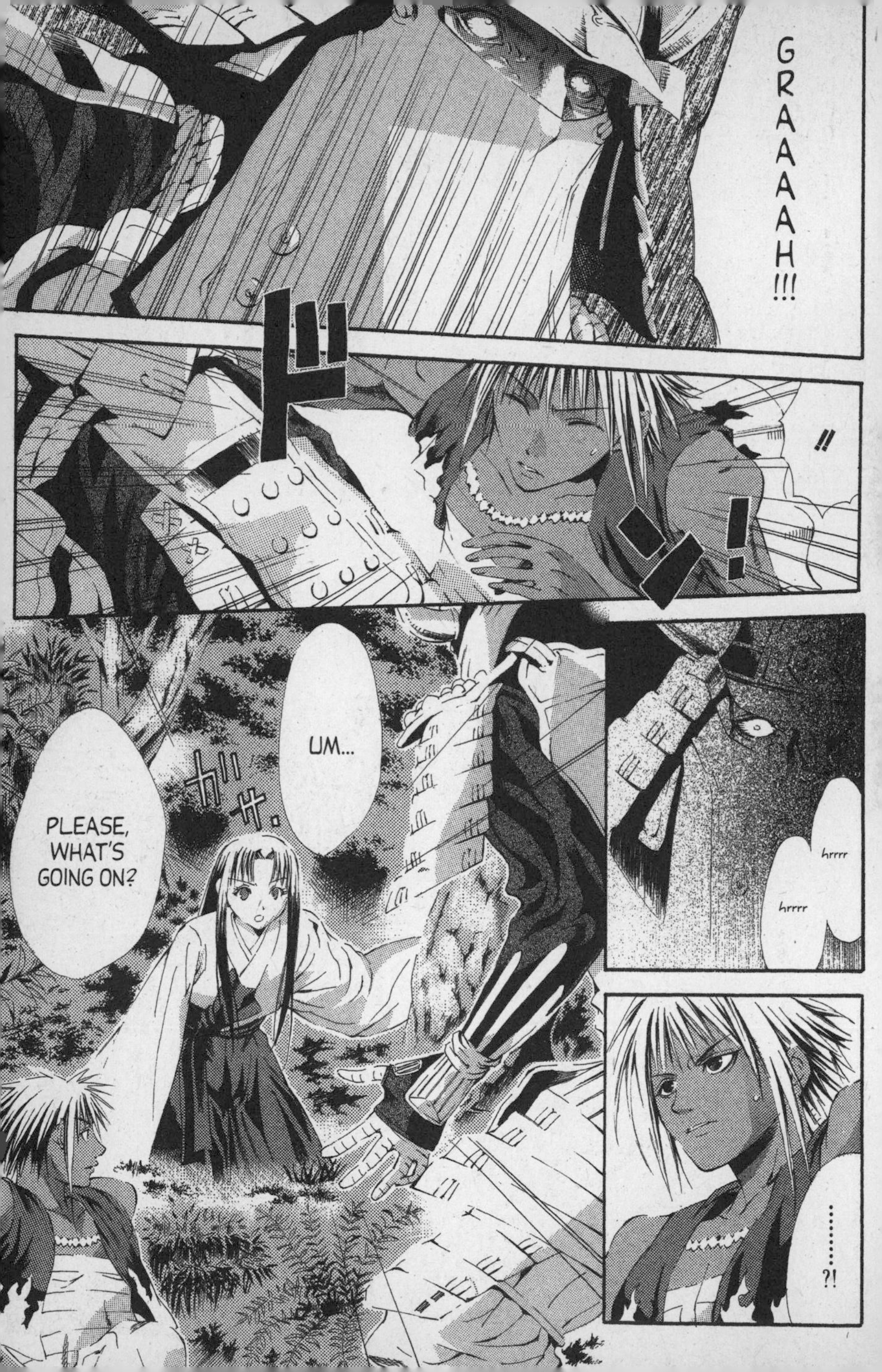
GRAAAAAH!!!
!!
UM...
PLEASE, WHAT'S GOING ON?
hrrrr
hrrrr
.......?!

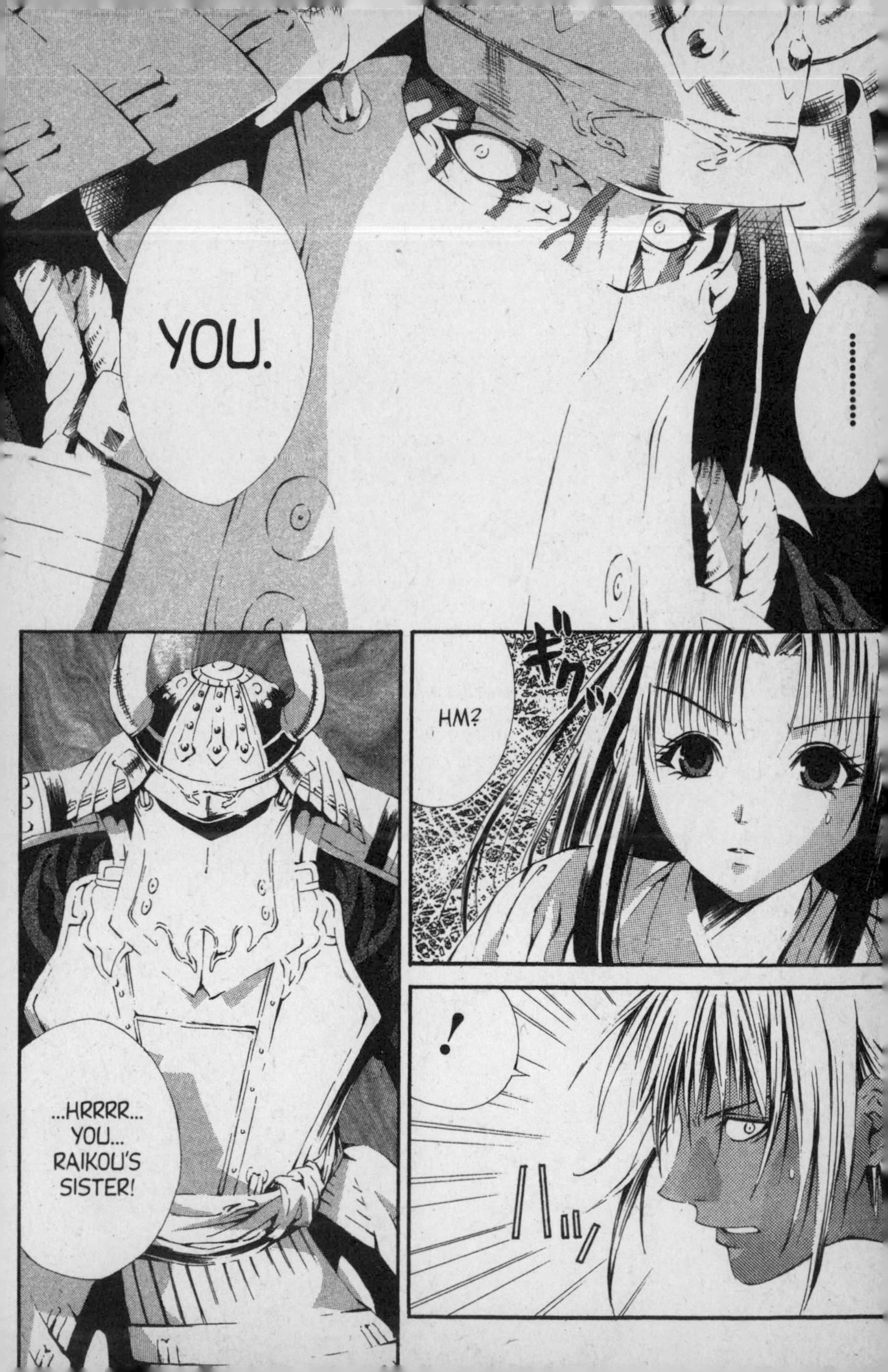
......
YOU.
HM?
!
...HRRRR... YOU... RAIKOU'S SISTER!

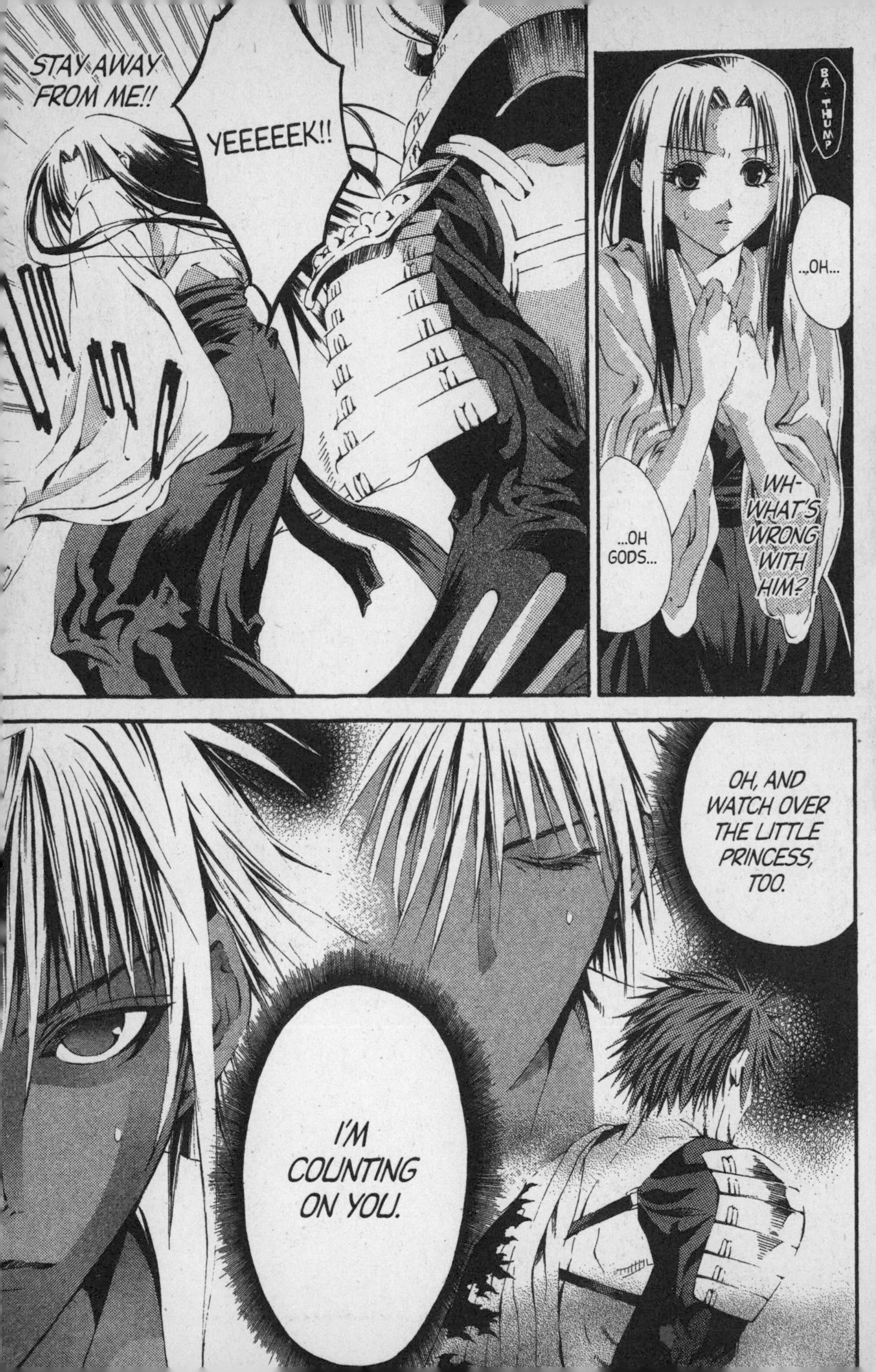
BA-THUMP
...OH...
WH-WHAT'S WRONG WITH HIM?
...OH GODS...
YEEEEEK!!
STAY AWAY FROM ME!!
OH, AND WATCH OVER THE LITTLE PRINCESS, TOO.
I'M COUNTING ON YOU.

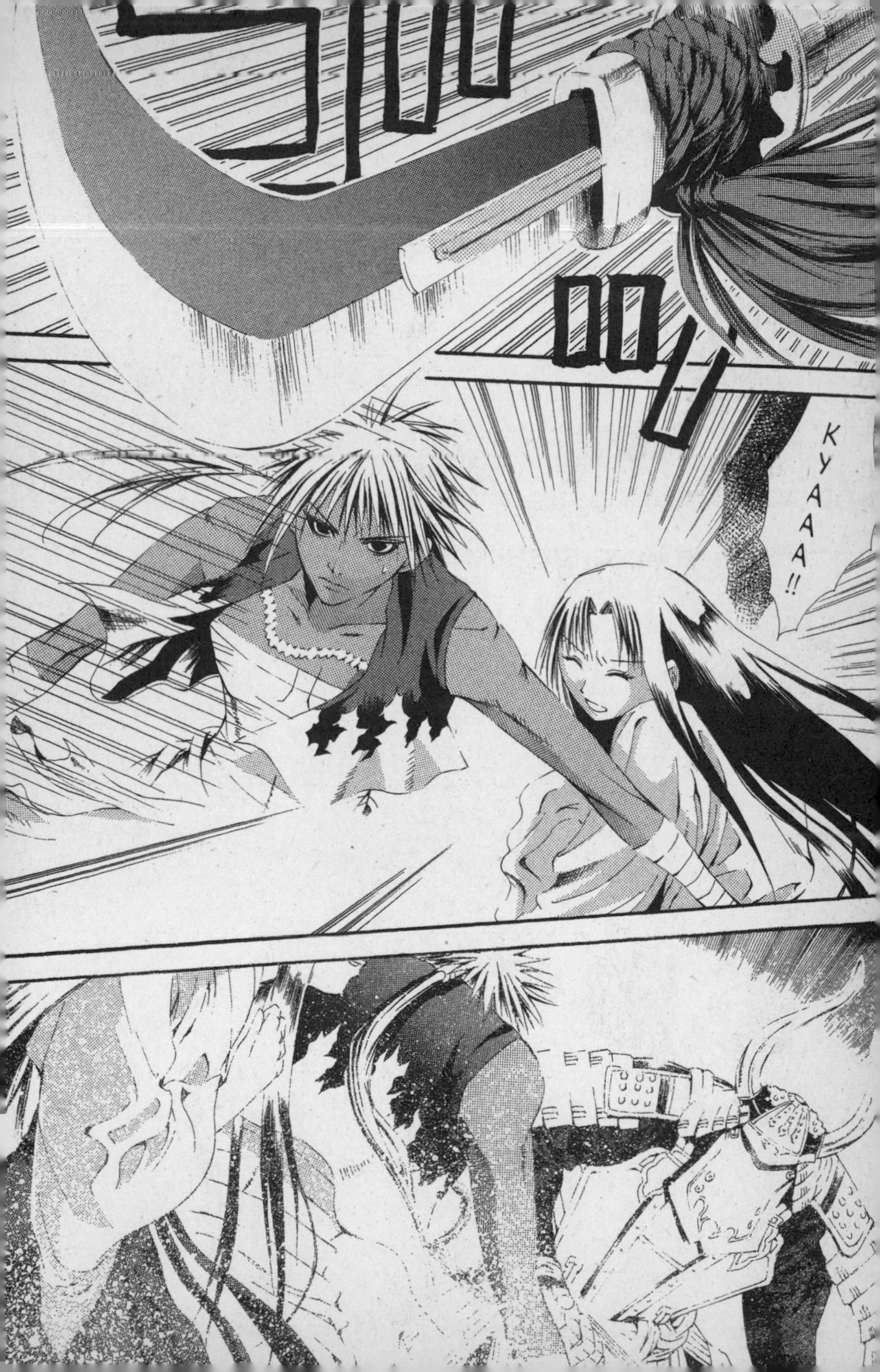
KYAAAA!!

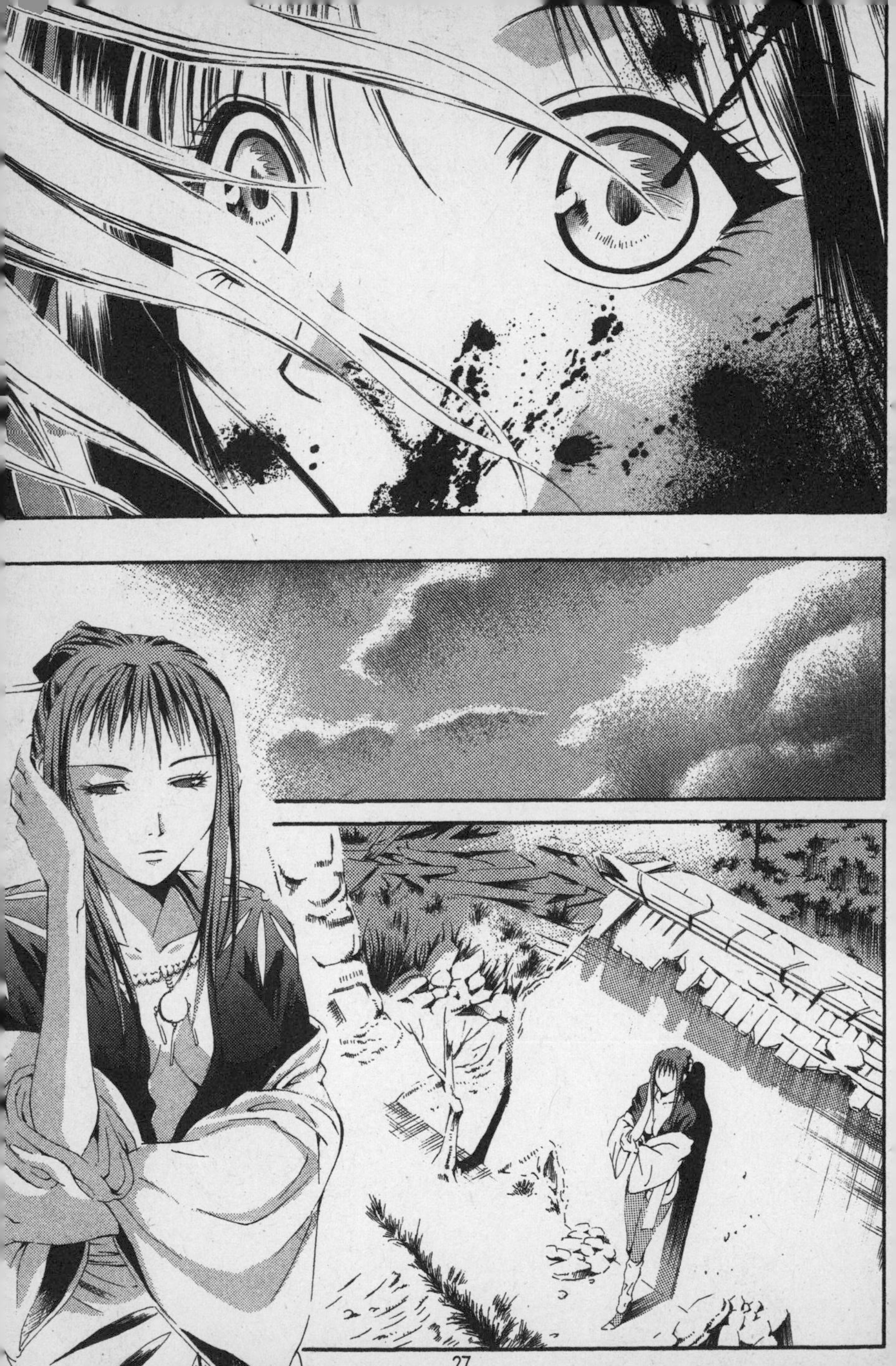

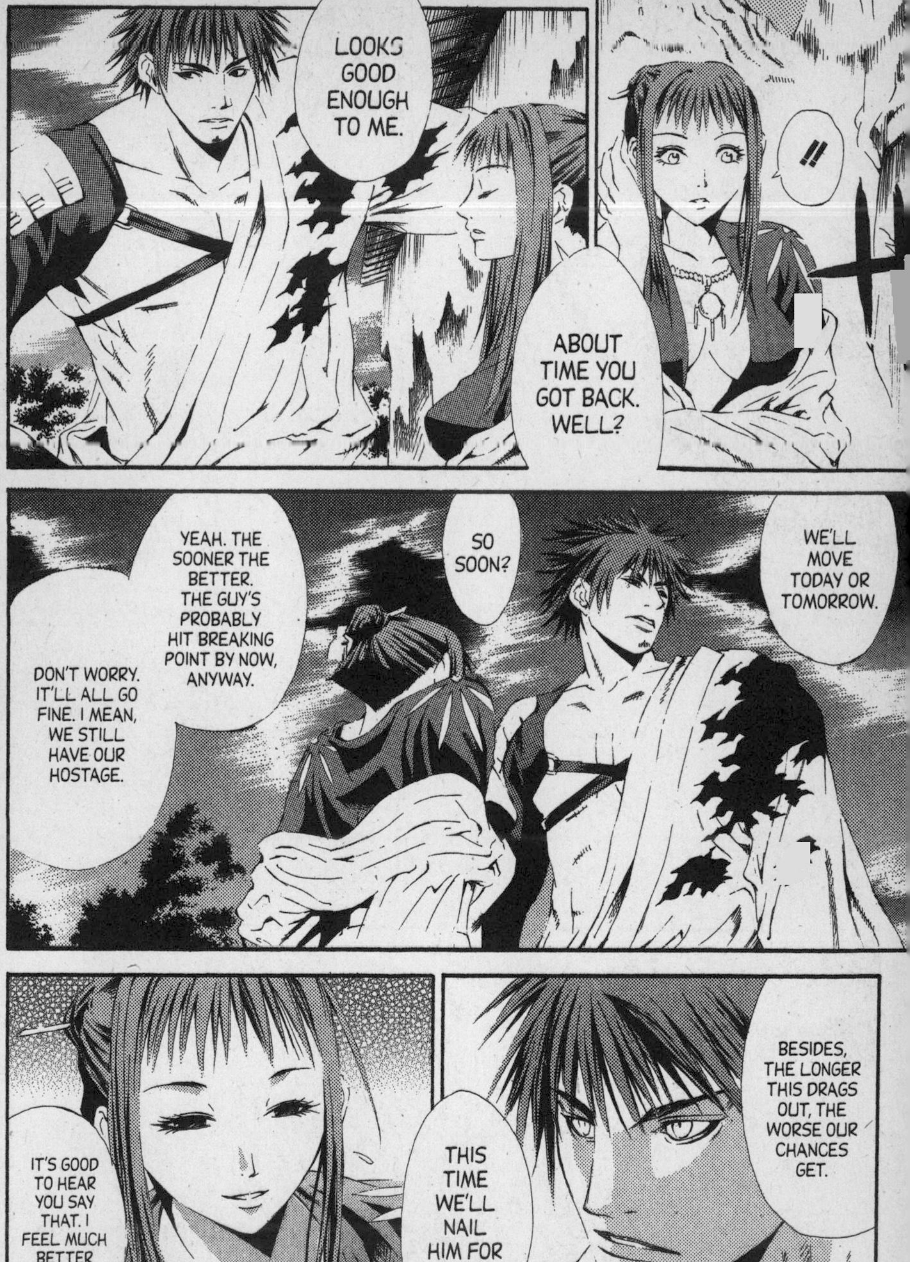

!!
ABOUT TIME YOU GOT BACK. WELL?
LOOKS GOOD ENOUGH TO ME.
WE'LL MOVE TODAY OR TOMORROW.
SO SOON?
YEAH. THE SOONER THE BETTER. THE GUY'S PROBABLY HIT BREAKING POINT BY NOW, ANYWAY.
DON'T WORRY. IT'LL ALL GO FINE. I MEAN, WE STILL HAVE OUR HOSTAGE.
BESIDES, THE LONGER THIS DRAGS OUT, THE WORSE OUR CHANCES GET.
THIS TIME WE'LL NAIL HIM FOR SURE!
IT'S GOOD TO HEAR YOU SAY THAT. I FEEL MUCH BETTER NOW.

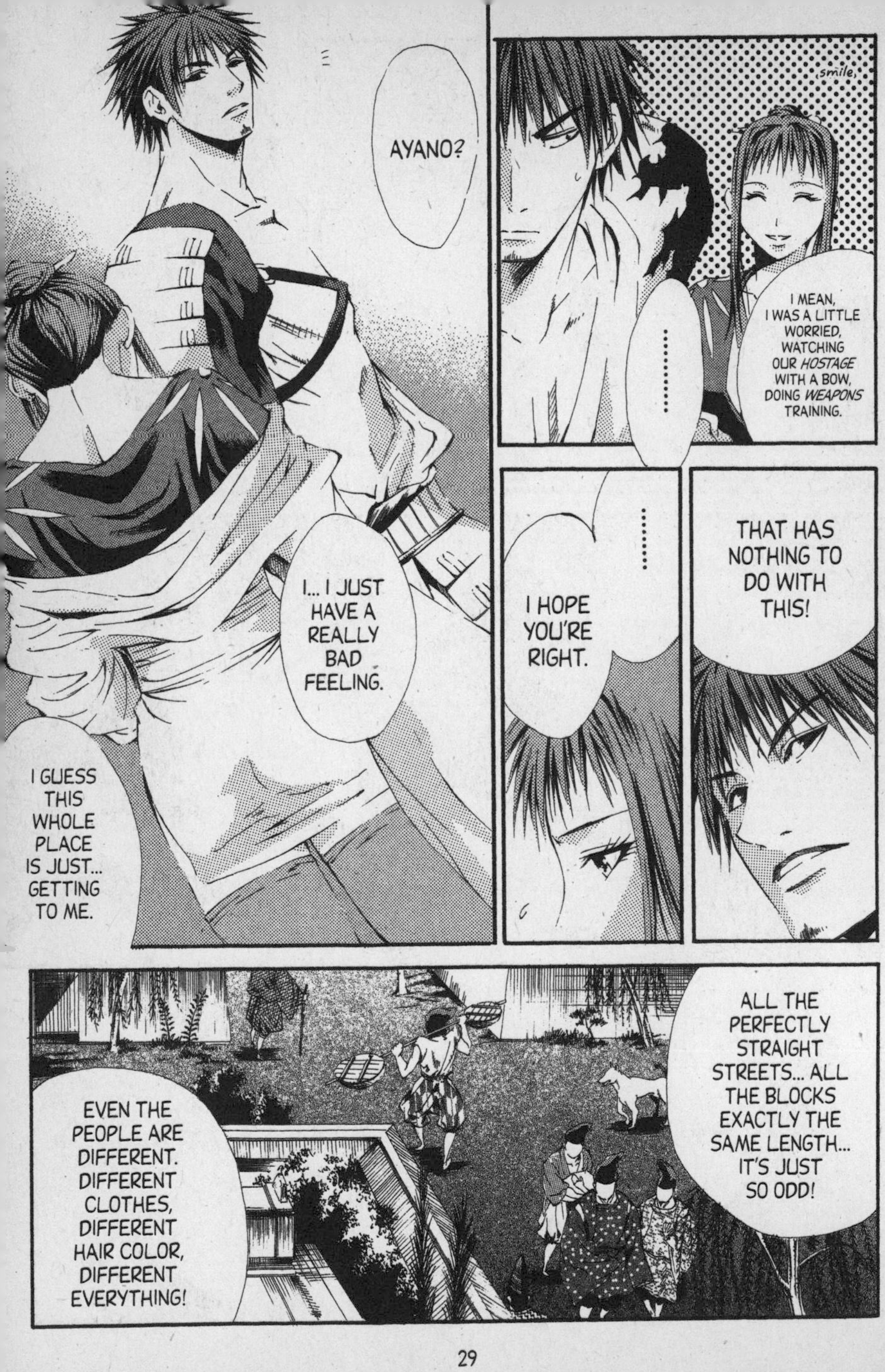
smile
I MEAN, I WAS A LITTLE WORRIED, WATCHING OUR *HOSTAGE* WITH A BOW, DOING *WEAPONS* TRAINING.
......
THAT HAS NOTHING TO DO WITH THIS!
......
I HOPE YOU'RE RIGHT.
AYANO?
I... I JUST HAVE A REALLY BAD FEELING.
I GUESS THIS WHOLE PLACE IS JUST... GETTING TO ME.
ALL THE PERFECTLY STRAIGHT STREETS... ALL THE BLOCKS EXACTLY THE SAME LENGTH... IT'S JUST SO ODD!
EVEN THE PEOPLE ARE DIFFERENT. DIFFERENT CLOTHES, DIFFERENT HAIR COLOR, DIFFERENT EVERYTHING!

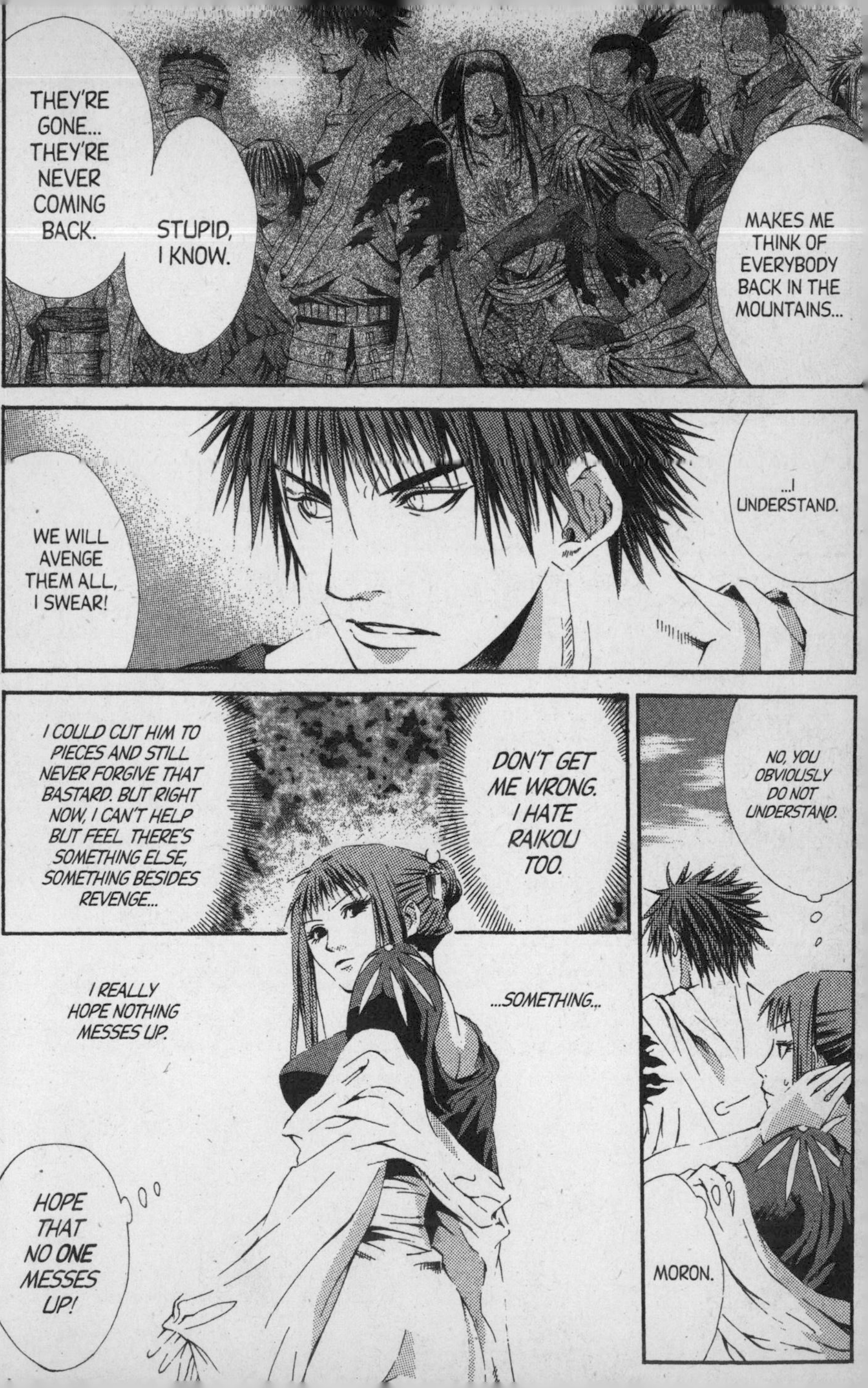
MAKES ME THINK OF EVERYBODY BACK IN THE MOUNTAINS...
THEY'RE GONE... THEY'RE NEVER COMING BACK.
STUPID, I KNOW.
WE WILL AVENGE THEM ALL, I SWEAR!
...I UNDERSTAND.
NO, YOU OBVIOUSLY DO NOT UNDERSTAND.
DON'T GET ME WRONG. I HATE RAIKOU TOO.
I COULD CUT HIM TO PIECES AND STILL NEVER FORGIVE THAT BASTARD. BUT RIGHT NOW, I CAN'T HELP BUT FEEL THERE'S SOMETHING ELSE, SOMETHING BESIDES REVENGE...
...SOMETHING...
I REALLY HOPE NOTHING MESSES UP.
HOPE THAT NO ONE MESSES UP!
MORON.

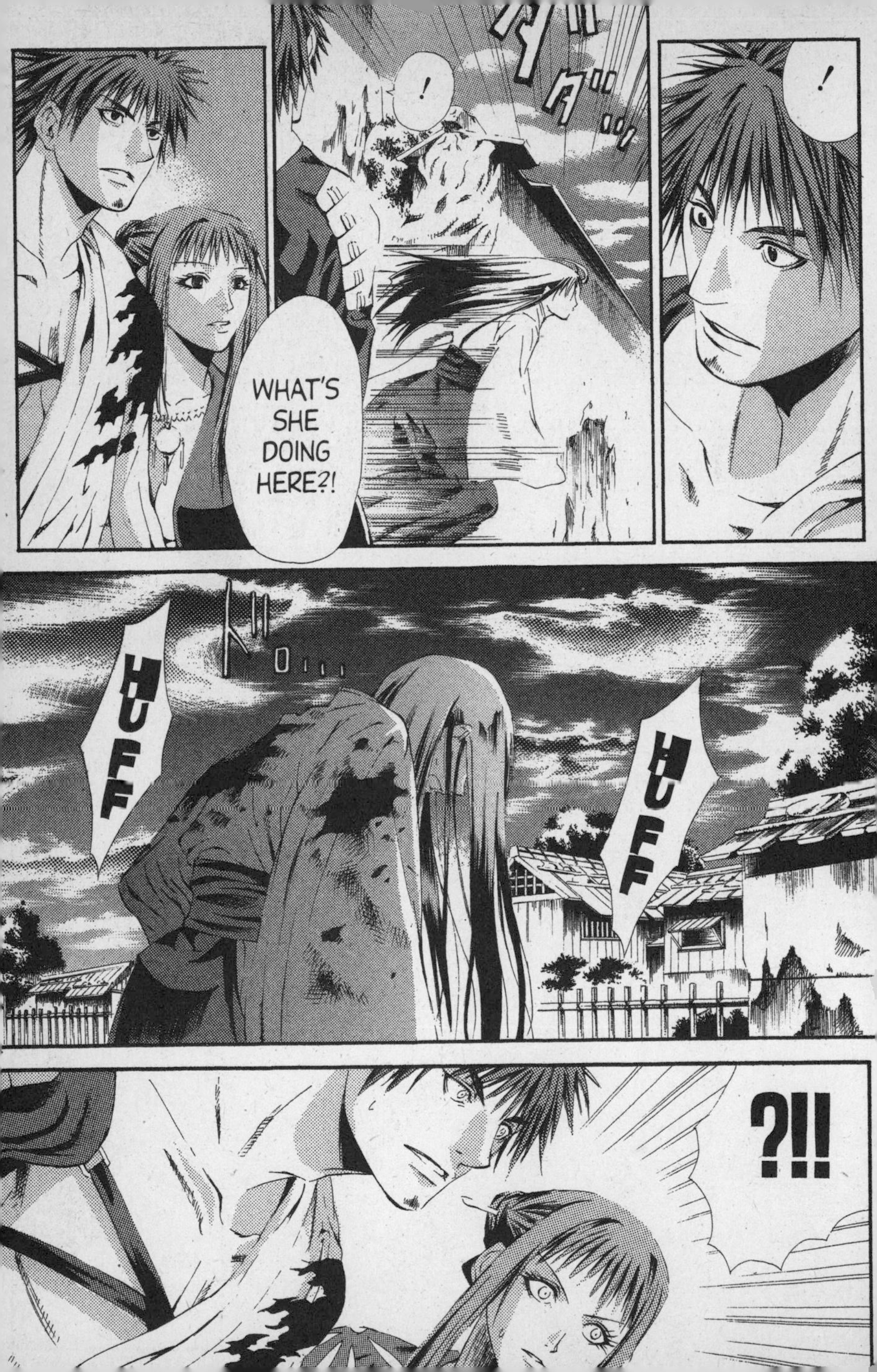
!
!
WHAT'S SHE DOING HERE?!
HUFF
HUFF
?!!

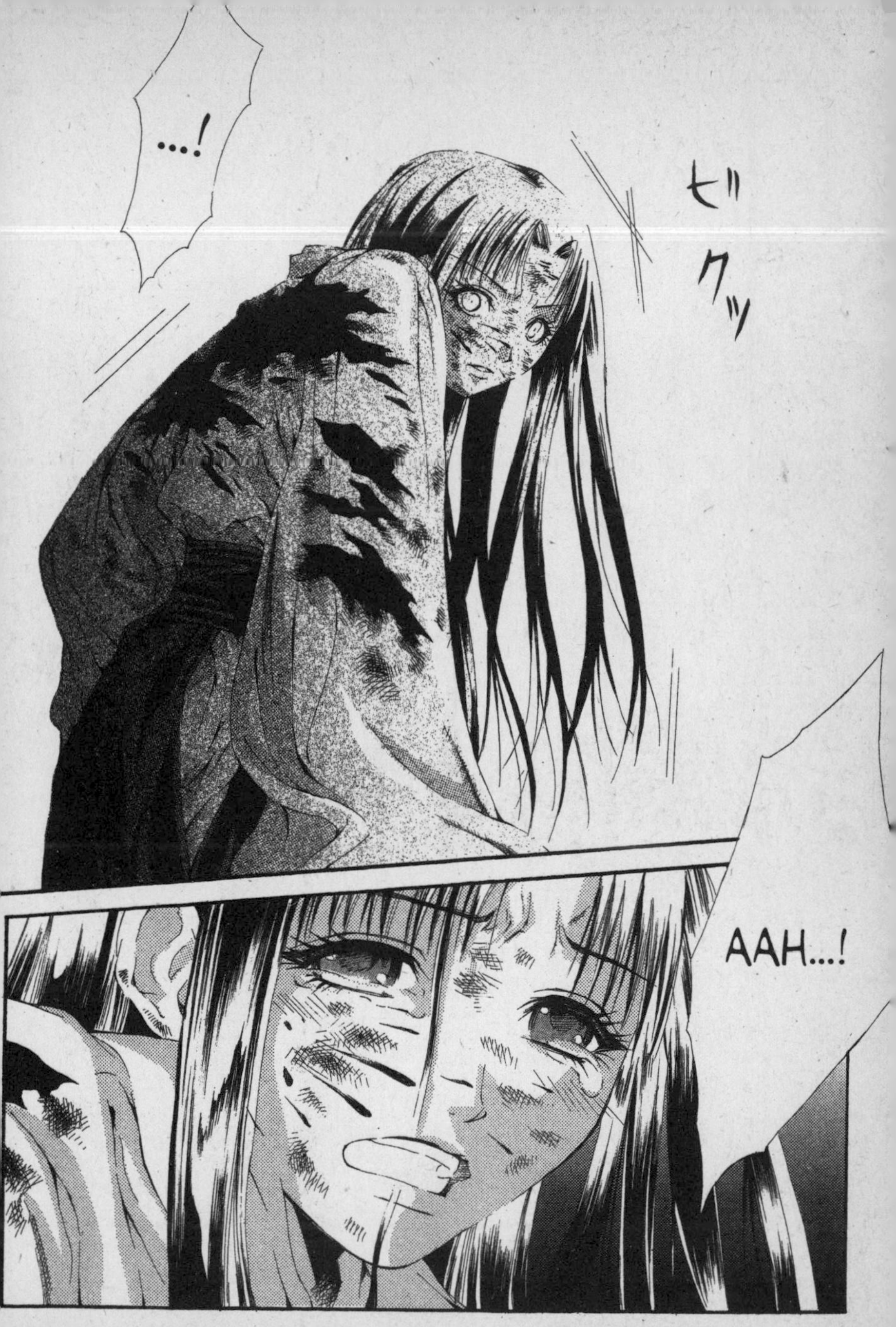
ビクッ
...!
AAH...!

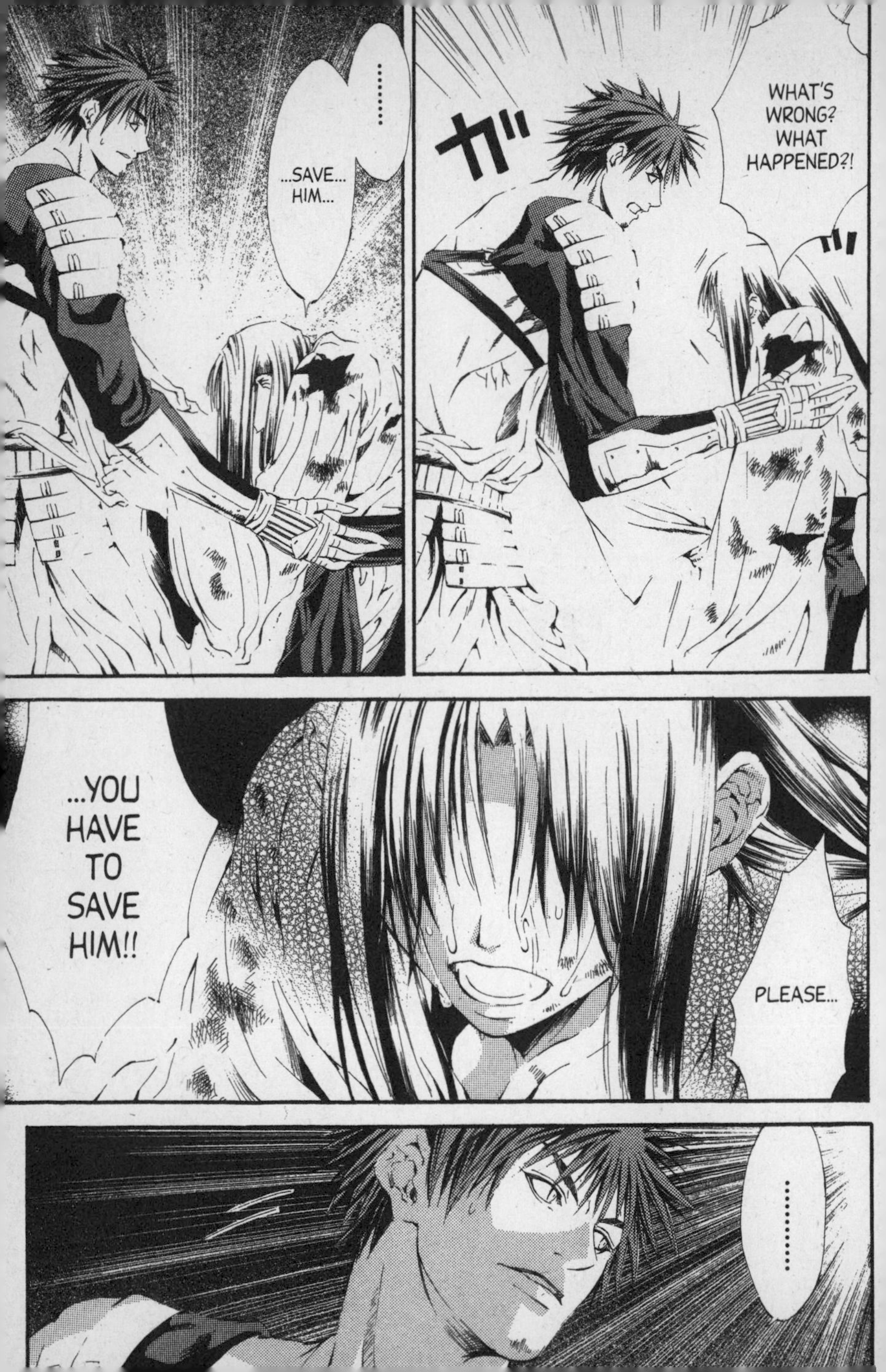
ガ
WHAT'S WRONG? WHAT HAPPENED?!
......
...SAVE... HIM...
PLEASE...
...YOU HAVE TO SAVE HIM!!
......

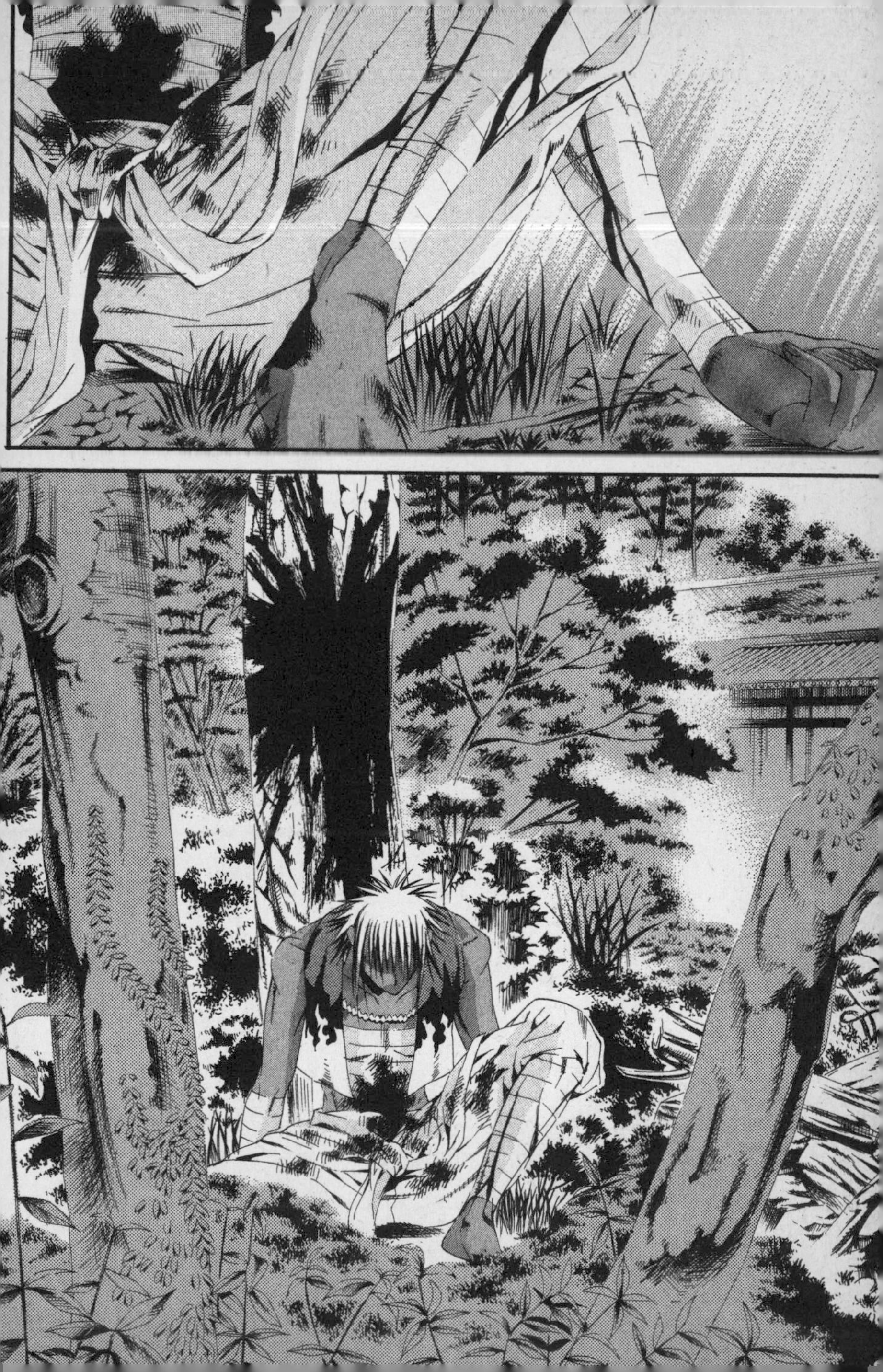

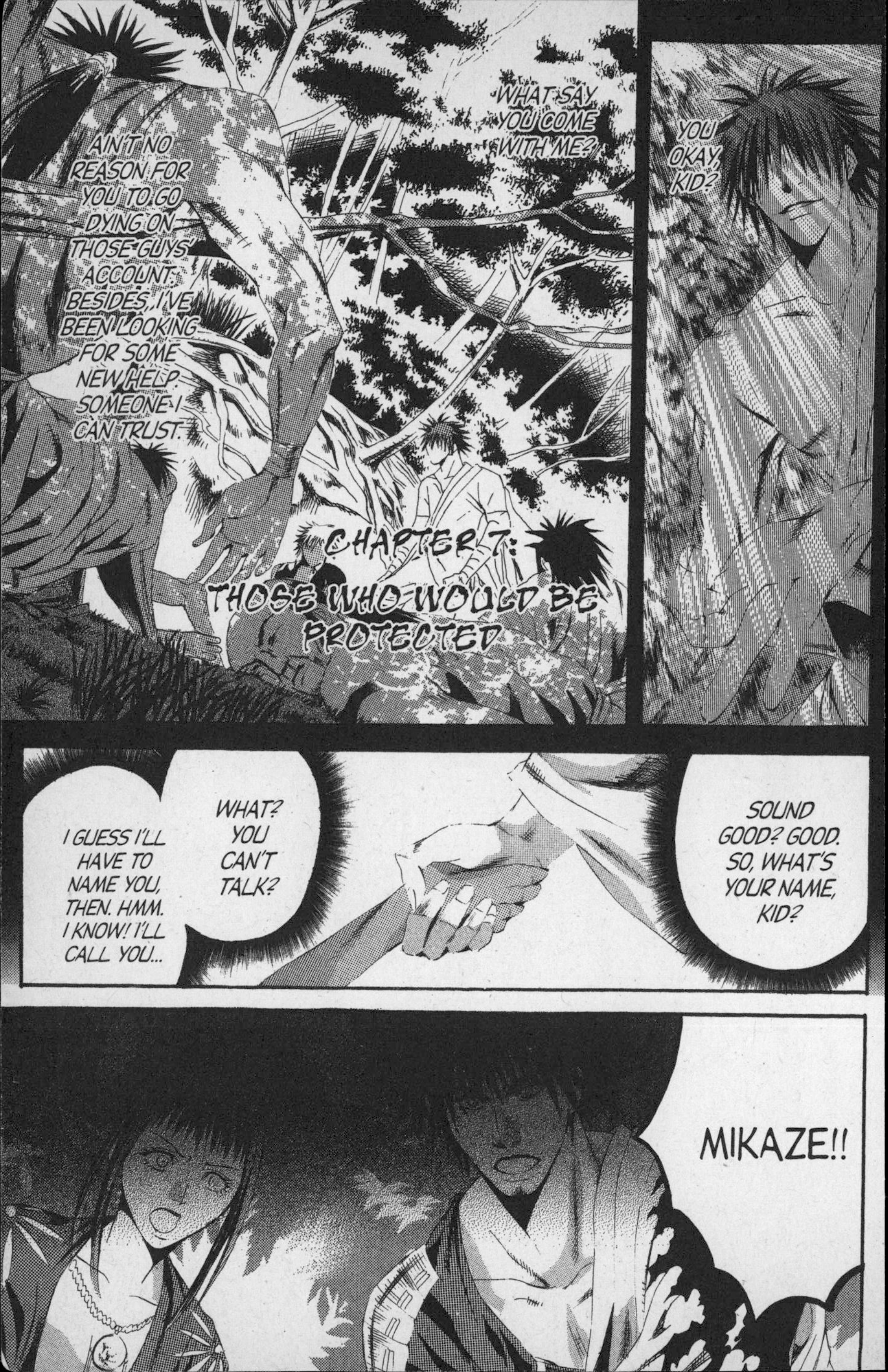
YOU OKAY, KID?
WHAT SAY YOU COME WITH ME?
AIN'T NO REASON FOR YOU TO GO DYING ON THOSE GUYS' ACCOUNT. BESIDES, I'VE BEEN LOOKING FOR SOME NEW HELP. SOMEONE I CAN TRUST.
CHAPTER 7: THOSE WHO WOULD BE PROTECTED
SOUND GOOD? GOOD. SO, WHAT'S YOUR NAME, KID?
WHAT? YOU CAN'T TALK?
I GUESS I'LL HAVE TO NAME YOU, THEN. HMM. I KNOW! I'LL CALL YOU...
MIKAZE!!

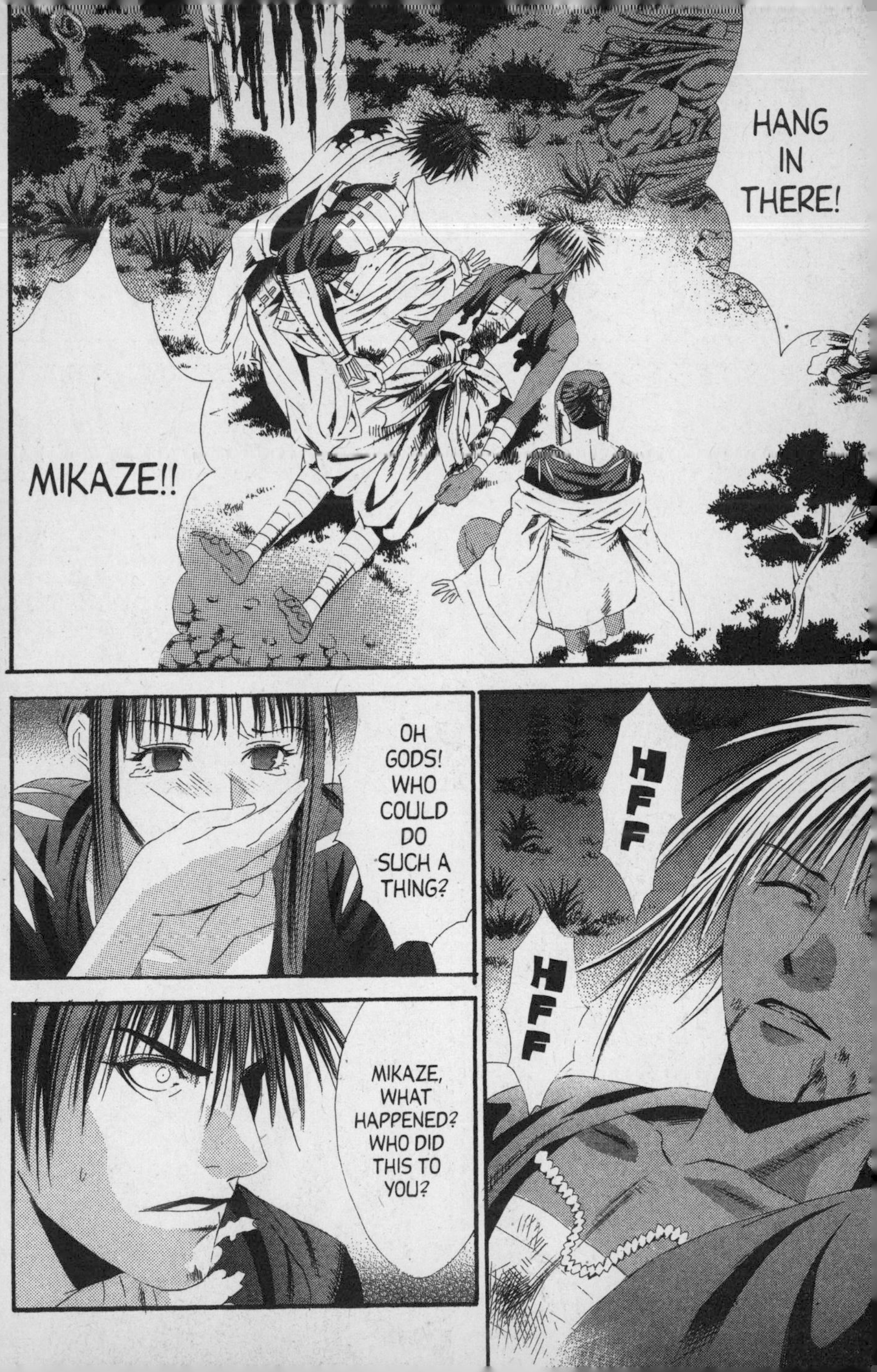
HANG IN THERE!
MIKAZE!!
HFF
HFF
OH GODS! WHO COULD DO SUCH A THING?
MIKAZE, WHAT HAPPENED? WHO DID THIS TO YOU?

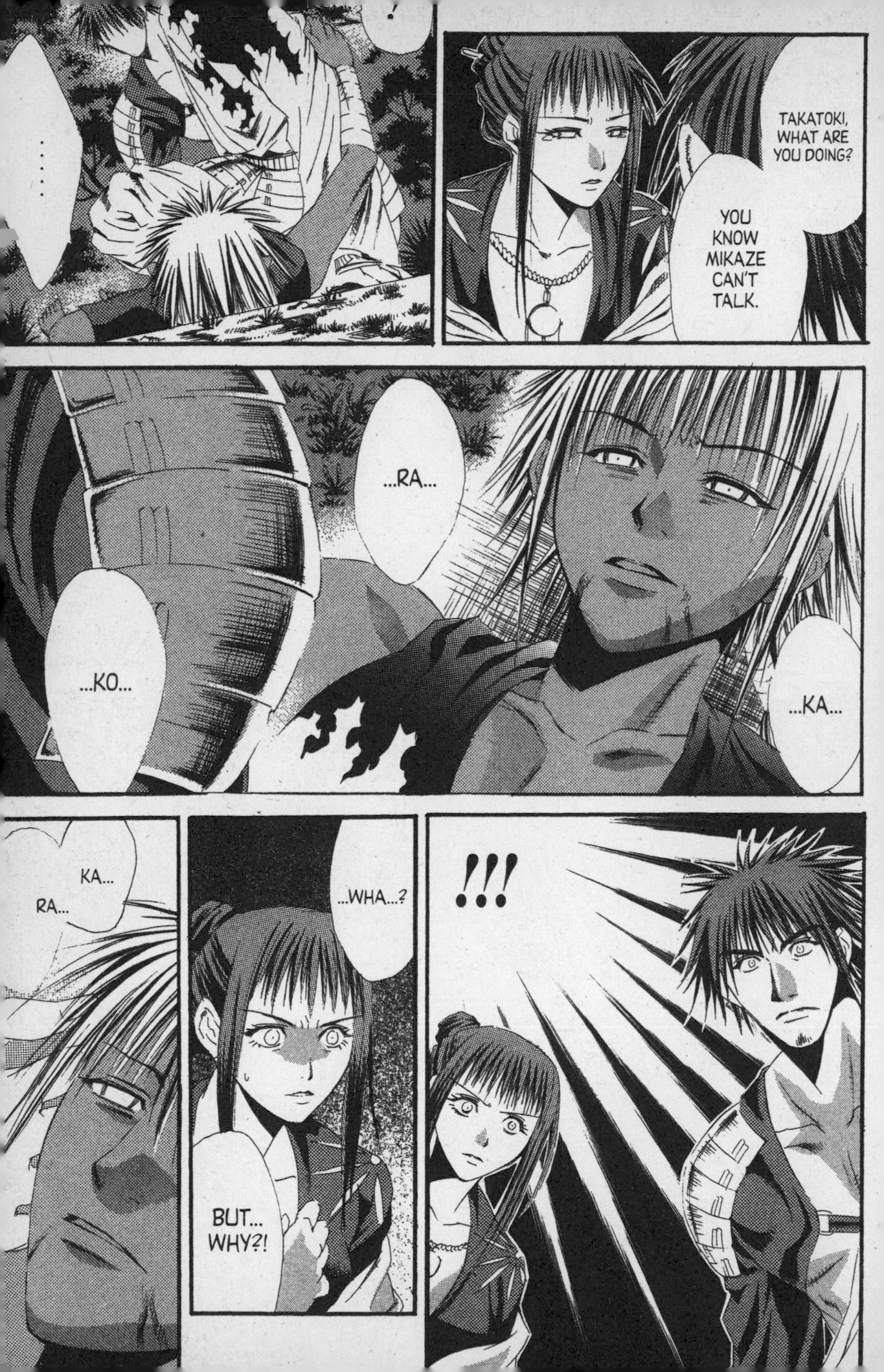
TAKATOKI, WHAT ARE YOU DOING?
YOU KNOW MIKAZE CAN'T TALK.
!
......
...KA...
...RA...
...KO...
!!!
...WHA...?
BUT... WHY?!
KA... RA...

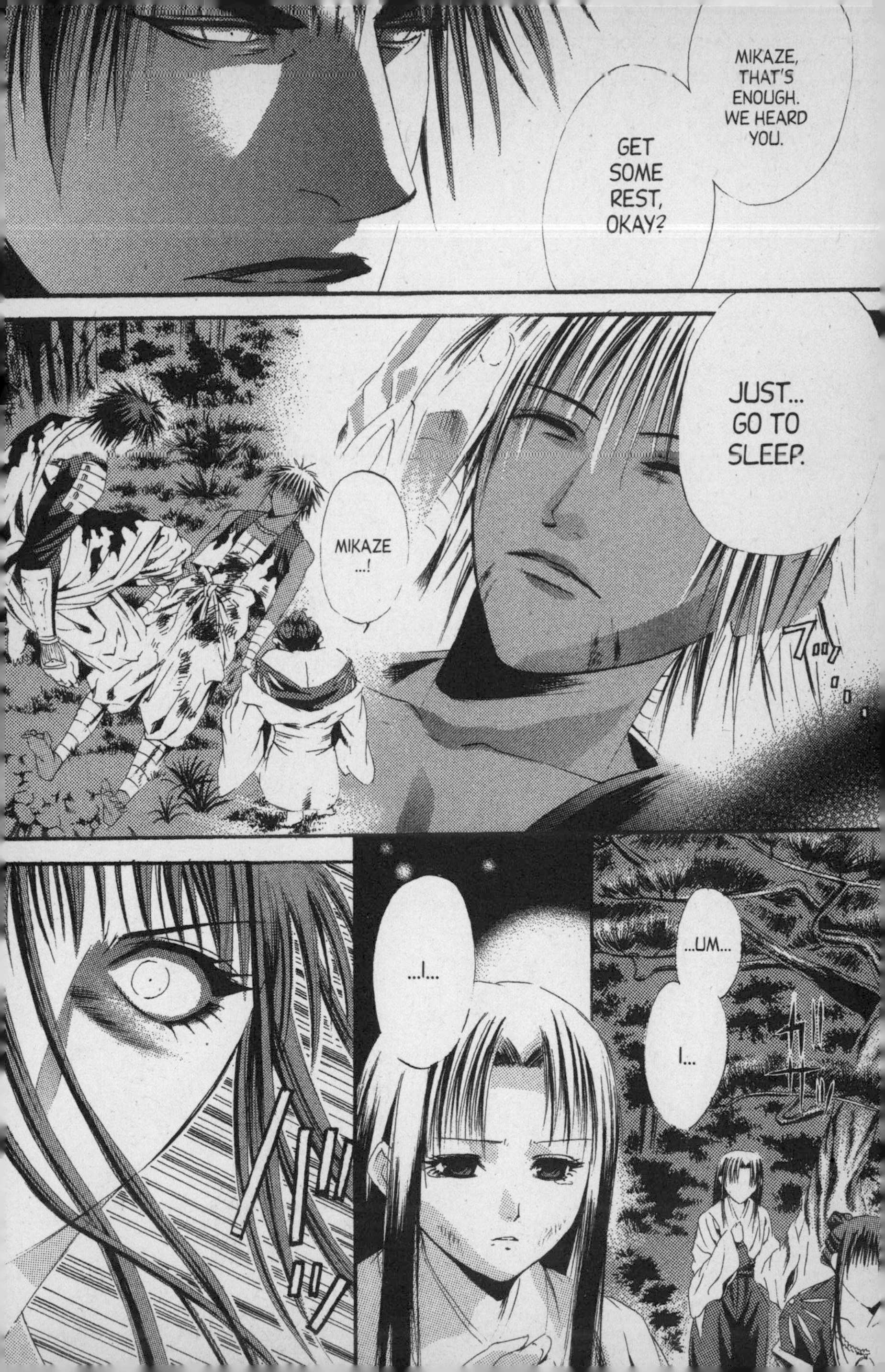
MIKAZE, THAT'S ENOUGH. WE HEARD YOU.
GET SOME REST, OKAY?
JUST... GO TO SLEEP.
MIKAZE ...!
...UM...
I...
...I...

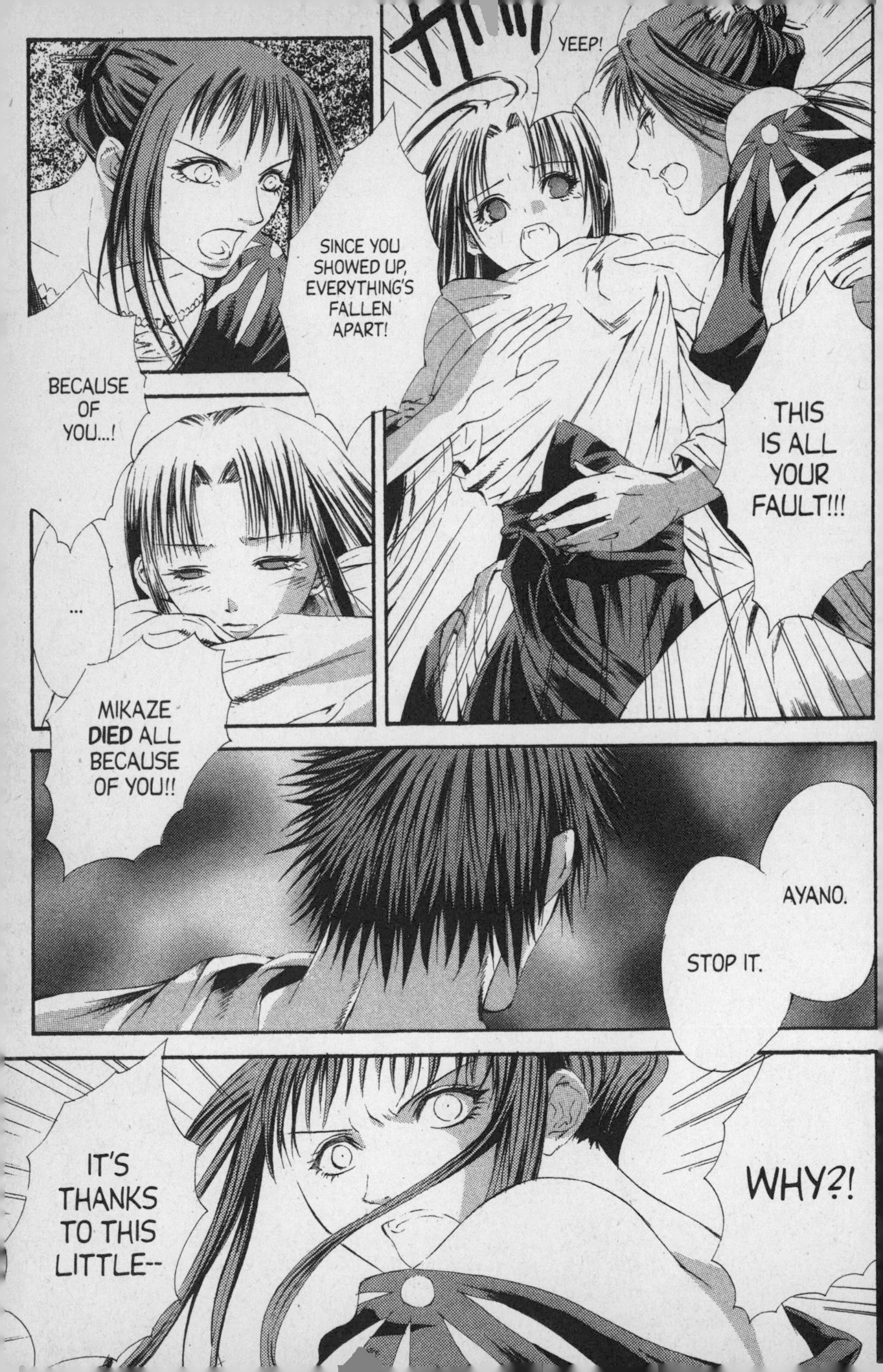

YEEP!
THIS IS ALL YOUR FAULT!!!
SINCE YOU SHOWED UP, EVERYTHING'S FALLEN APART!
BECAUSE OF YOU...!
...
MIKAZE **DIED** ALL BECAUSE OF YOU!!
AYANO.
STOP IT.
WHY?!
IT'S THANKS TO THIS LITTLE--

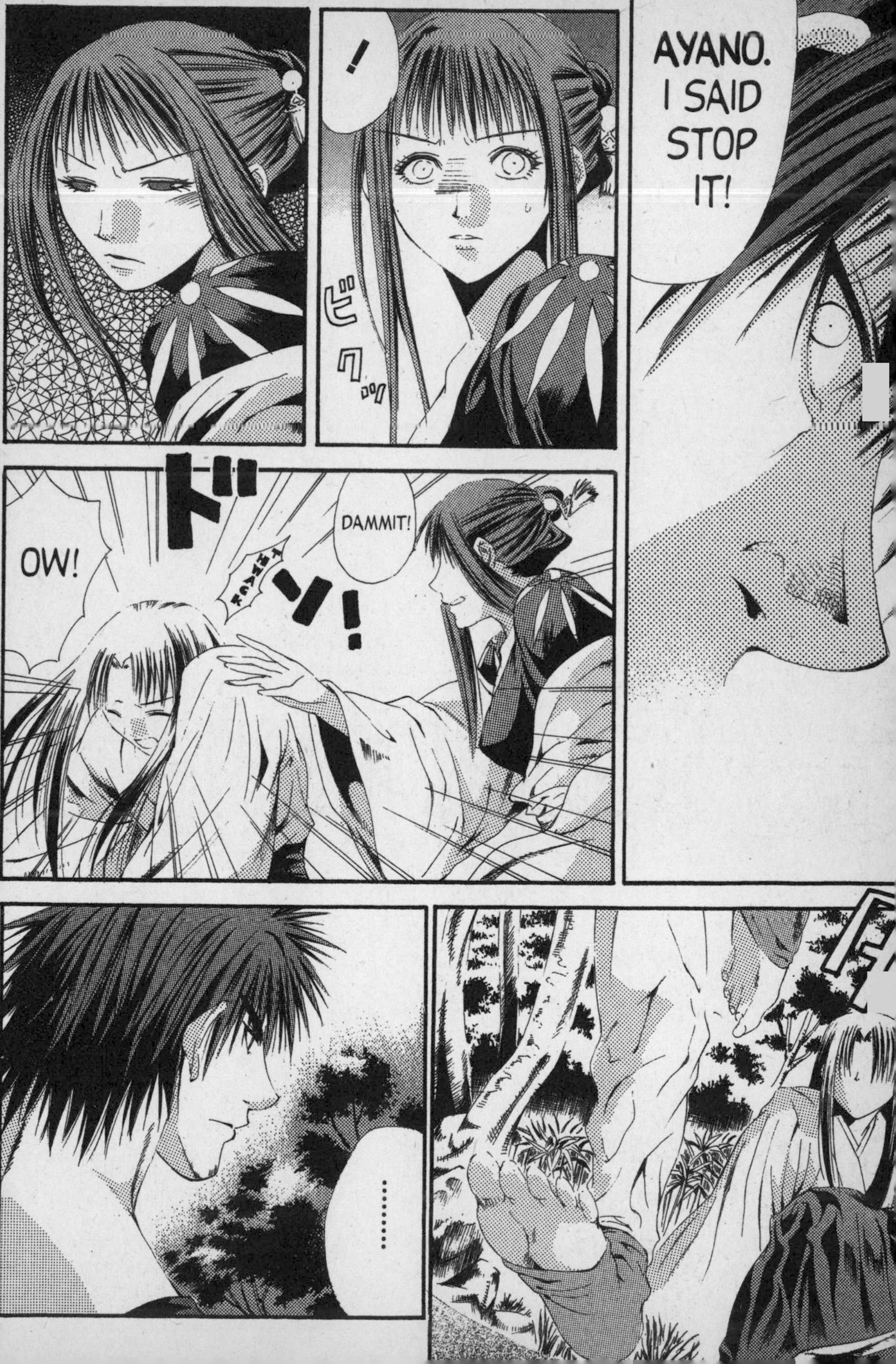
AYANO. I SAID STOP IT!
!
ビク
ドン!
DAMMIT!
THWACK
OW!
......

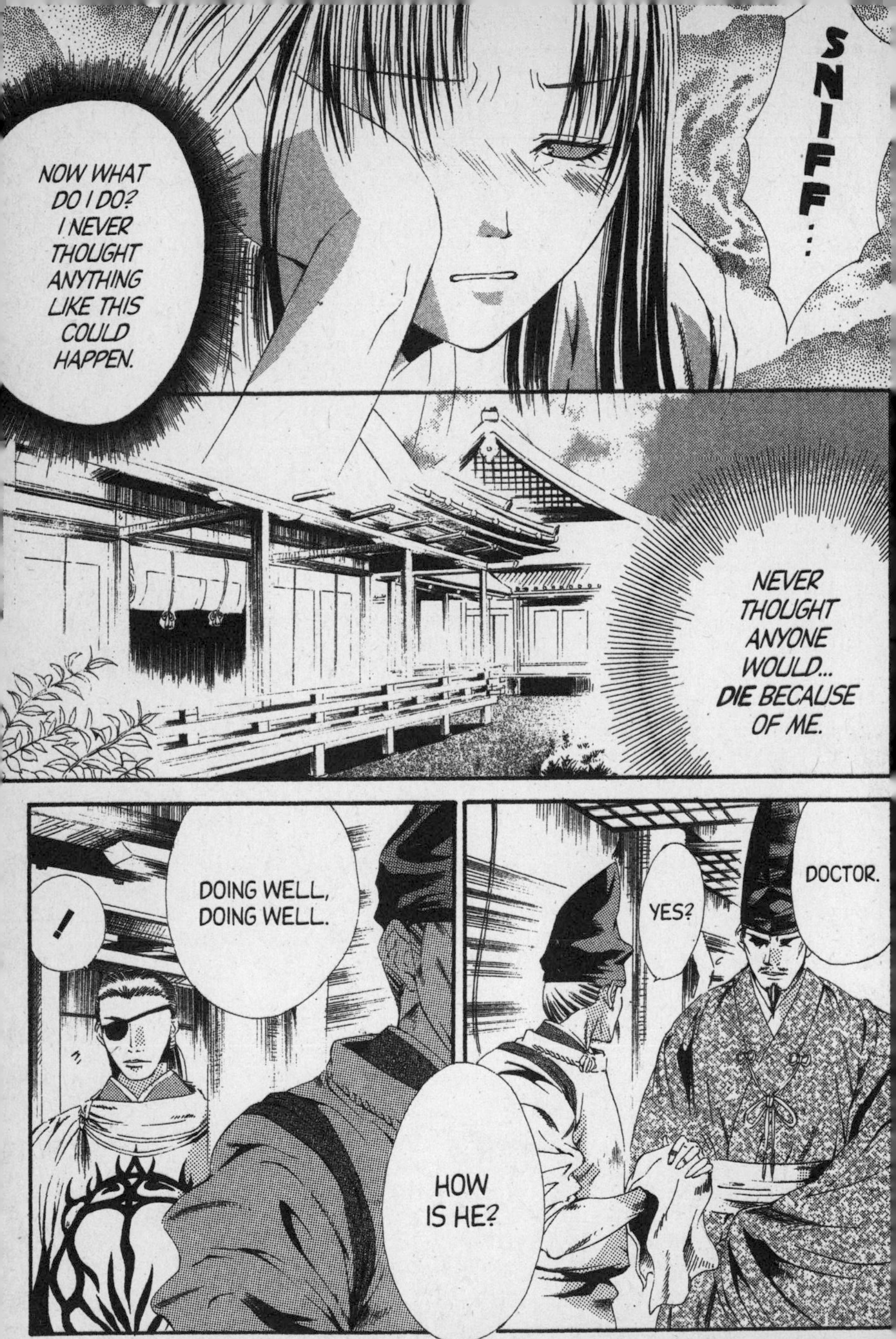
SNIFF...
NOW WHAT DO I DO? I NEVER THOUGHT ANYTHING LIKE THIS COULD HAPPEN.
NEVER THOUGHT ANYONE WOULD... DIE BECAUSE OF ME.
DOCTOR.
YES?
HOW IS HE?
DOING WELL, DOING WELL.
!

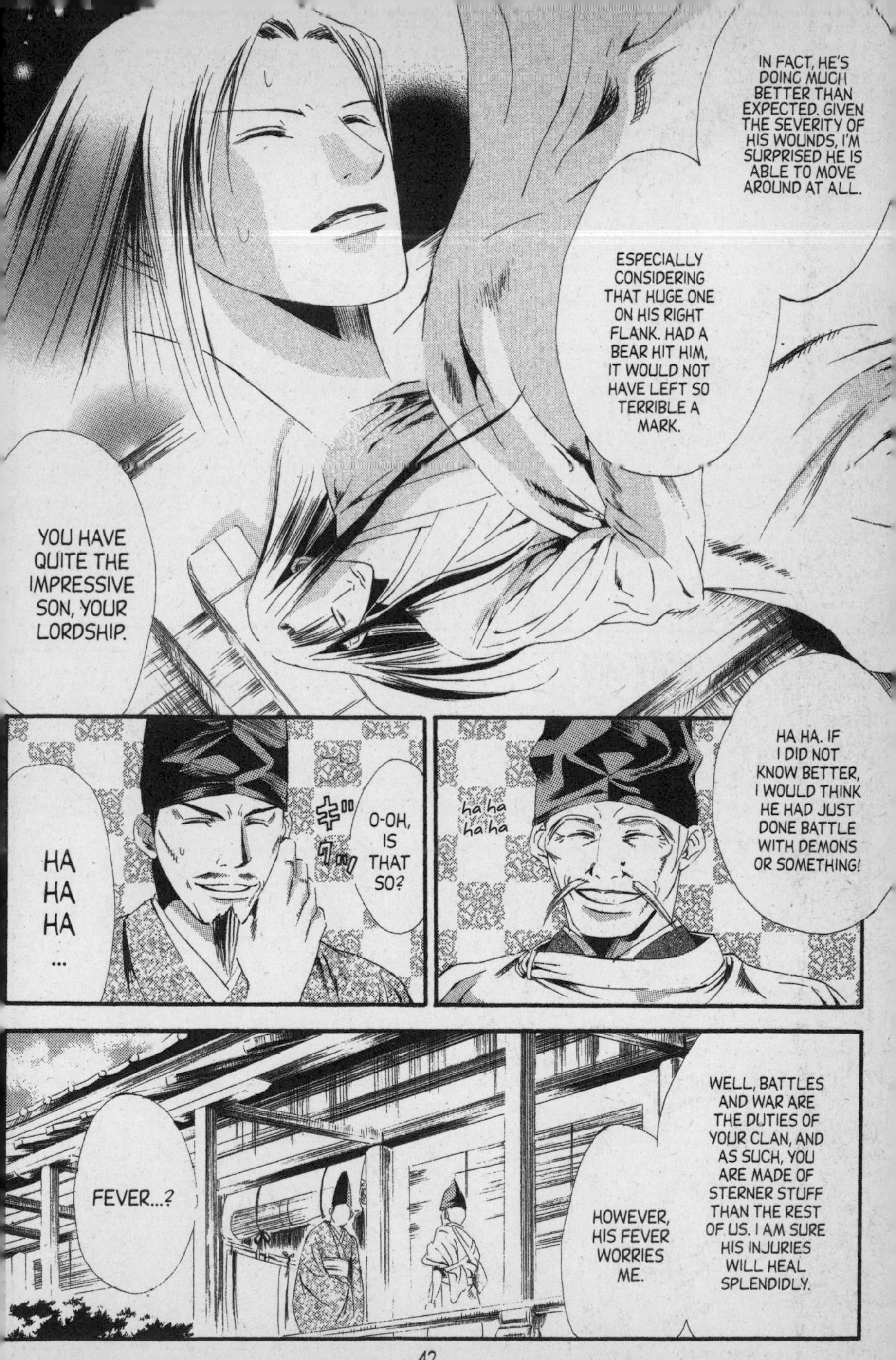
IN FACT, HE'S DOING MUCH BETTER THAN EXPECTED. GIVEN THE SEVERITY OF HIS WOUNDS, I'M SURPRISED HE IS ABLE TO MOVE AROUND AT ALL.
ESPECIALLY CONSIDERING THAT HUGE ONE ON HIS RIGHT FLANK. HAD A BEAR HIT HIM, IT WOULD NOT HAVE LEFT SO TERRIBLE A MARK.
YOU HAVE QUITE THE IMPRESSIVE SON, YOUR LORDSHIP.
HA HA. IF I DID NOT KNOW BETTER, I WOULD THINK HE HAD JUST DONE BATTLE WITH DEMONS OR SOMETHING!
ha ha ha ha
O-OH, IS THAT SO?
HA HA HA ...
WELL, BATTLES AND WAR ARE THE DUTIES OF YOUR CLAN, AND AS SUCH, YOU ARE MADE OF STERNER STUFF THAN THE REST OF US. I AM SURE HIS INJURIES WILL HEAL SPLENDIDLY.
HOWEVER, HIS FEVER WORRIES ME.
FEVER...?

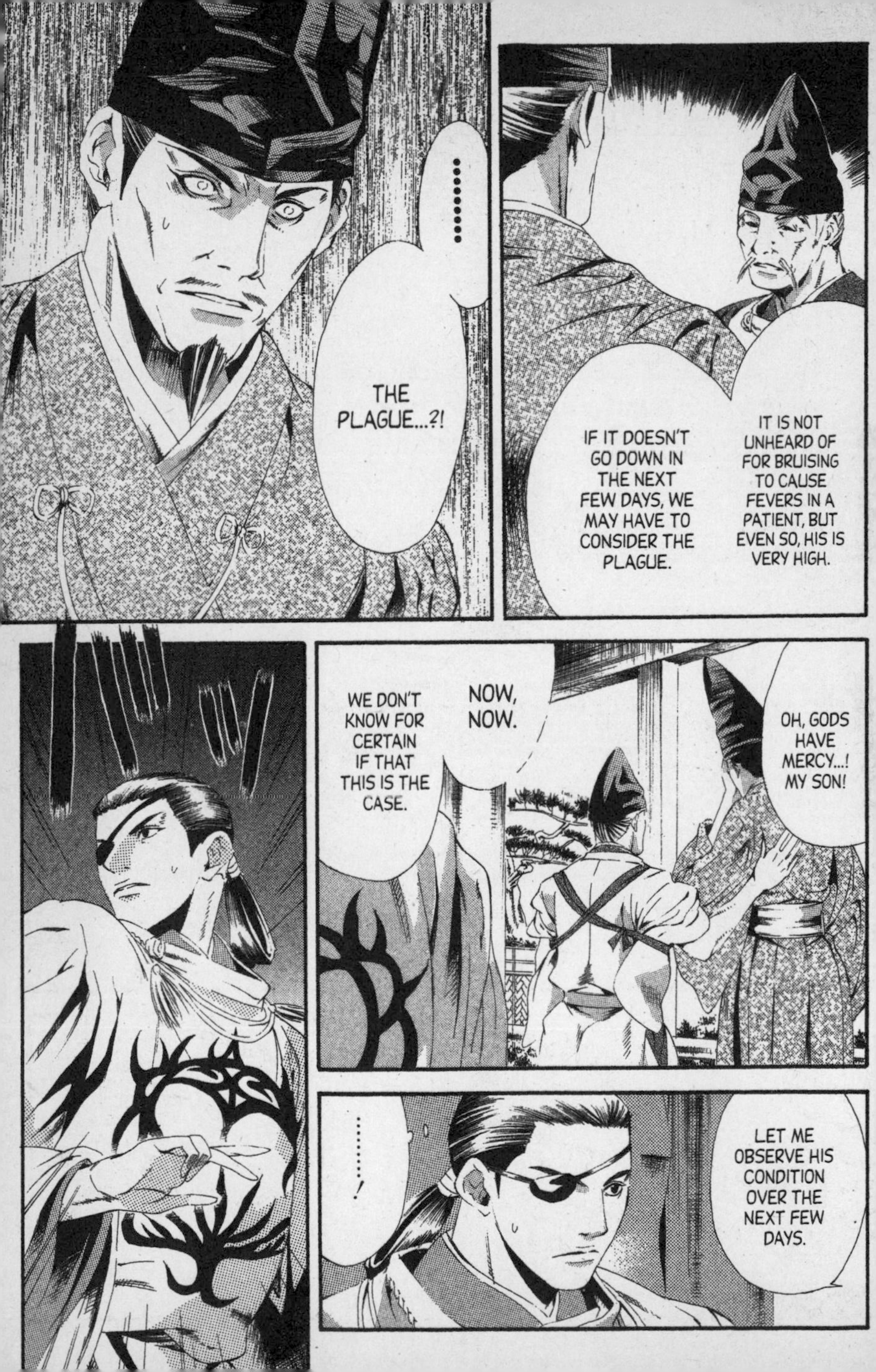
IT IS NOT UNHEARD OF FOR BRUISING TO CAUSE FEVERS IN A PATIENT, BUT EVEN SO, HIS IS VERY HIGH.
IF IT DOESN'T GO DOWN IN THE NEXT FEW DAYS, WE MAY HAVE TO CONSIDER THE PLAGUE.
....
THE PLAGUE...?!
OH, GODS HAVE MERCY...! MY SON!
NOW, NOW.
WE DON'T KNOW FOR CERTAIN IF THAT THIS IS THE CASE.
LET ME OBSERVE HIS CONDITION OVER THE NEXT FEW DAYS.
......!

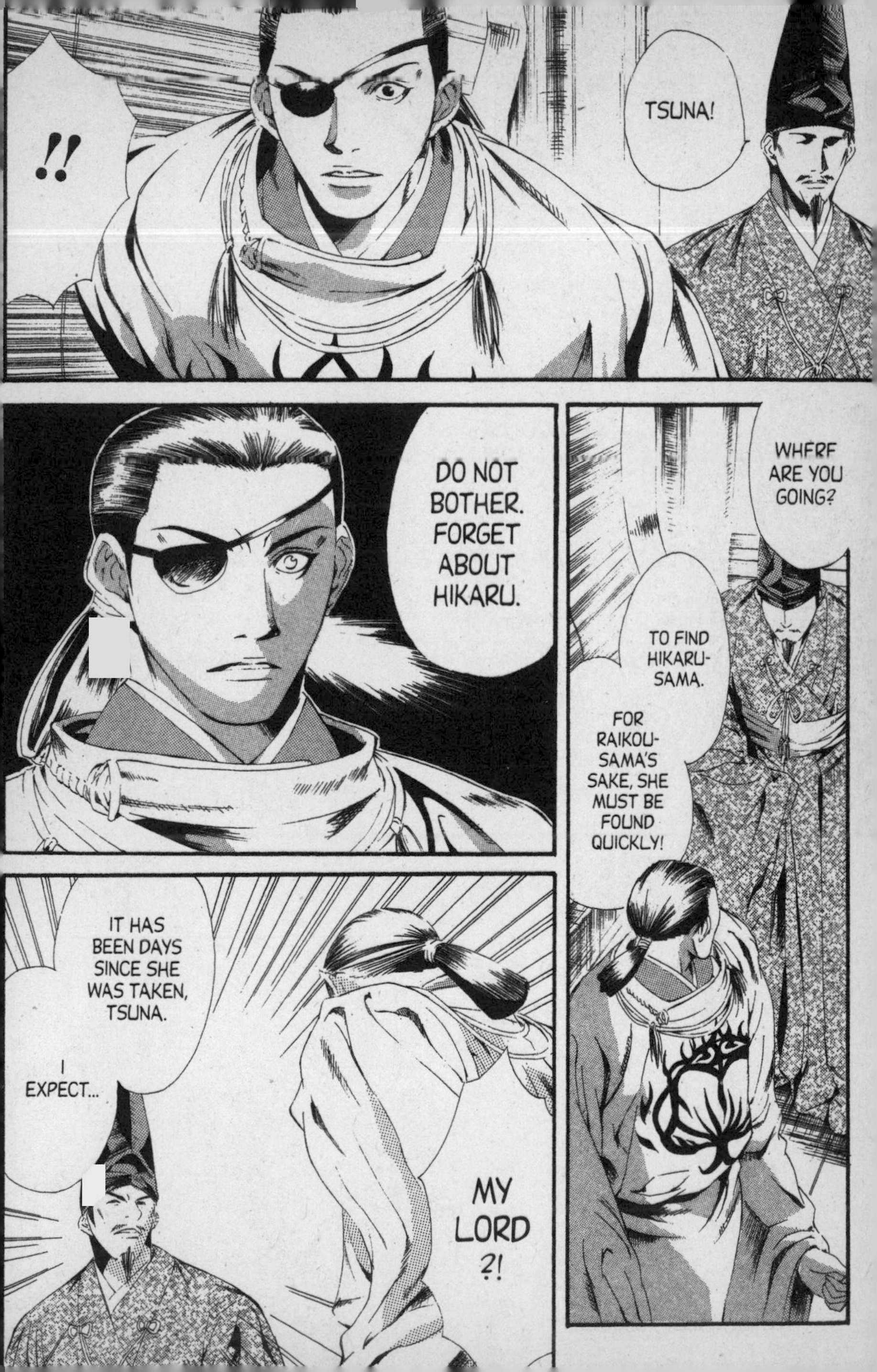
TSUNA!
!!
WHERE ARE YOU GOING?
DO NOT BOTHER. FORGET ABOUT HIKARU.
TO FIND HIKARU-SAMA.
FOR RAIKOU-SAMA'S SAKE, SHE MUST BE FOUND QUICKLY!
MY LORD ?!
IT HAS BEEN DAYS SINCE SHE WAS TAKEN, TSUNA.
I EXPECT...

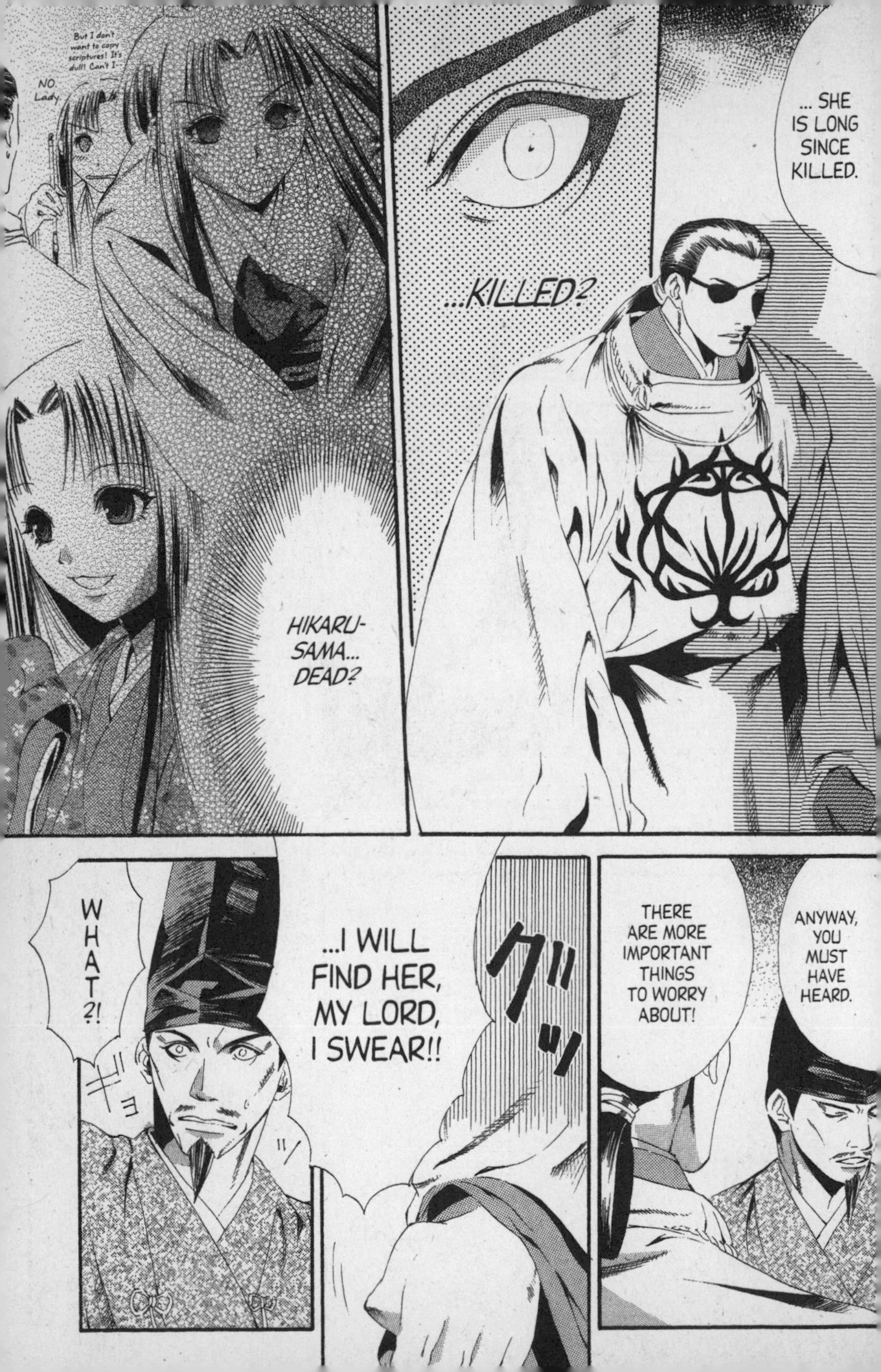

... SHE IS LONG SINCE KILLED.
...KILLED?
HIKARU-SAMA... DEAD?
But I don't want to copy scriptures! It's dull! Can't I--
NO. Lady.
ANYWAY, YOU MUST HAVE HEARD.
THERE ARE MORE IMPORTANT THINGS TO WORRY ABOUT!
...I WILL FIND HER, MY LORD, I SWEAR!!
WHAT?!

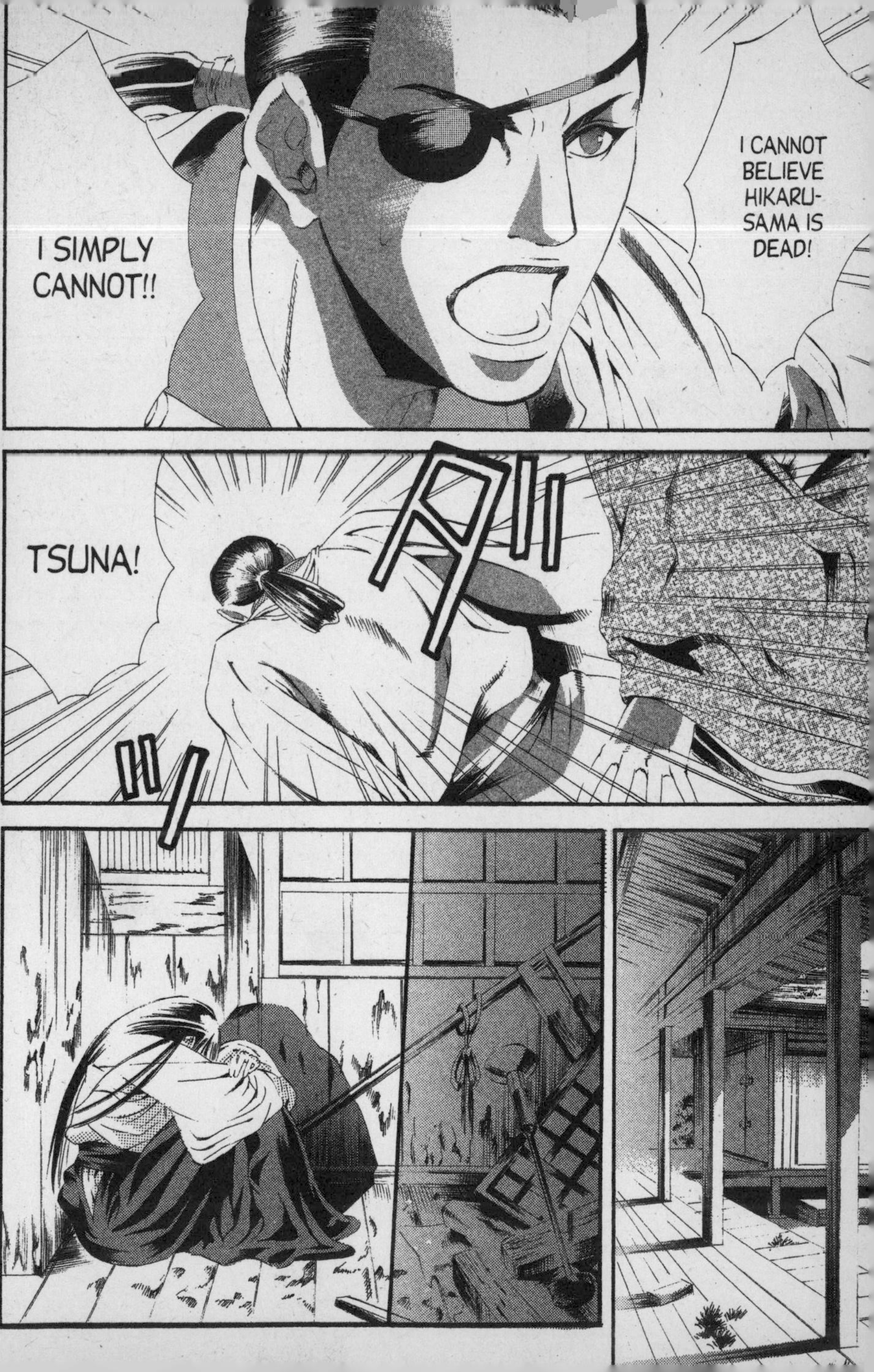
I CANNOT BELIEVE HIKARU-SAMA IS DEAD!
I SIMPLY CANNOT!!
TSUNA!

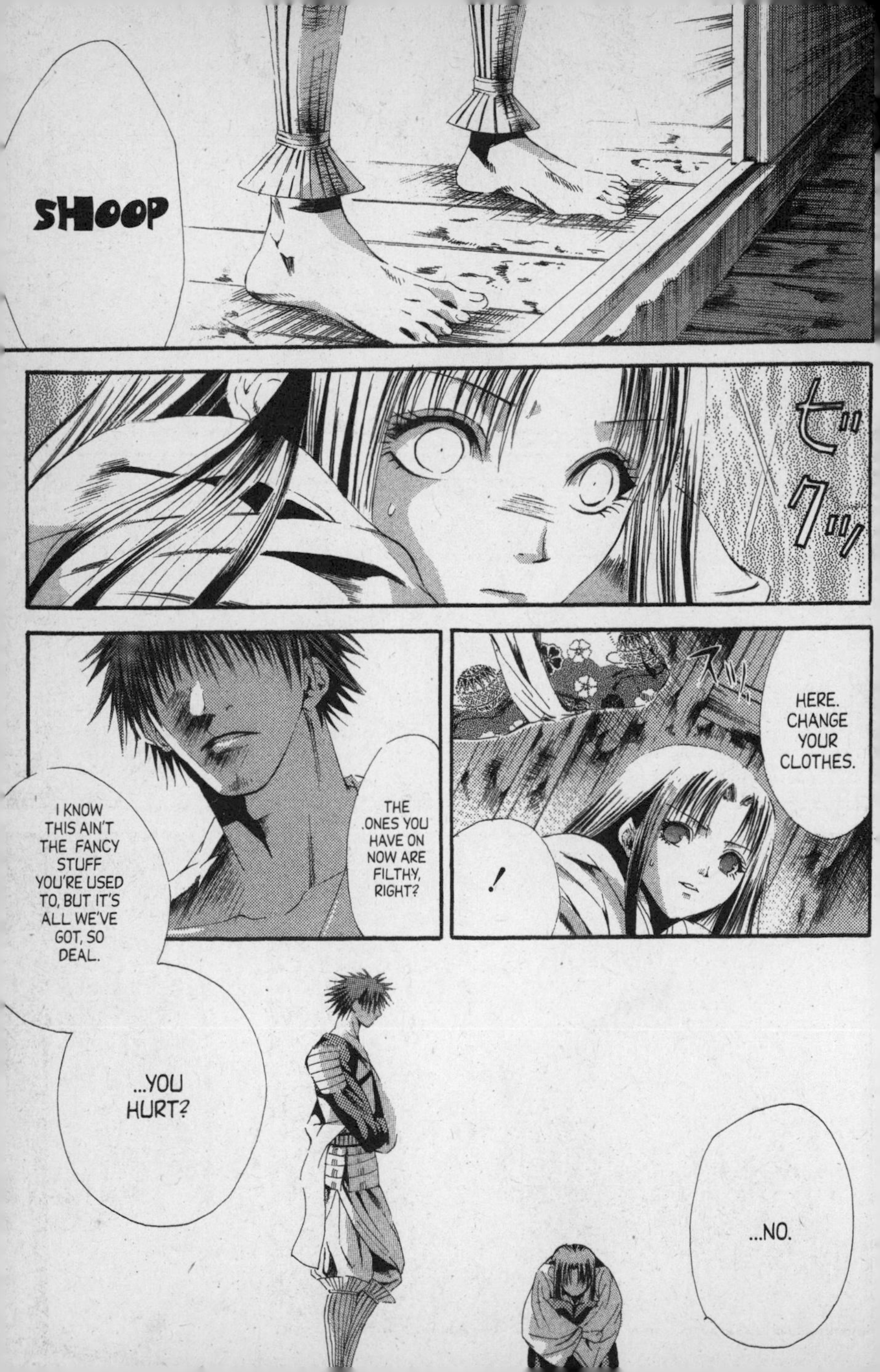
SHOOP
ビクッ
HERE. CHANGE YOUR CLOTHES.
!
THE ONES YOU HAVE ON NOW ARE FILTHY, RIGHT?
I KNOW THIS AIN'T THE FANCY STUFF YOU'RE USED TO, BUT IT'S ALL WE'VE GOT, SO DEAL.
...YOU HURT?
...NO.

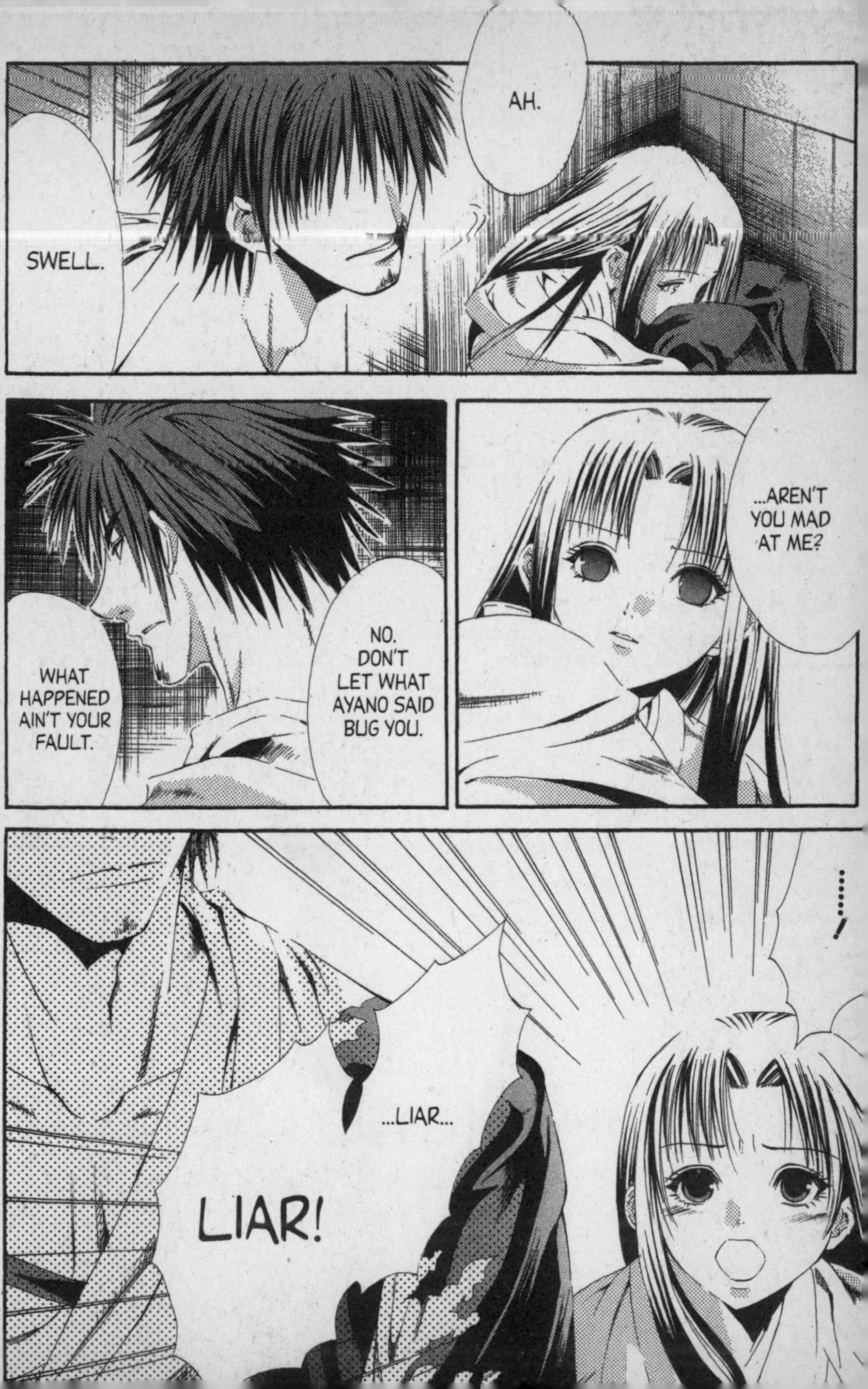
AH.
SWELL.
...AREN'T YOU MAD AT ME?
NO. DON'T LET WHAT AYANO SAID BUG YOU.
WHAT HAPPENED AIN'T YOUR FAULT.
......!
...LIAR...
LIAR!

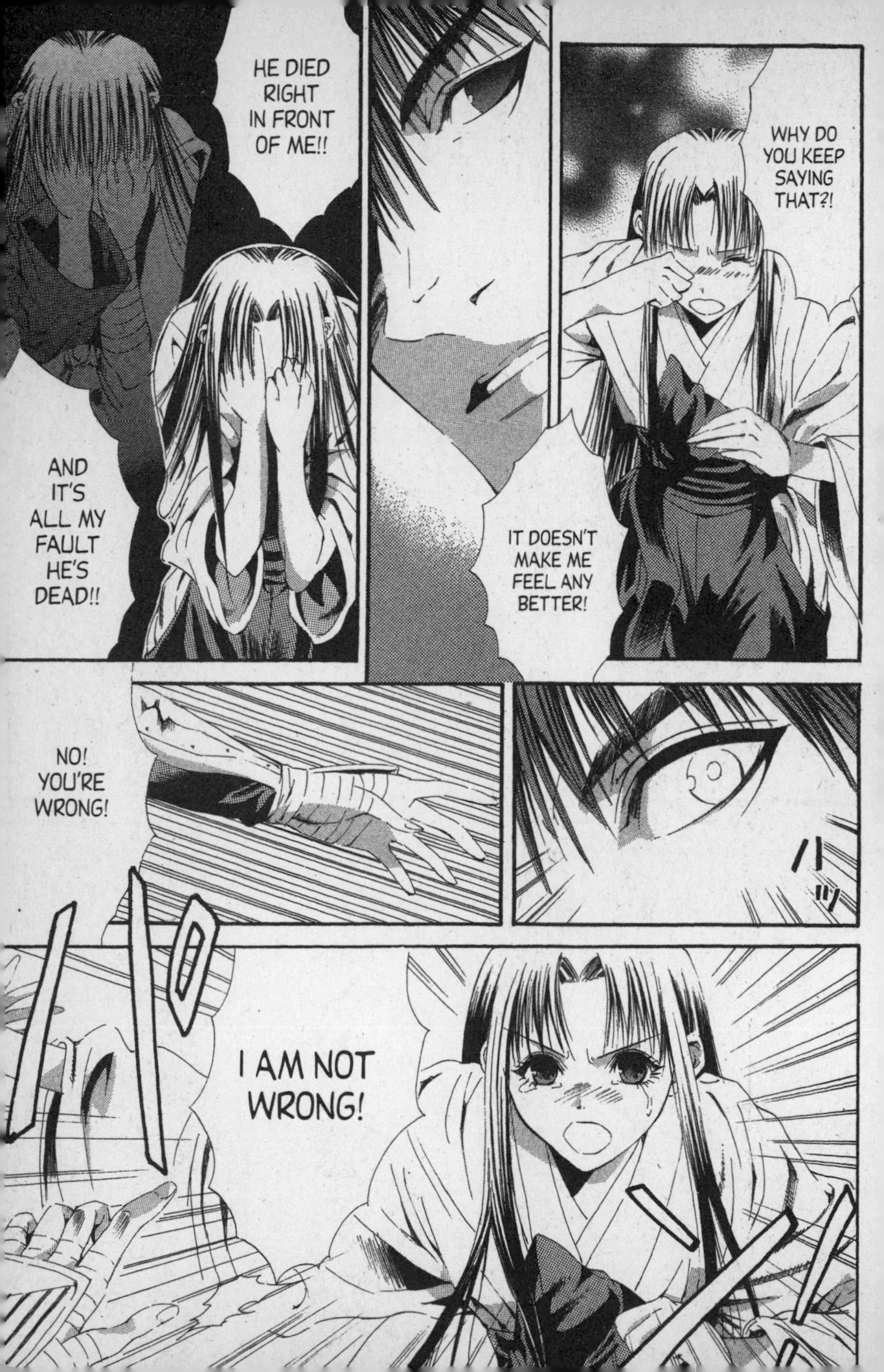
WHY DO YOU KEEP SAYING THAT?!
IT DOESN'T MAKE ME FEEL ANY BETTER!
HE DIED RIGHT IN FRONT OF ME!!
AND IT'S ALL MY FAULT HE'S DEAD!!
NO! YOU'RE WRONG!
ハッ
I AM NOT WRONG!

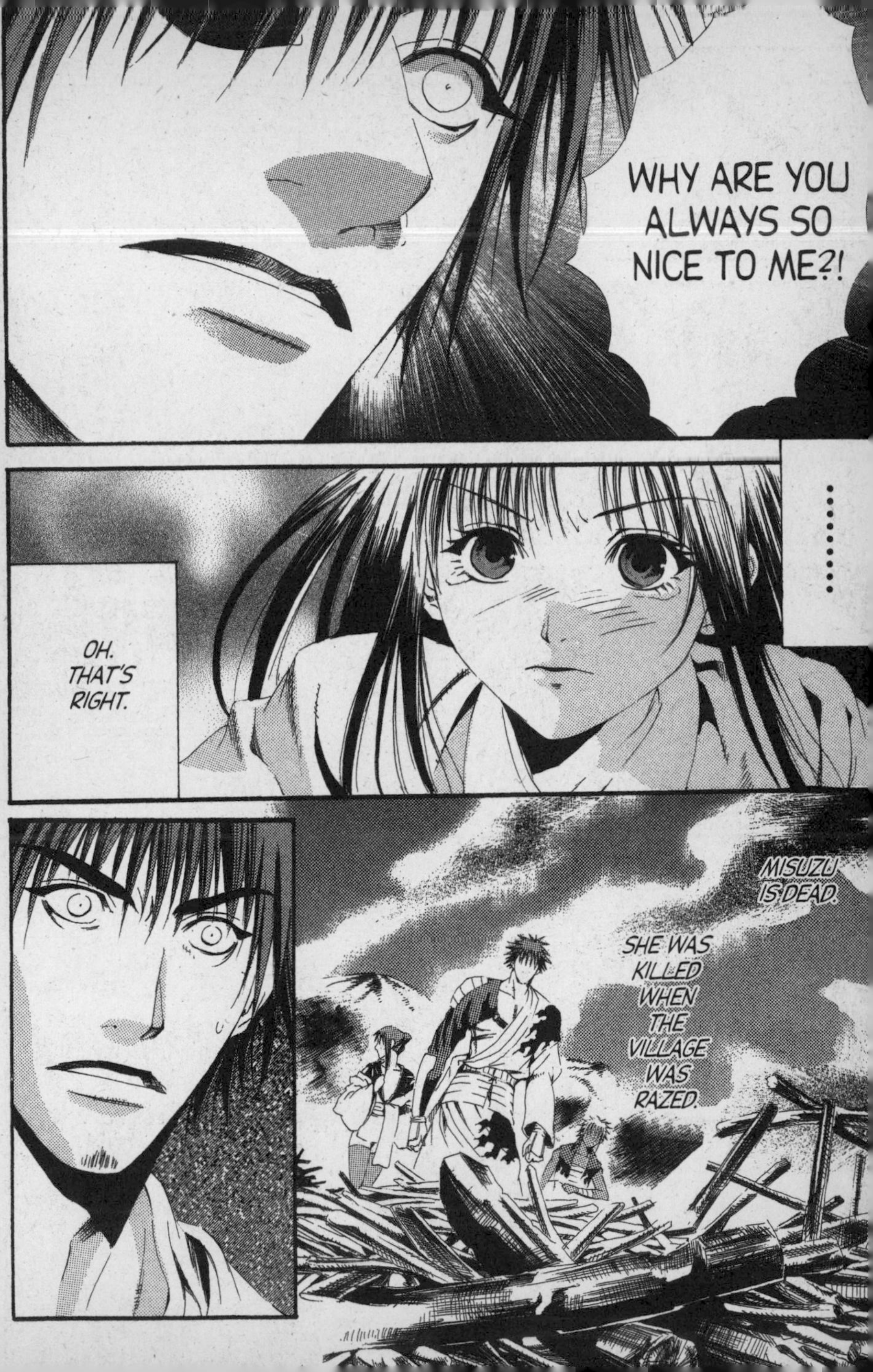
WHY ARE YOU ALWAYS SO NICE TO ME?!
....
OH. THAT'S RIGHT.
MISUZU IS DEAD.
SHE WAS KILLED WHEN THE VILLAGE WAS RAZED.

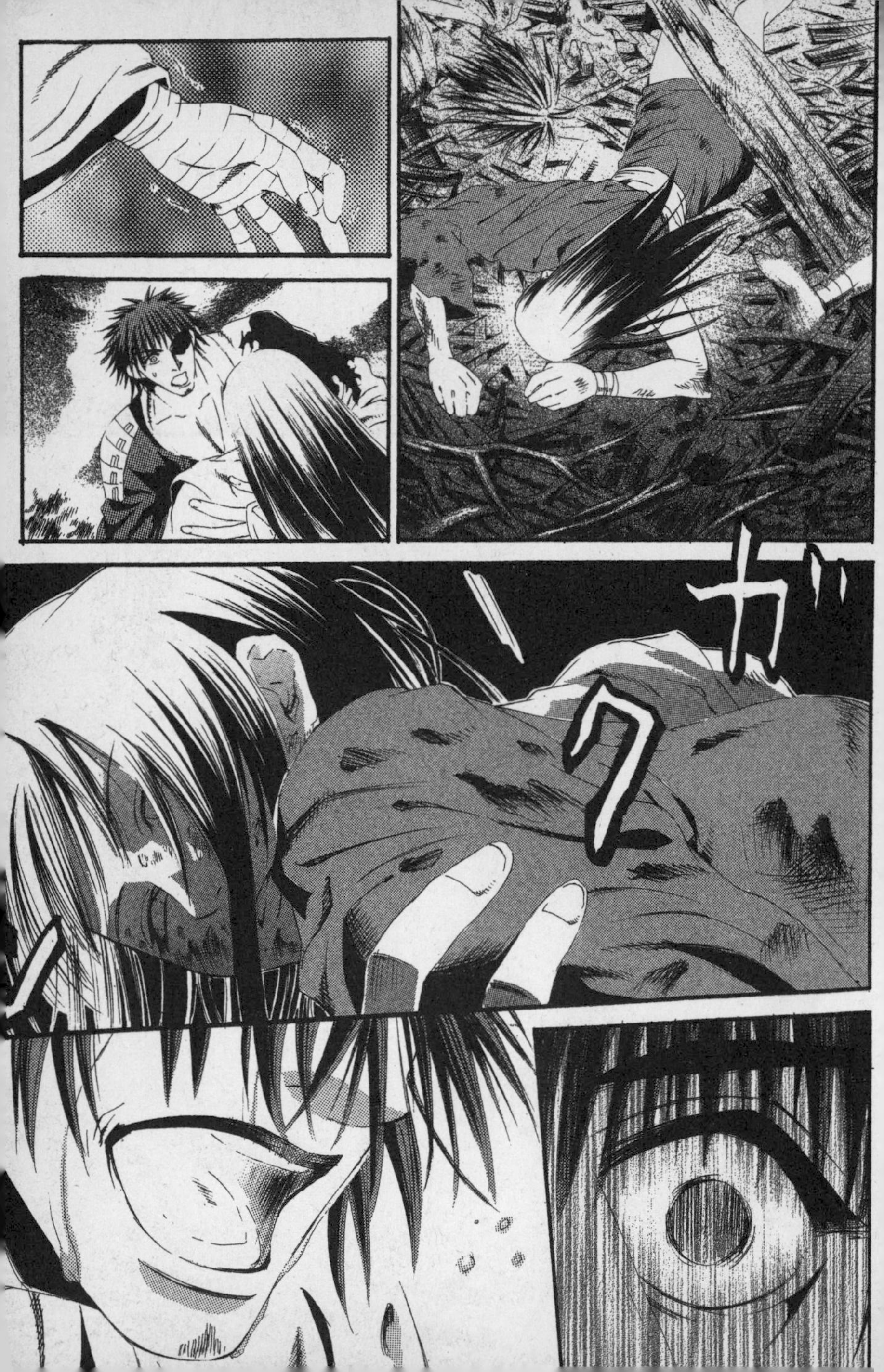
ガク

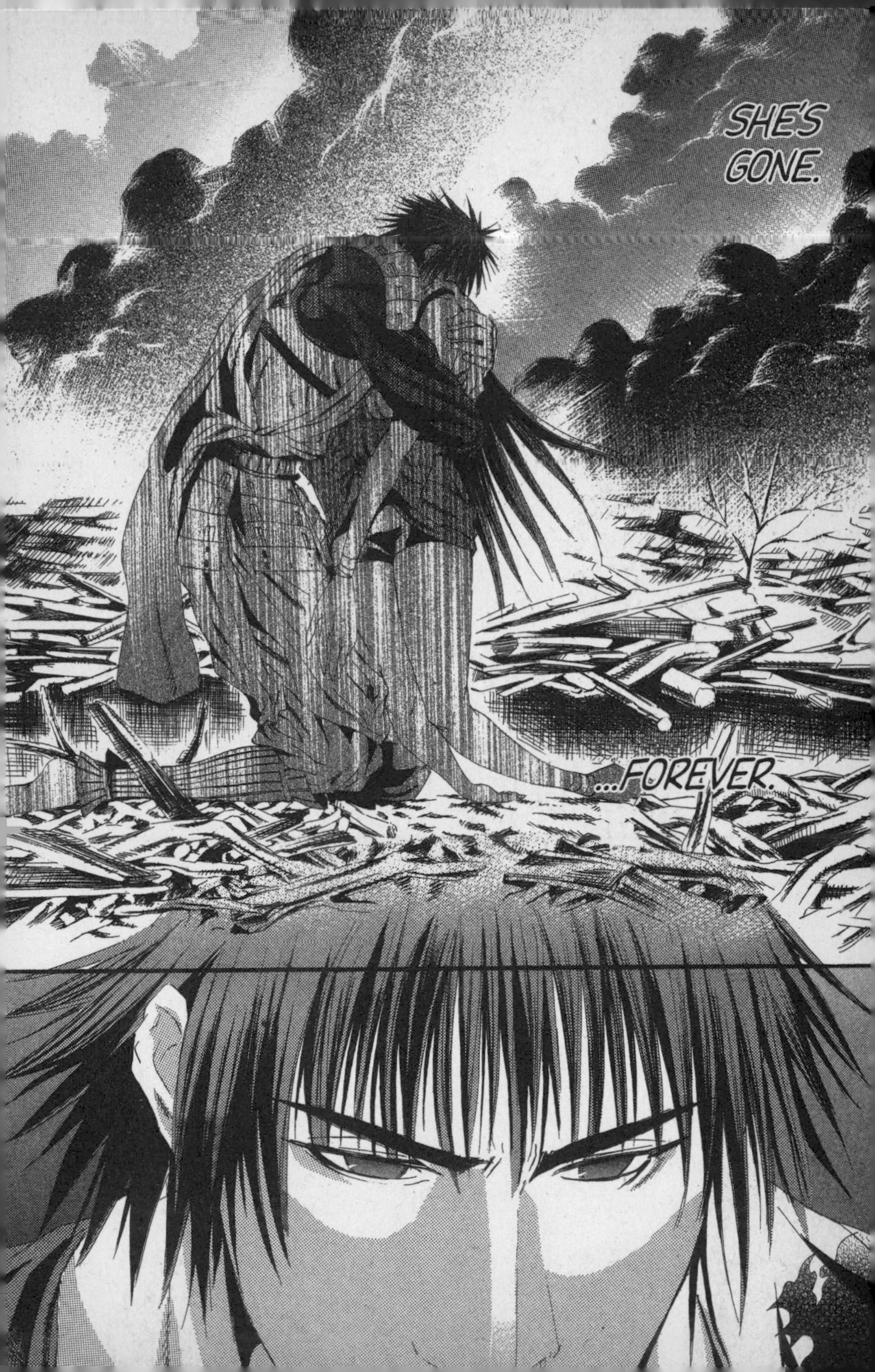
SHE'S GONE.
...FOREVER.

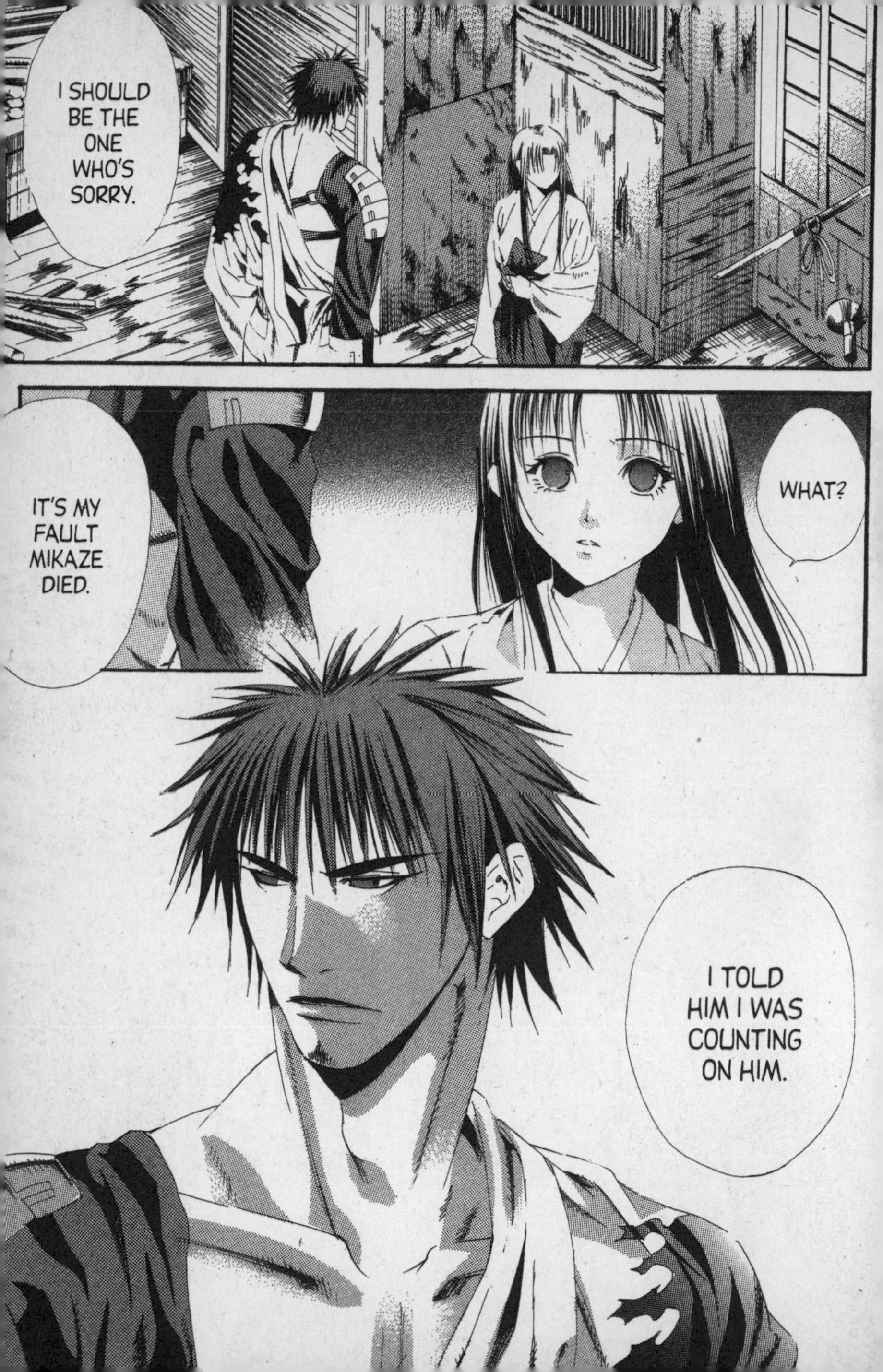
I SHOULD BE THE ONE WHO'S SORRY.
WHAT?
IT'S MY FAULT MIKAZE DIED.
I TOLD HIM I WAS COUNTING ON HIM.

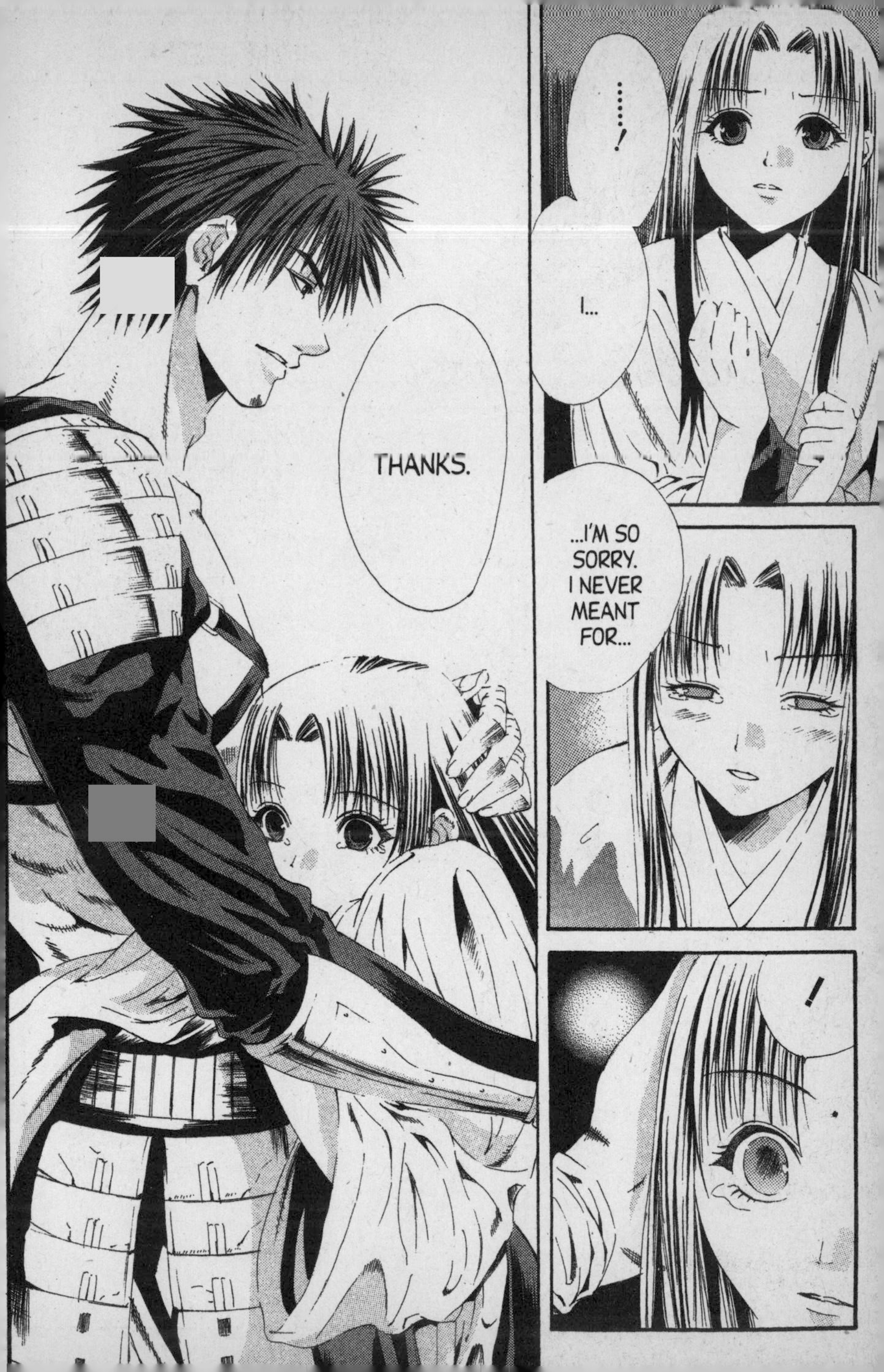

......!
I...
...I'M SO SORRY. I NEVER MEANT FOR...
!
THANKS.

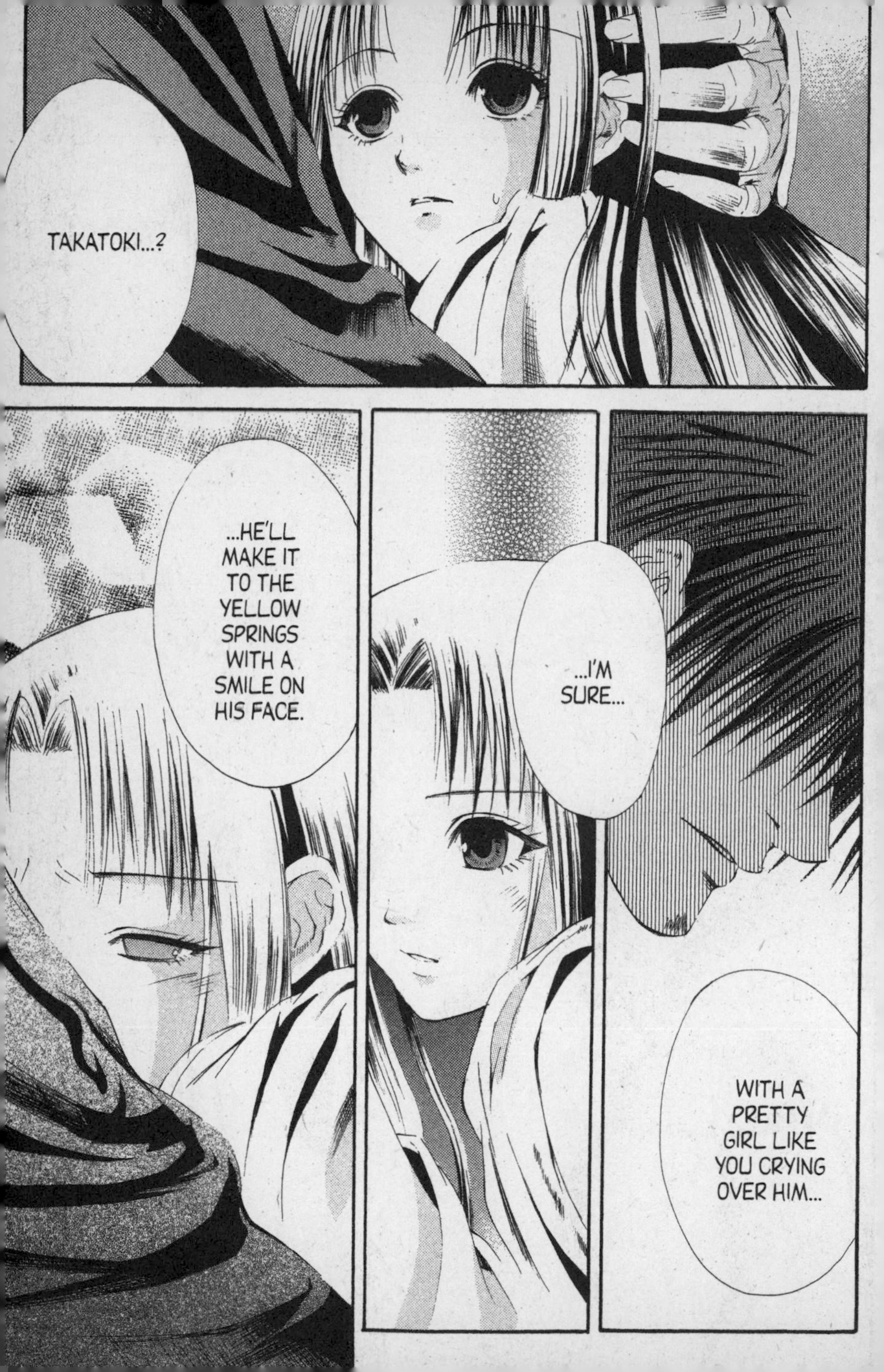
TAKATOKI...?
...I'M SURE...
...HE'LL MAKE IT TO THE YELLOW SPRINGS WITH A SMILE ON HIS FACE.
WITH A PRETTY GIRL LIKE YOU CRYING OVER HIM...

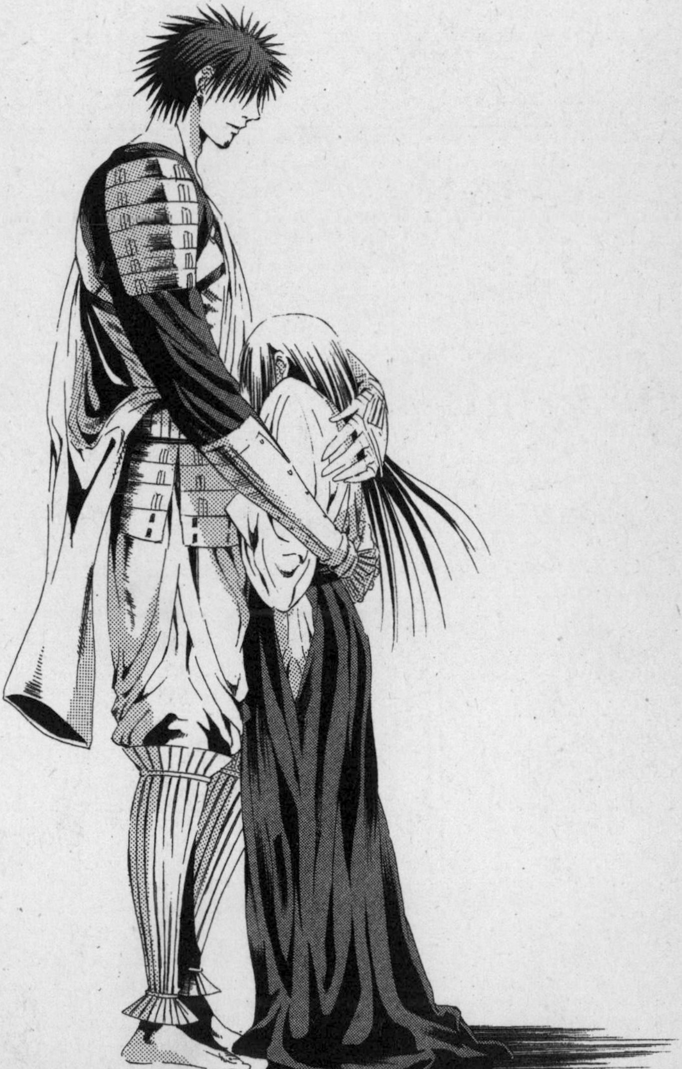

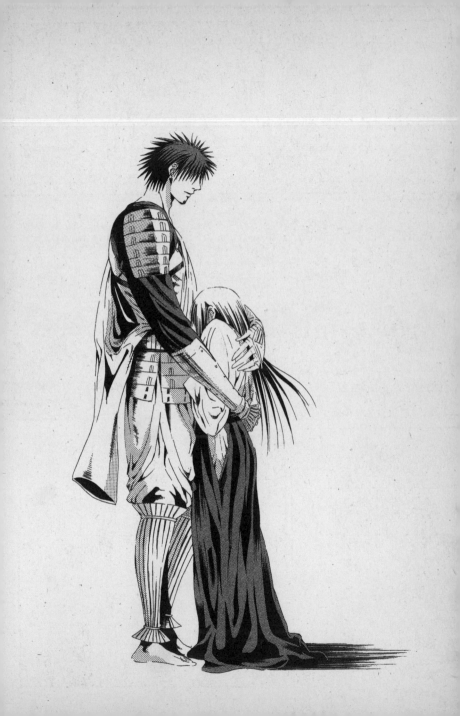

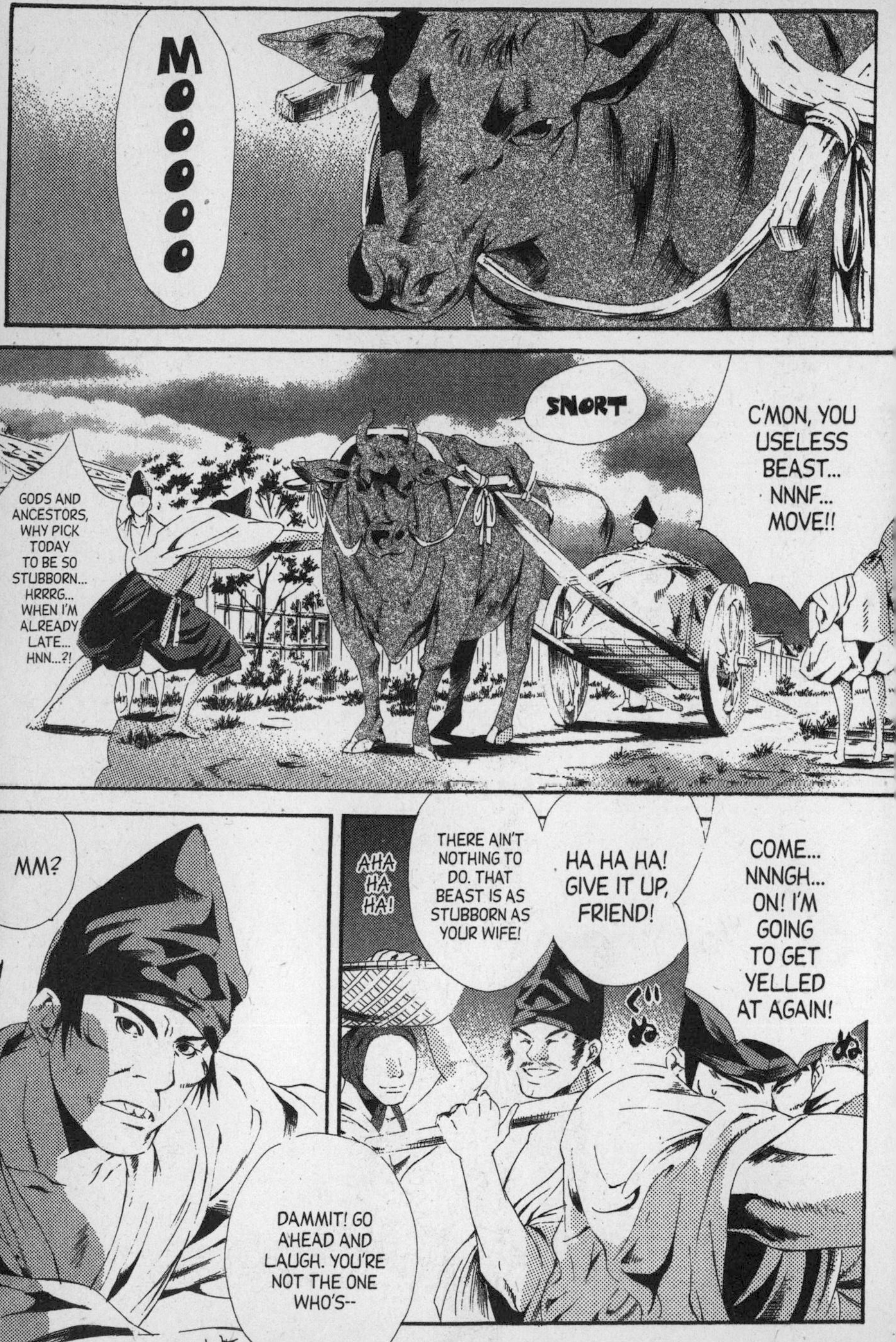
MOOOOOO
C'MON, YOU USELESS BEAST... NNNF... MOVE!!
SNORT
GODS AND ANCESTORS, WHY PICK TODAY TO BE SO STUBBORN... HRRRG... WHEN I'M ALREADY LATE... HNN...?!
COME... NNNGH... ON! I'M GOING TO GET YELLED AT AGAIN!
HA HA HA! GIVE IT UP, FRIEND!
THERE AIN'T NOTHING TO DO. THAT BEAST IS AS STUBBORN AS YOUR WIFE!
AHA HA HA!
MM?
DAMMIT! GO AHEAD AND LAUGH. YOU'RE NOT THE ONE WHO'S--

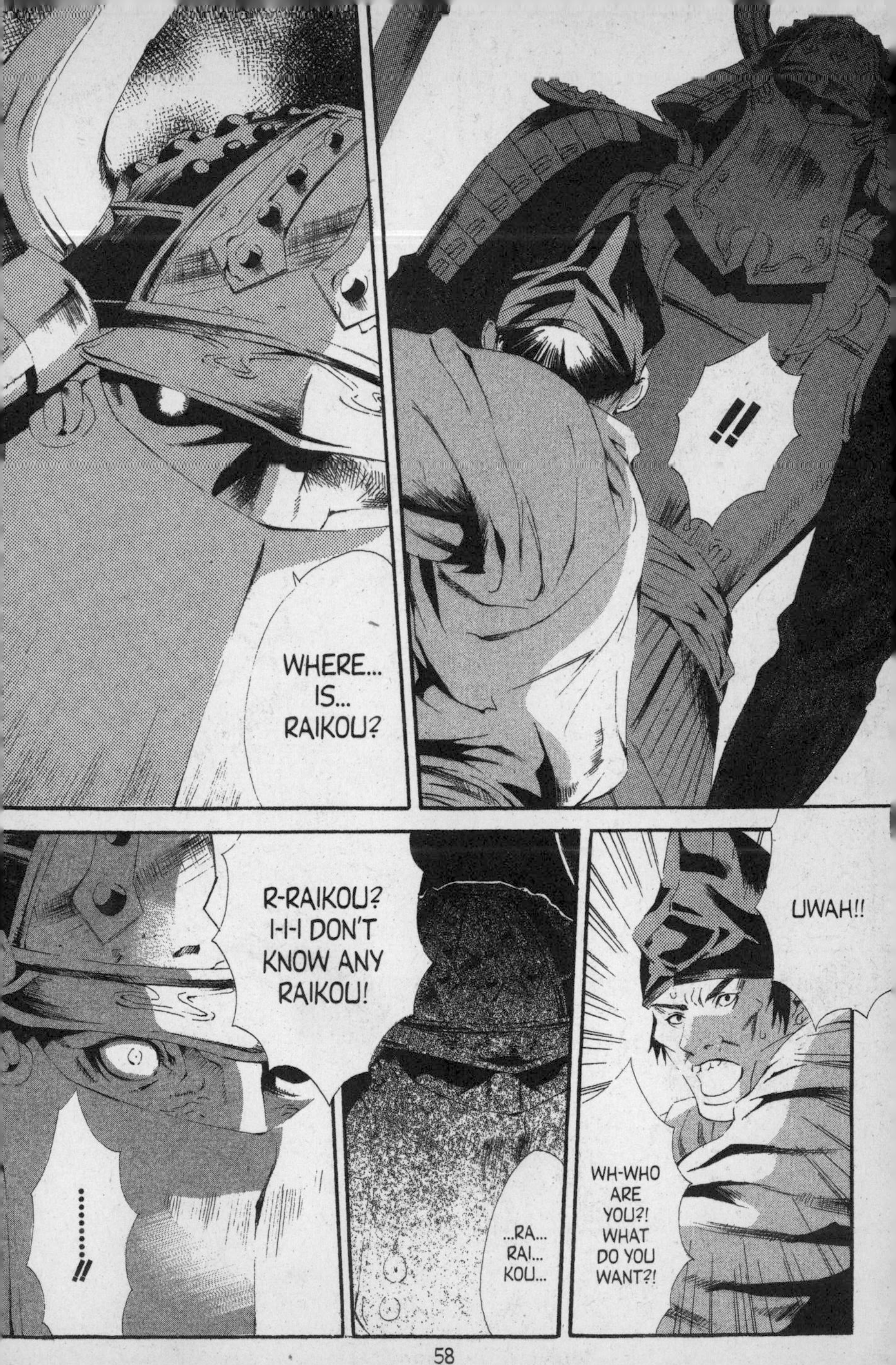

!!
WHERE... IS... RAIKOU?
UWAH!!
WH-WHO ARE YOU?! WHAT DO YOU WANT?!
...RA... RAI... KOU...
R-RAIKOU? I-I-I DON'T KNOW ANY RAIKOU!
.........!!

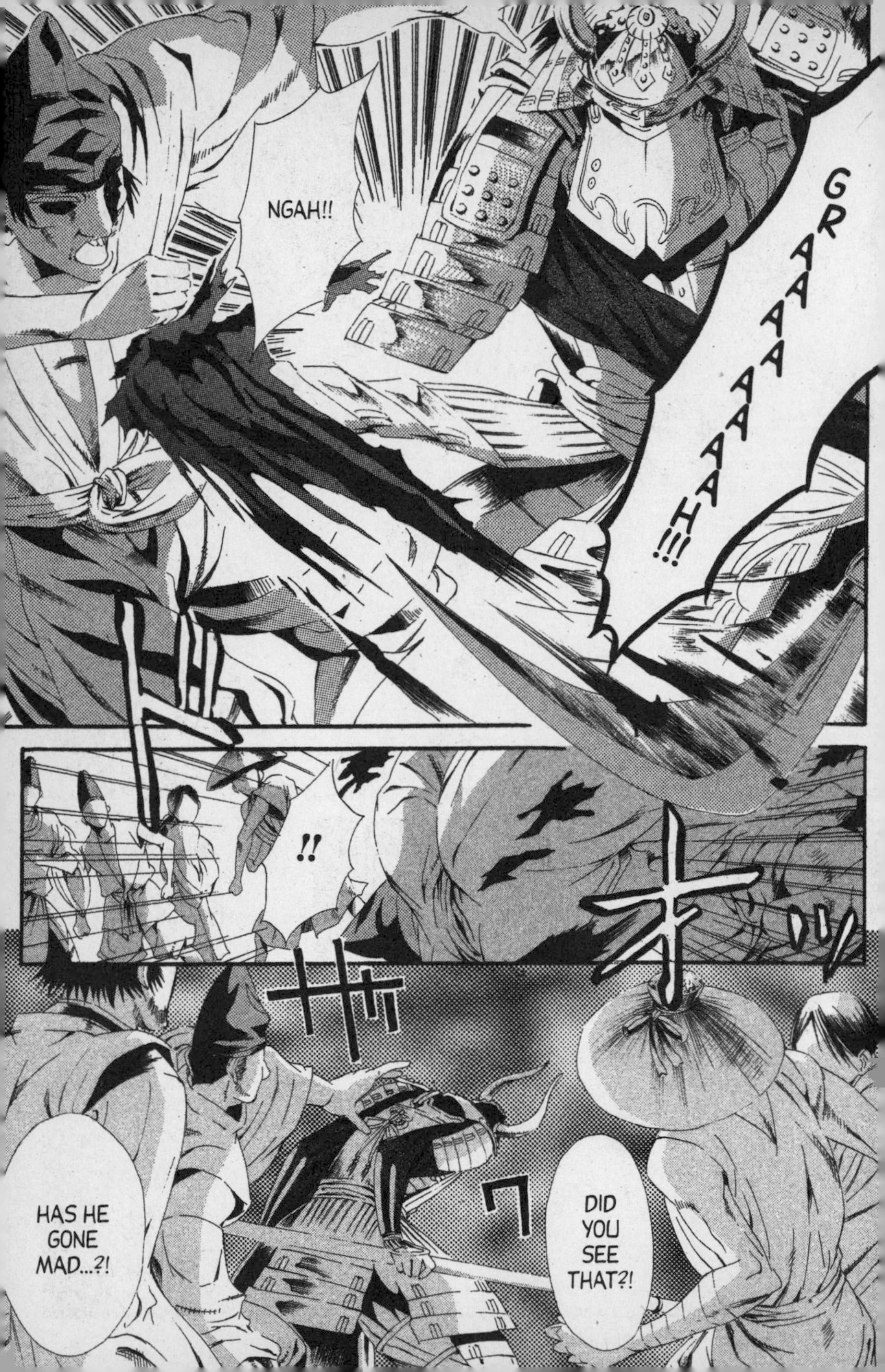

GRAAAAAAAAH!!!
NGAH!!
!!
DID YOU SEE THAT?!
HAS HE GONE MAD...?!

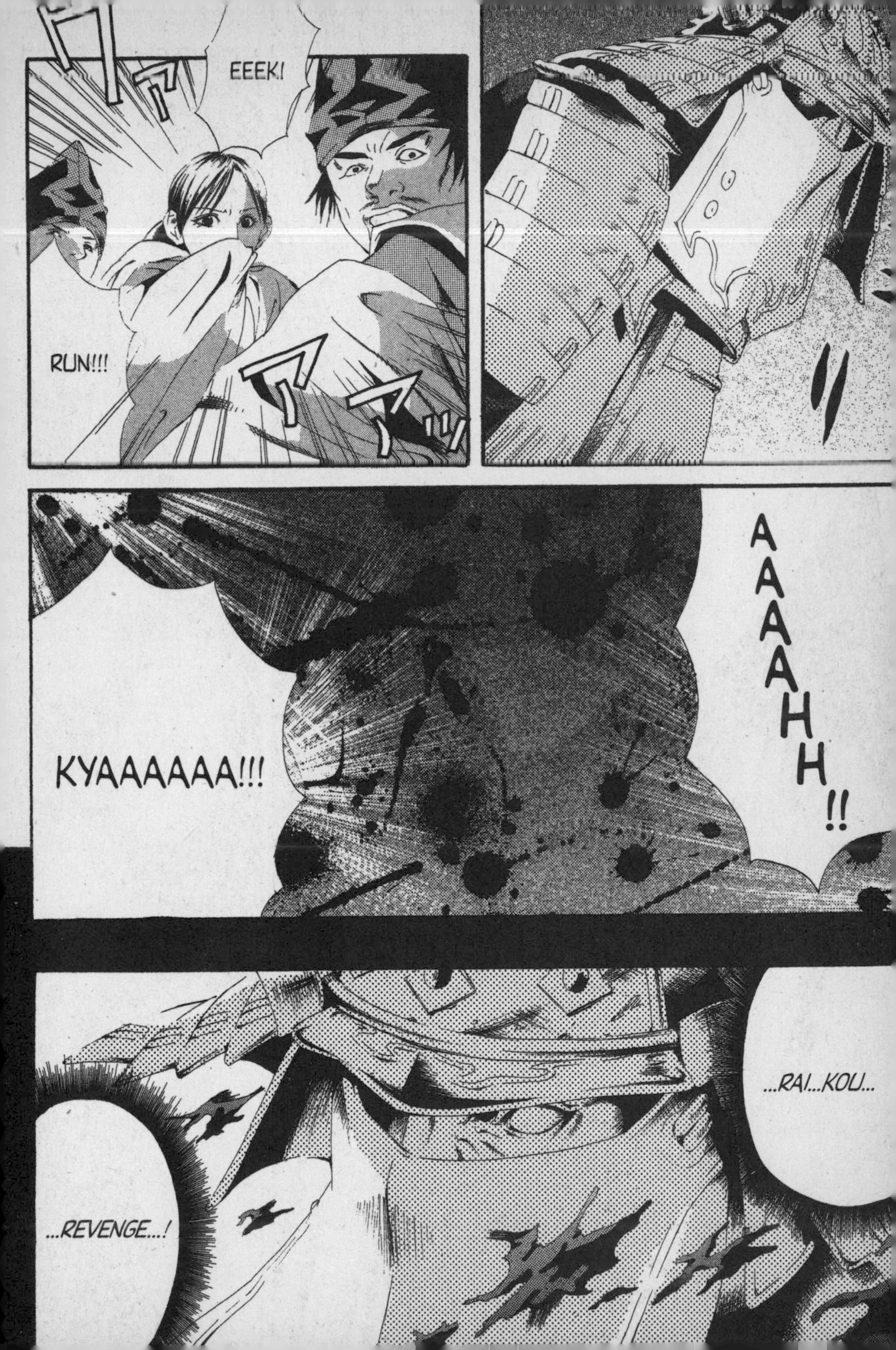

EEEK!
RUN!!!
AAAAHH!!
KYAAAAAA!!!
...RAI...KOU...
...REVENGE...!

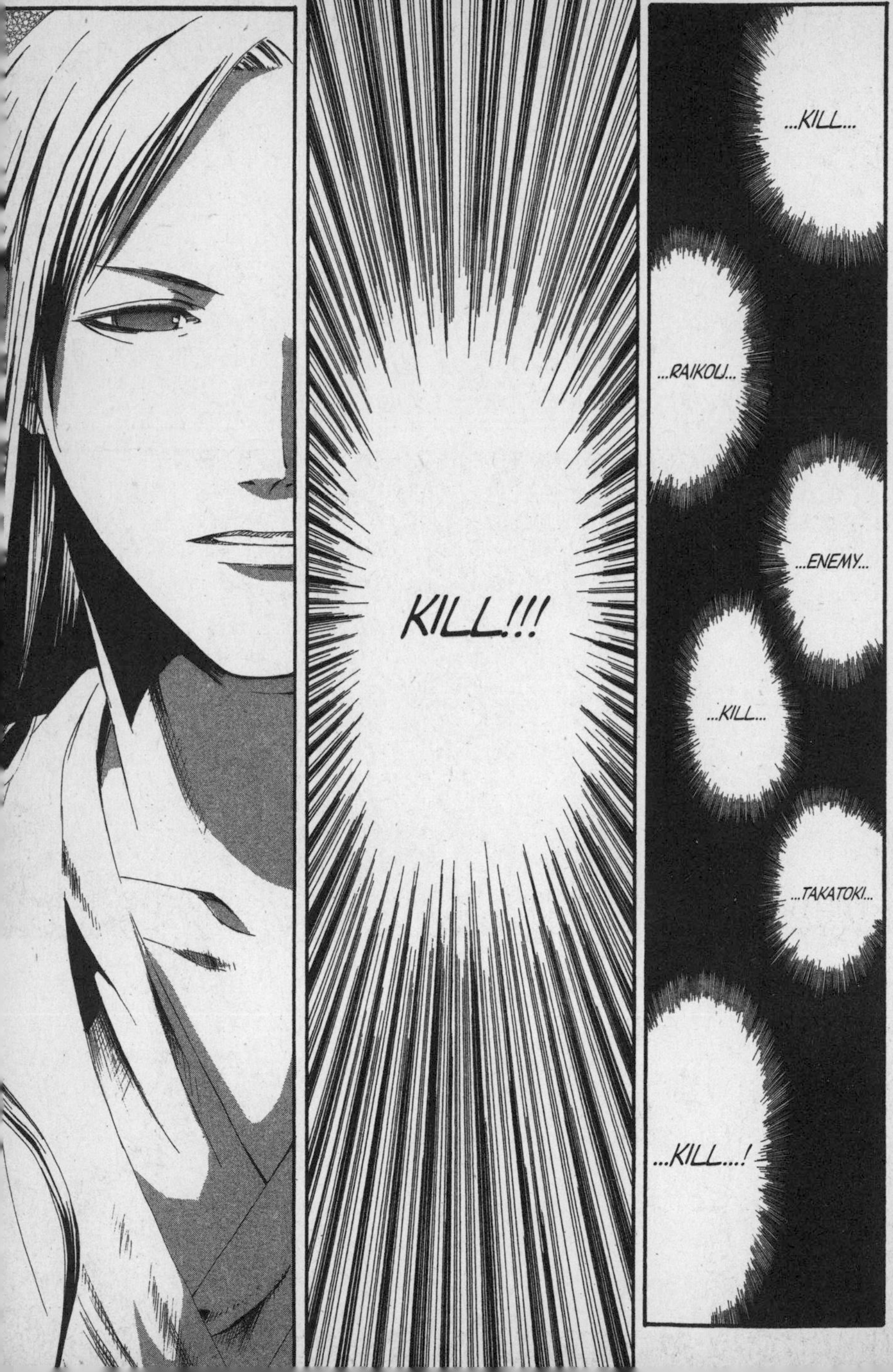
...KILL...
...RAIKOU...
...ENEMY...
...KILL...
...TAKATOKI...
...KILL...!
KILL!!!

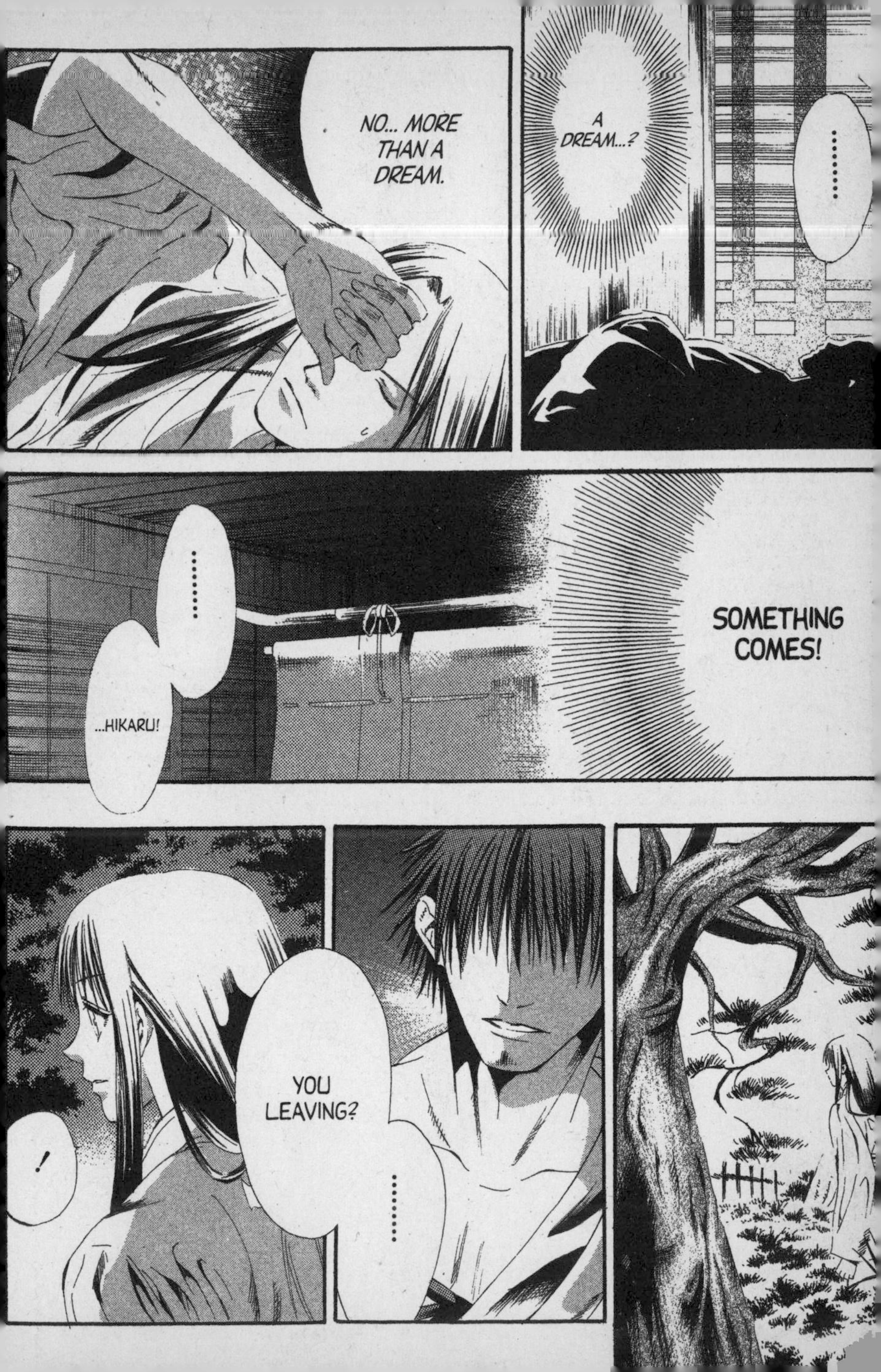
......
A DREAM...?
NO... MORE THAN A DREAM.
SOMETHING COMES!
......
...HIKARU!
!
YOU LEAVING?
......

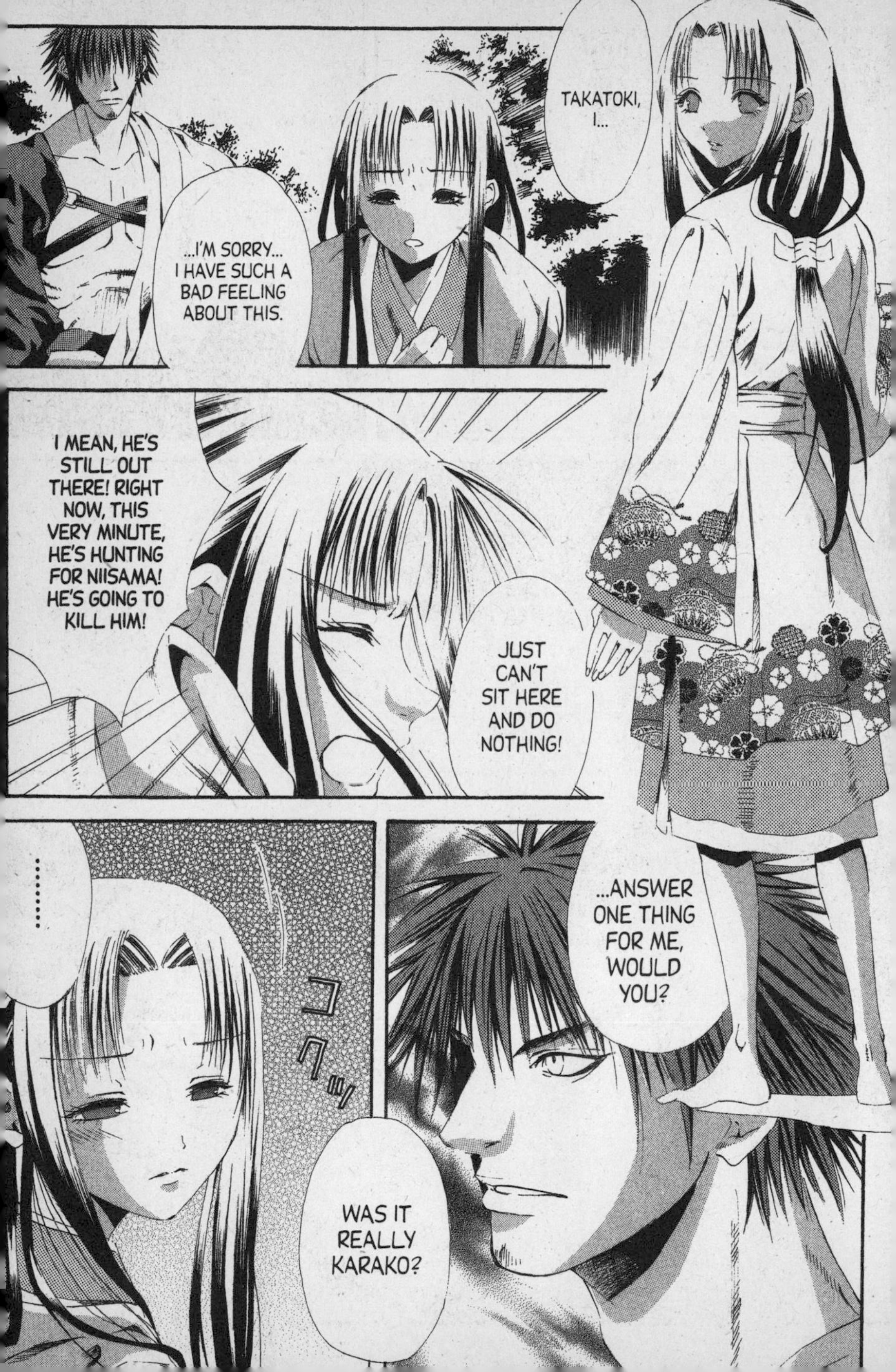
TAKATOKI, I...
...I'M SORRY... I HAVE SUCH A BAD FEELING ABOUT THIS.
JUST CAN'T SIT HERE AND DO NOTHING!
I MEAN, HE'S STILL OUT THERE! RIGHT NOW, THIS VERY MINUTE, HE'S HUNTING FOR NIISAMA! HE'S GOING TO KILL HIM!
...ANSWER ONE THING FOR ME, WOULD YOU?
WAS IT REALLY KARAKO?
....

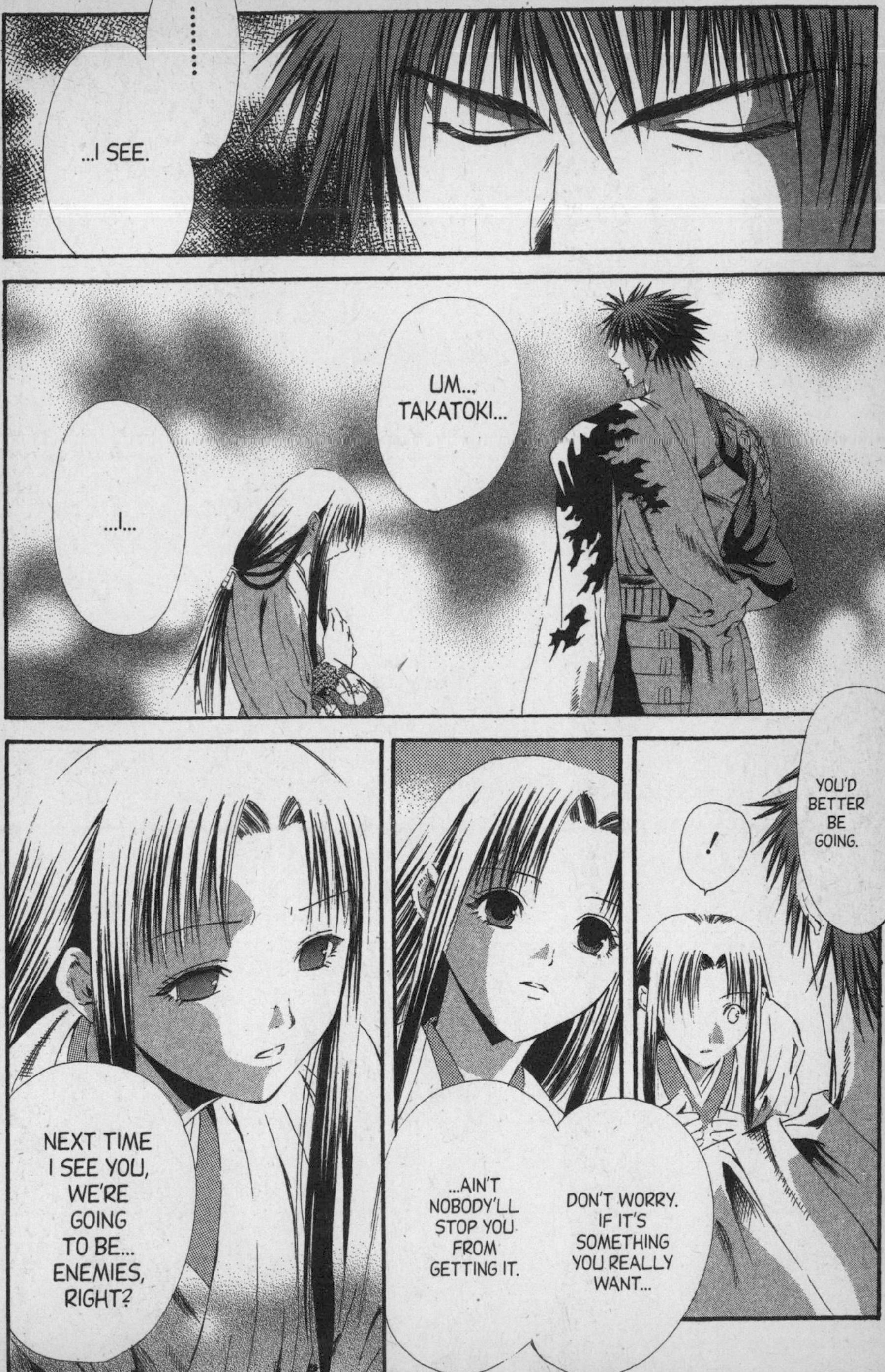
......
...I SEE.
UM... TAKATOKI...
...I...
YOU'D BETTER BE GOING.
!
DON'T WORRY. IF IT'S SOMETHING YOU REALLY WANT...
...AIN'T NOBODY'LL STOP YOU FROM GETTING IT.
NEXT TIME I SEE YOU, WE'RE GOING TO BE... ENEMIES, RIGHT?

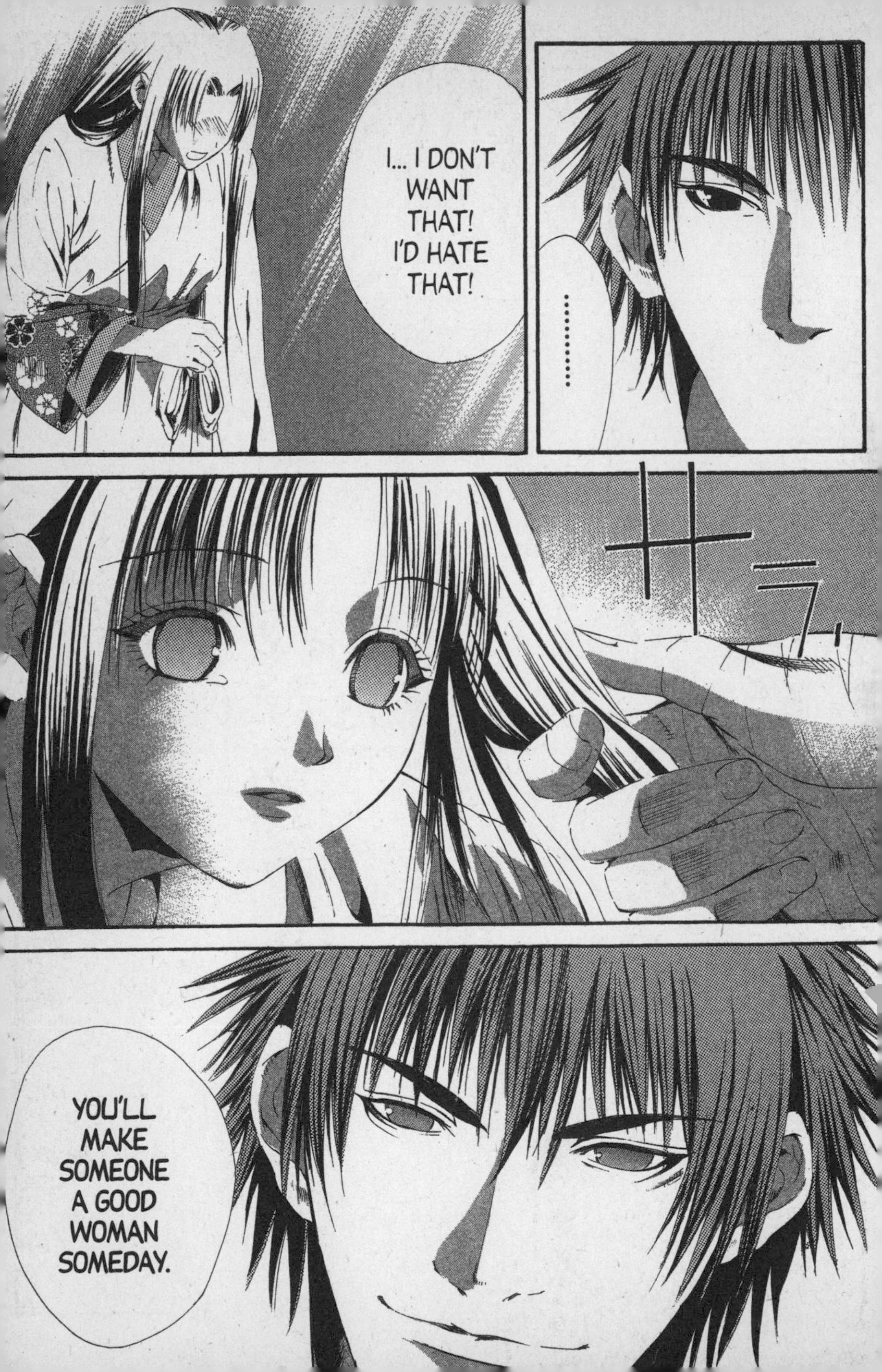
……
I... I DON'T WANT THAT! I'D HATE THAT!
サラ
YOU'LL MAKE SOMEONE A GOOD WOMAN SOMEDAY.

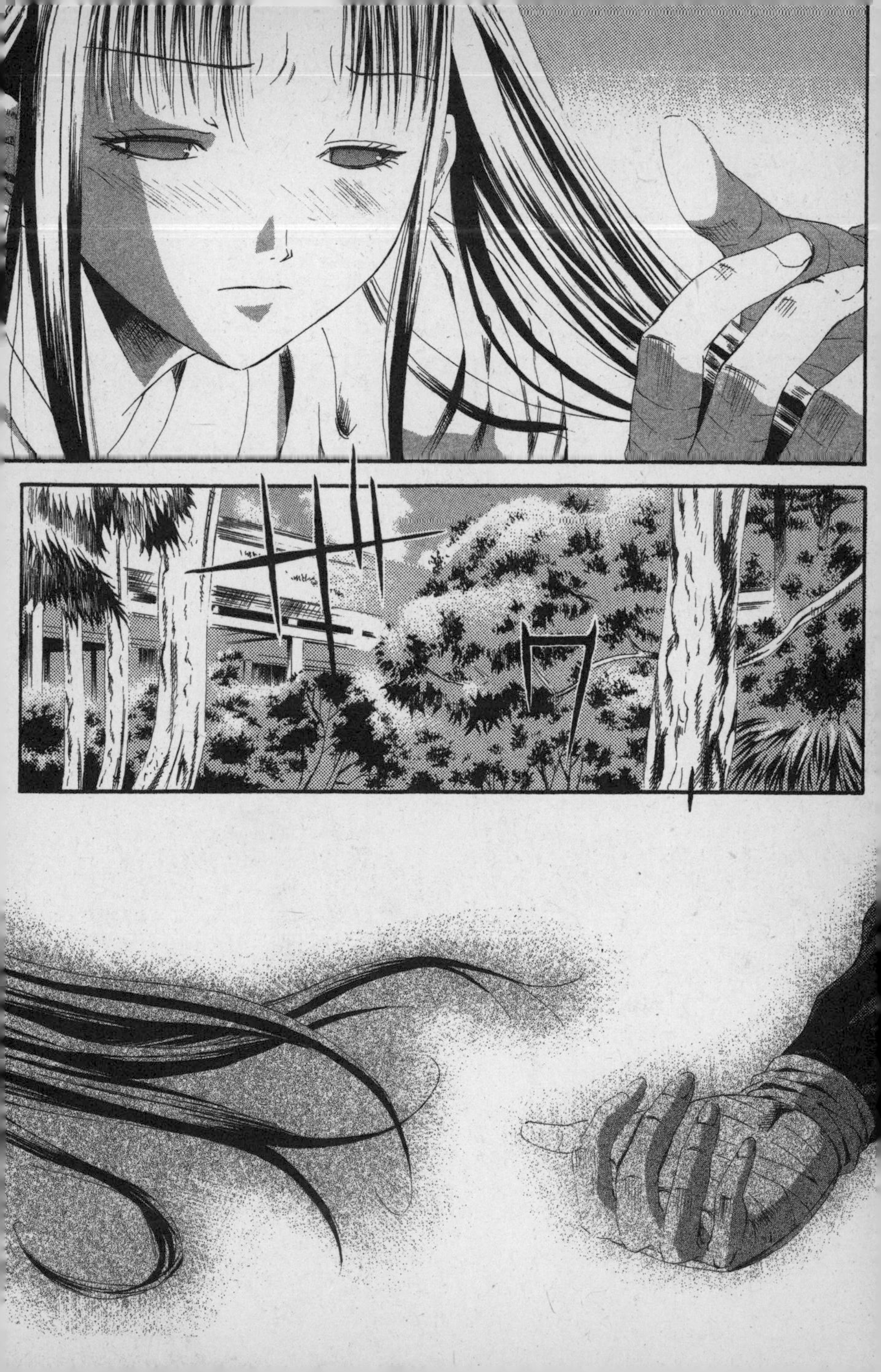

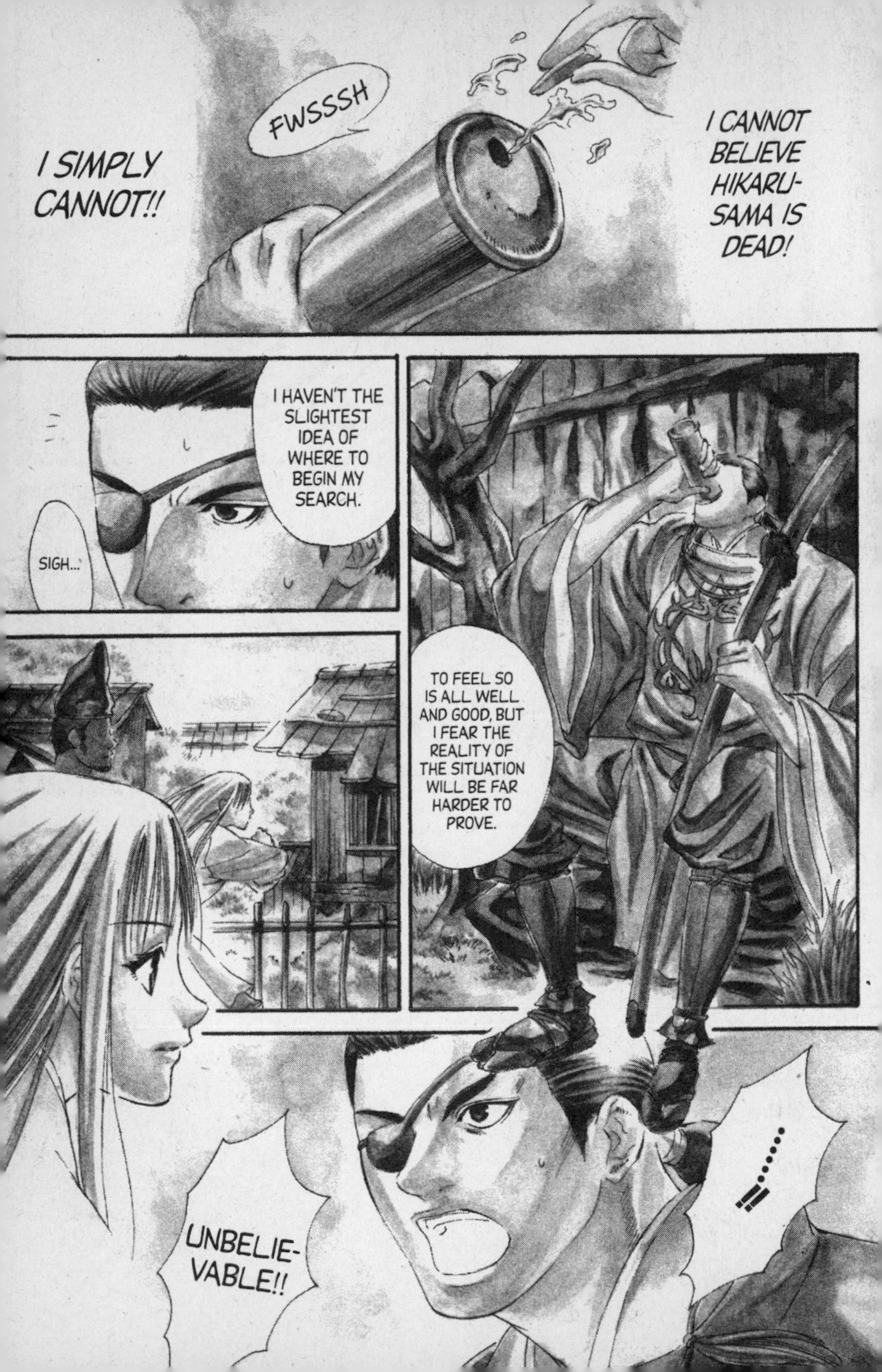

I CANNOT BELIEVE HIKARU-SAMA IS DEAD!
FWSSSH
I SIMPLY CANNOT!!
TO FEEL SO IS ALL WELL AND GOOD, BUT I FEAR THE REALITY OF THE SITUATION WILL BE FAR HARDER TO PROVE.
I HAVEN'T THE SLIGHTEST IDEA OF WHERE TO BEGIN MY SEARCH.
SIGH...
!!......
UNBELIE-VABLE!!

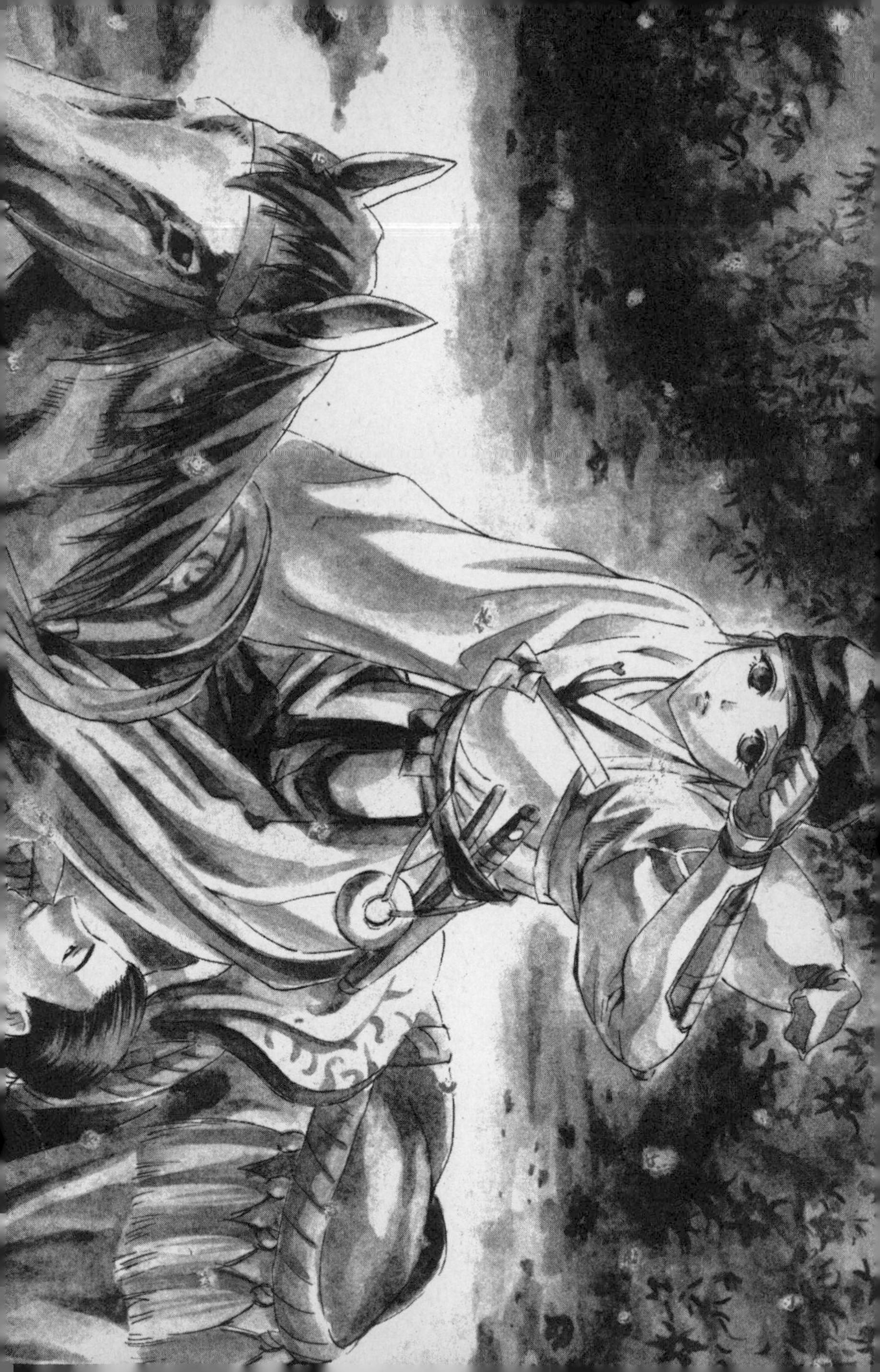

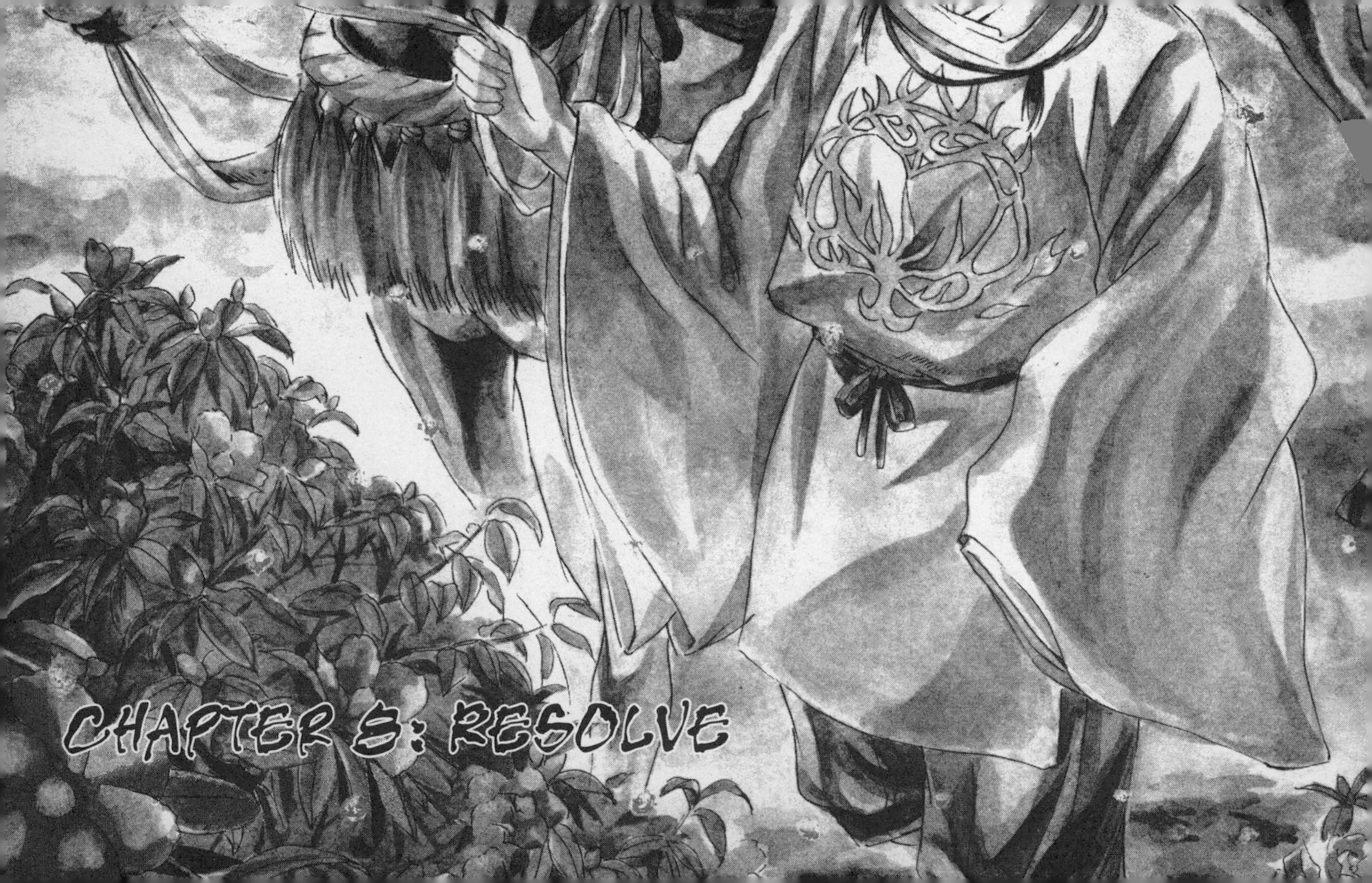
CHAPTER 8: RESOLVE

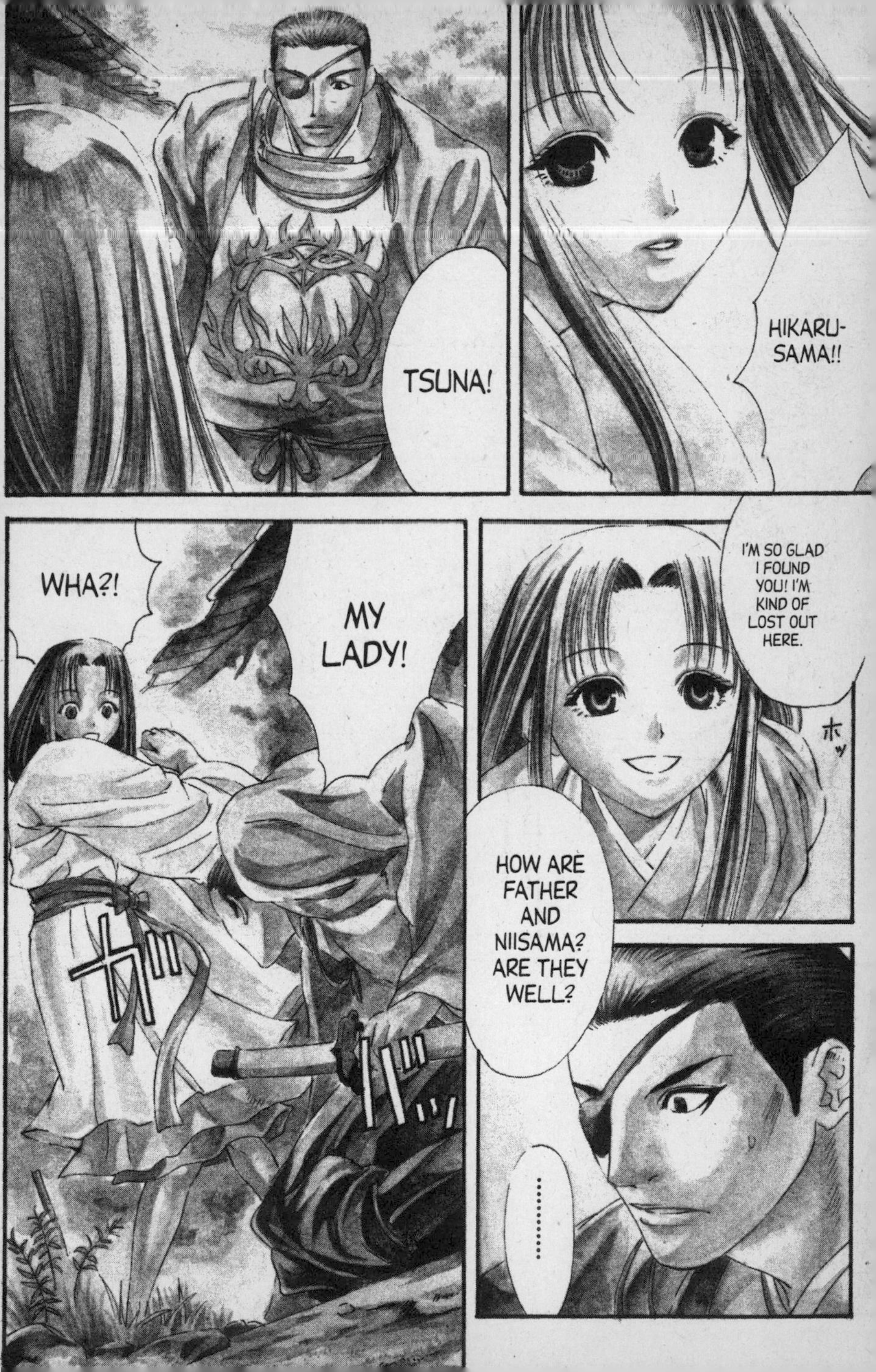
HIKARU-SAMA!!
TSUNA!
I'M SO GLAD I FOUND YOU! I'M KIND OF LOST OUT HERE.
ホッ
HOW ARE FATHER AND NIISAMA? ARE THEY WELL?
......
MY LADY!
WHA?!

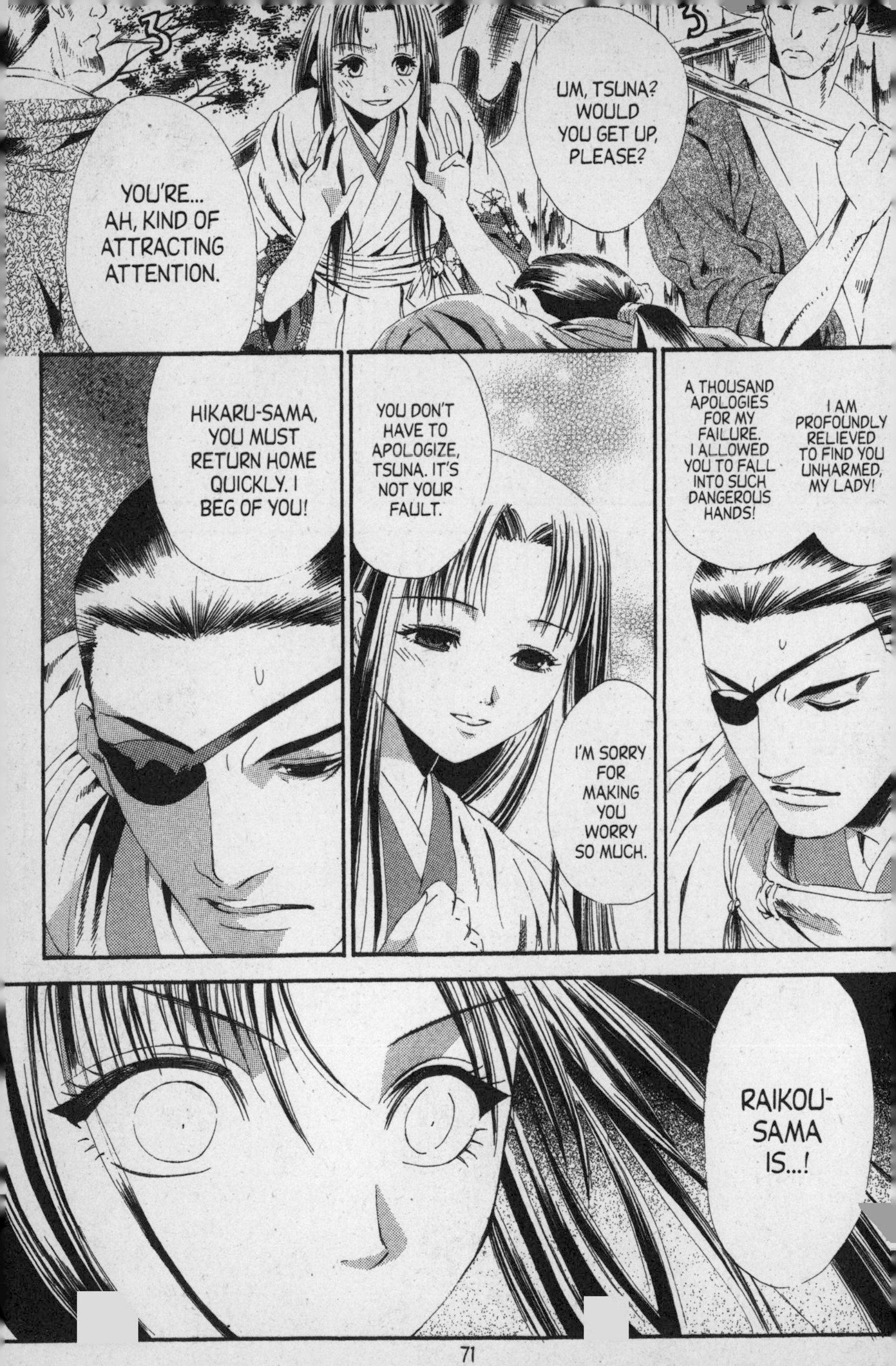
UM, TSUNA? WOULD YOU GET UP, PLEASE?
YOU'RE... AH, KIND OF ATTRACTING ATTENTION.
I AM PROFOUNDLY RELIEVED TO FIND YOU UNHARMED, MY LADY!
A THOUSAND APOLOGIES FOR MY FAILURE. I ALLOWED YOU TO FALL INTO SUCH DANGEROUS HANDS!
YOU DON'T HAVE TO APOLOGIZE, TSUNA. IT'S NOT YOUR FAULT.
I'M SORRY FOR MAKING YOU WORRY SO MUCH.
HIKARU-SAMA, YOU MUST RETURN HOME QUICKLY. I BEG OF YOU!
RAIKOU-SAMA IS...!

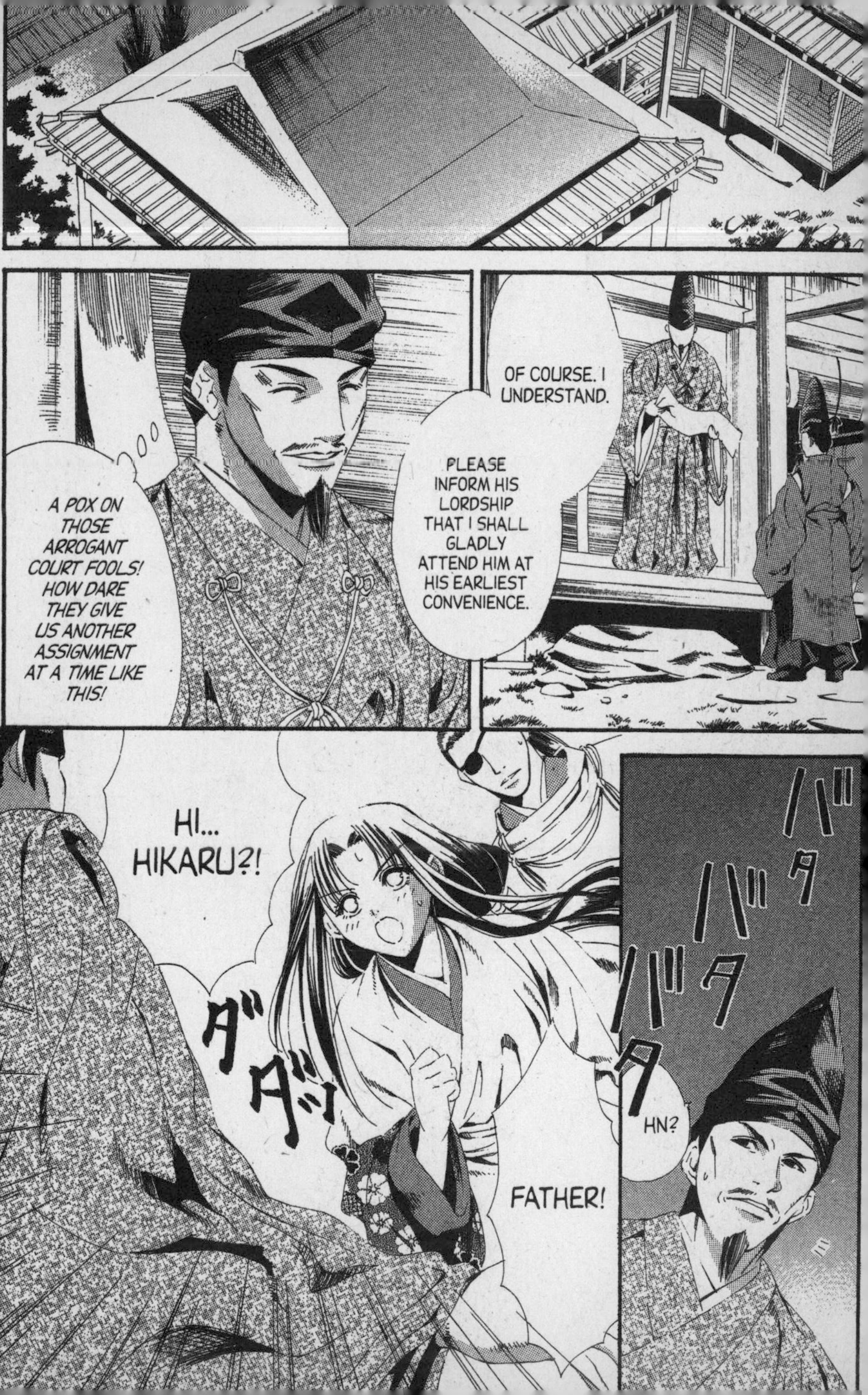
OF COURSE. I UNDERSTAND.
PLEASE INFORM HIS LORDSHIP THAT I SHALL GLADLY ATTEND HIM AT HIS EARLIEST CONVENIENCE.
A POX ON THOSE ARROGANT COURT FOOLS! HOW DARE THEY GIVE US ANOTHER ASSIGNMENT AT A TIME LIKE THIS!
バタバタバタ
HN?
HI... HIKARU?!
FATHER!
ダダッ

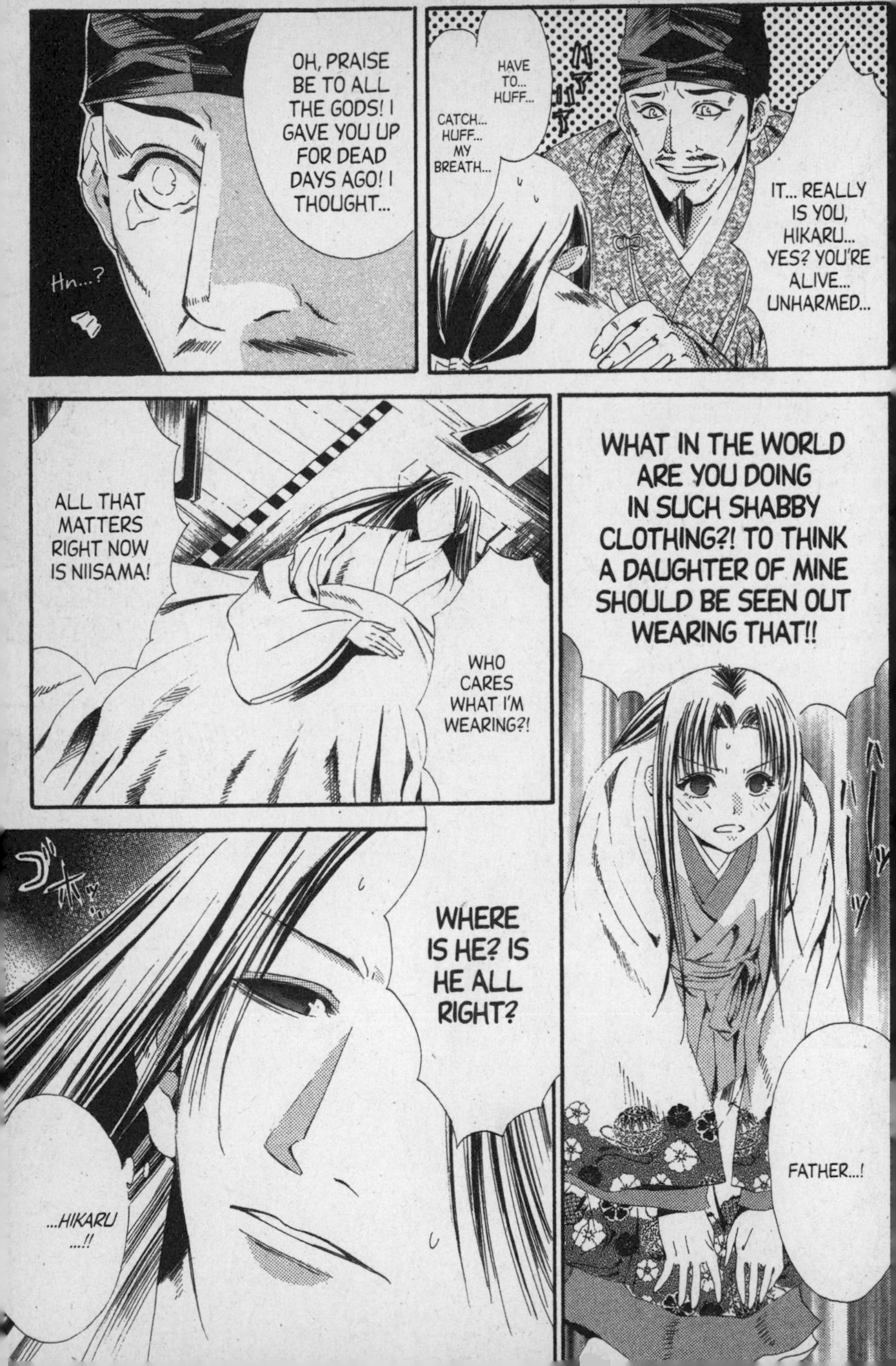
IT... REALLY IS YOU, HIKARU... YES? YOU'RE ALIVE... UNHARMED...
HAVE TO... HUFF...
CATCH... HUFF... MY BREATH...
OH, PRAISE BE TO ALL THE GODS! I GAVE YOU UP FOR DEAD DAYS AGO! I THOUGHT...
Hn...?
WHAT IN THE WORLD ARE YOU DOING IN SUCH SHABBY CLOTHING?! TO THINK A DAUGHTER OF MINE SHOULD BE SEEN OUT WEARING THAT!!
FATHER...!
WHO CARES WHAT I'M WEARING?!
ALL THAT MATTERS RIGHT NOW IS NIISAMA!
WHERE IS HE? IS HE ALL RIGHT?
...HIKARU ....!!

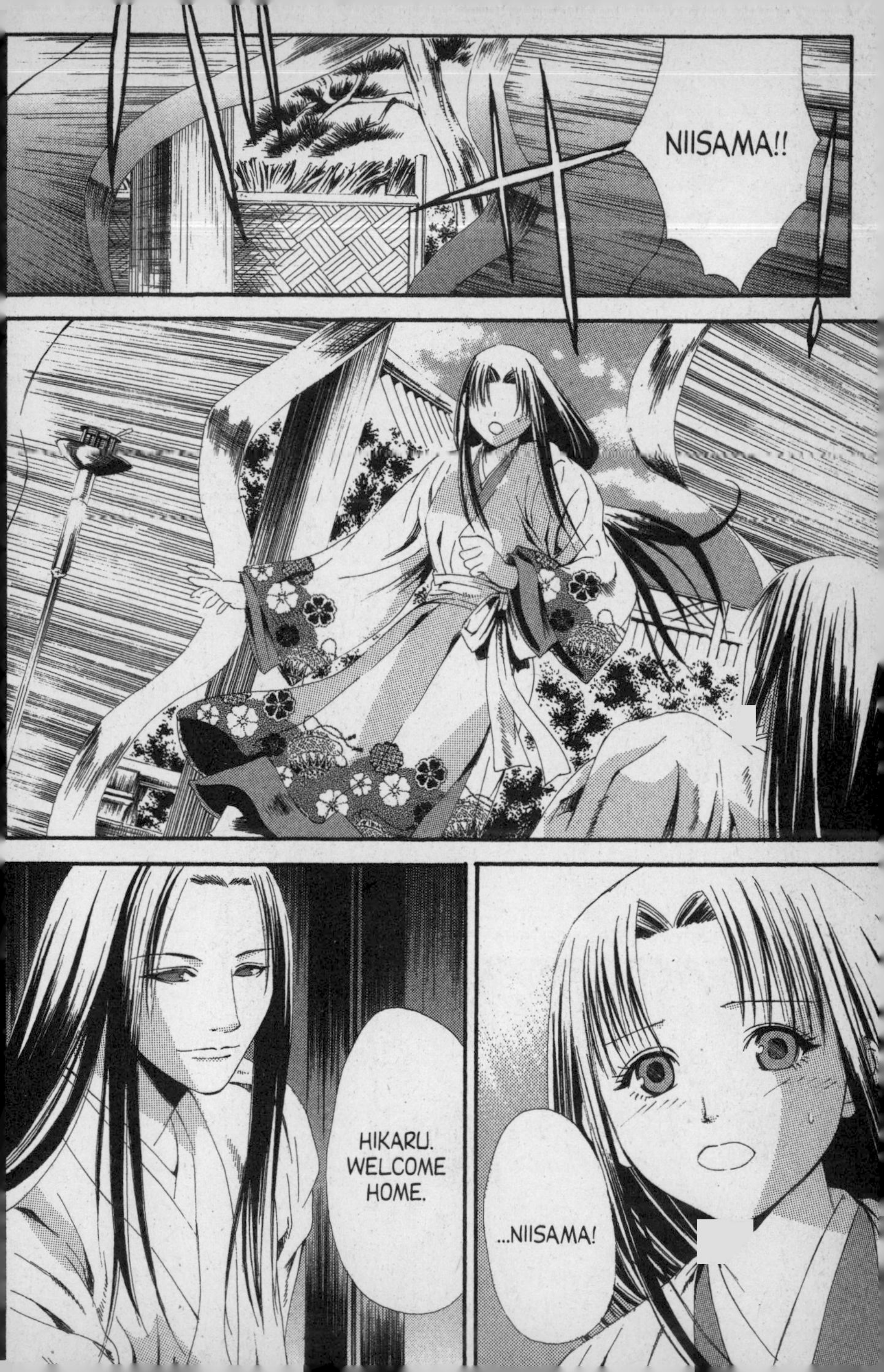
NIISAMA!!
HIKARU. WELCOME HOME.
...NIISAMA!

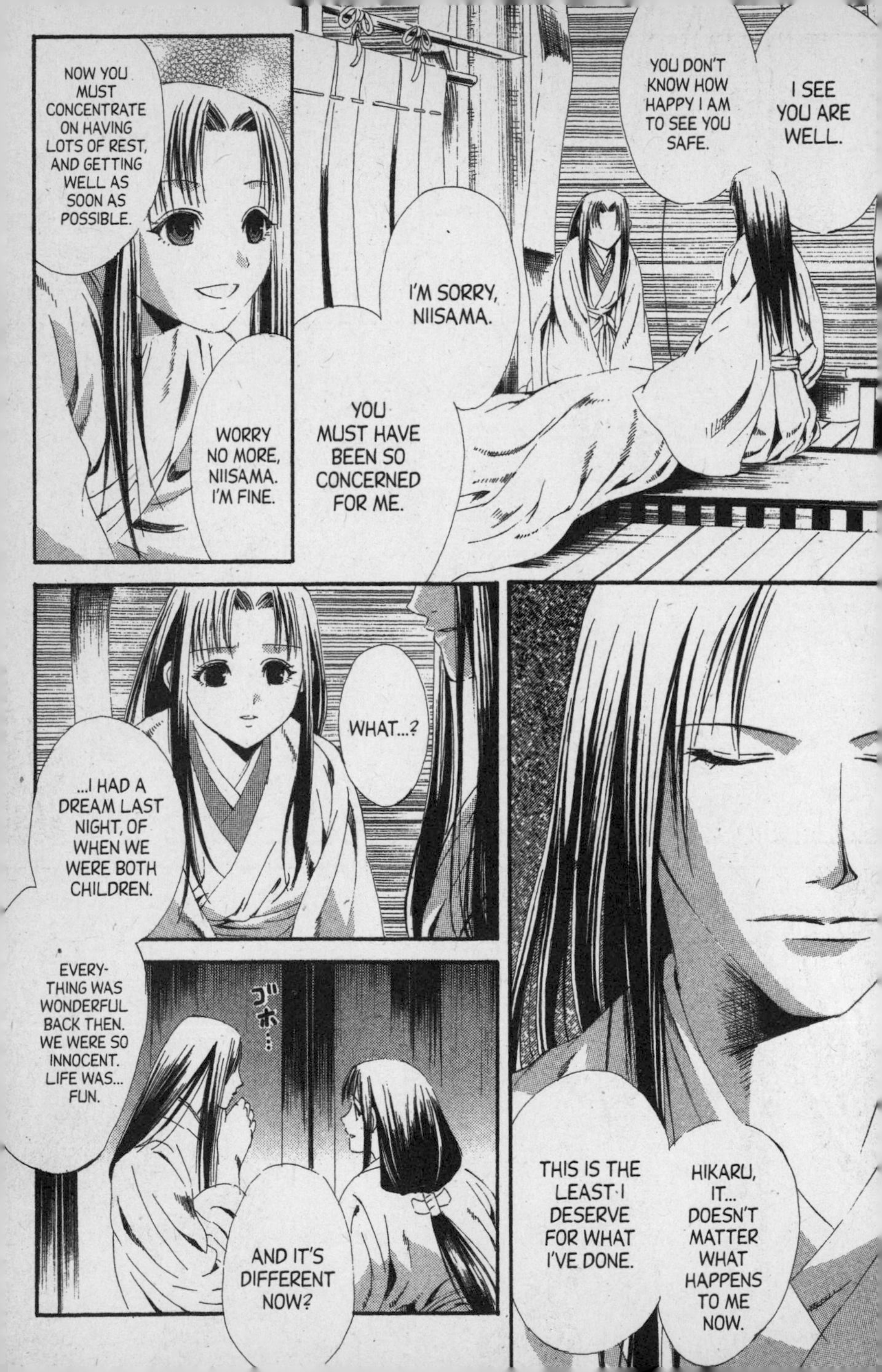
I SEE YOU ARE WELL.
YOU DON'T KNOW HOW HAPPY I AM TO SEE YOU SAFE.
I'M SORRY, NIISAMA.
YOU MUST HAVE BEEN SO CONCERNED FOR ME.
WORRY NO MORE, NIISAMA. I'M FINE.
NOW YOU MUST CONCENTRATE ON HAVING LOTS OF REST, AND GETTING WELL AS SOON AS POSSIBLE.
HIKARU, IT... DOESN'T MATTER WHAT HAPPENS TO ME NOW.
THIS IS THE LEAST I DESERVE FOR WHAT I'VE DONE.
WHAT...?
...I HAD A DREAM LAST NIGHT, OF WHEN WE WERE BOTH CHILDREN.
ゴホ…
EVERY-THING WAS WONDERFUL BACK THEN. WE WERE SO INNOCENT. LIFE WAS... FUN.
AND IT'S DIFFERENT NOW?

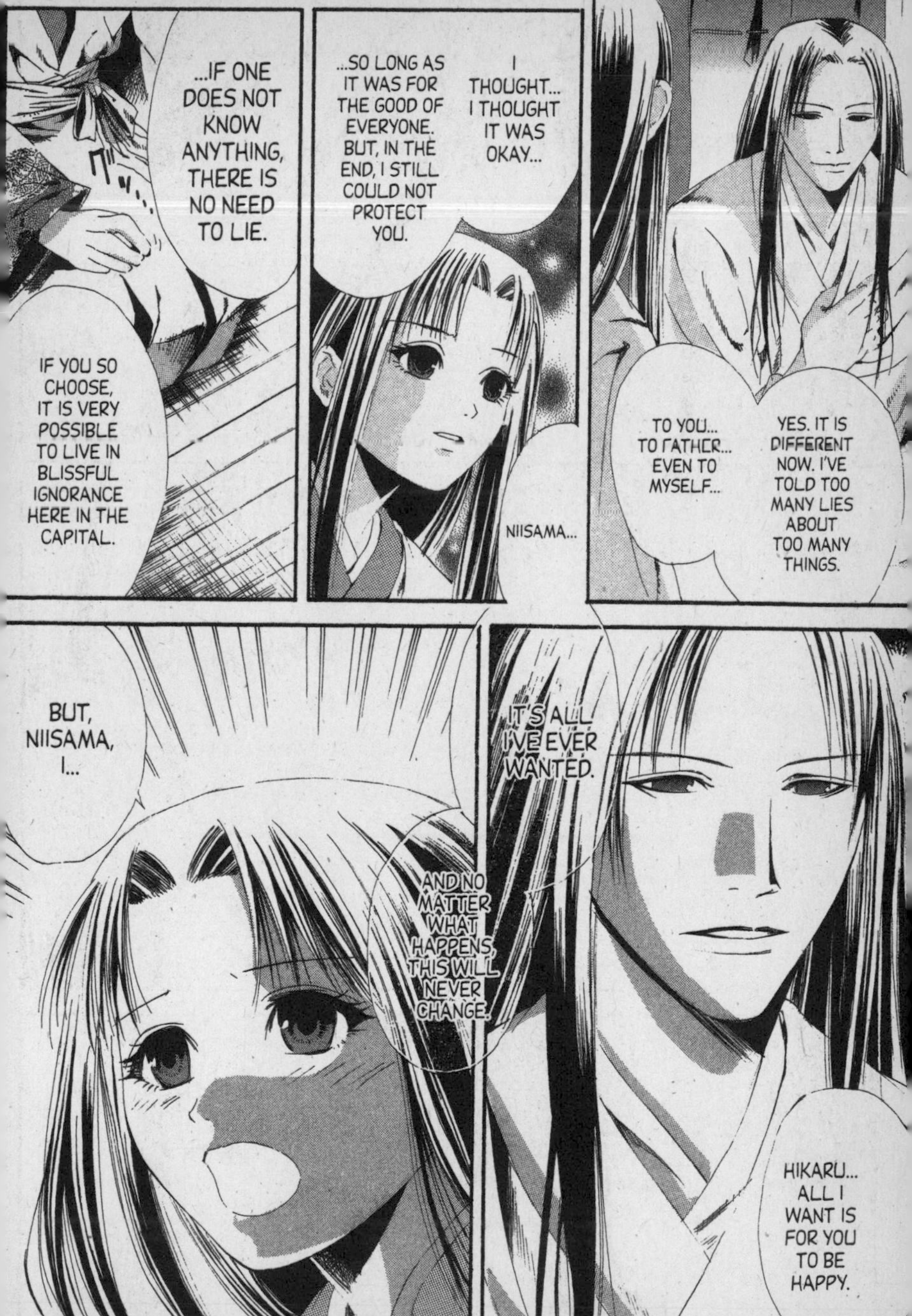
YES. IT IS DIFFERENT NOW. I'VE TOLD TOO MANY LIES ABOUT TOO MANY THINGS.
TO YOU... TO FATHER... EVEN TO MYSELF...
I THOUGHT... I THOUGHT IT WAS OKAY...
...SO LONG AS IT WAS FOR THE GOOD OF EVERYONE. BUT, IN THE END, I STILL COULD NOT PROTECT YOU.
NIISAMA...
...IF ONE DOES NOT KNOW ANYTHING, THERE IS NO NEED TO LIE.
IF YOU SO CHOOSE, IT IS VERY POSSIBLE TO LIVE IN BLISSFUL IGNORANCE HERE IN THE CAPITAL.
HIKARU... ALL I WANT IS FOR YOU TO BE HAPPY.
IT'S ALL I'VE EVER WANTED.
AND NO MATTER WHAT HAPPENS, THIS WILL NEVER CHANGE.
BUT, NIISAMA, I...

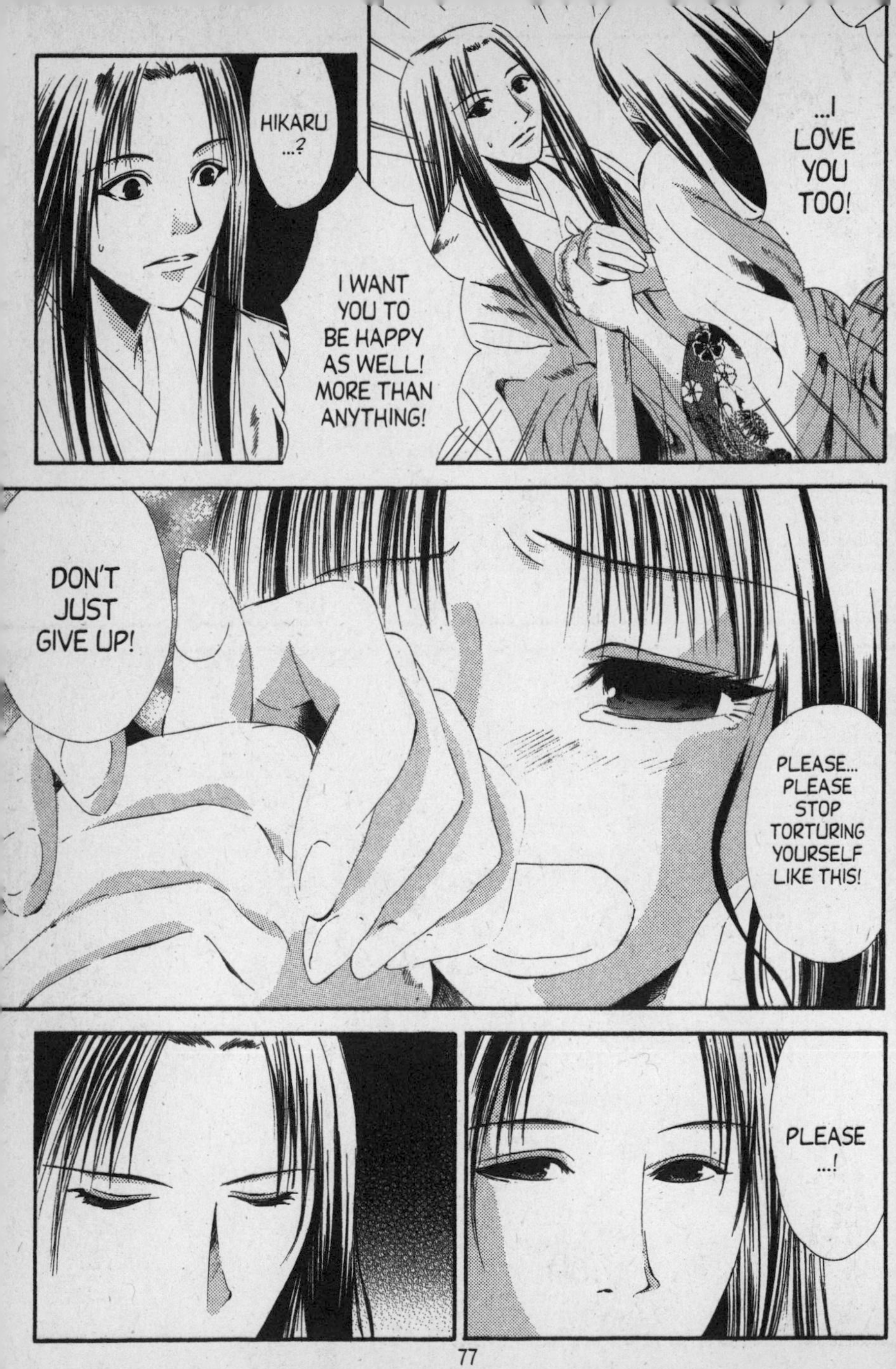
...I LOVE YOU TOO!
I WANT YOU TO BE HAPPY AS WELL! MORE THAN ANYTHING!
HIKARU ...?
PLEASE... PLEASE STOP TORTURING YOURSELF LIKE THIS!
DON'T JUST GIVE UP!
PLEASE ...!

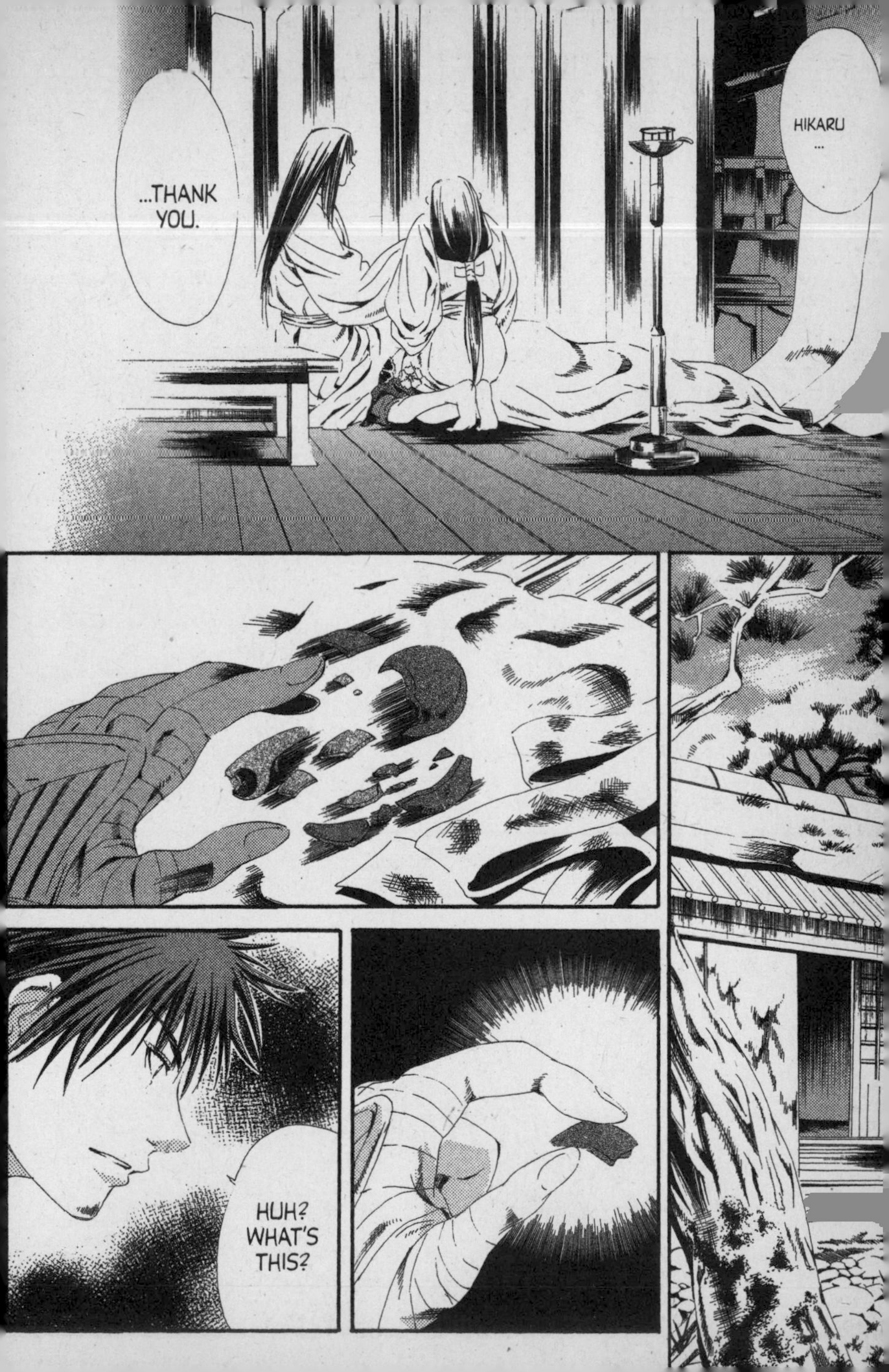
HIKARU ...
...THANK YOU.
HUH? WHAT'S THIS?

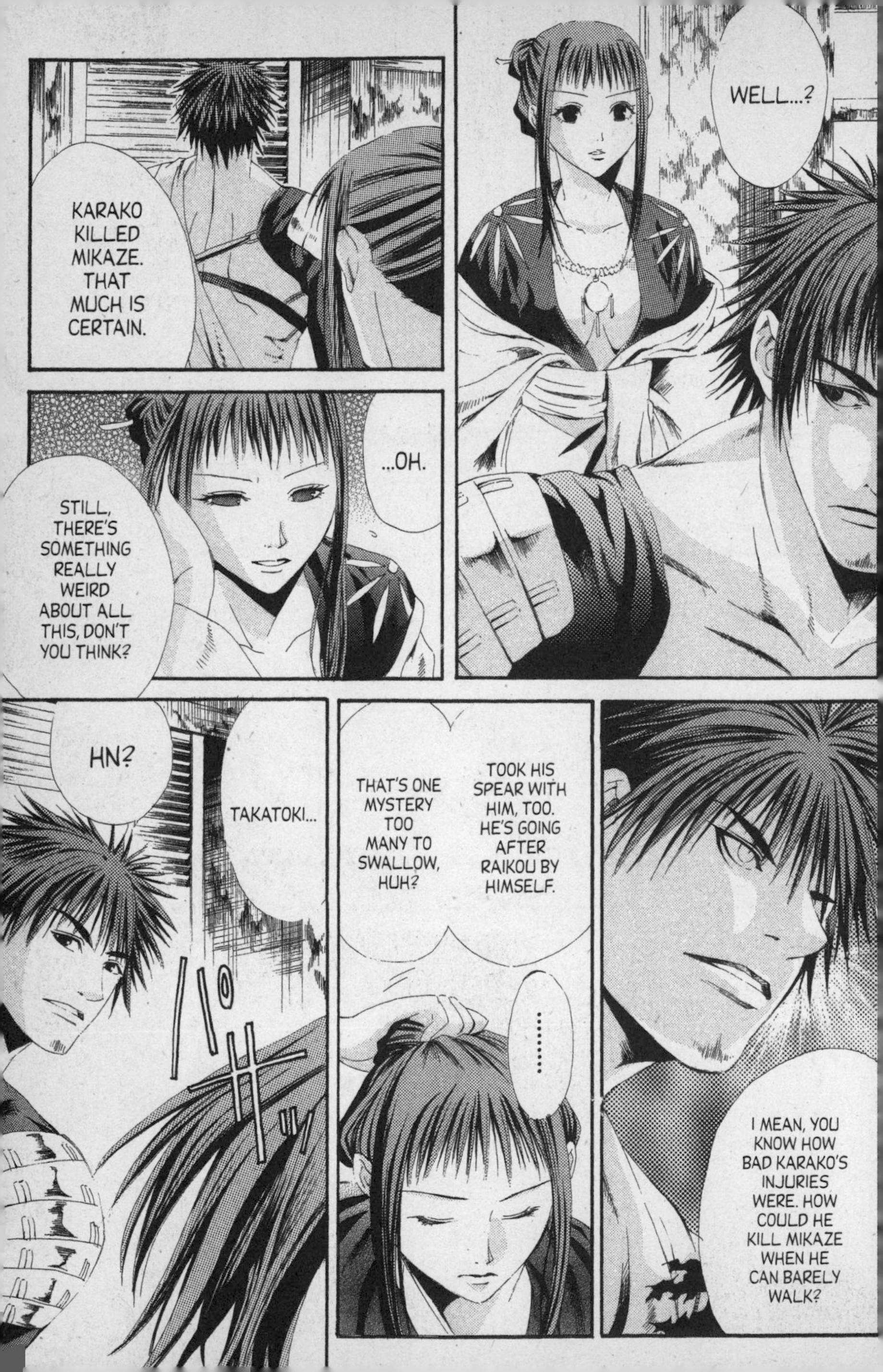
WELL...?
KARAKO KILLED MIKAZE. THAT MUCH IS CERTAIN.
...OH.
STILL, THERE'S SOMETHING REALLY WEIRD ABOUT ALL THIS, DON'T YOU THINK?
I MEAN, YOU KNOW HOW BAD KARAKO'S INJURIES WERE. HOW COULD HE KILL MIKAZE WHEN HE CAN BARELY WALK?
TOOK HIS SPEAR WITH HIM, TOO. HE'S GOING AFTER RAIKOU BY HIMSELF.
THAT'S ONE MYSTERY TOO MANY TO SWALLOW, HUH?
......
TAKATOKI...
HN?

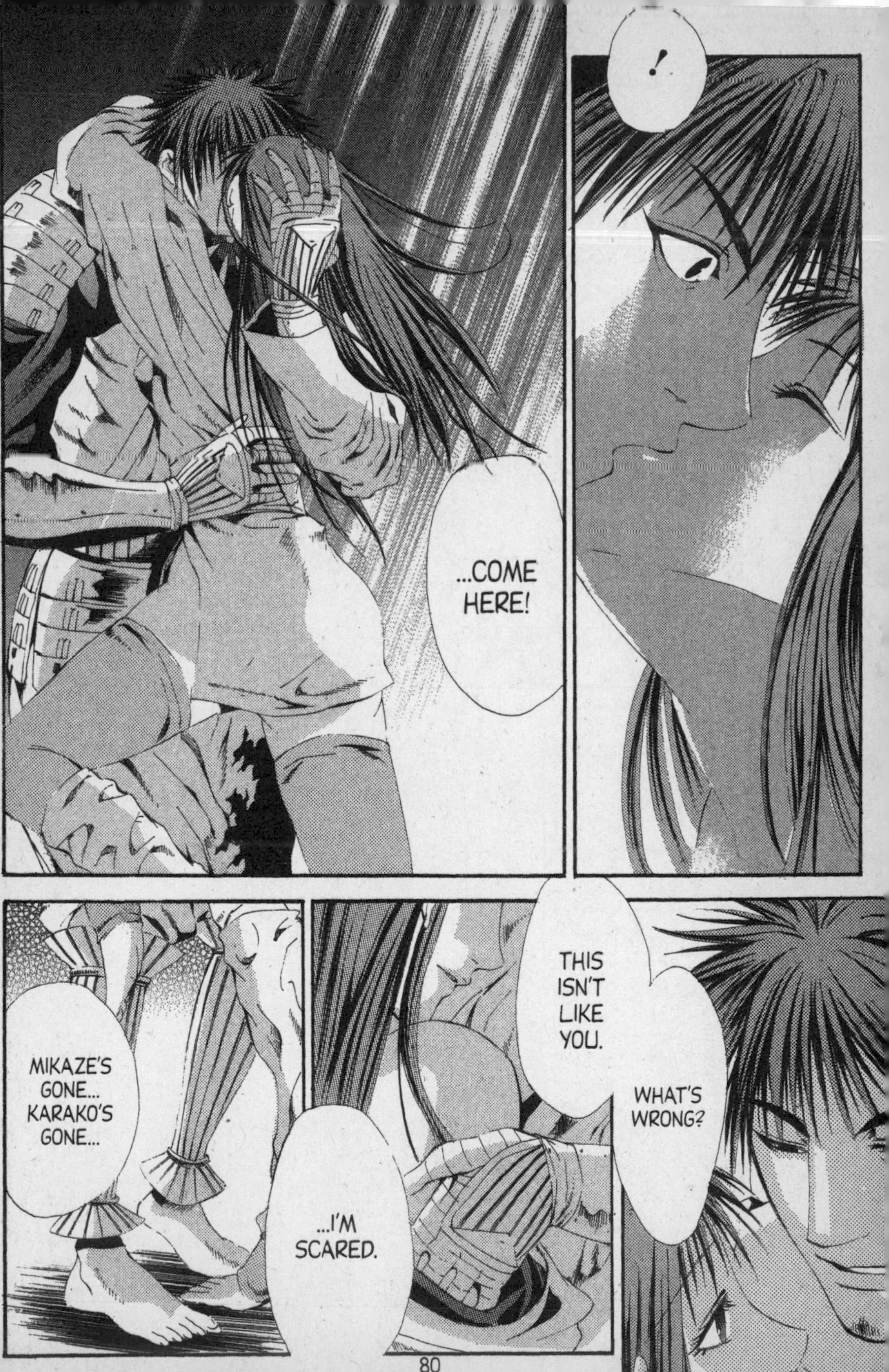
!
...COME HERE!
THIS ISN'T LIKE YOU.
WHAT'S WRONG?
...I'M SCARED.
MIKAZE'S GONE... KARAKO'S GONE...

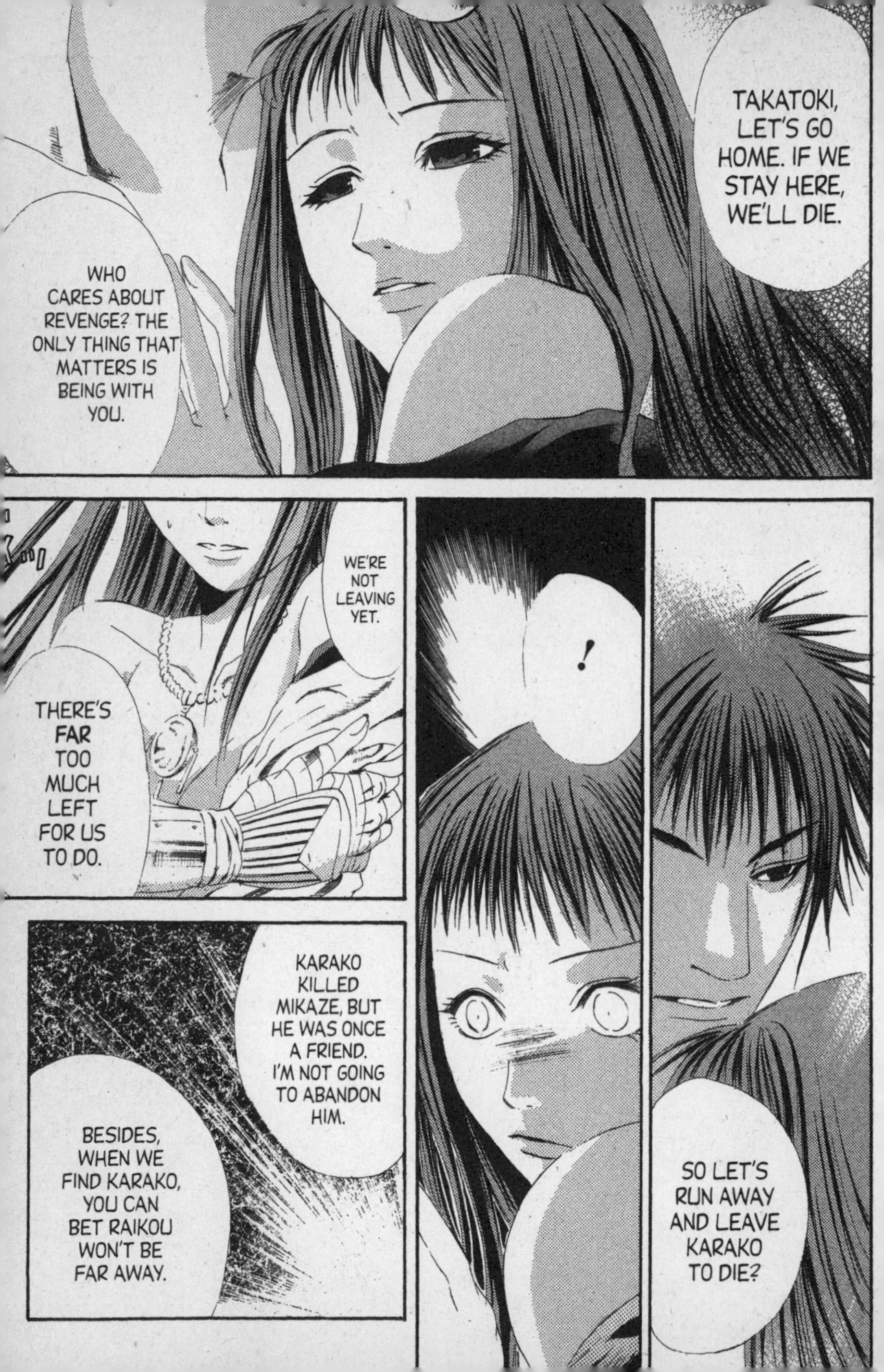
TAKATOKI, LET'S GO HOME. IF WE STAY HERE, WE'LL DIE.
WHO CARES ABOUT REVENGE? THE ONLY THING THAT MATTERS IS BEING WITH YOU.
WE'RE NOT LEAVING YET.
THERE'S FAR TOO MUCH LEFT FOR US TO DO.
!
SO LET'S RUN AWAY AND LEAVE KARAKO TO DIE?
KARAKO KILLED MIKAZE, BUT HE WAS ONCE A FRIEND. I'M NOT GOING TO ABANDON HIM.
BESIDES, WHEN WE FIND KARAKO, YOU CAN BET RAIKOU WON'T BE FAR AWAY.

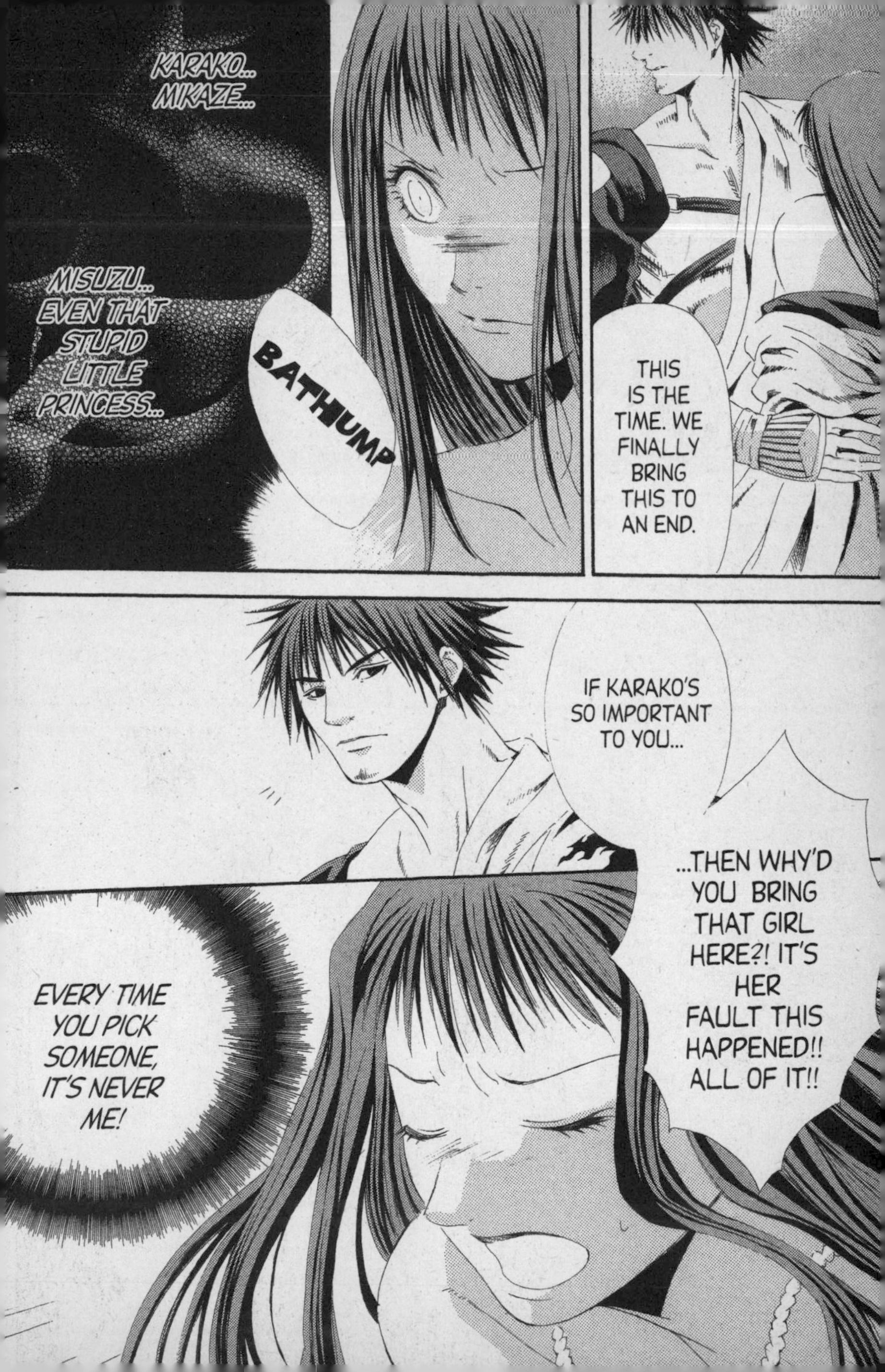
THIS IS THE TIME. WE FINALLY BRING THIS TO AN END.
BATHUMP
KARAKO... MIKAZE...
MISUZU... EVEN THAT STUPID LITTLE PRINCESS...
IF KARAKO'S SO IMPORTANT TO YOU...
...THEN WHY'D YOU BRING THAT GIRL HERE?! IT'S HER FAULT THIS HAPPENED!! ALL OF IT!!
EVERY TIME YOU PICK SOMEONE, IT'S NEVER ME!

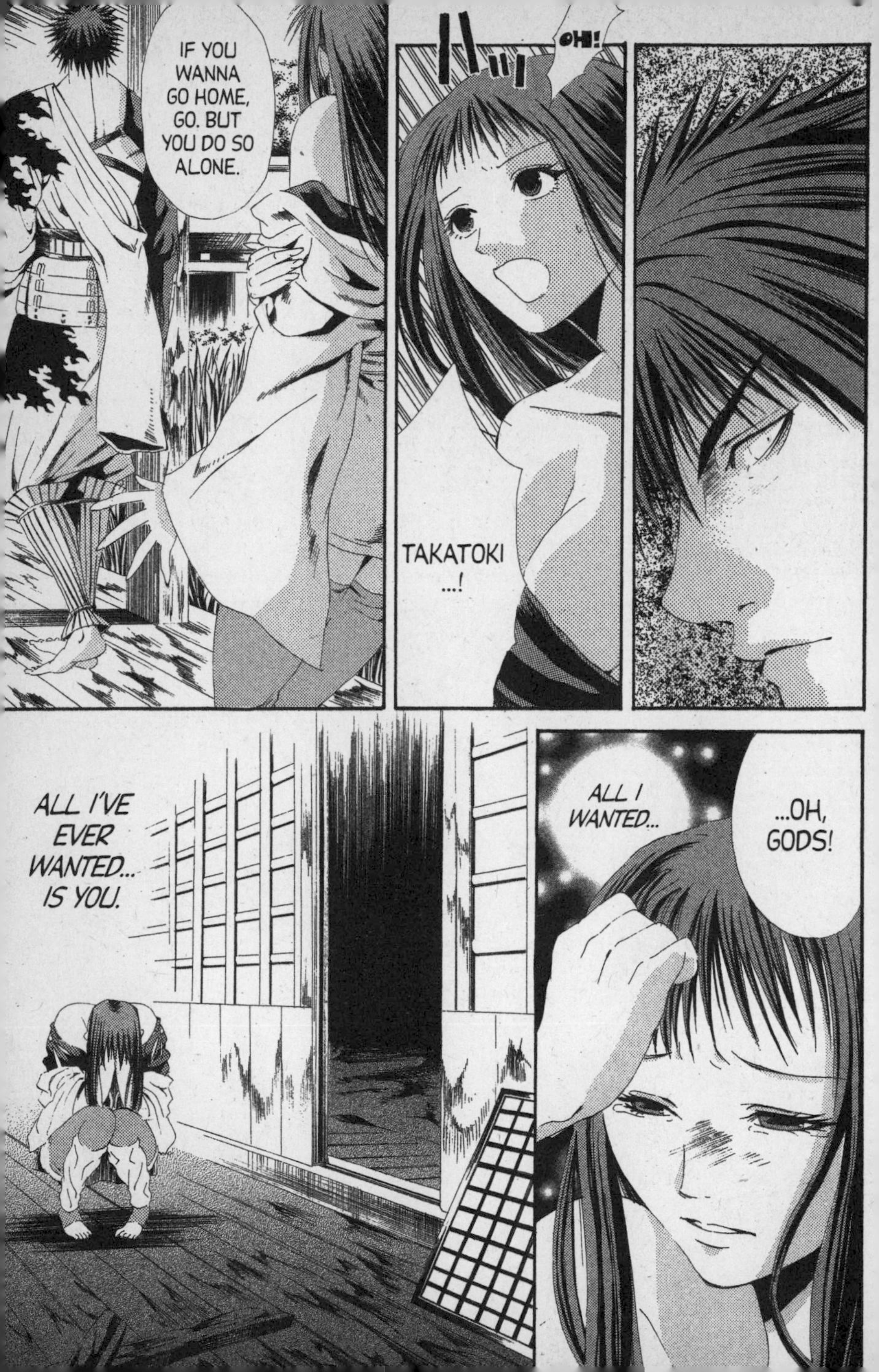
OH!
TAKATOKI ...!
IF YOU WANNA GO HOME, GO. BUT YOU DO SO ALONE.
...OH, GODS!
ALL I WANTED...
ALL I'VE EVER WANTED... IS YOU.

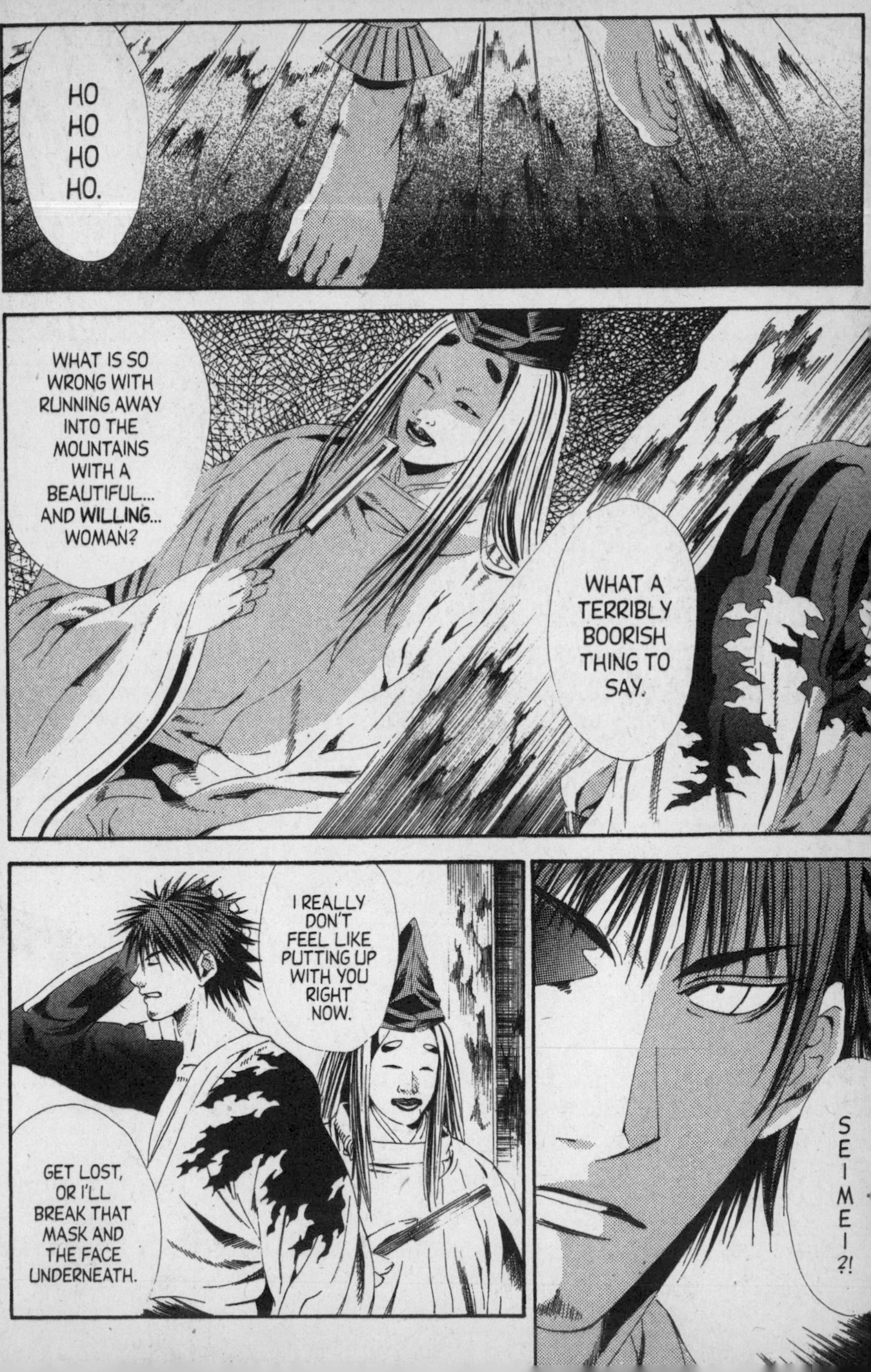
HO HO HO HO.
WHAT A TERRIBLY BOORISH THING TO SAY.
WHAT IS SO WRONG WITH RUNNING AWAY INTO THE MOUNTAINS WITH A BEAUTIFUL... AND WILLING... WOMAN?
SEIMEI?!
I REALLY DON'T FEEL LIKE PUTTING UP WITH YOU RIGHT NOW.
GET LOST, OR I'LL BREAK THAT MASK AND THE FACE UNDERNEATH.

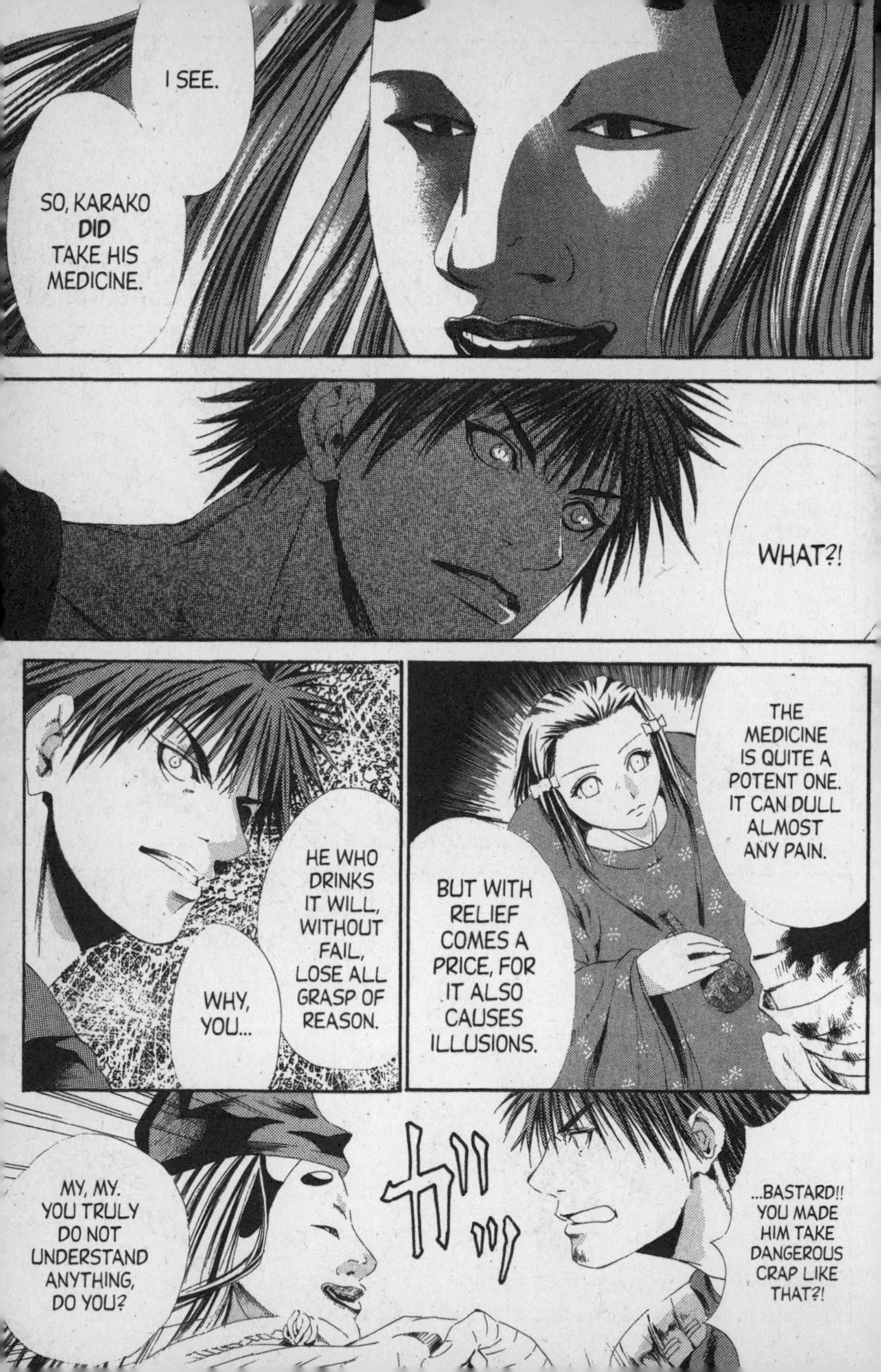
I SEE.
SO, KARAKO DID TAKE HIS MEDICINE.
WHAT?!
THE MEDICINE IS QUITE A POTENT ONE. IT CAN DULL ALMOST ANY PAIN.
BUT WITH RELIEF COMES A PRICE, FOR IT ALSO CAUSES ILLUSIONS.
HE WHO DRINKS IT WILL, WITHOUT FAIL, LOSE ALL GRASP OF REASON.
WHY, YOU...
...BASTARD!! YOU MADE HIM TAKE DANGEROUS CRAP LIKE THAT?!
ガッ
MY, MY. YOU TRULY DO NOT UNDERSTAND ANYTHING, DO YOU?

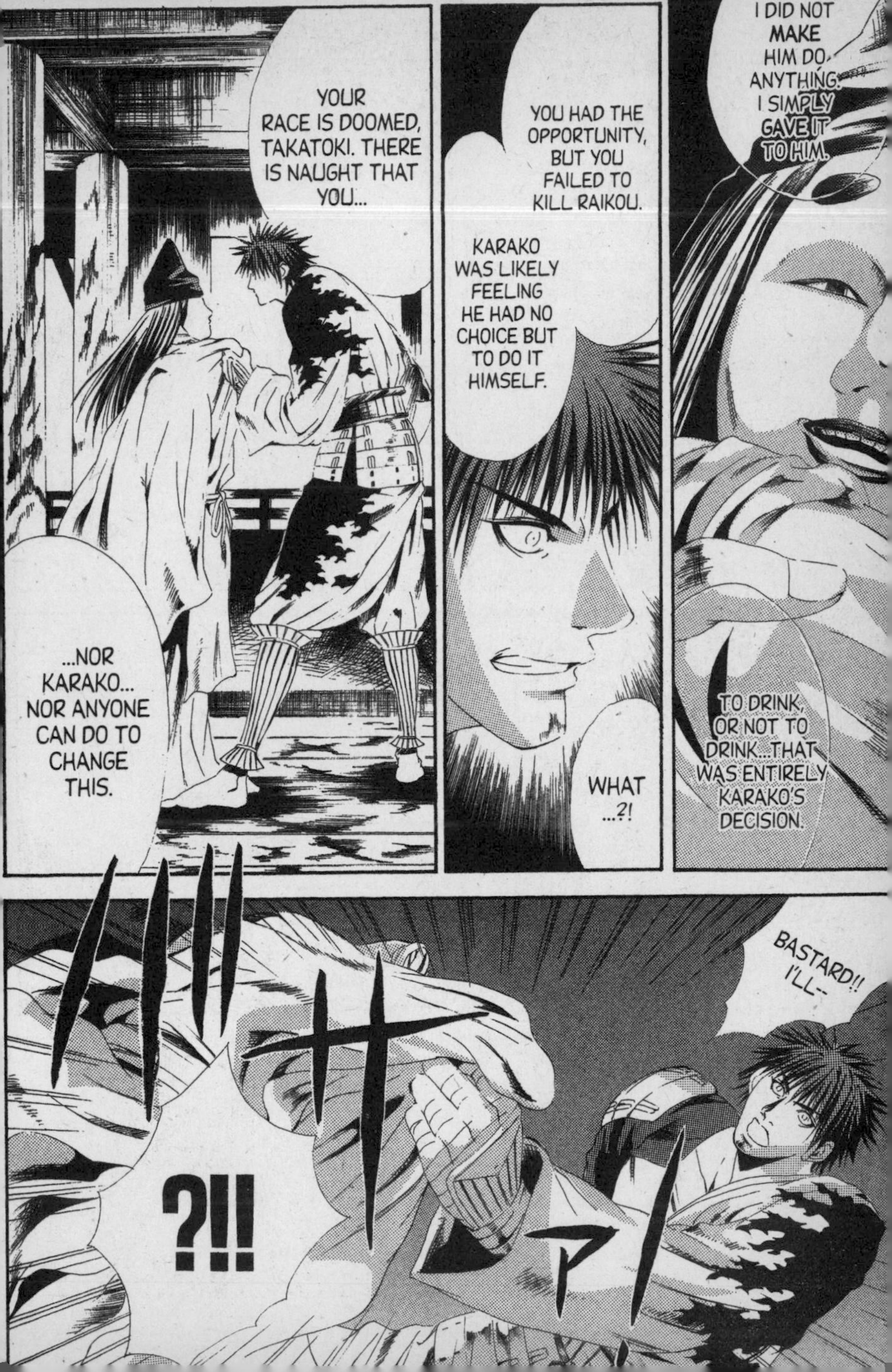

I DID NOT MAKE HIM DO ANYTHING. I SIMPLY GAVE IT TO HIM.
TO DRINK, OR NOT TO DRINK...THAT WAS ENTIRELY KARAKO'S DECISION.
YOU HAD THE OPPORTUNITY, BUT YOU FAILED TO KILL RAIKOU.
KARAKO WAS LIKELY FEELING HE HAD NO CHOICE BUT TO DO IT HIMSELF.
WHAT ...?!
YOUR RACE IS DOOMED, TAKATOKI. THERE IS NAUGHT THAT YOU...
...NOR KARAKO... NOR ANYONE CAN DO TO CHANGE THIS.
BASTARD!! I'LL--
?!!

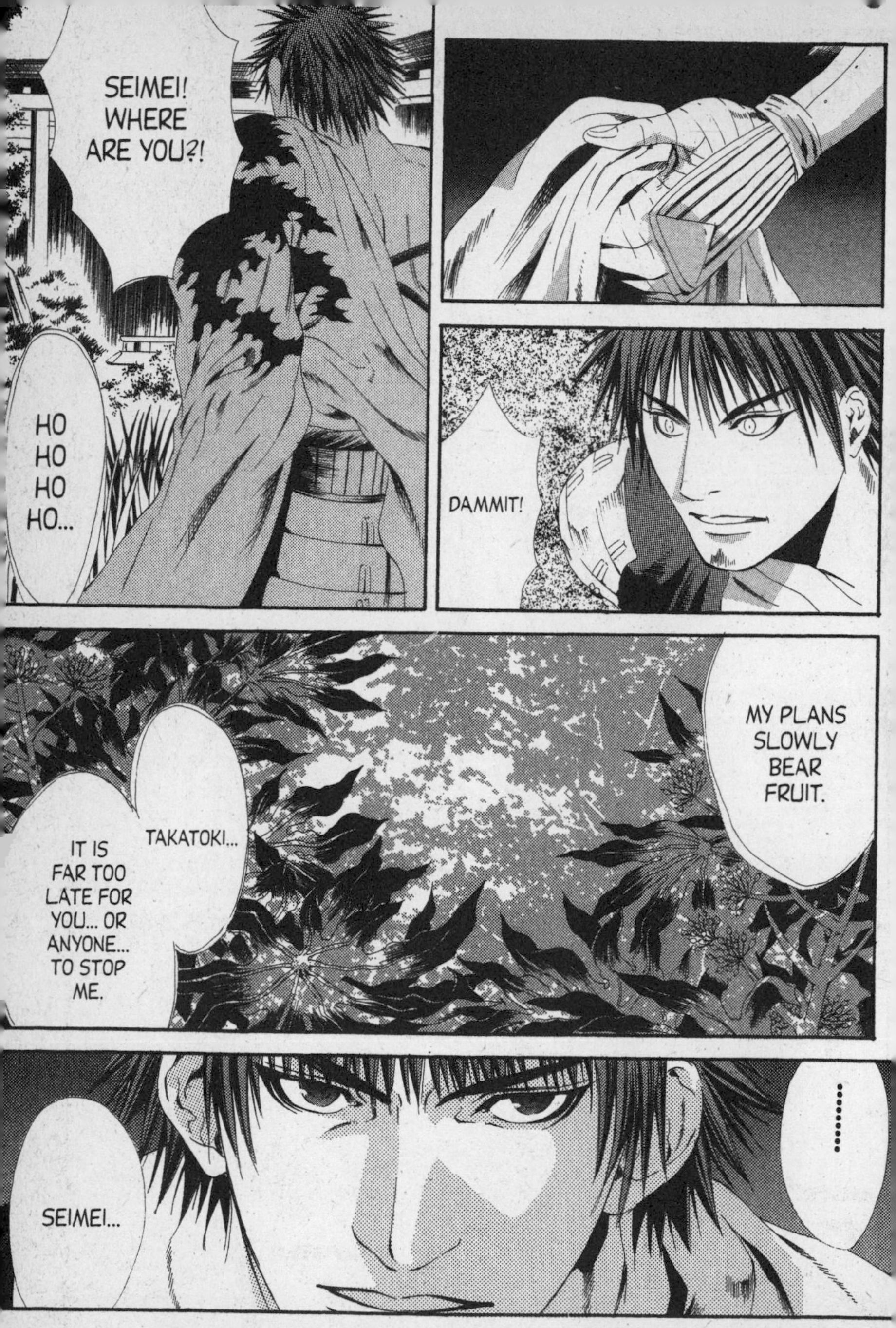
SEIMEI! WHERE ARE YOU?!
HO HO HO HO...
DAMMIT!
MY PLANS SLOWLY BEAR FRUIT.
TAKATOKI...
IT IS FAR TOO LATE FOR YOU... OR ANYONE... TO STOP ME.
....
SEIMEI...

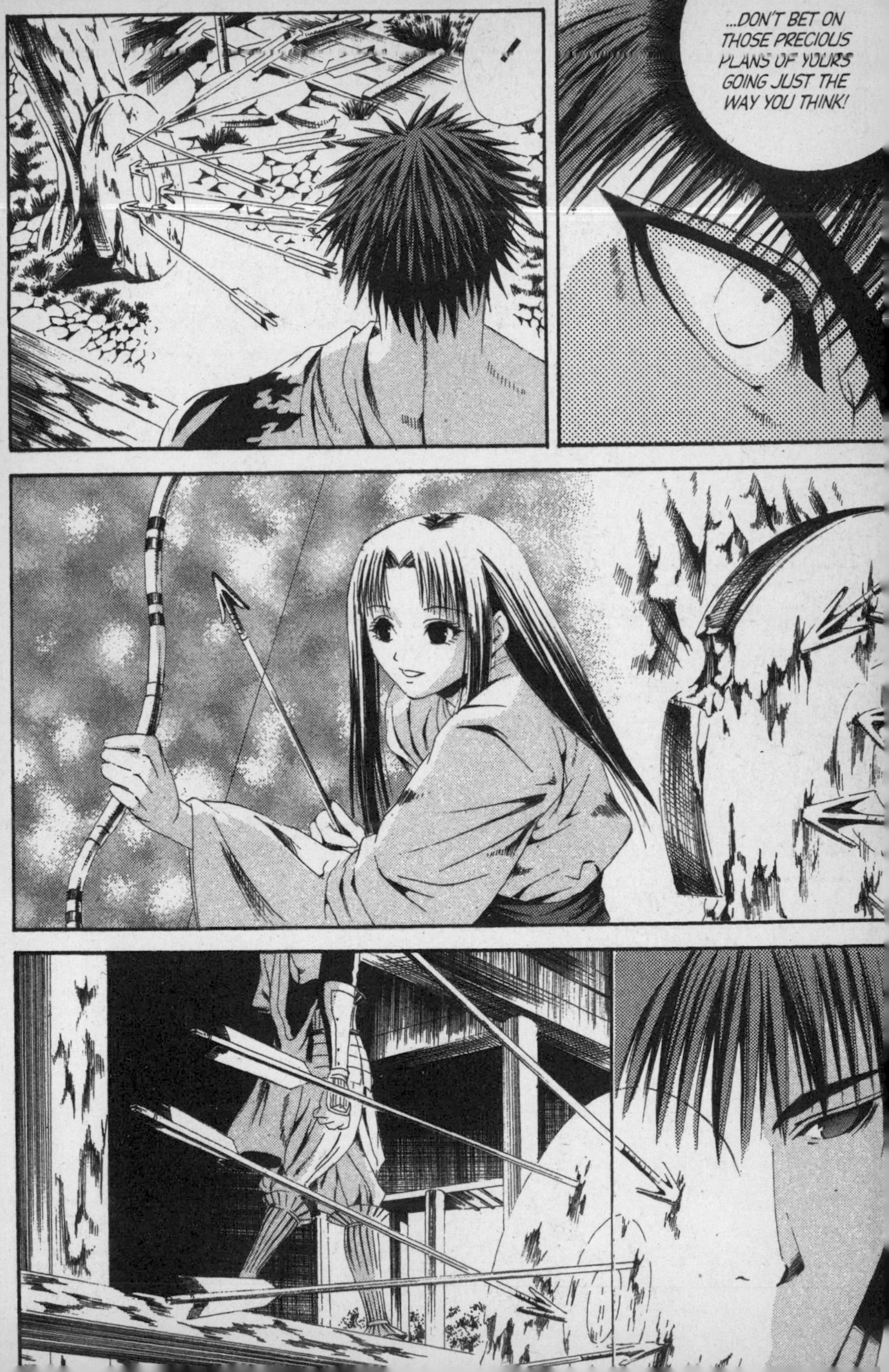

...DON'T BET ON THOSE PRECIOUS PLANS OF YOURS GOING JUST THE WAY YOU THINK!
!

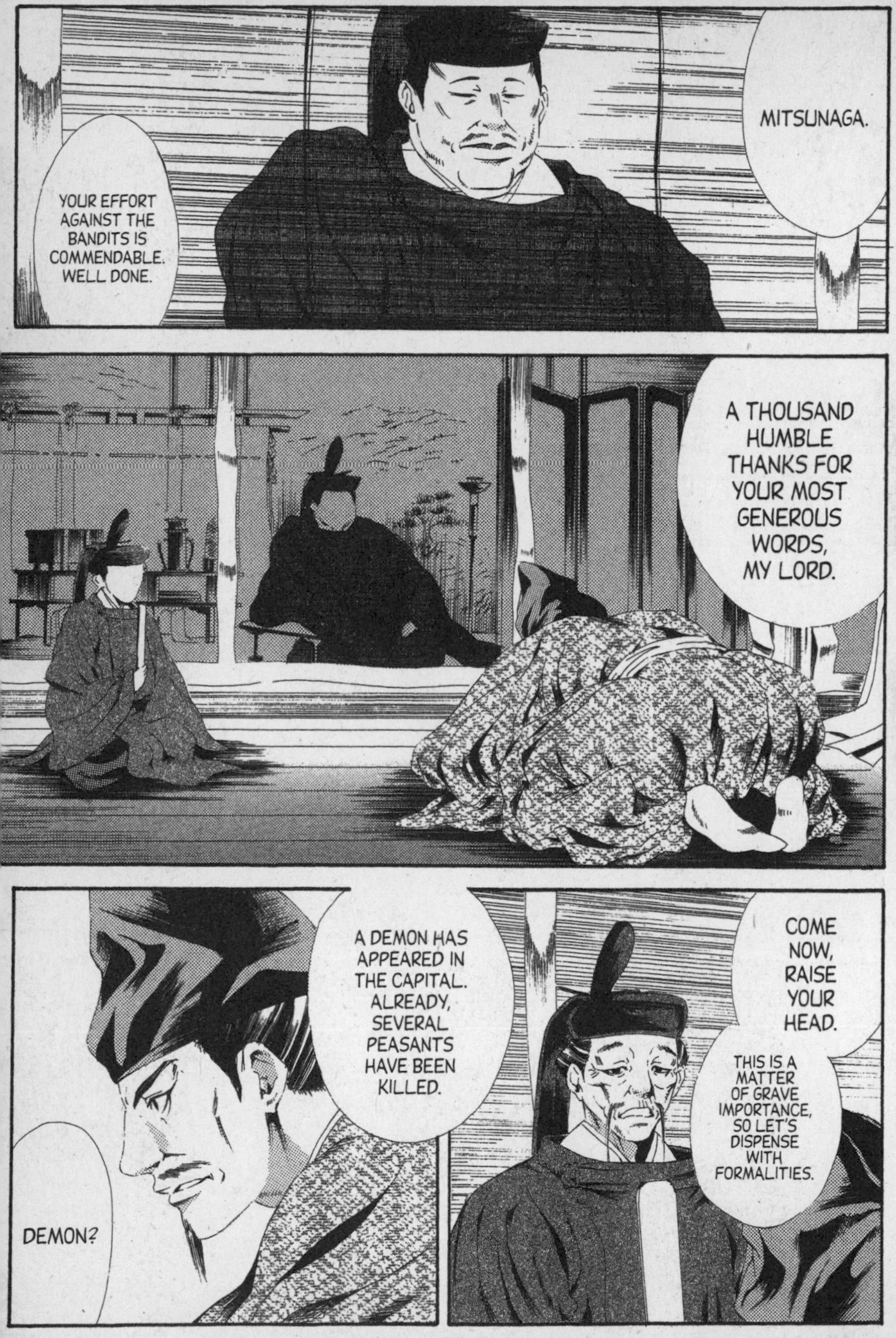
MITSUNAGA.
YOUR EFFORT AGAINST THE BANDITS IS COMMENDABLE. WELL DONE.
A THOUSAND HUMBLE THANKS FOR YOUR MOST GENEROUS WORDS, MY LORD.
COME NOW, RAISE YOUR HEAD.
THIS IS A MATTER OF GRAVE IMPORTANCE, SO LET'S DISPENSE WITH FORMALITIES.
A DEMON HAS APPEARED IN THE CAPITAL. ALREADY, SEVERAL PEASANTS HAVE BEEN KILLED.
DEMON?

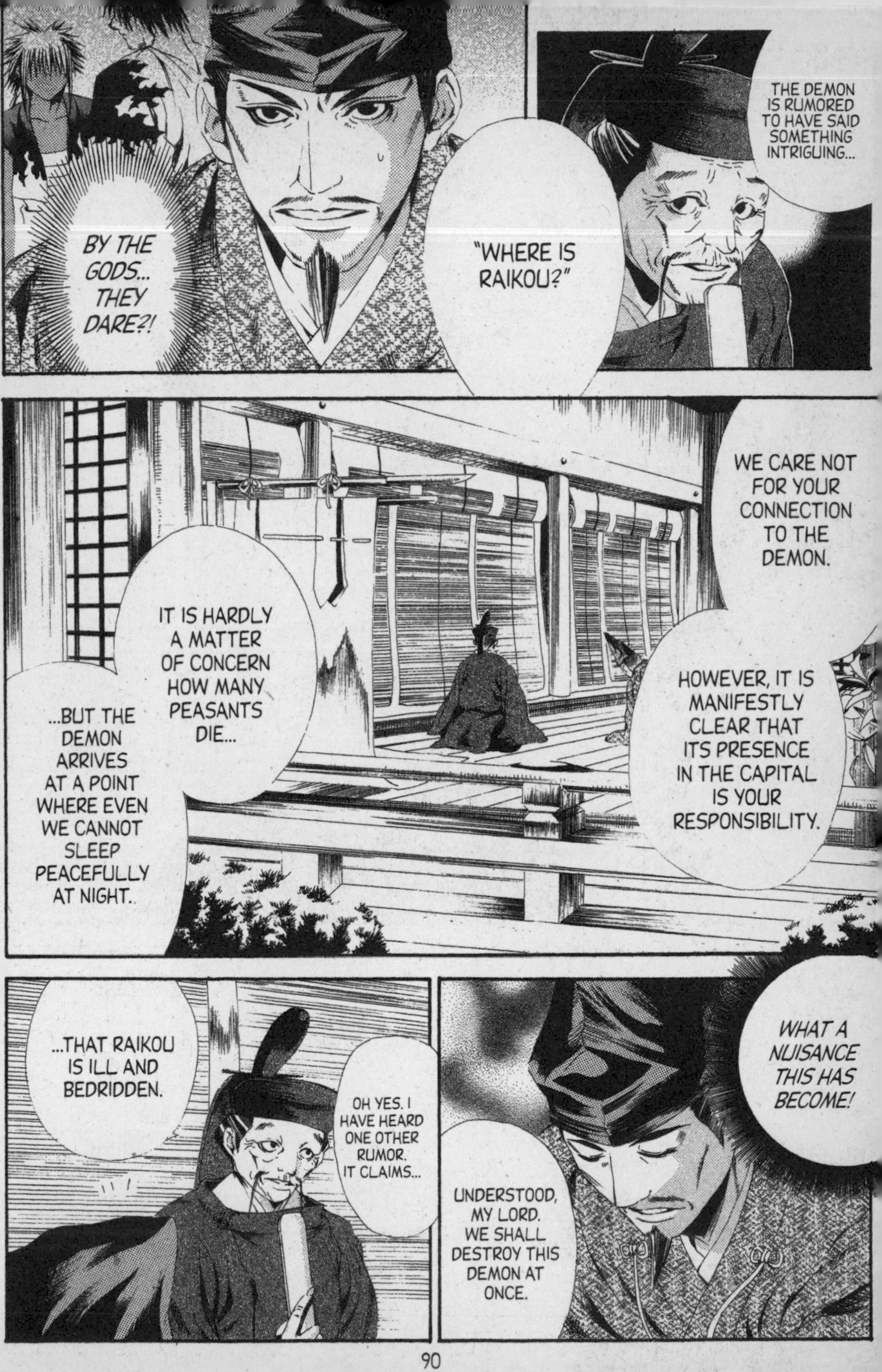
THE DEMON IS RUMORED TO HAVE SAID SOMETHING INTRIGUING...
"WHERE IS RAIKOU?"
BY THE GODS... THEY DARE?!
WE CARE NOT FOR YOUR CONNECTION TO THE DEMON.
HOWEVER, IT IS MANIFESTLY CLEAR THAT ITS PRESENCE IN THE CAPITAL IS YOUR RESPONSIBILITY.
IT IS HARDLY A MATTER OF CONCERN HOW MANY PEASANTS DIE...
...BUT THE DEMON ARRIVES AT A POINT WHERE EVEN WE CANNOT SLEEP PEACEFULLY AT NIGHT..
WHAT A NUISANCE THIS HAS BECOME!
UNDERSTOOD, MY LORD. WE SHALL DESTROY THIS DEMON AT ONCE.
OH YES. I HAVE HEARD ONE OTHER RUMOR. IT CLAIMS...
...THAT RAIKOU IS ILL AND BEDRIDDEN.

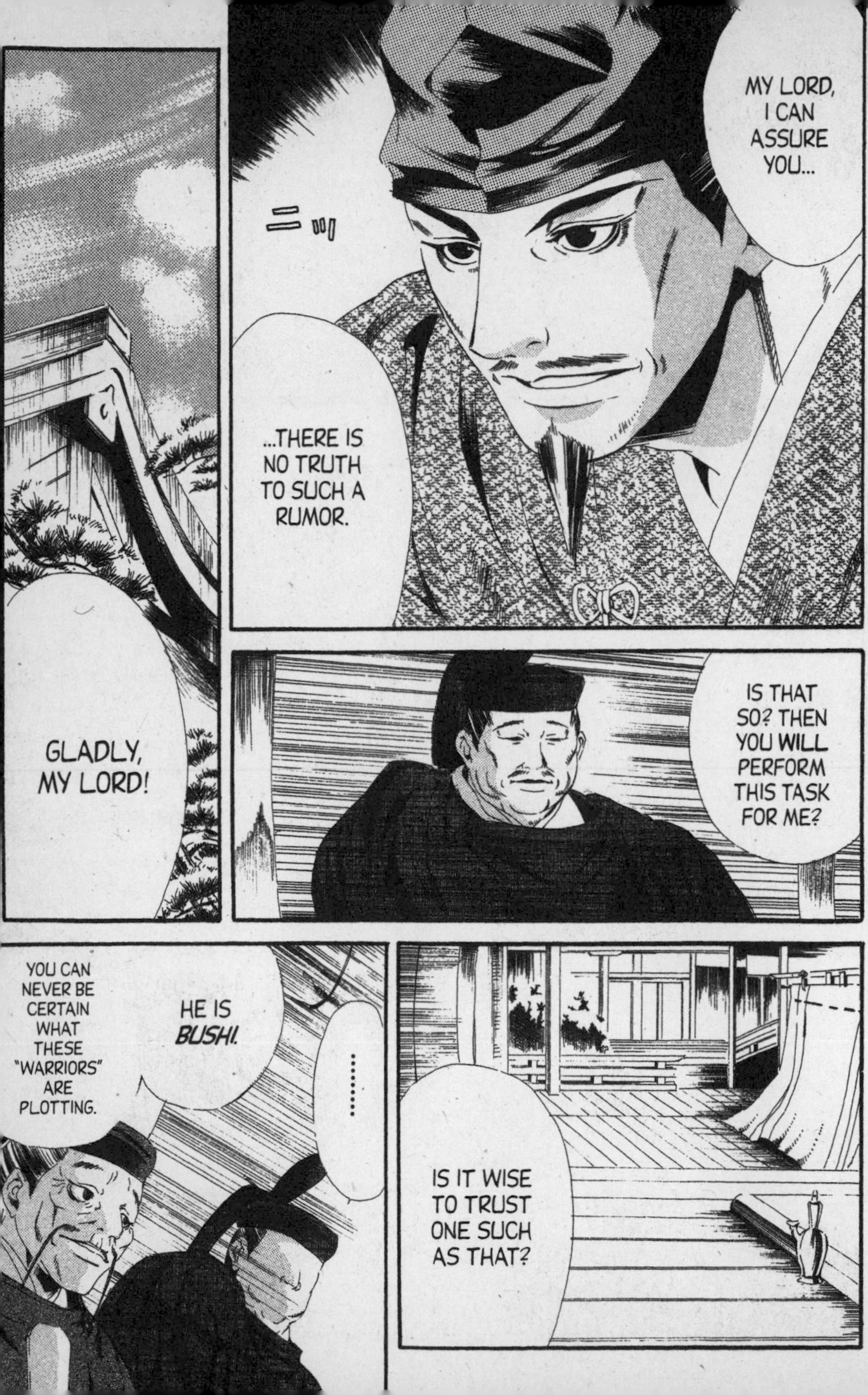
MY LORD, I CAN ASSURE YOU...
...THERE IS NO TRUTH TO SUCH A RUMOR.
IS THAT SO? THEN YOU WILL PERFORM THIS TASK FOR ME?
GLADLY, MY LORD!
IS IT WISE TO TRUST ONE SUCH AS THAT?
......
HE IS *BUSHI*.
YOU CAN NEVER BE CERTAIN WHAT THESE "WARRIORS" ARE PLOTTING.

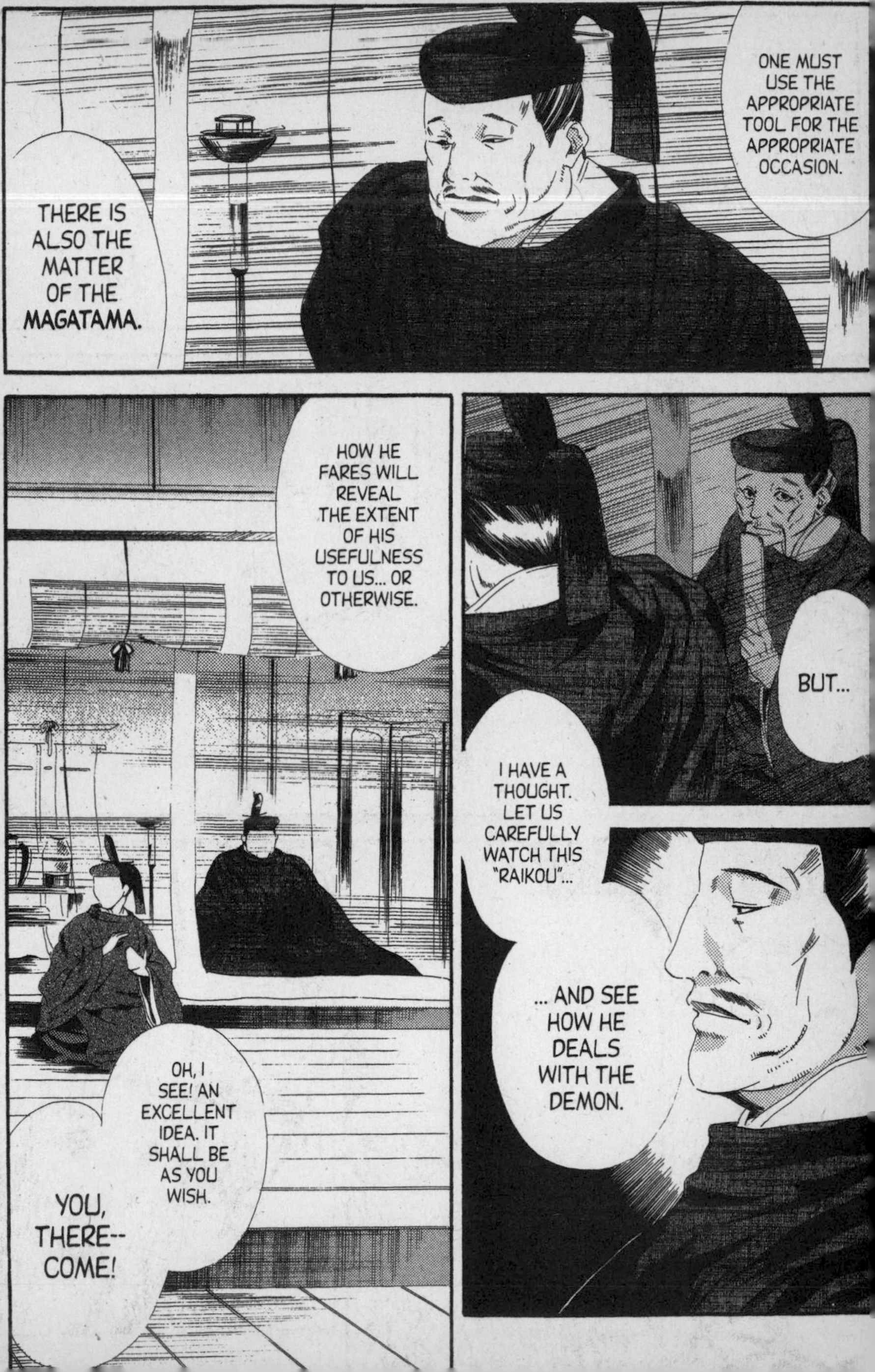
ONE MUST USE THE APPROPRIATE TOOL FOR THE APPROPRIATE OCCASION.
THERE IS ALSO THE MATTER OF THE MAGATAMA.
BUT...
I HAVE A THOUGHT. LET US CAREFULLY WATCH THIS "RAIKOU"...
... AND SEE HOW HE DEALS WITH THE DEMON.
HOW HE FARES WILL REVEAL THE EXTENT OF HIS USEFULNESS TO US... OR OTHERWISE.
OH, I SEE! AN EXCELLENT IDEA. IT SHALL BE AS YOU WISH.
YOU, THERE--COME!

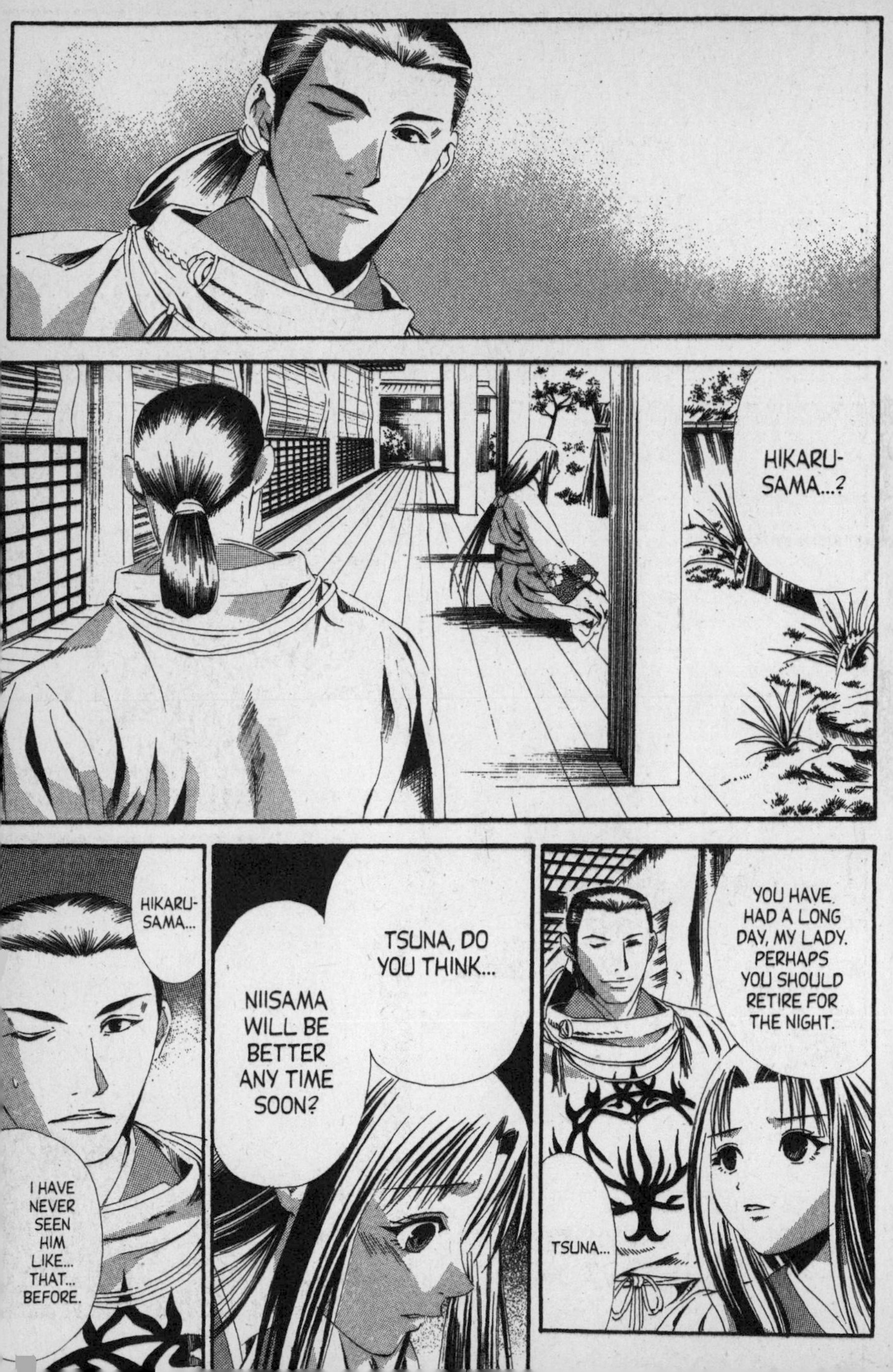
HIKARU-SAMA...?
YOU HAVE HAD A LONG DAY, MY LADY. PERHAPS YOU SHOULD RETIRE FOR THE NIGHT.
TSUNA...
TSUNA, DO YOU THINK...
NIISAMA WILL BE BETTER ANY TIME SOON?
HIKARU-SAMA...
I HAVE NEVER SEEN HIM LIKE... THAT... BEFORE.

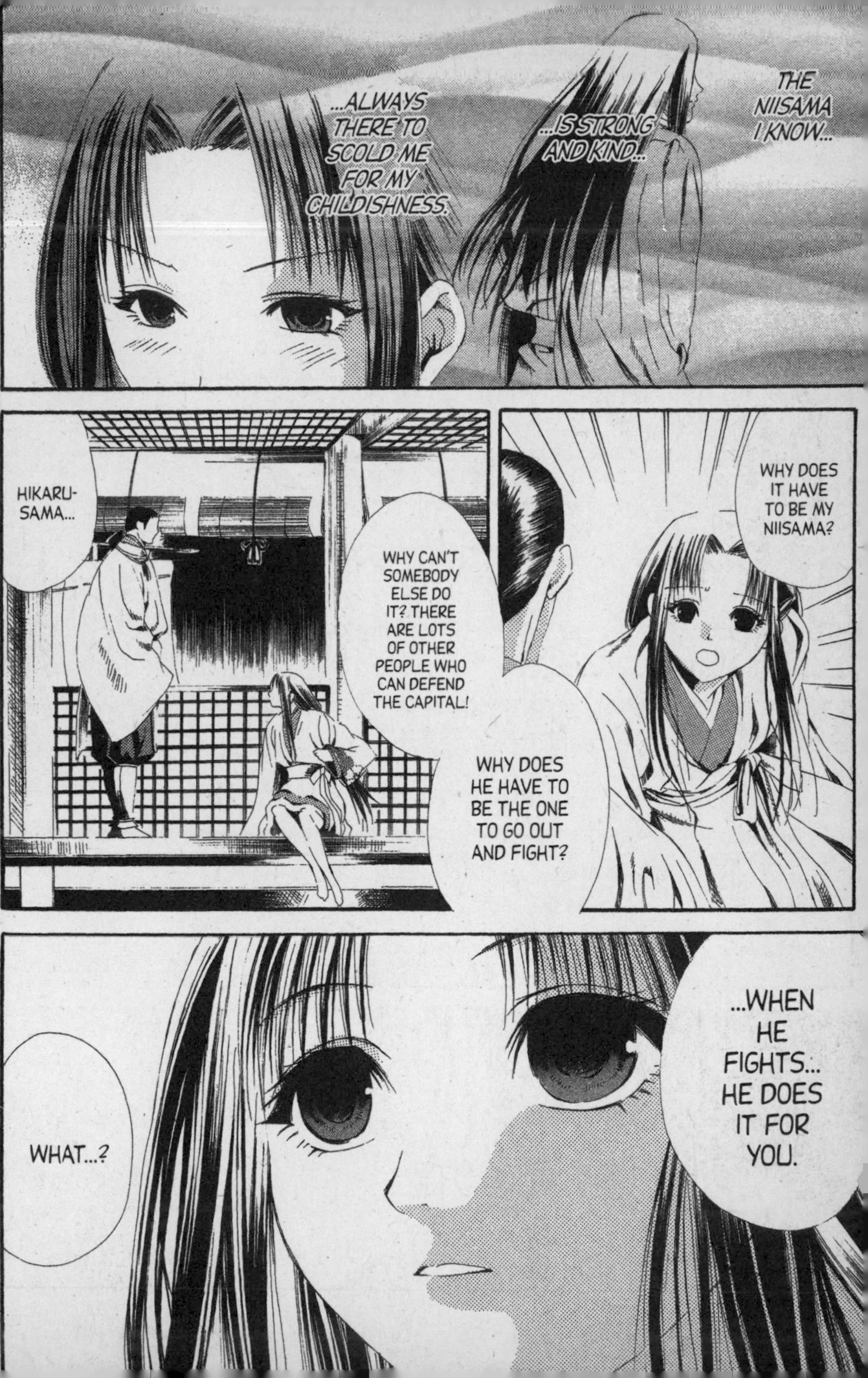
THE NIISAMA I KNOW...
...IS STRONG AND KIND...
...ALWAYS THERE TO SCOLD ME FOR MY CHILDISHNESS.
WHY DOES IT HAVE TO BE MY NIISAMA?
WHY CAN'T SOMEBODY ELSE DO IT? THERE ARE LOTS OF OTHER PEOPLE WHO CAN DEFEND THE CAPITAL!
WHY DOES HE HAVE TO BE THE ONE TO GO OUT AND FIGHT?
HIKARU-SAMA...
...WHEN HE FIGHTS... HE DOES IT FOR YOU.
WHAT...?

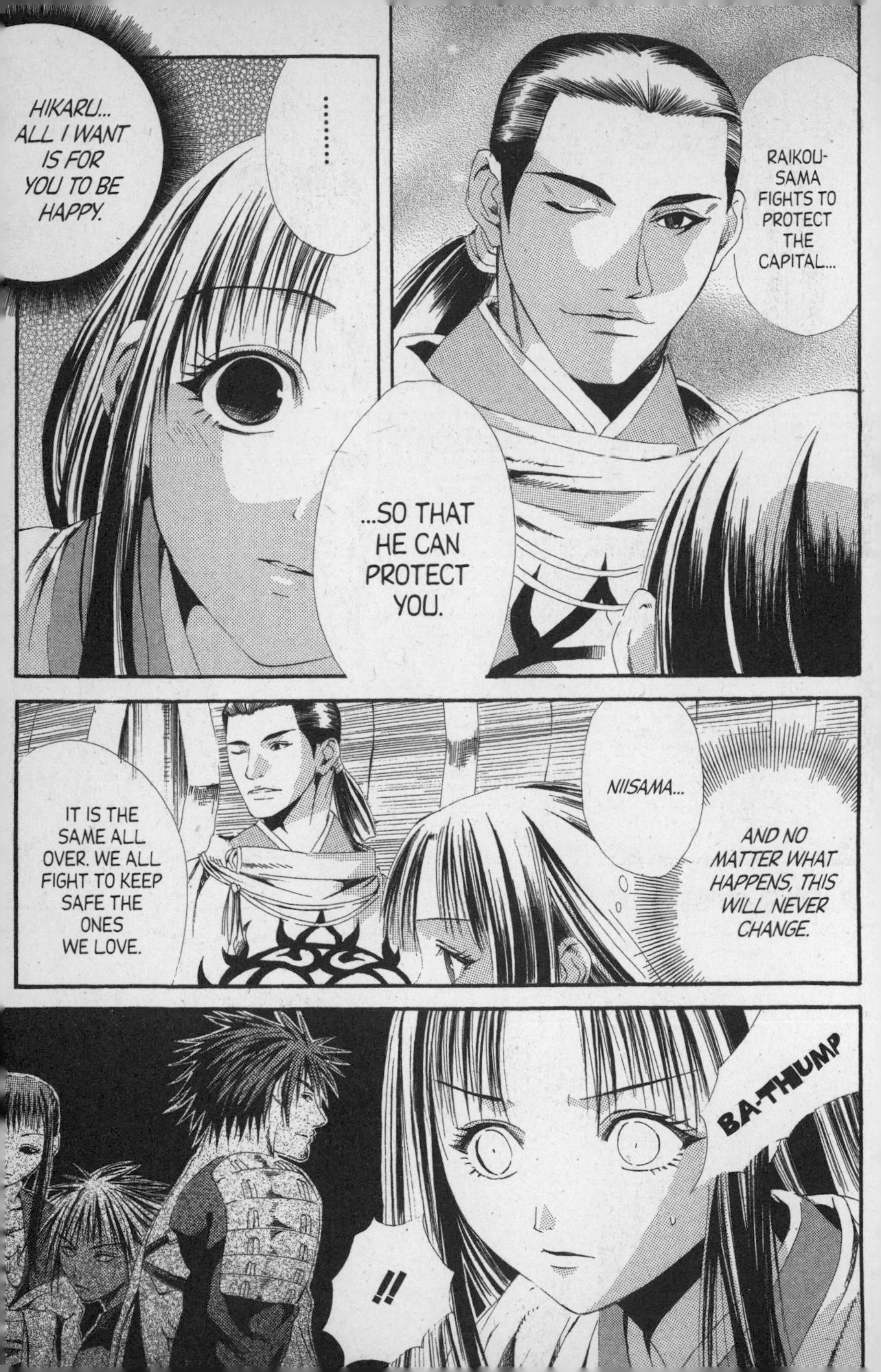
RAIKOU-SAMA FIGHTS TO PROTECT THE CAPITAL...
...SO THAT HE CAN PROTECT YOU.
......
HIKARU... ALL I WANT IS FOR YOU TO BE HAPPY.
NIISAMA...
AND NO MATTER WHAT HAPPENS, THIS WILL NEVER CHANGE.
IT IS THE SAME ALL OVER. WE ALL FIGHT TO KEEP SAFE THE ONES WE LOVE.
BA-THUMP
!!

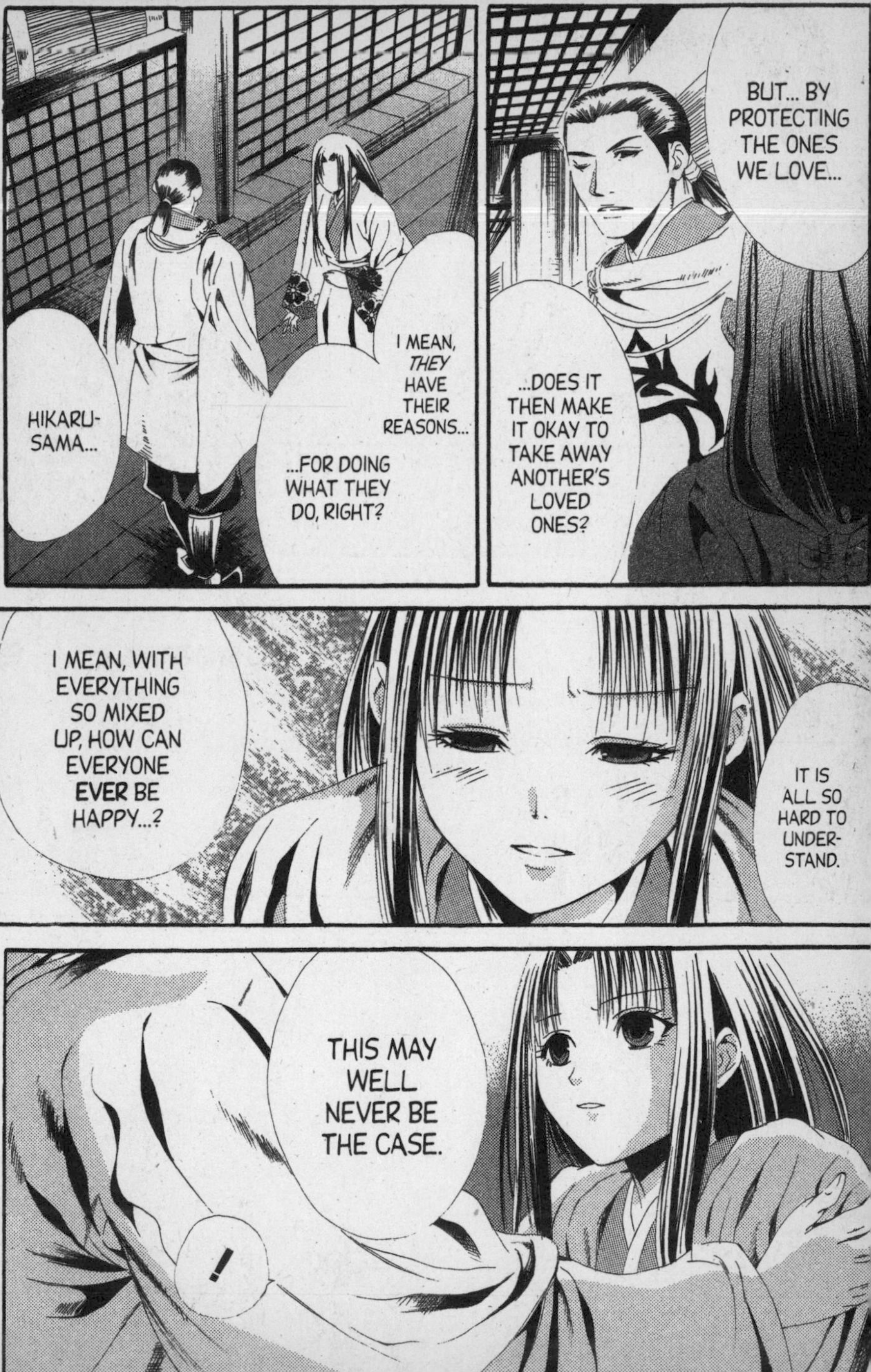
BUT... BY PROTECTING THE ONES WE LOVE...
...DOES IT THEN MAKE IT OKAY TO TAKE AWAY ANOTHER'S LOVED ONES?
I MEAN, *THEY* HAVE THEIR REASONS...
...FOR DOING WHAT THEY DO, RIGHT?
HIKARU-SAMA...
IT IS ALL SO HARD TO UNDERSTAND.
I MEAN, WITH EVERYTHING SO MIXED UP, HOW CAN EVERYONE EVER BE HAPPY...?
THIS MAY WELL NEVER BE THE CASE.
!

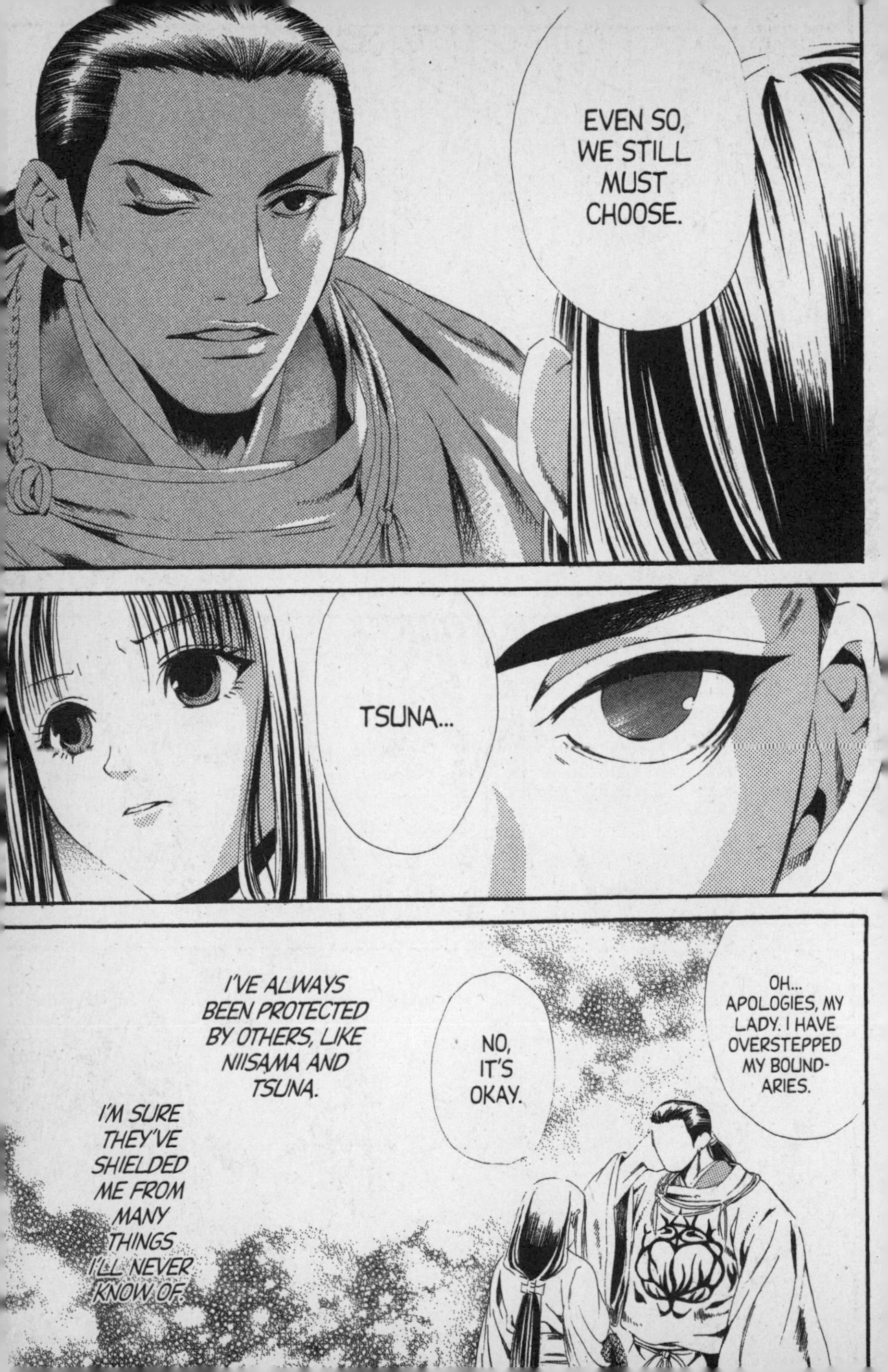
EVEN SO, WE STILL MUST CHOOSE.
TSUNA...
OH... APOLOGIES, MY LADY. I HAVE OVERSTEPPED MY BOUNDARIES.
NO, IT'S OKAY.
I'VE ALWAYS BEEN PROTECTED BY OTHERS, LIKE NIISAMA AND TSUNA.
I'M SURE THEY'VE SHIELDED ME FROM MANY THINGS I'LL NEVER KNOW OF.

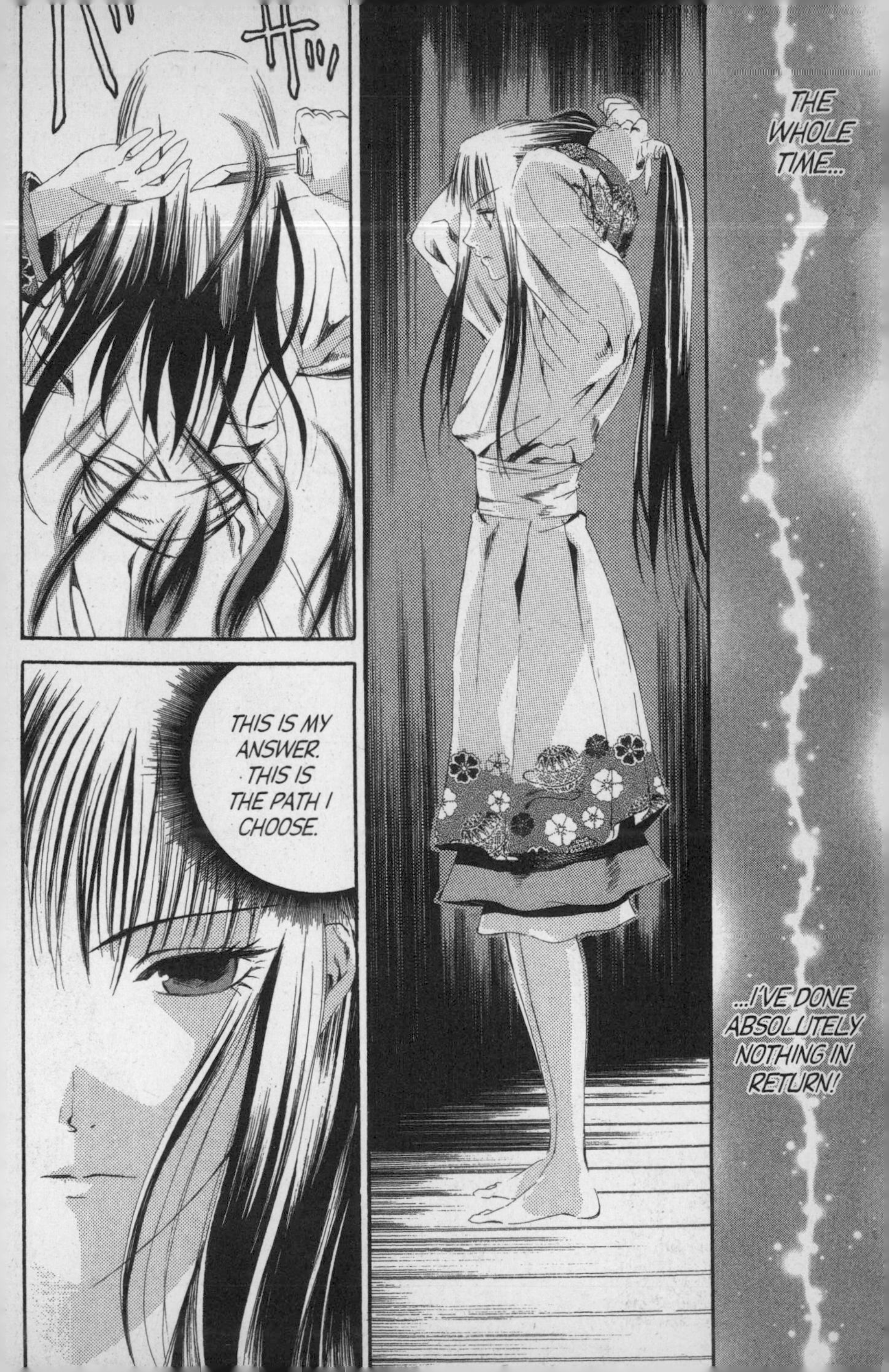
THE WHOLE TIME...
...I'VE DONE ABSOLUTELY NOTHING IN RETURN!
THIS IS MY ANSWER. THIS IS THE PATH I CHOOSE.

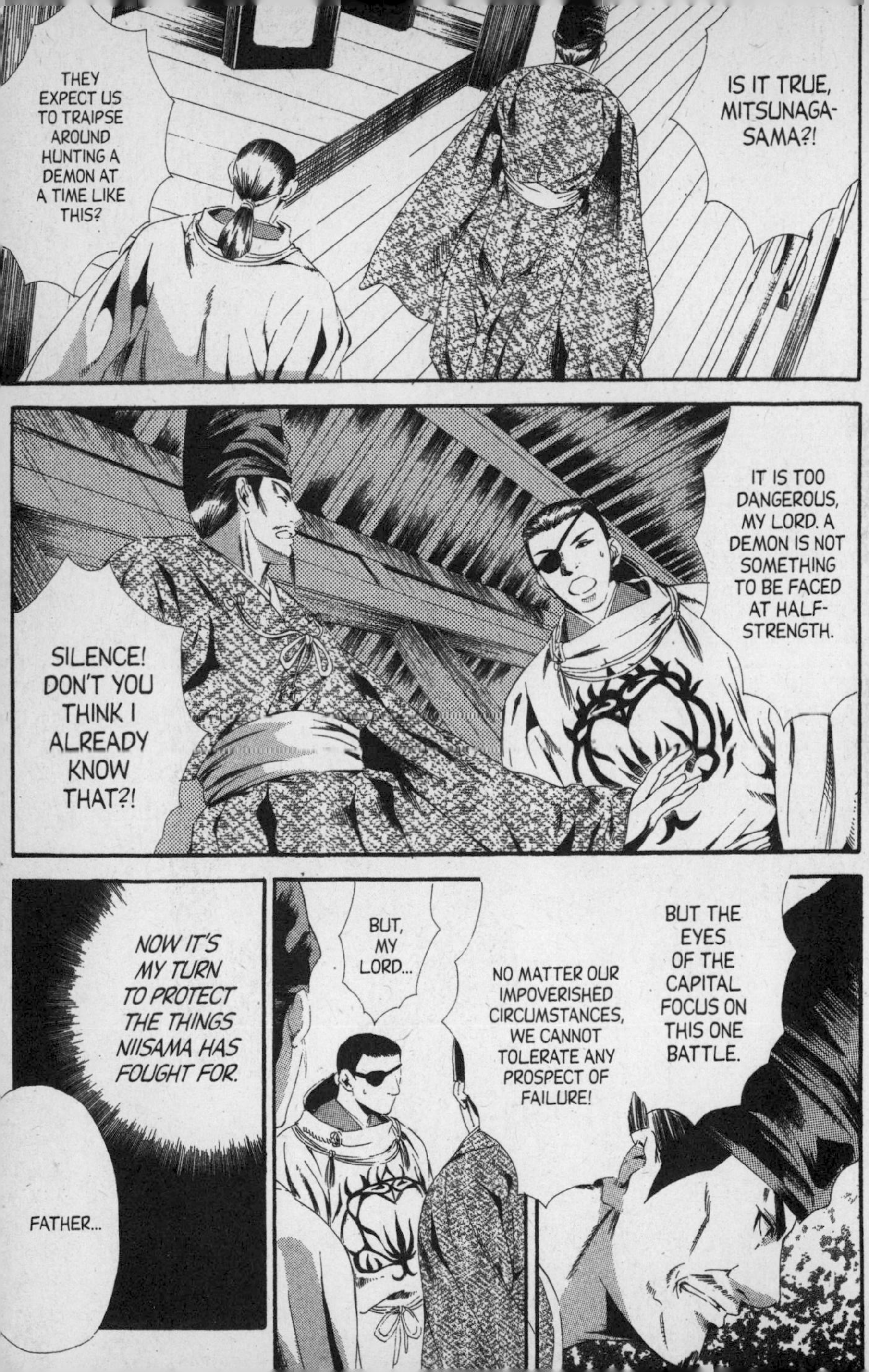
IS IT TRUE, MITSUNAGA-SAMA?!
THEY EXPECT US TO TRAIPSE AROUND HUNTING A DEMON AT A TIME LIKE THIS?
IT IS TOO DANGEROUS, MY LORD. A DEMON IS NOT SOMETHING TO BE FACED AT HALF-STRENGTH.
SILENCE! DON'T YOU THINK I ALREADY KNOW THAT?!
BUT THE EYES OF THE CAPITAL FOCUS ON THIS ONE BATTLE.
NO MATTER OUR IMPOVERISHED CIRCUMSTANCES, WE CANNOT TOLERATE ANY PROSPECT OF FAILURE!
BUT, MY LORD...
NOW IT'S MY TURN TO PROTECT THE THINGS NIISAMA HAS FOUGHT FOR.
FATHER...

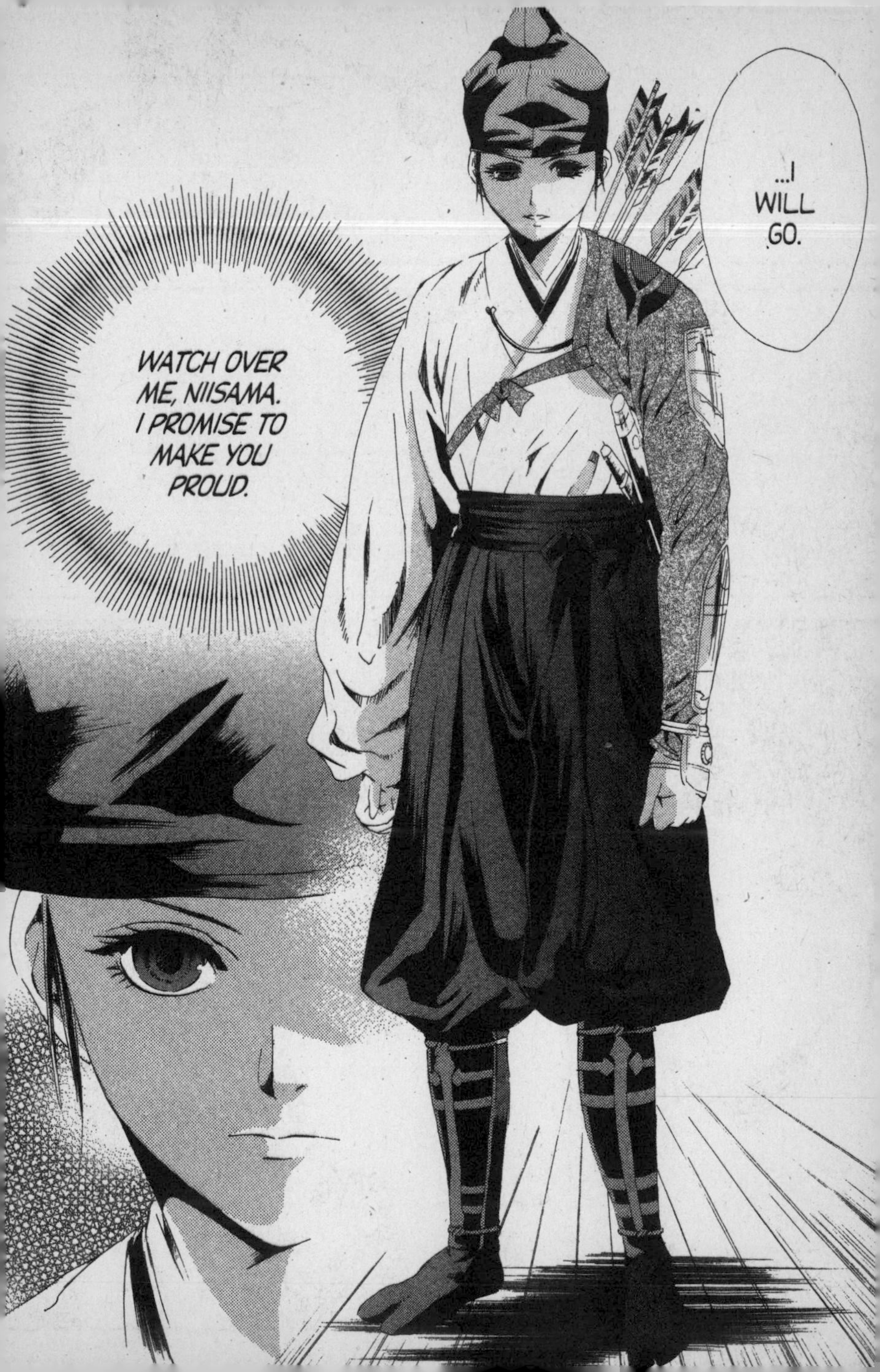
...I WILL GO.
WATCH OVER ME, NIISAMA. I PROMISE TO MAKE YOU PROUD.

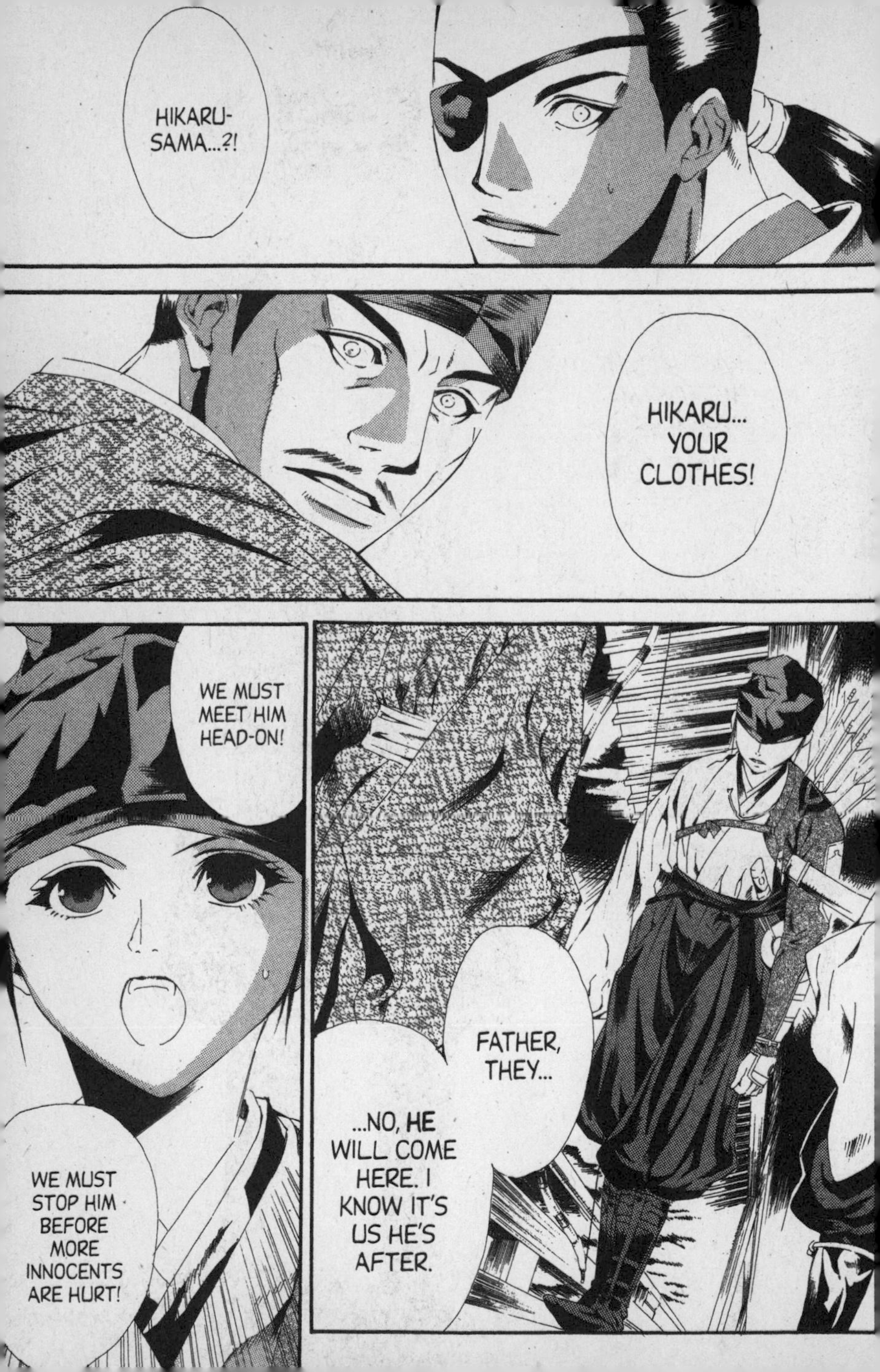
HIKARU-SAMA...?!
HIKARU... YOUR CLOTHES!
FATHER, THEY...
...NO, HE WILL COME HERE. I KNOW IT'S US HE'S AFTER.
WE MUST MEET HIM HEAD-ON!
WE MUST STOP HIM BEFORE MORE INNOCENTS ARE HURT!

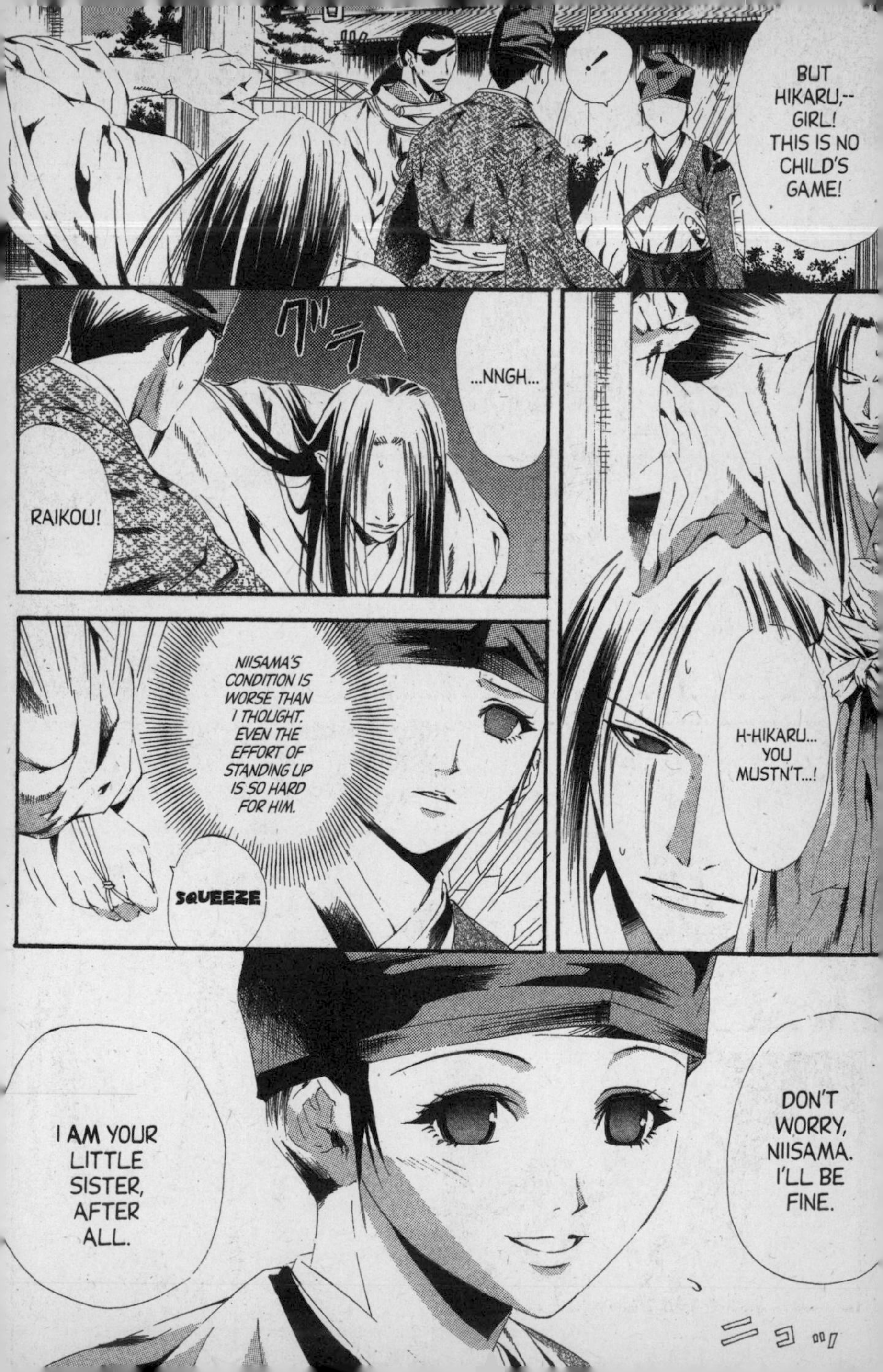
!
BUT HIKARU,-- GIRL! THIS IS NO CHILD'S GAME!
グラ
...NNGH...
RAIKOU!
H-HIKARU... YOU MUSTN'T...!
NIISAMA'S CONDITION IS WORSE THAN I THOUGHT. EVEN THE EFFORT OF STANDING UP IS SO HARD FOR HIM.
SQUEEZE
DON'T WORRY, NIISAMA. I'LL BE FINE.
I AM YOUR LITTLE SISTER, AFTER ALL.
ニコッ

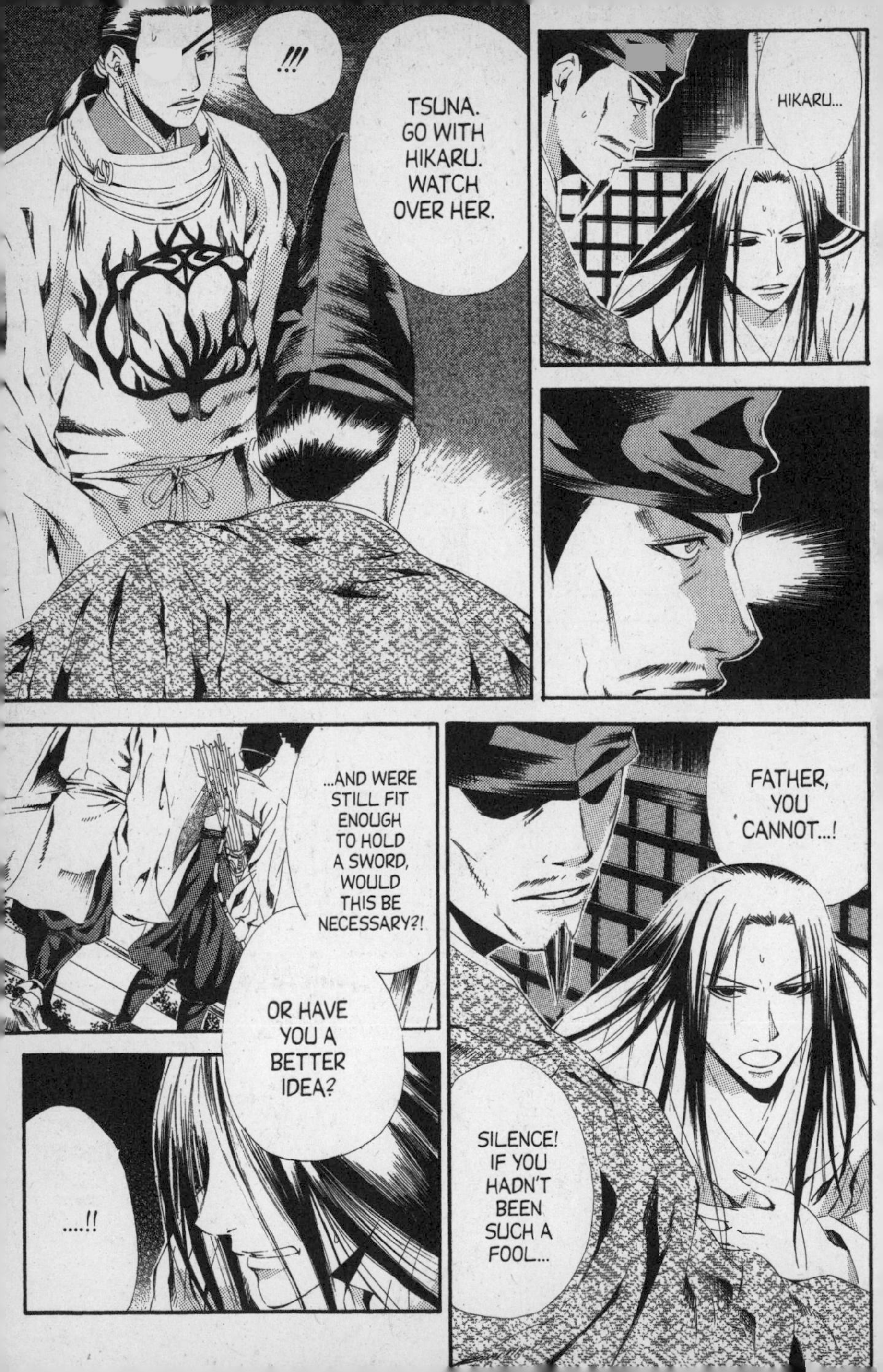
HIKARU...
TSUNA. GO WITH HIKARU. WATCH OVER HER.
!!!
FATHER, YOU CANNOT...!
SILENCE! IF YOU HADN'T BEEN SUCH A FOOL...
...AND WERE STILL FIT ENOUGH TO HOLD A SWORD, WOULD THIS BE NECESSARY?!
OR HAVE YOU A BETTER IDEA?
....!!

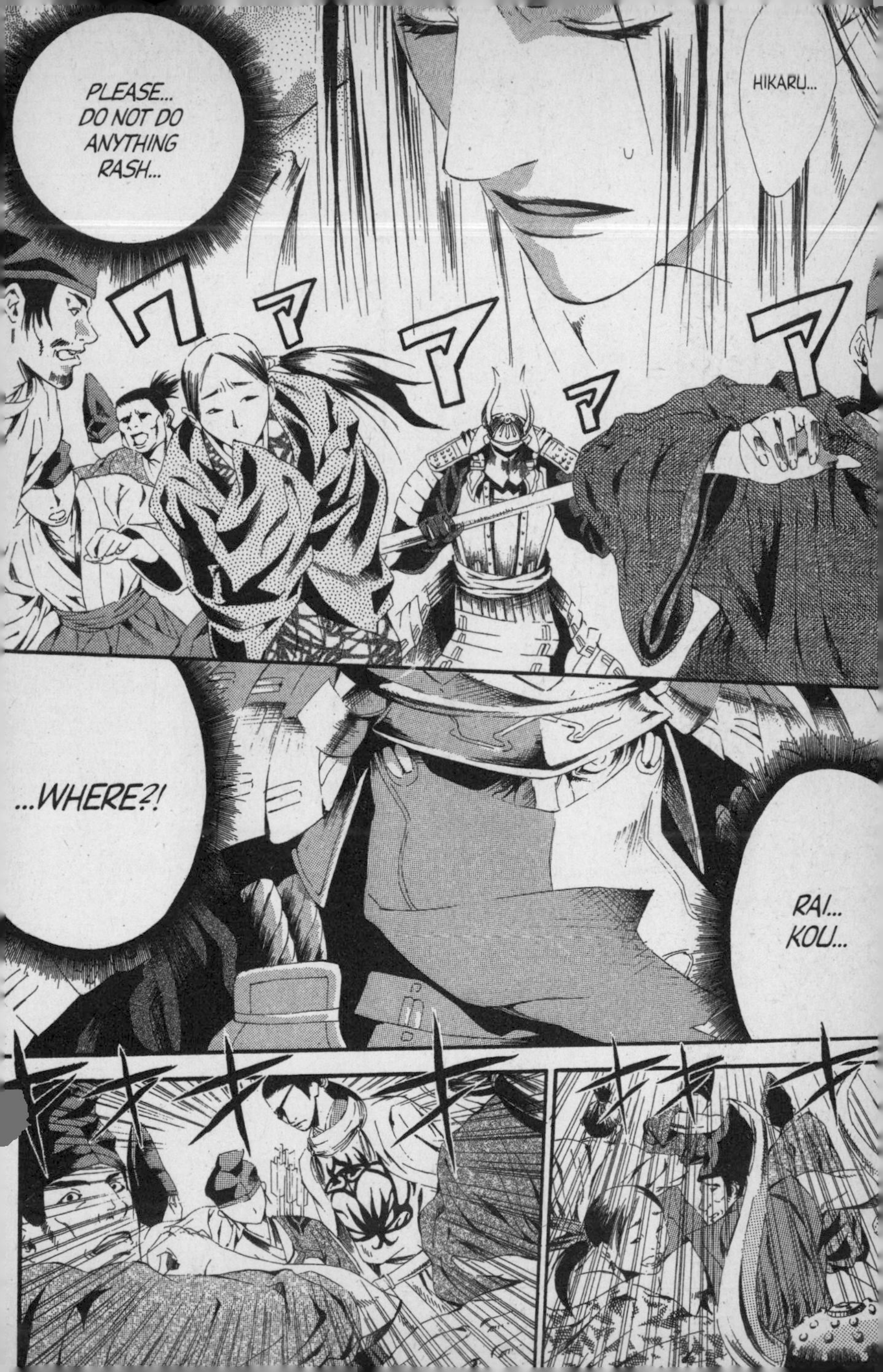
HIKARU...
PLEASE... DO NOT DO ANYTHING RASH...
RAI... KOU...
...WHERE?!

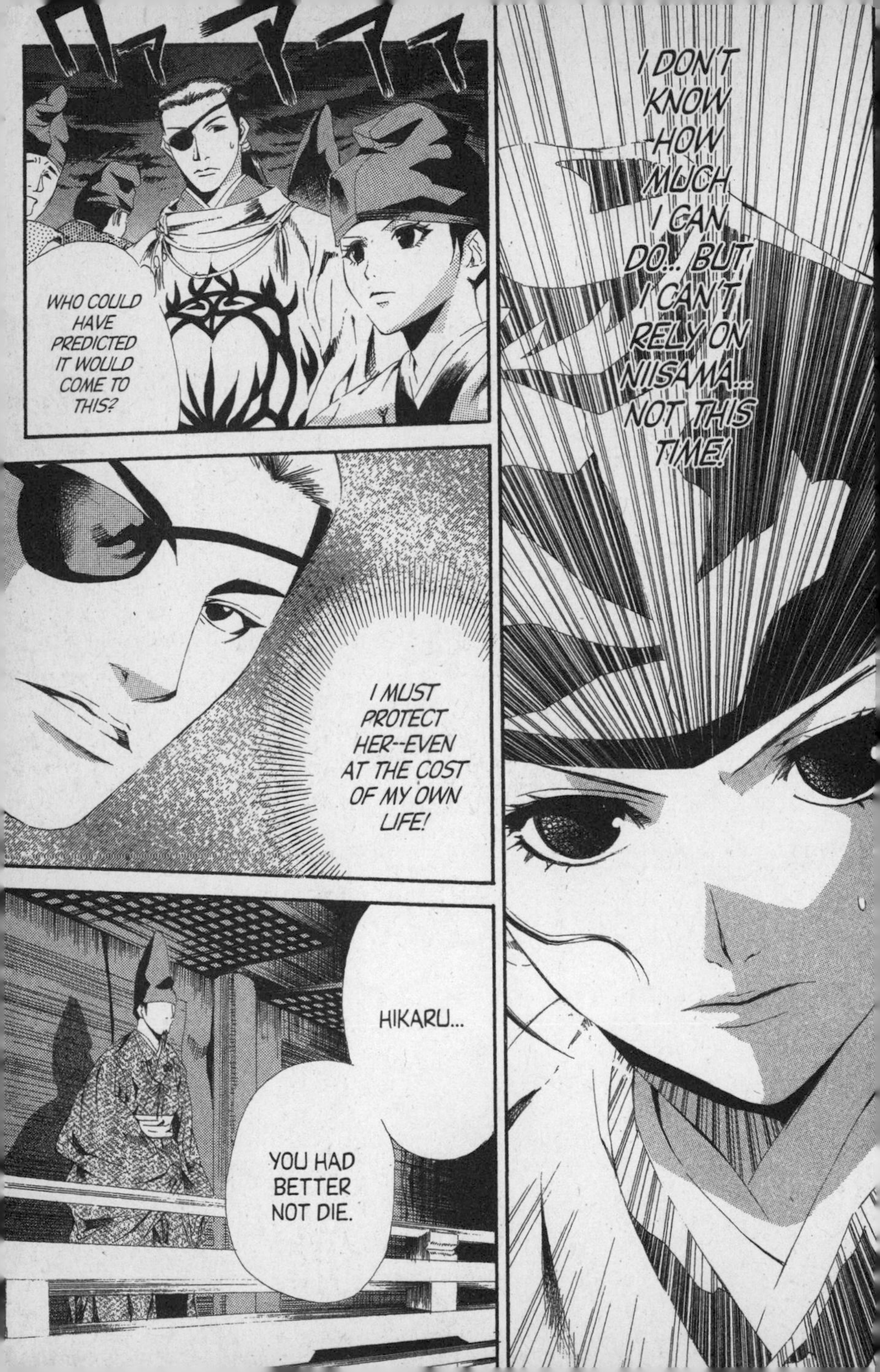
I DON'T KNOW HOW MUCH I CAN DO... BUT I CAN'T RELY ON NIISAMA... NOT THIS TIME!
WHO COULD HAVE PREDICTED IT WOULD COME TO THIS?
I MUST PROTECT HER--EVEN AT THE COST OF MY OWN LIFE!
HIKARU...
YOU HAD BETTER NOT DIE.

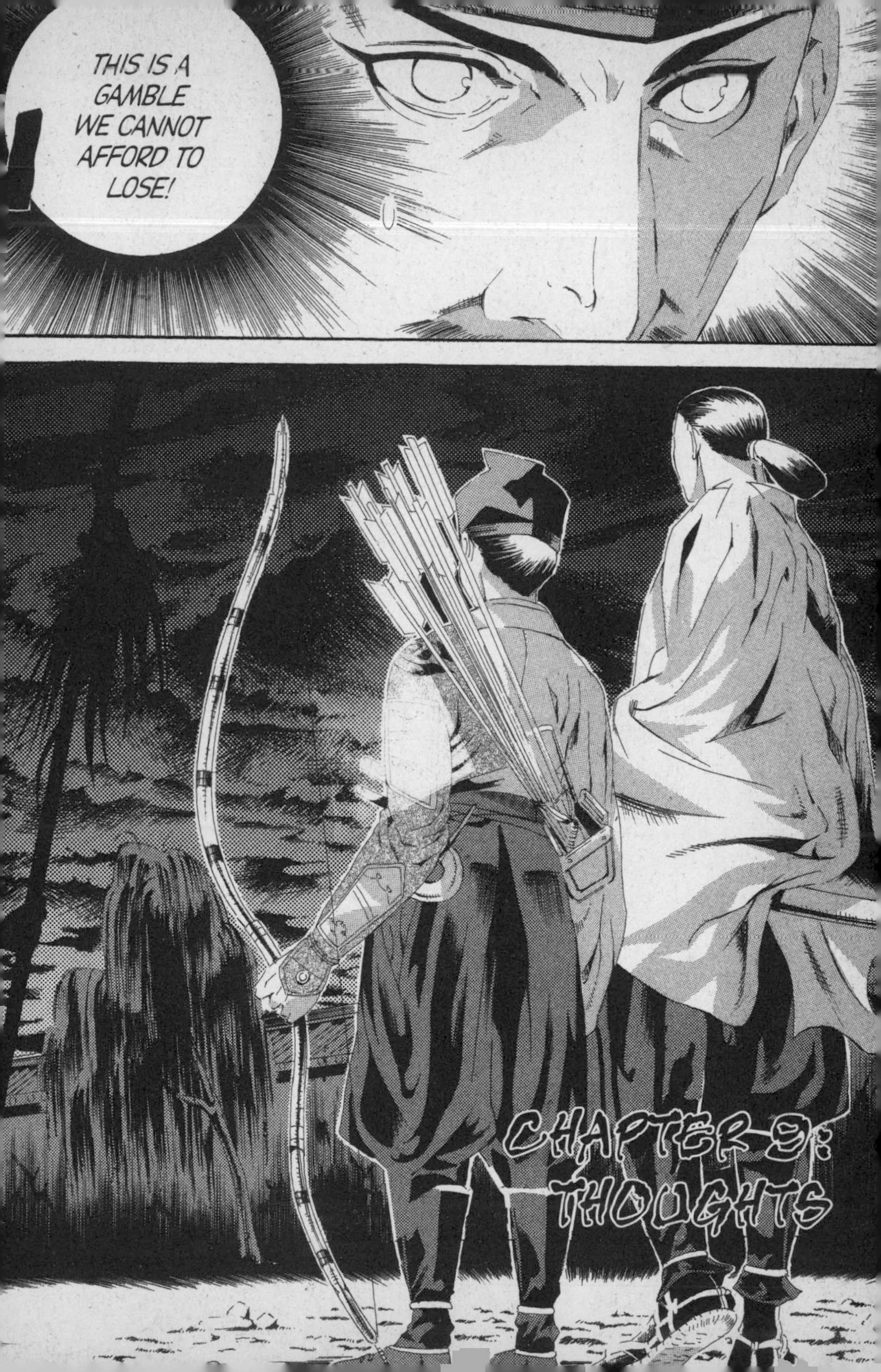
THIS IS A GAMBLE WE CANNOT AFFORD TO LOSE!
CHAPTER 9: THOUGHTS

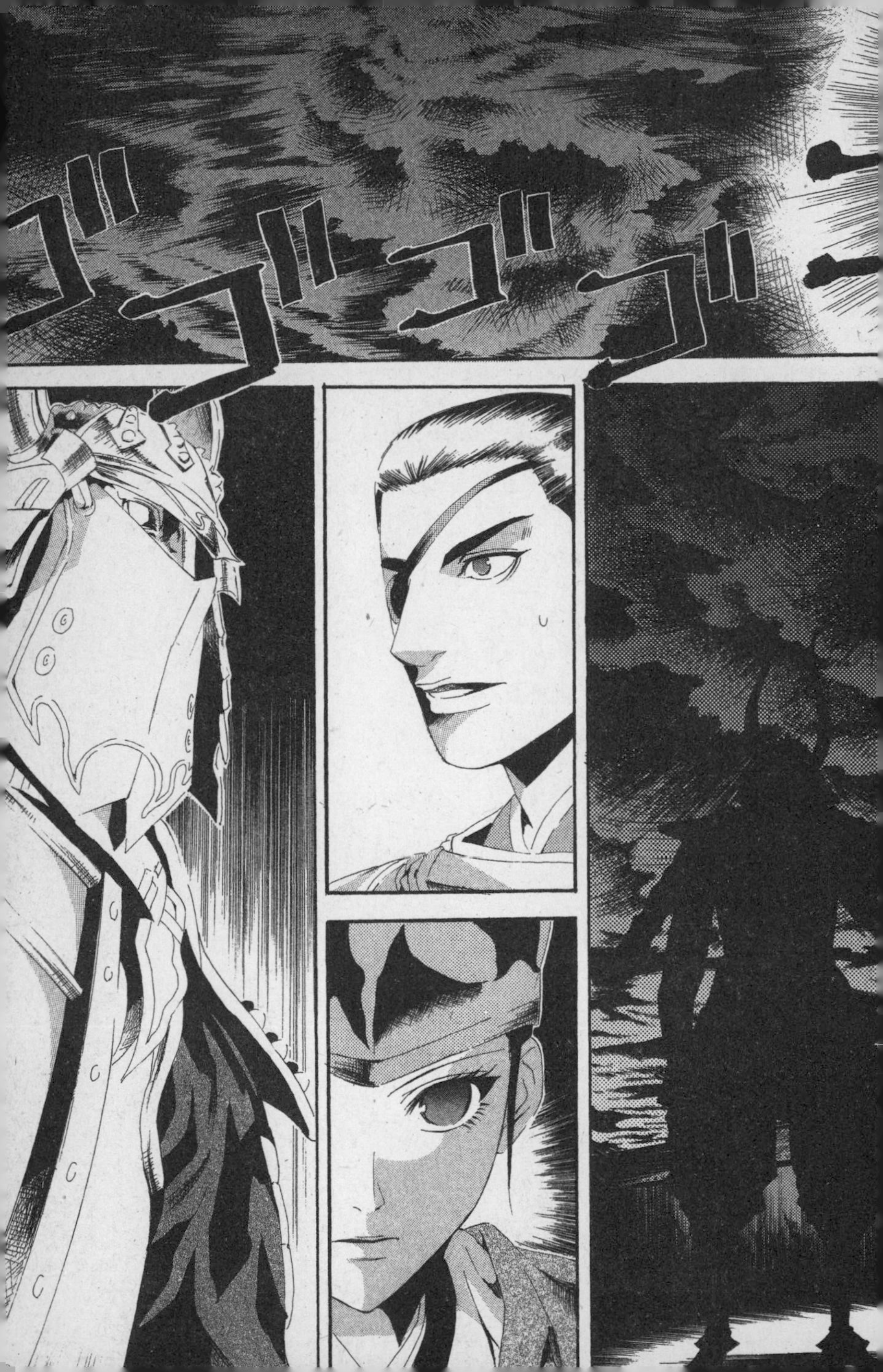
ゴゴゴゴ

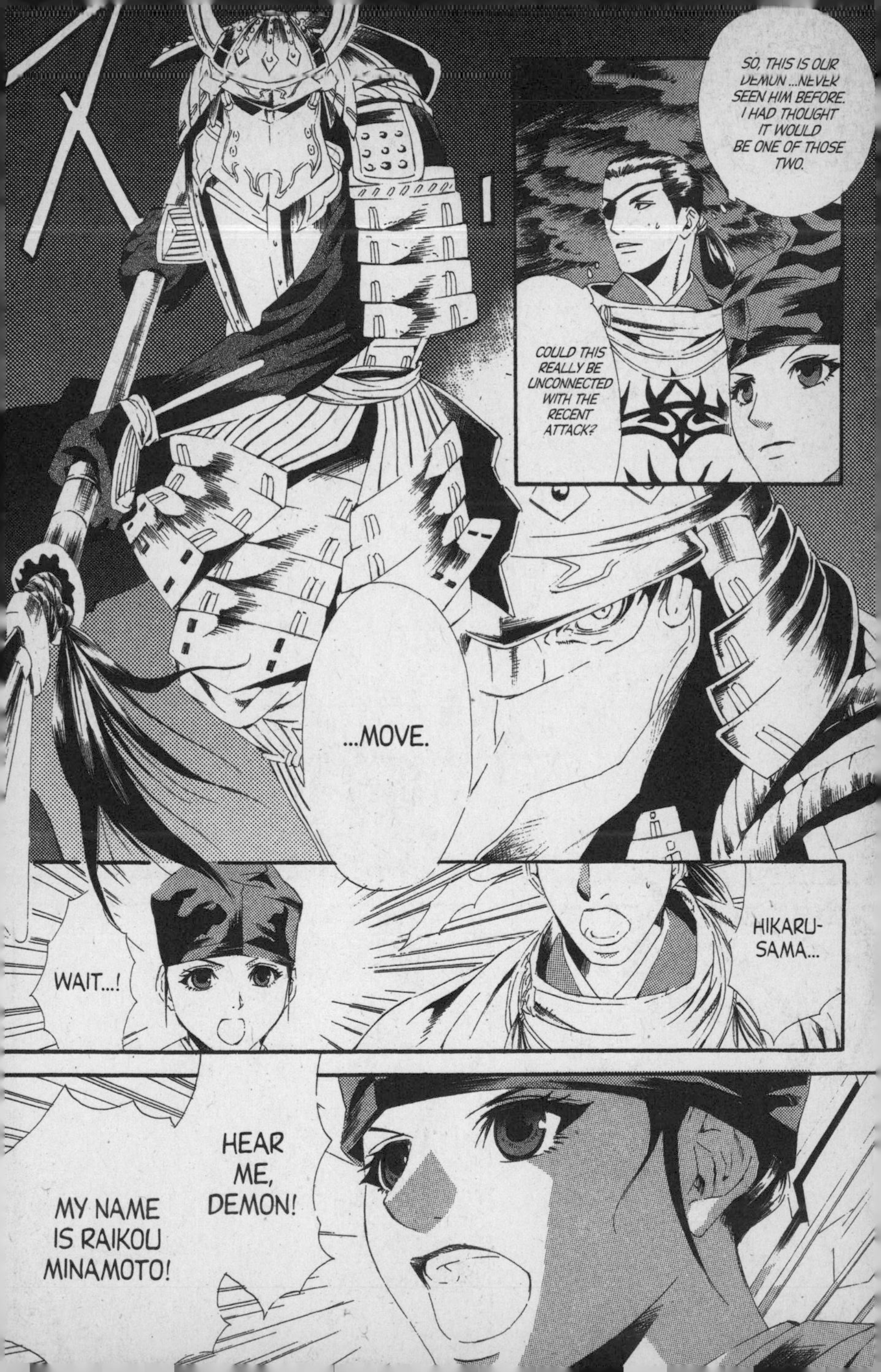
SO, THIS IS OUR DEMON ...NEVER SEEN HIM BEFORE. I HAD THOUGHT IT WOULD BE ONE OF THOSE TWO.
COULD THIS REALLY BE UNCONNECTED WITH THE RECENT ATTACK?
...MOVE.
HIKARU-SAMA...
WAIT...!
HEAR ME, DEMON!
MY NAME IS RAIKOU MINAMOTO!

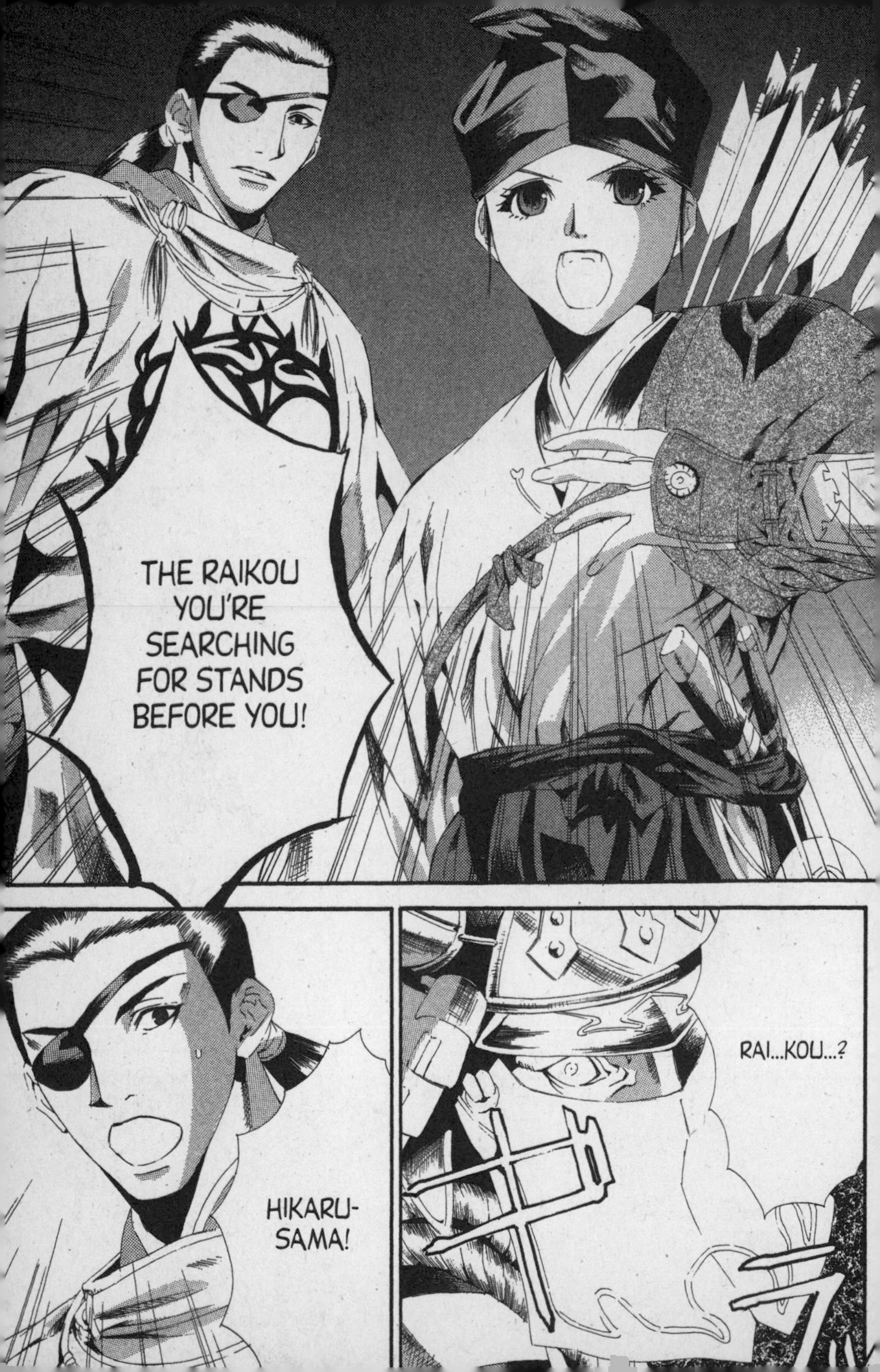
THE RAIKOU YOU'RE SEARCHING FOR STANDS BEFORE YOU!
RAI...KOU...?
HIKARU-SAMA!

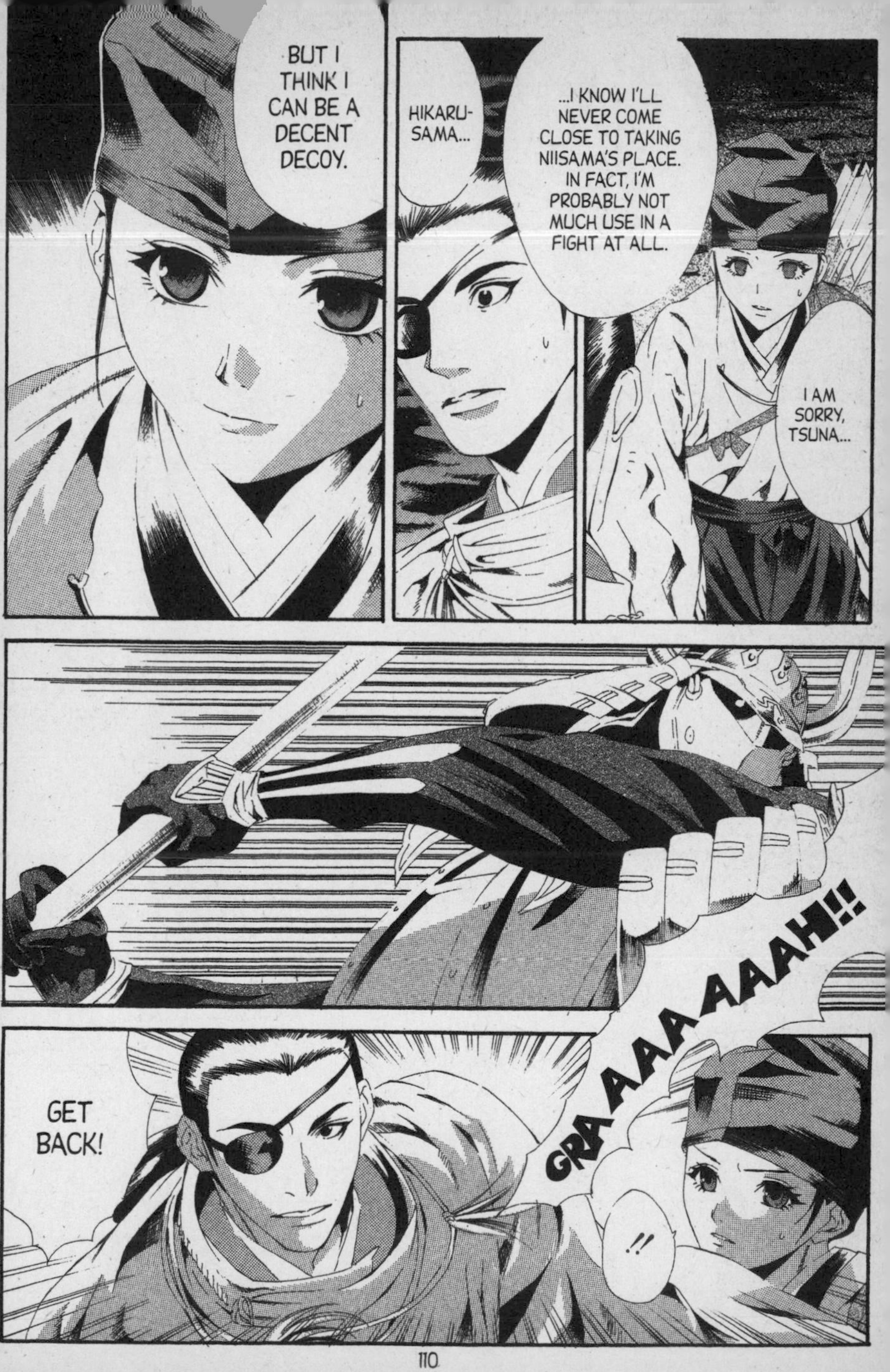
...I KNOW I'LL NEVER COME CLOSE TO TAKING NIISAMA'S PLACE. IN FACT, I'M PROBABLY NOT MUCH USE IN A FIGHT AT ALL.
HIKARU-SAMA...
BUT I THINK I CAN BE A DECENT DECOY.
I AM SORRY, TSUNA...
GRAAAAAAAAH!!
!!
GET BACK!

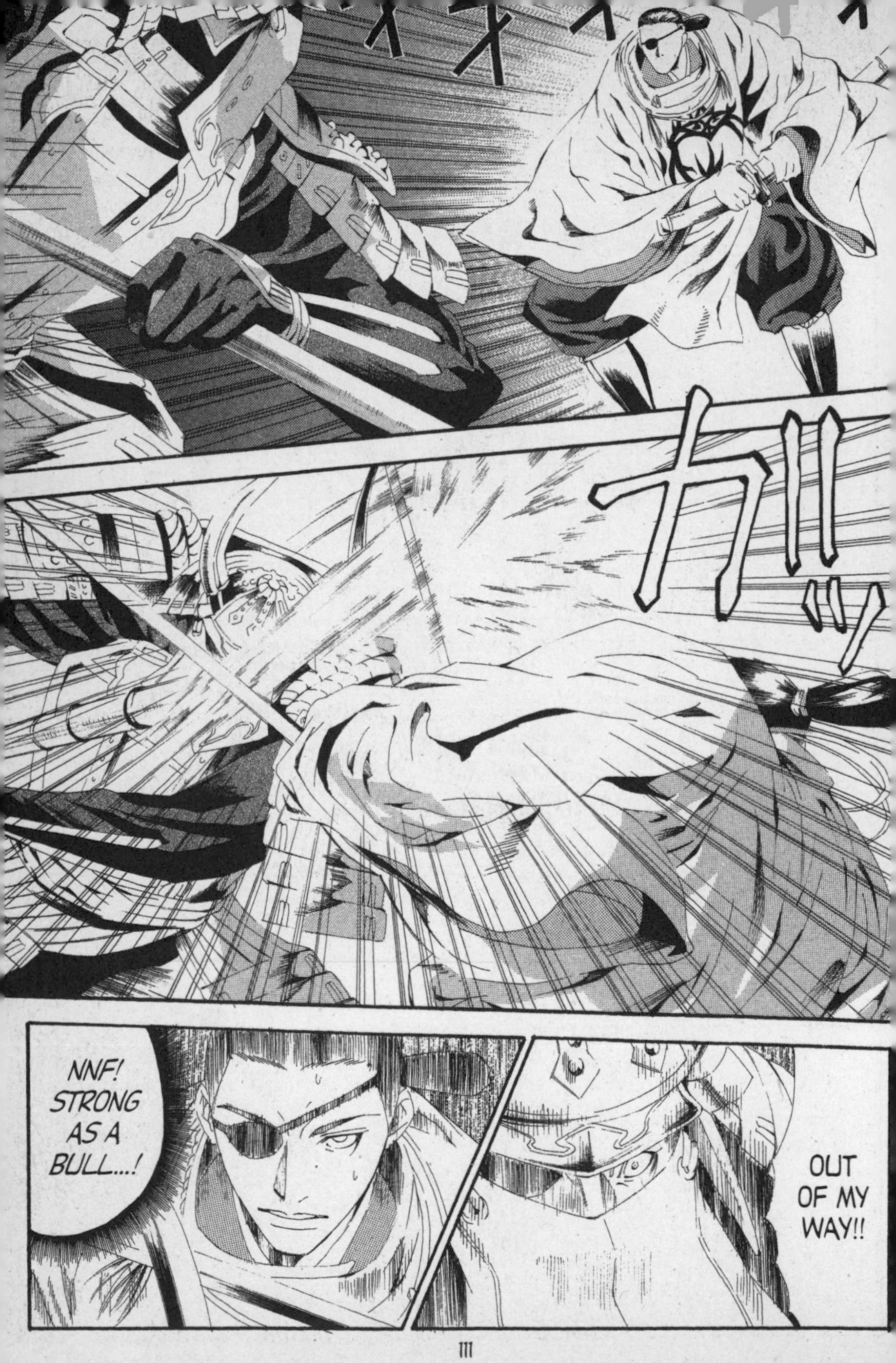
カッ
NNF! STRONG AS A BULL...!
OUT OF MY WAY!!

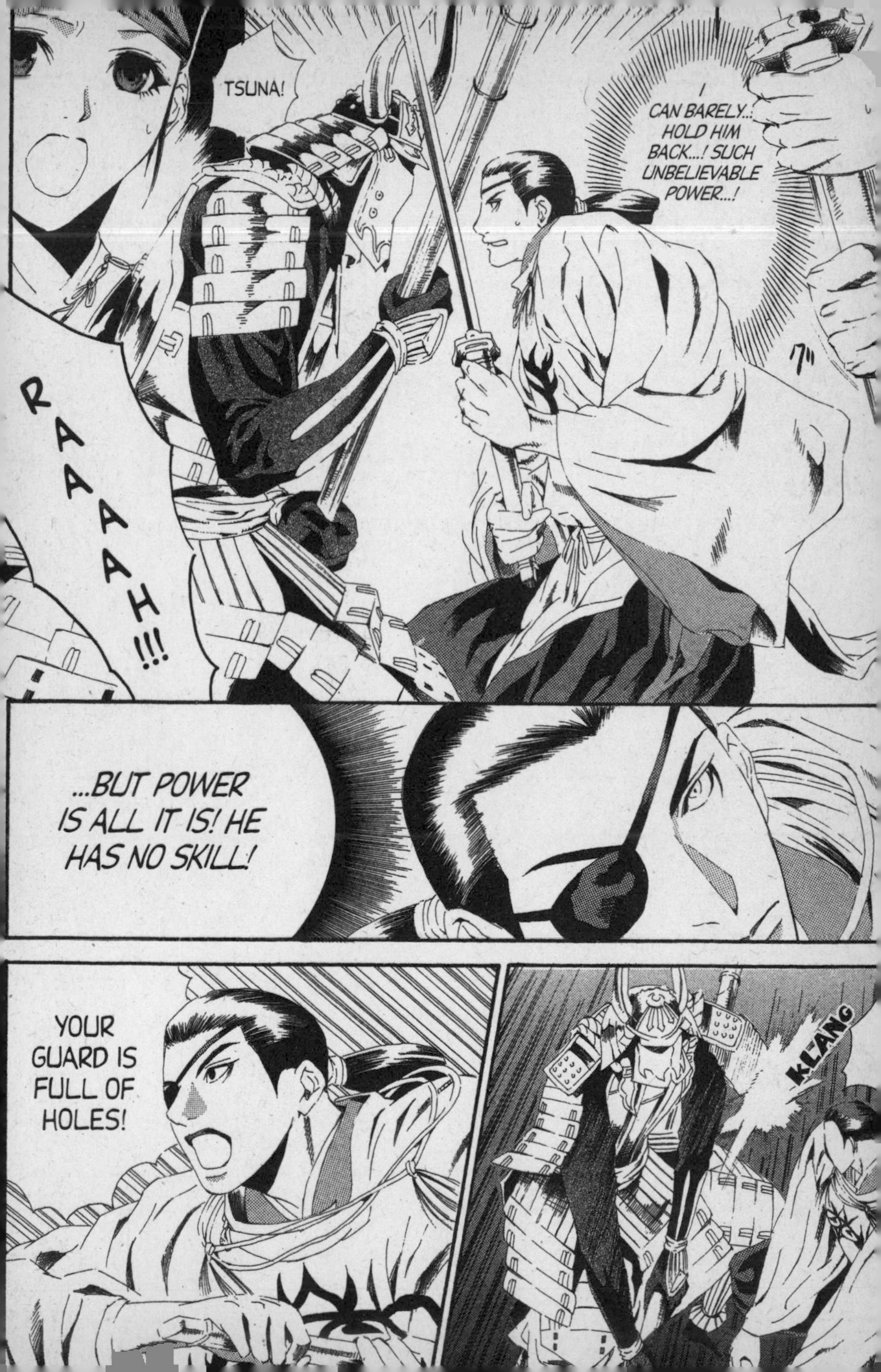
I CAN BARELY... HOLD HIM BACK...! SUCH UNBELIEVABLE POWER...!
TSUNA!
RAAAAH!!!
...BUT POWER IS ALL IT IS! HE HAS NO SKILL!
KLANG
YOUR GUARD IS FULL OF HOLES!

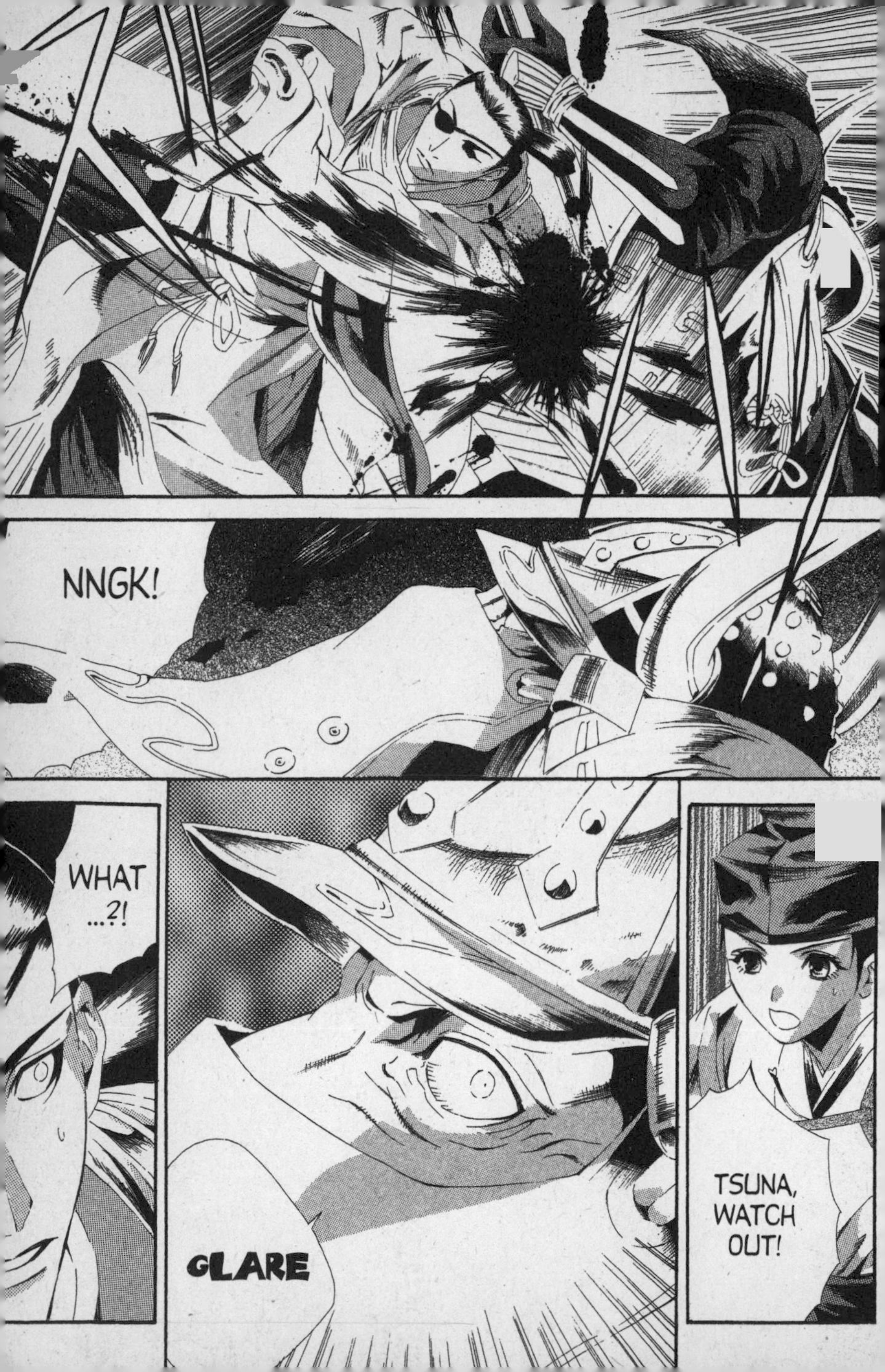
NNGK!
TSUNA, WATCH OUT!
GLARE
WHAT ...?!

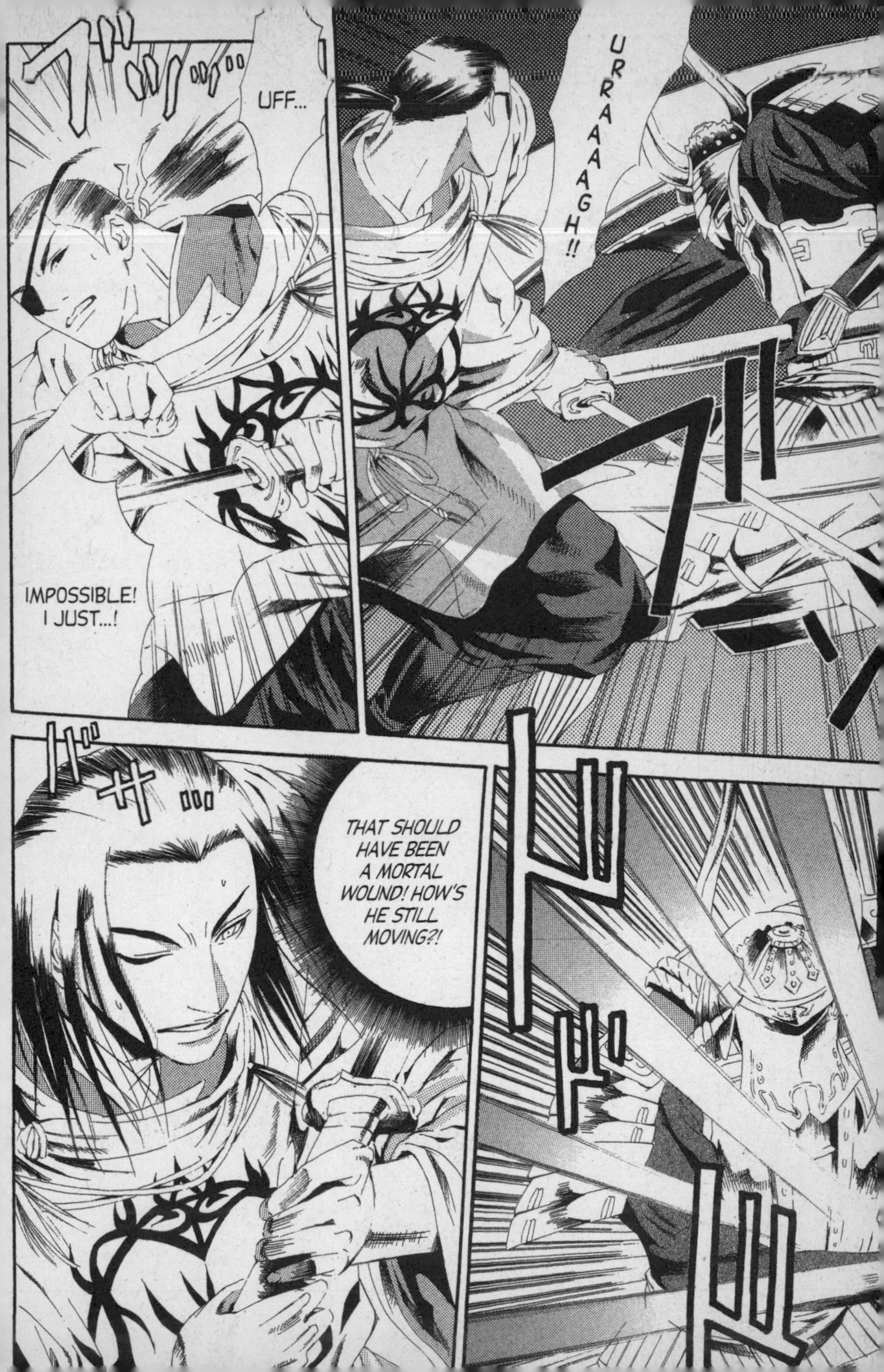
URRAAAAGH!!
UFF...
IMPOSSIBLE! I JUST...!
THAT SHOULD HAVE BEEN A MORTAL WOUND! HOW'S HE STILL MOVING?!

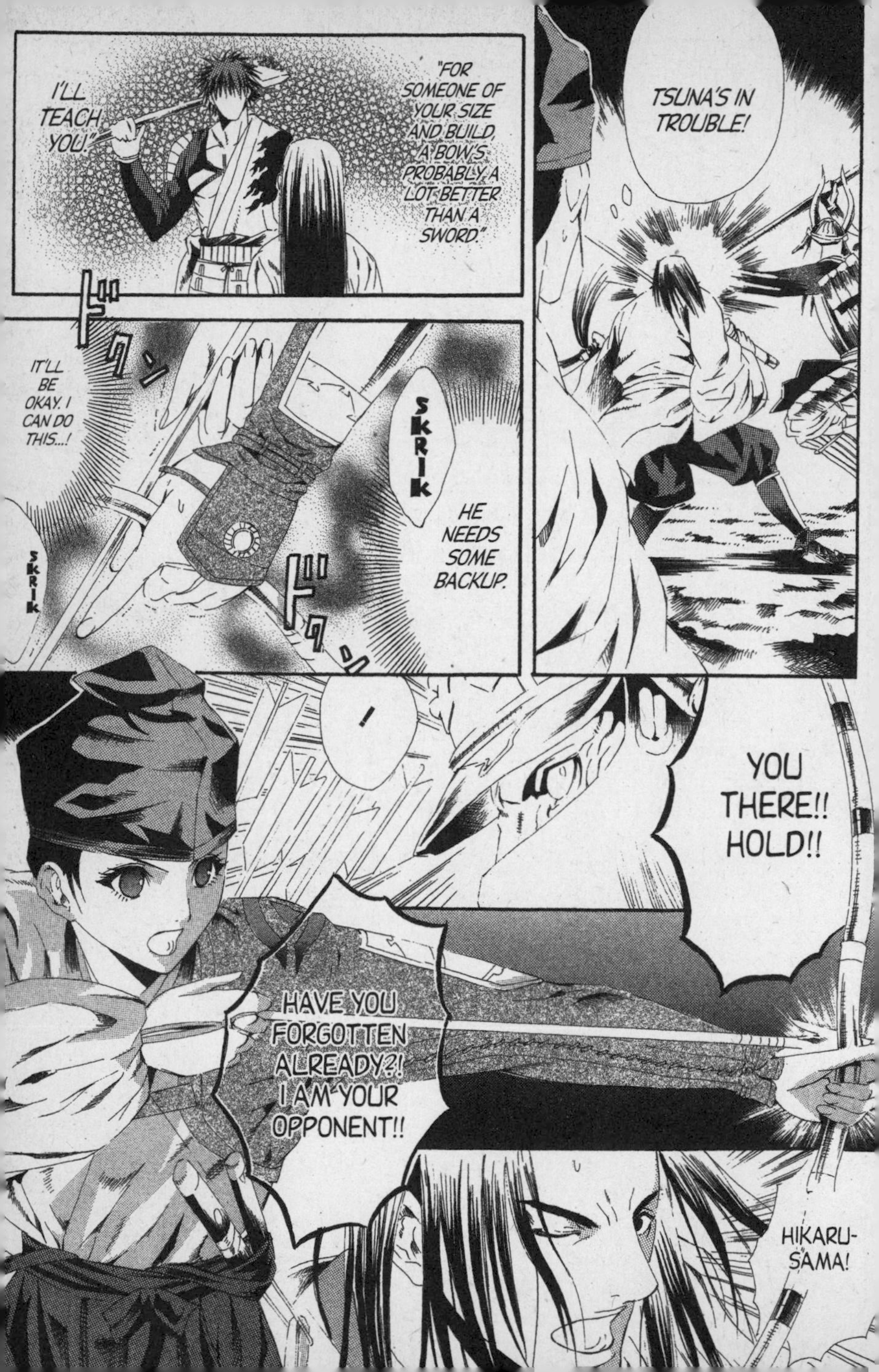
TSUNA'S IN TROUBLE!
"FOR SOMEONE OF YOUR SIZE AND BUILD, A BOW'S PROBABLY A LOT BETTER THAN A SWORD."
I'LL TEACH YOU."
SKRIK
HE NEEDS SOME BACKUP.
IT'LL BE OKAY. I CAN DO THIS...!
SKRIK
YOU THERE!! HOLD!!
!
HAVE YOU FORGOTTEN ALREADY?! I AM YOUR OPPONENT!!
HIKARU-SAMA!

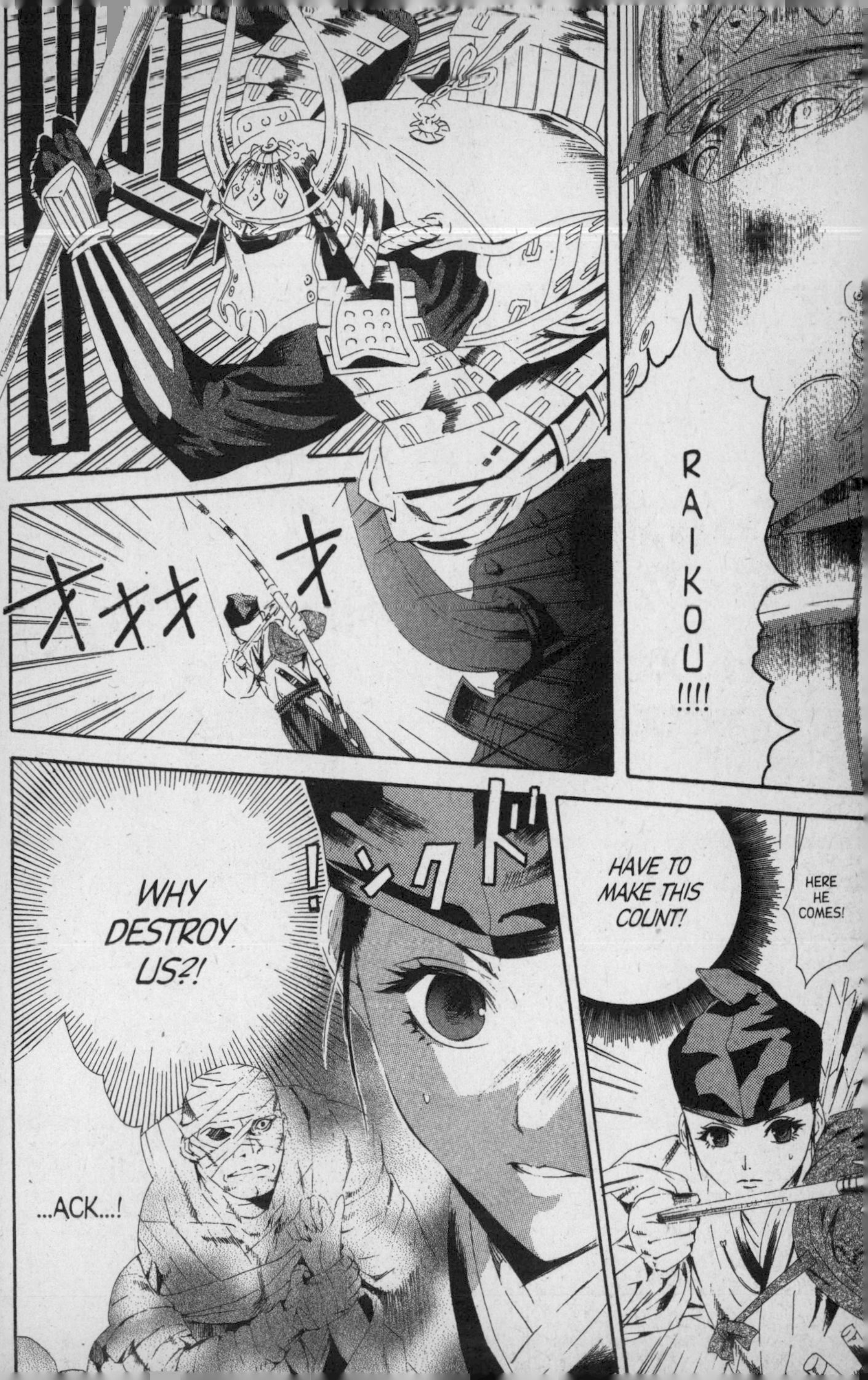

RAIKOU!!!!
HERE HE COMES!
HAVE TO MAKE THIS COUNT!
WHY DESTROY US?!
...ACK...!

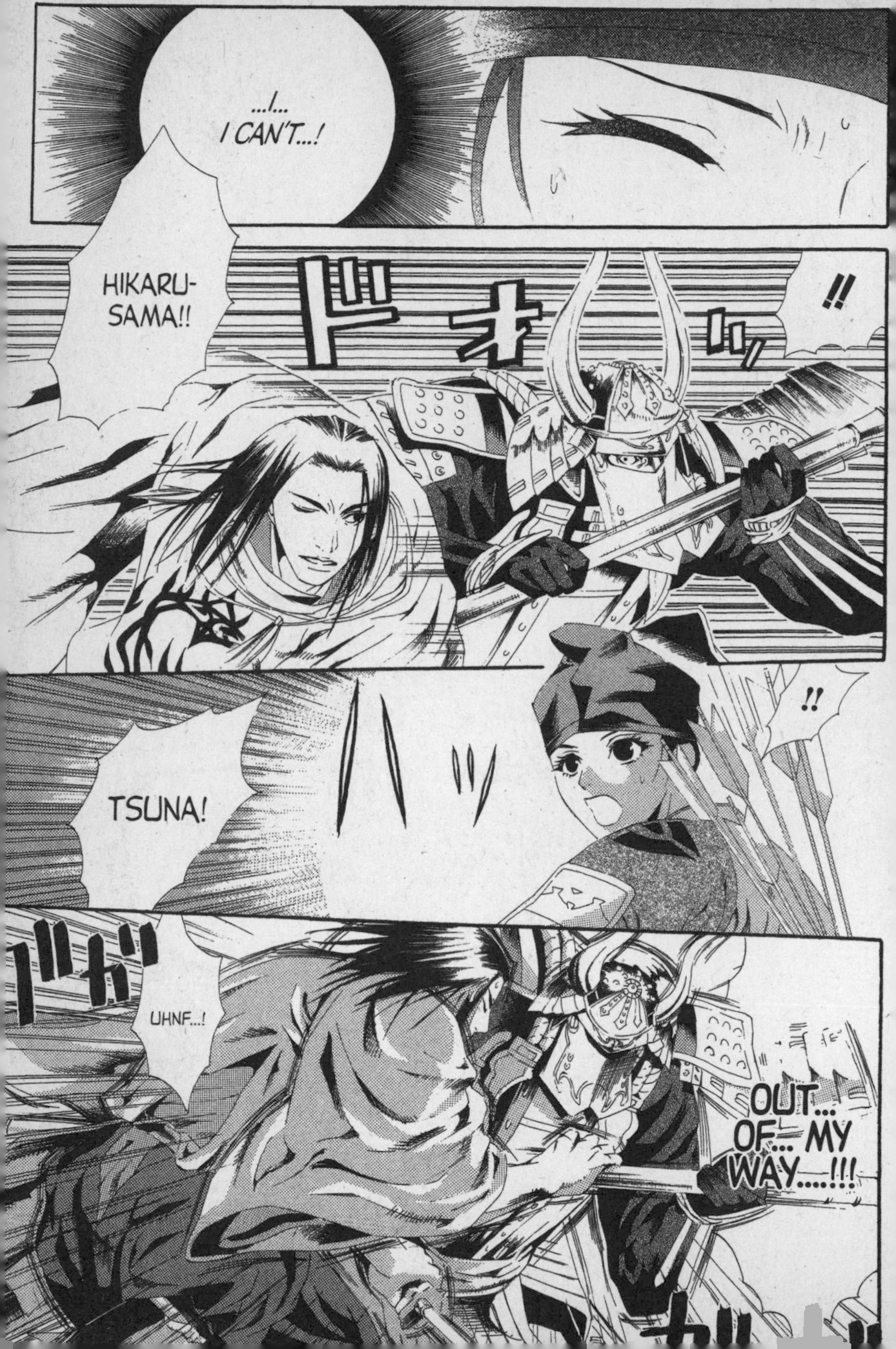
...I...
I CAN'T...!
HIKARU-
SAMA!!
ドオッ
!!
TSUNA!
ハッ
!!
ドガ
UHNF...!
OUT...
OF... MY
WAY....!!!

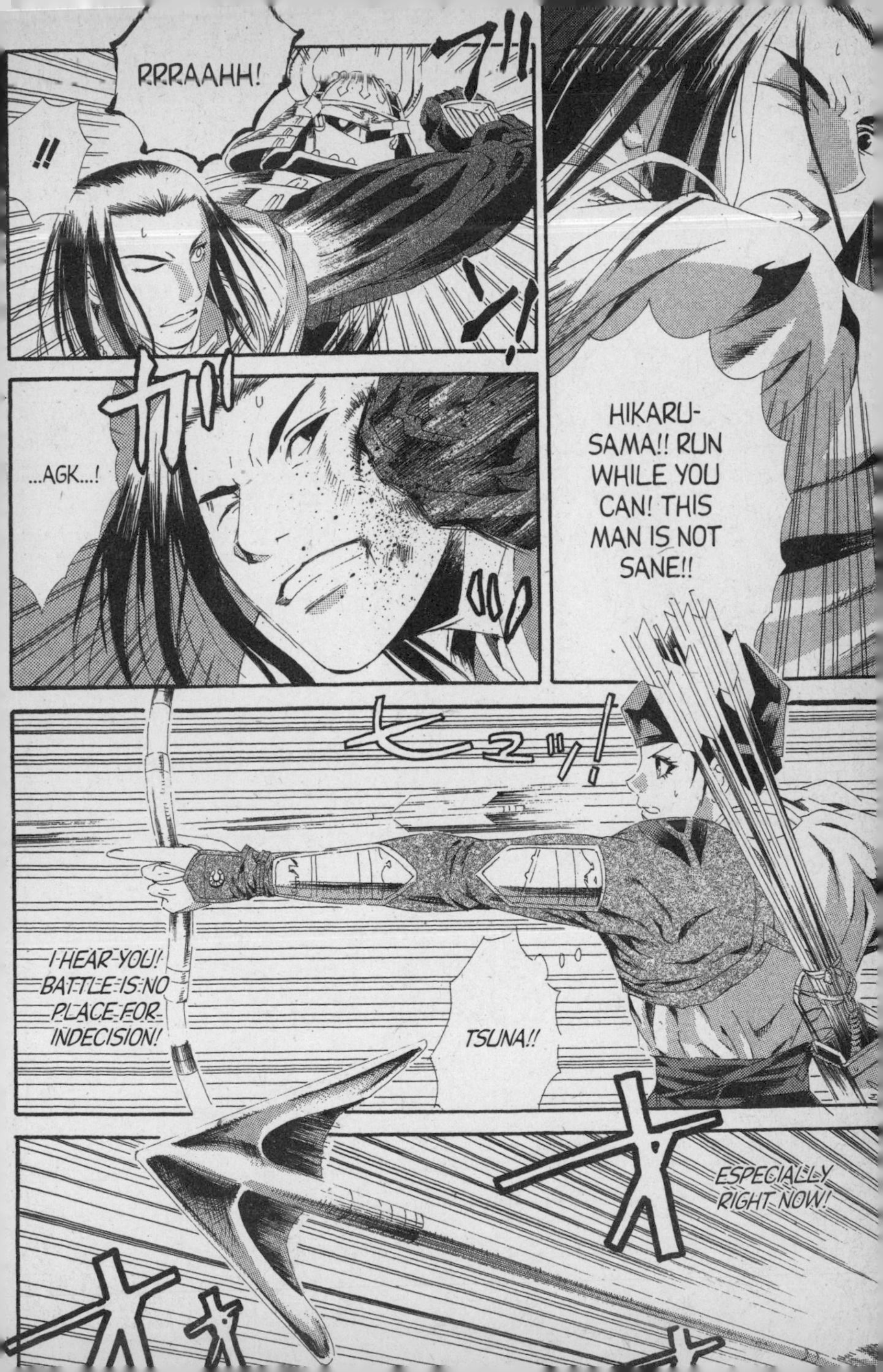
RRRAAHH!
!!
...AGK...!
HIKARU-SAMA!! RUN WHILE YOU CAN! THIS MAN IS NOT SANE!!
TSUNA!!
I HEAR YOU! BATTLE IS NO PLACE FOR INDECISION!
ESPECIALLY RIGHT NOW!

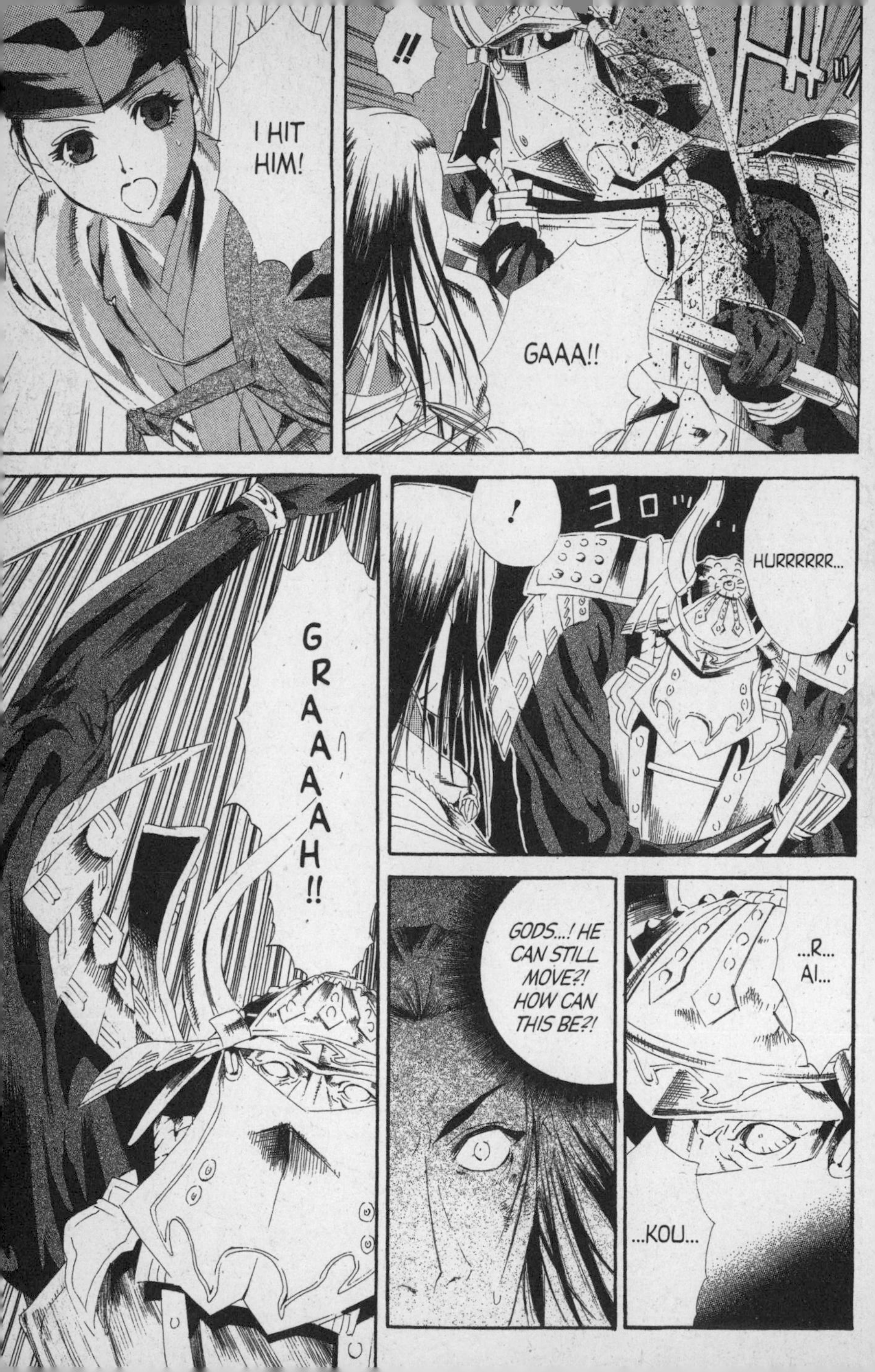
!!
I HIT HIM!
GAAA!!
HURRRRRR...
!
GRAAAAAH!!
...R... AI...
...KOU...
GODS...! HE CAN STILL MOVE?! HOW CAN THIS BE?!

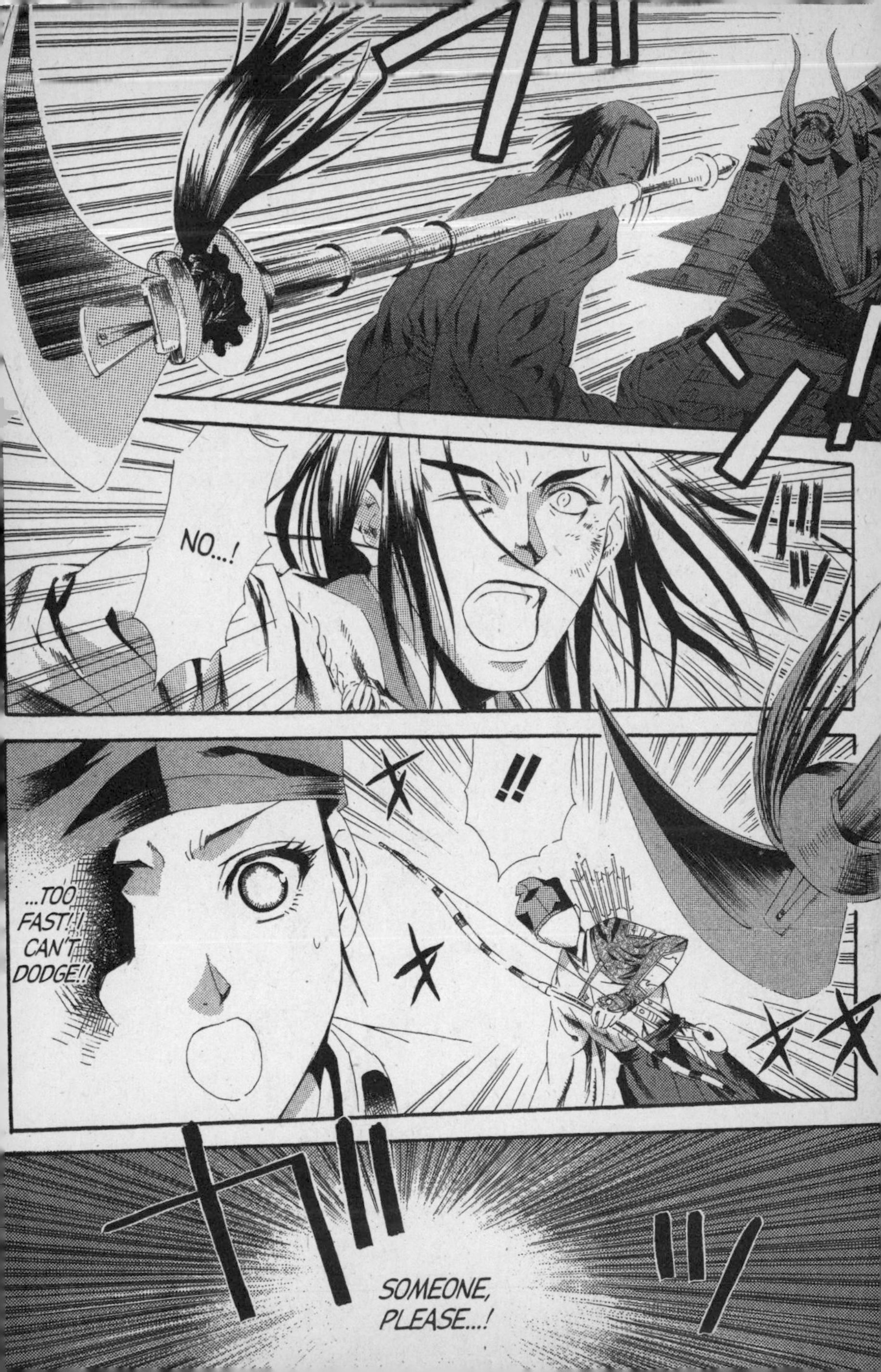
NO...!
!!
...TOO FAST!! I CAN'T DODGE!!
SOMEONE, PLEASE...!

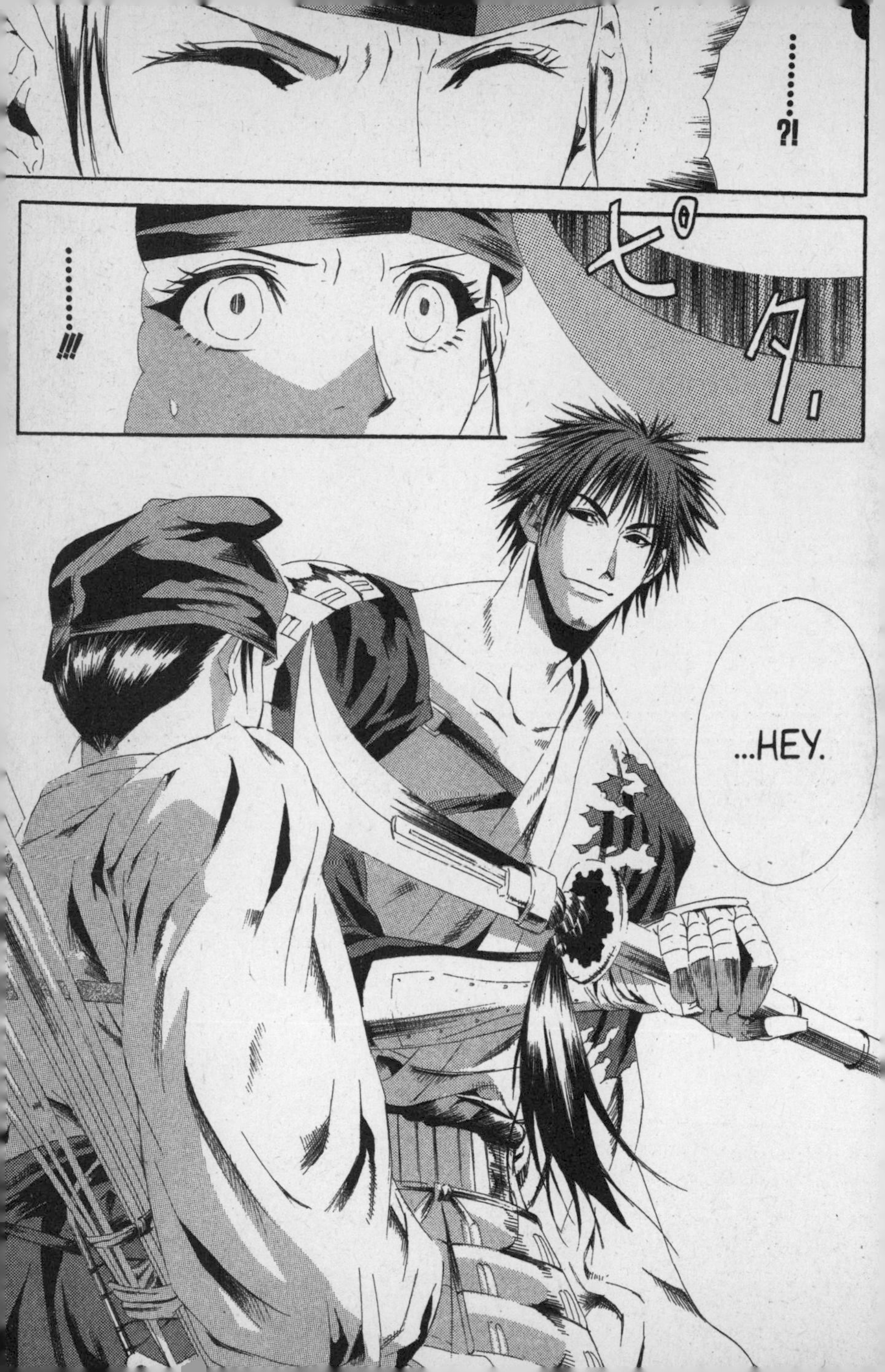
......?!
ピタ
......!!!
...HEY.

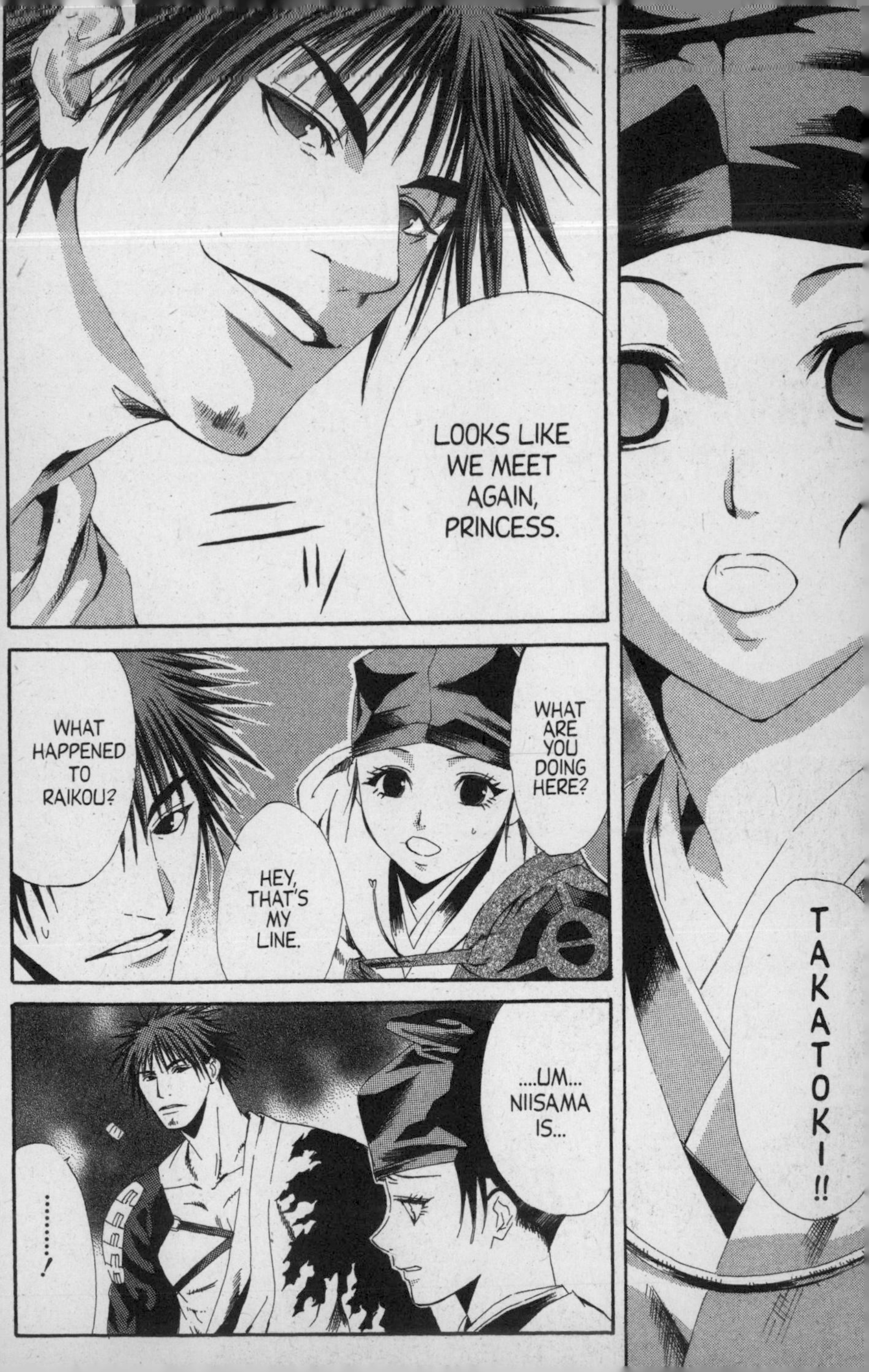
TAKATOKI!!
LOOKS LIKE WE MEET AGAIN, PRINCESS.
WHAT ARE YOU DOING HERE?
HEY, THAT'S MY LINE.
WHAT HAPPENED TO RAIKOU?
....UM... NIISAMA IS...
......!

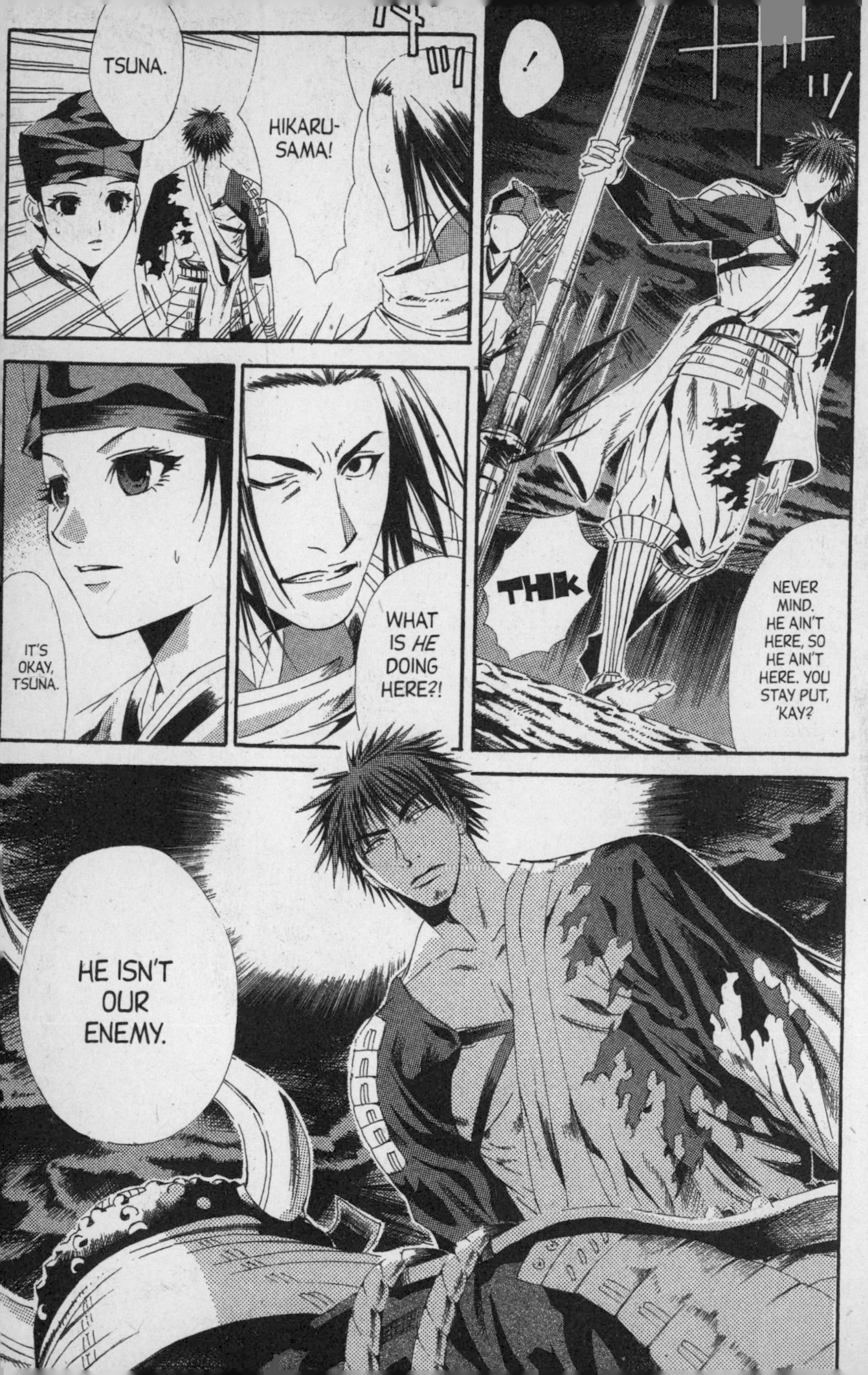
!
THK
NEVER MIND. HE AIN'T HERE, SO HE AIN'T HERE. YOU STAY PUT, 'KAY?
TSUNA.
HIKARU-SAMA!
WHAT IS *HE* DOING HERE?!
IT'S OKAY, TSUNA.
HE ISN'T OUR ENEMY.

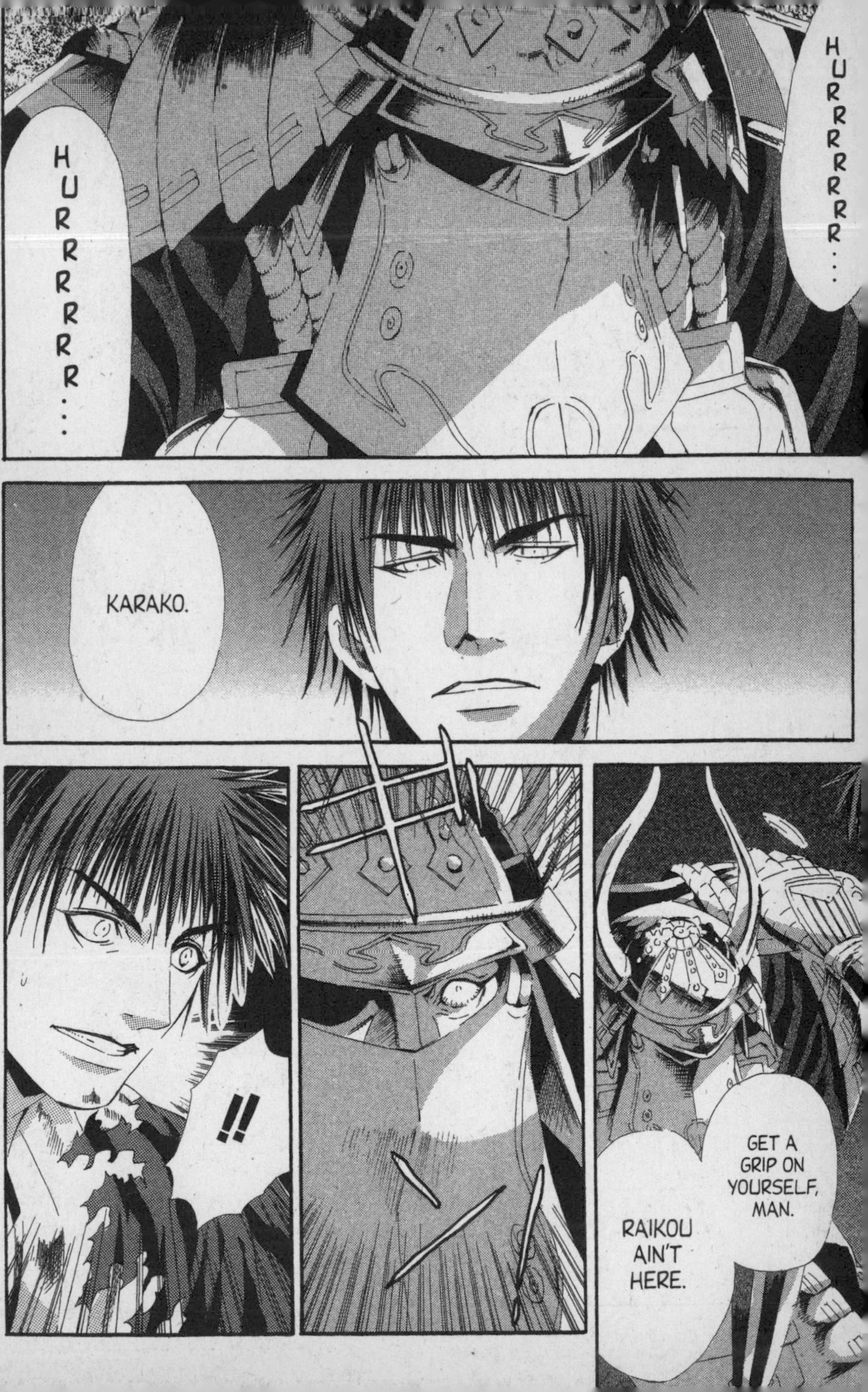
HURRRRRR...
HURRRRRR...
KARAKO.
!!
GET A GRIP ON YOURSELF, MAN.
RAIKOU AIN'T HERE.

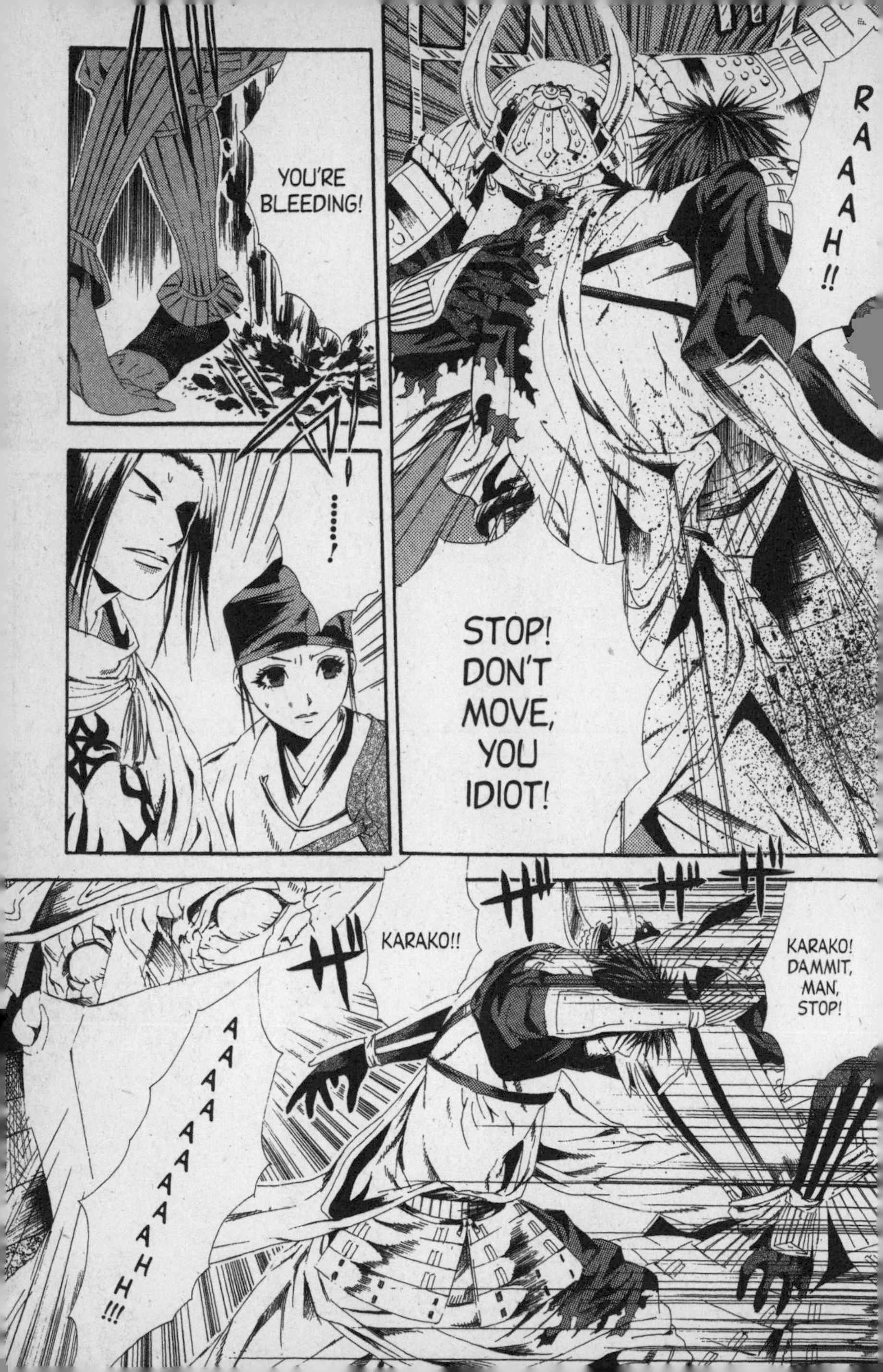
RAAAAH!!
STOP! DON'T MOVE, YOU IDIOT!
YOU'RE BLEEDING!
......!
KARAKO! DAMMIT, MAN, STOP!
KARAKO!!
AAAAAAAAAHH!!!

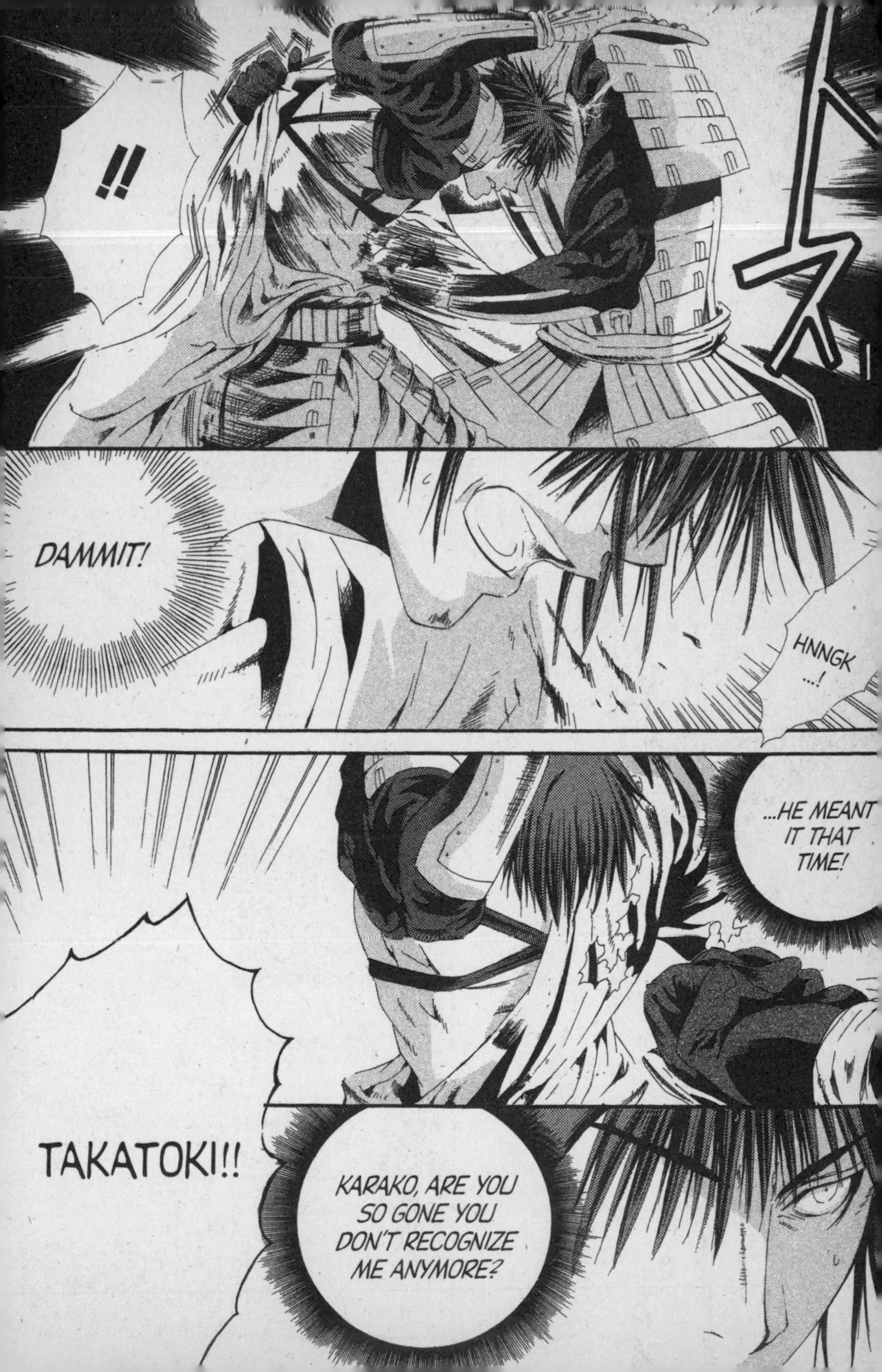
!!
HNNGK ...!
DAMMIT!
...HE MEANT IT THAT TIME!
TAKATOKI!!
KARAKO, ARE YOU SO GONE YOU DON'T RECOGNIZE ME ANYMORE?

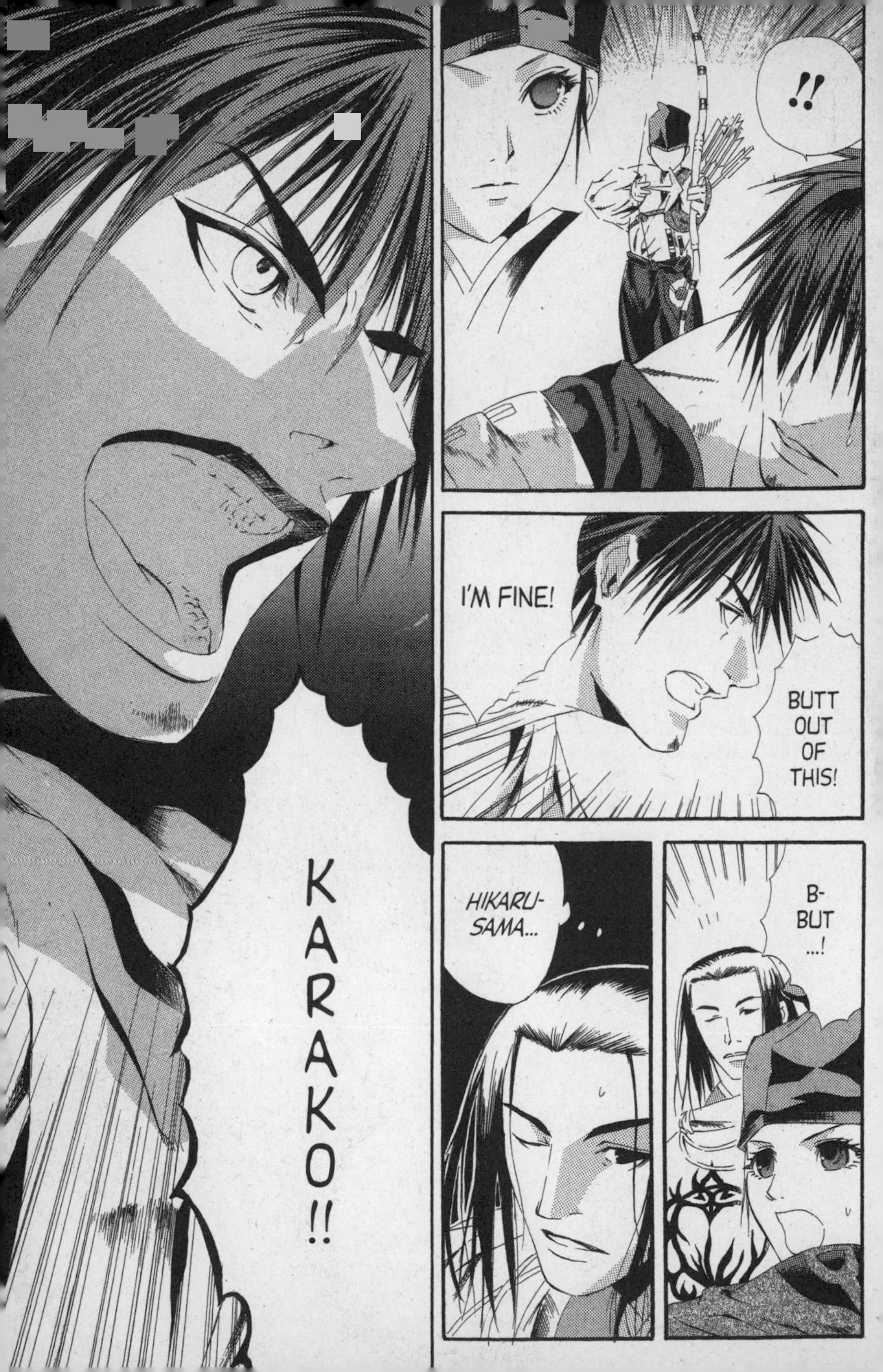
!!
I'M FINE!
BUTT OUT OF THIS!
B-BUT ...!
HIKARU-SAMA...
KARAKO!!

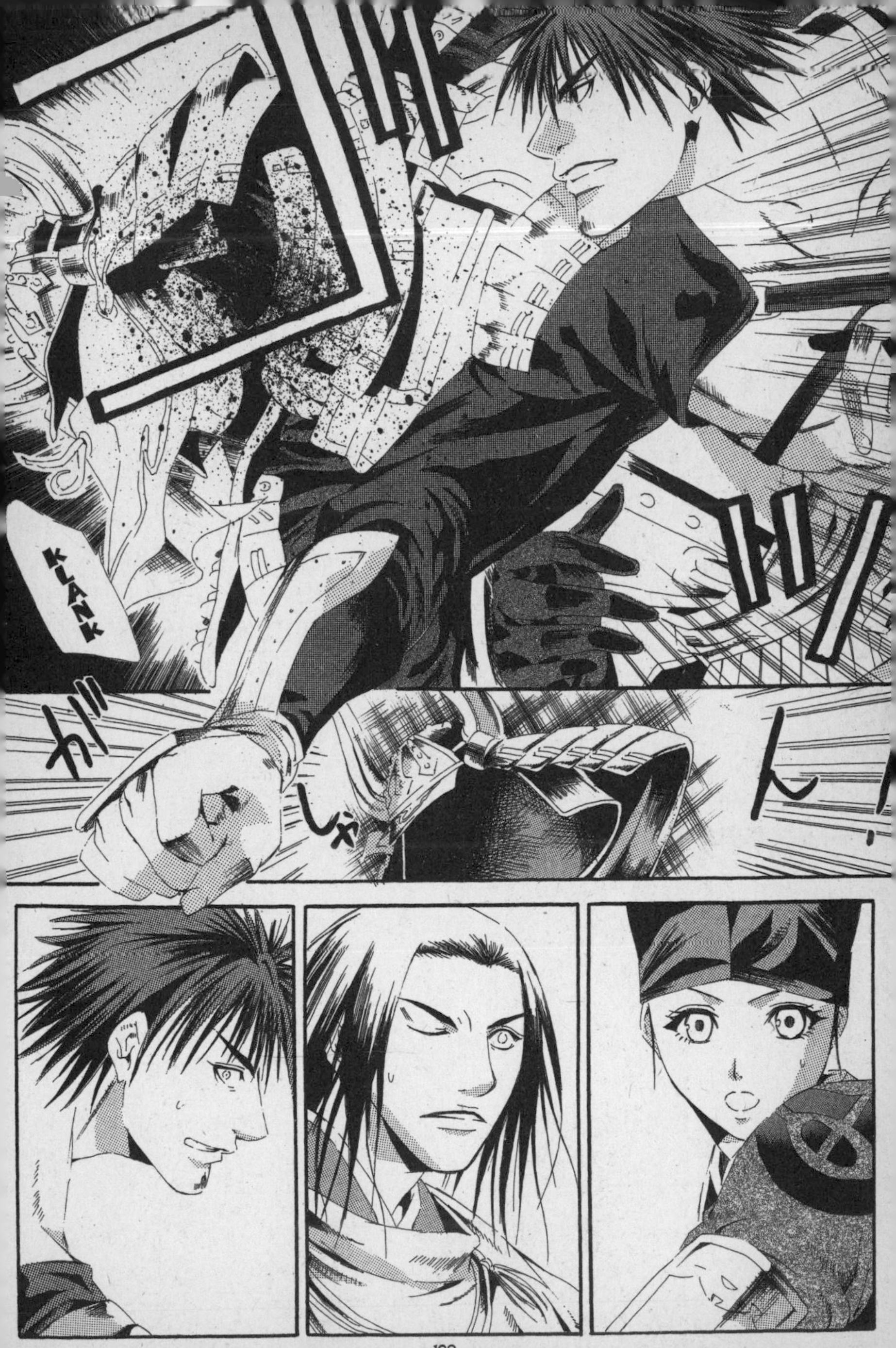
KLANK
がしゃん!

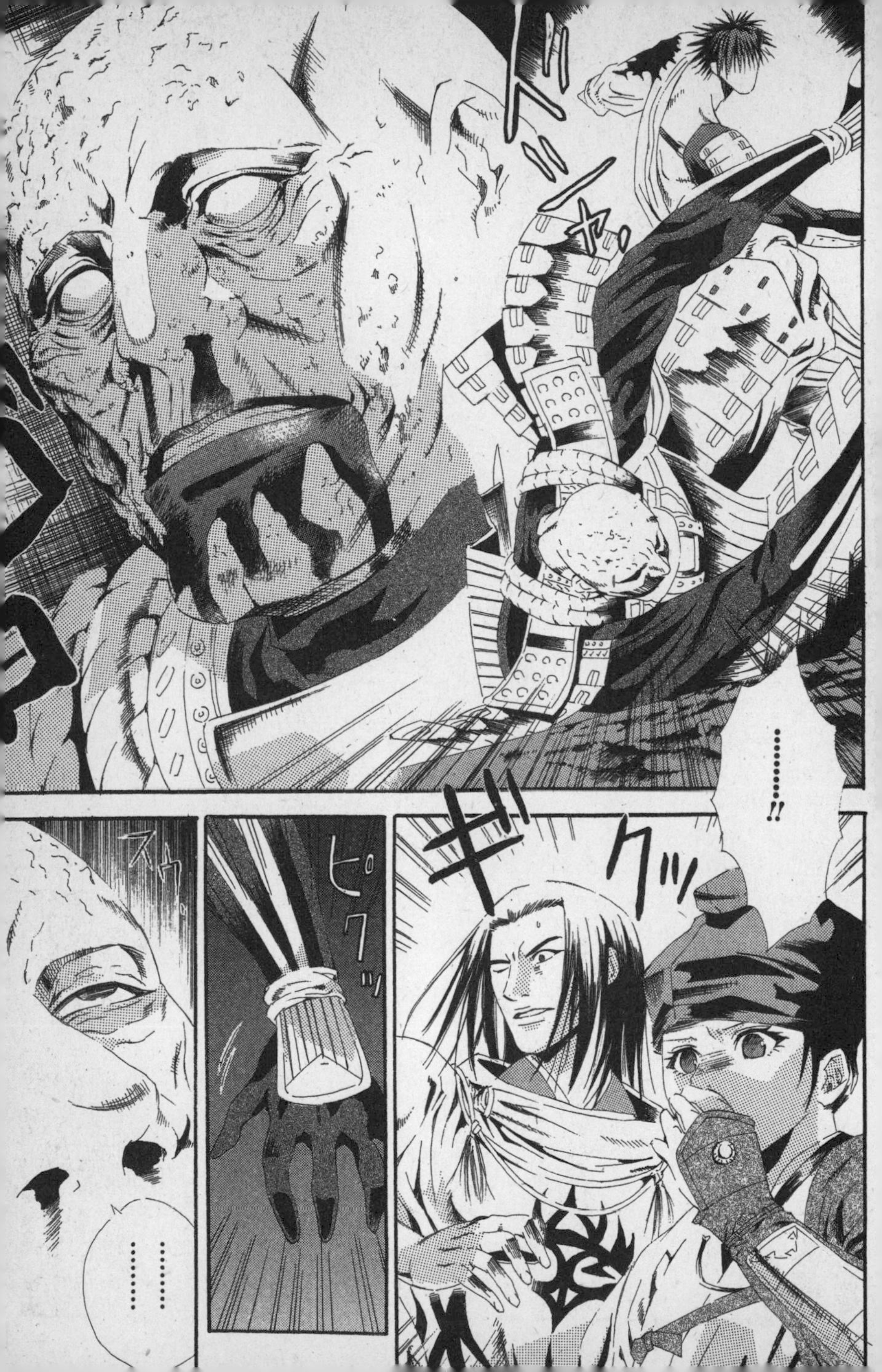
ドシャ
……!!
ギクッ
ピクッ
スゥ
……

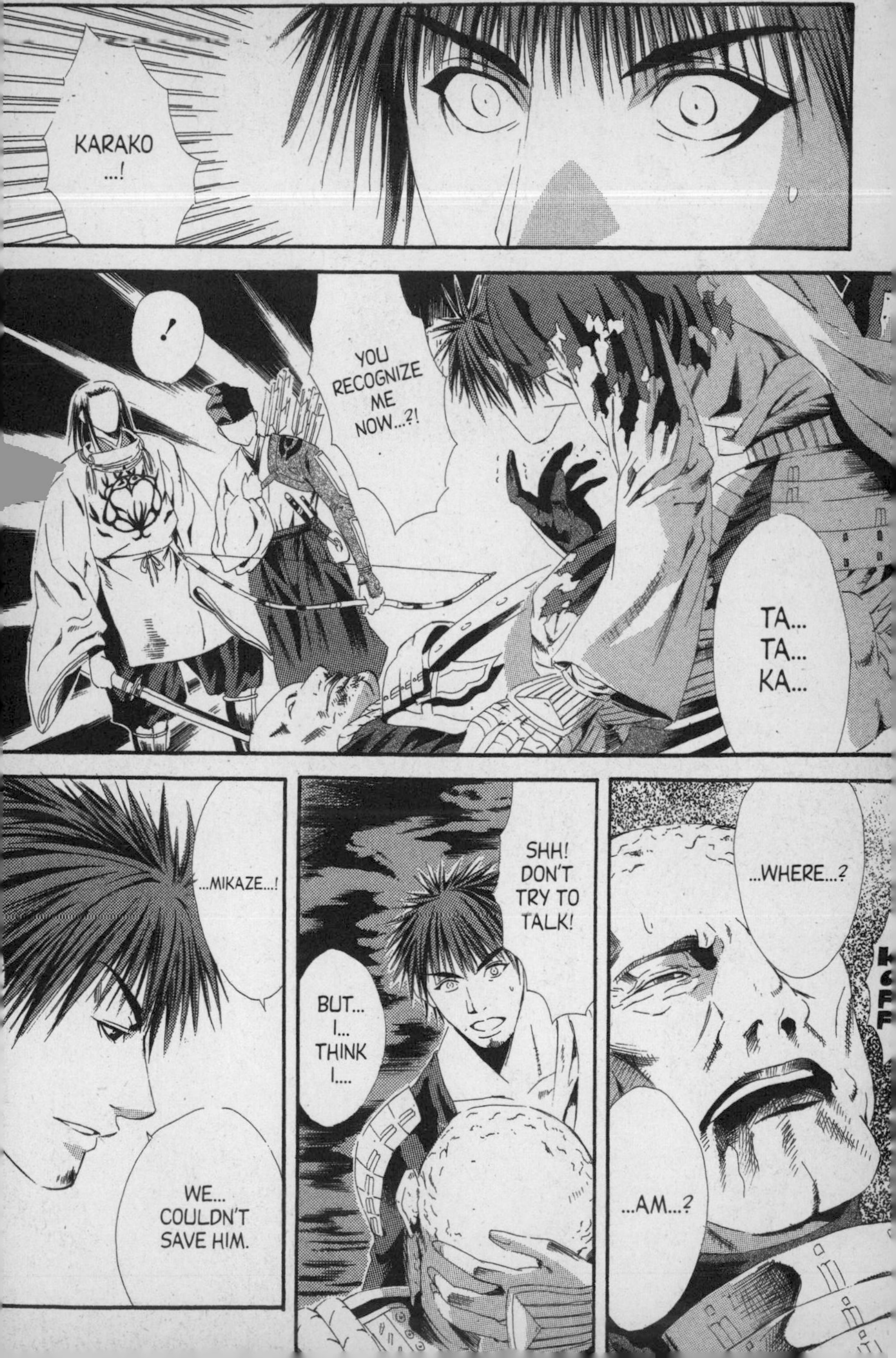
KARAKO ...!
TA... TA... KA...
YOU RECOGNIZE ME NOW...?!
!
...WHERE...?
...AM...?
SHH! DON'T TRY TO TALK!
BUT... I... THINK I....
...MIKAZE...!
WE... COULDN'T SAVE HIM.

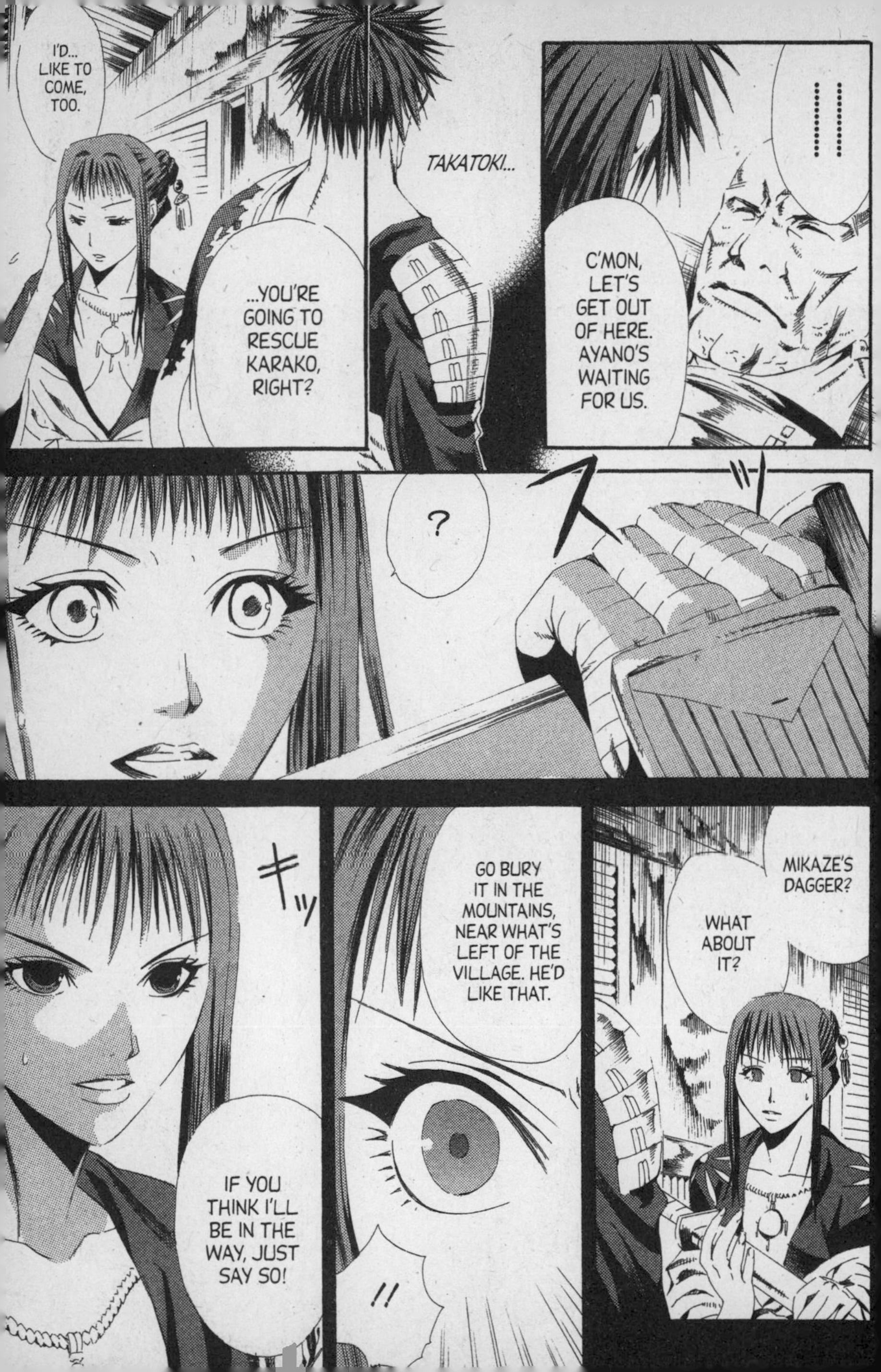
......
C'MON, LET'S GET OUT OF HERE. AYANO'S WAITING FOR US.
TAKATOKI...
...YOU'RE GOING TO RESCUE KARAKO, RIGHT?
I'D... LIKE TO COME, TOO.
スッ
?
MIKAZE'S DAGGER?
WHAT ABOUT IT?
GO BURY IT IN THE MOUNTAINS, NEAR WHAT'S LEFT OF THE VILLAGE. HE'D LIKE THAT.
!!
キッ
IF YOU THINK I'LL BE IN THE WAY, JUST SAY SO!

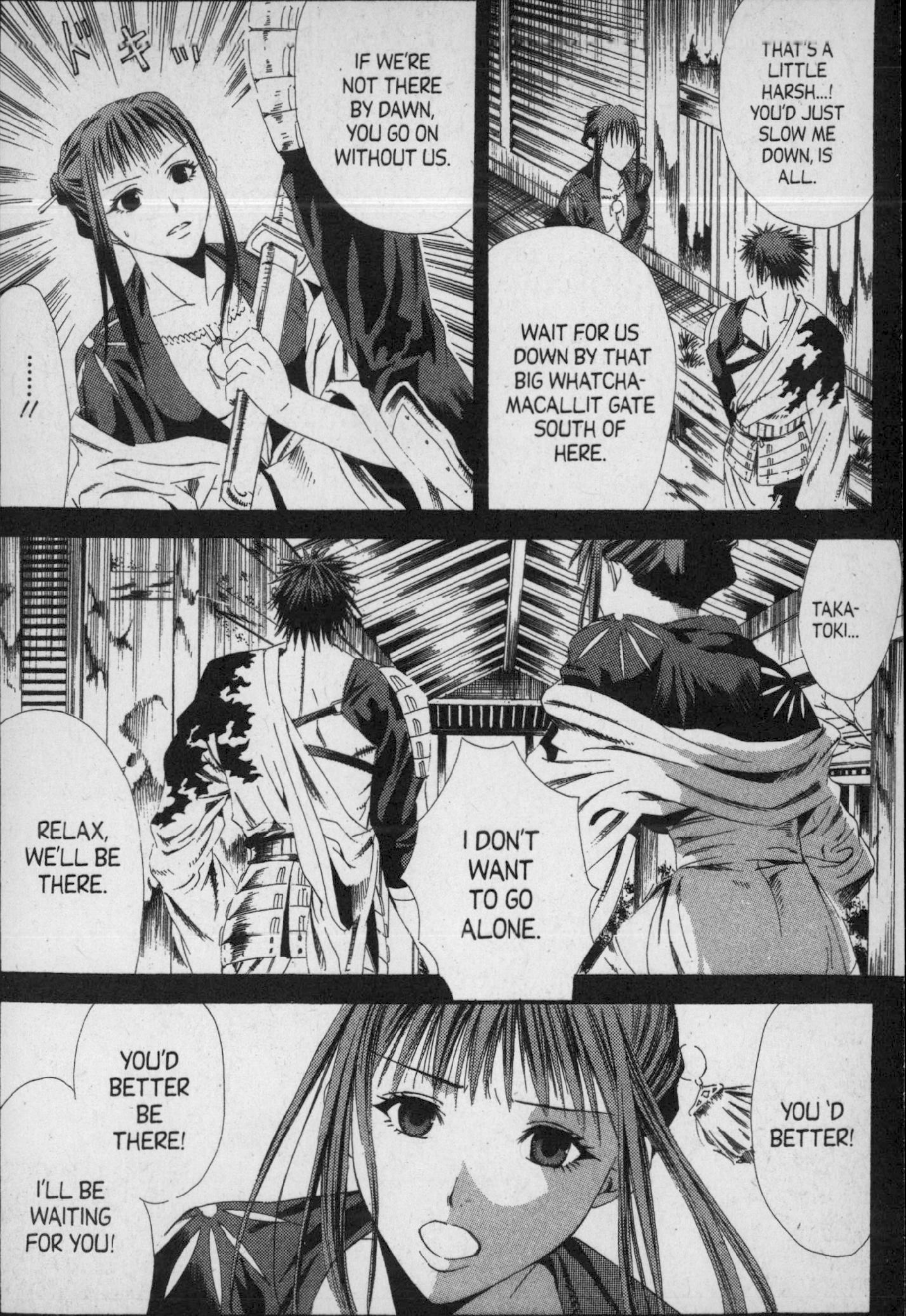
THAT'S A LITTLE HARSH...! YOU'D JUST SLOW ME DOWN, IS ALL.
WAIT FOR US DOWN BY THAT BIG WHATCHA-MACALLIT GATE SOUTH OF HERE.
IF WE'RE NOT THERE BY DAWN, YOU GO ON WITHOUT US.
ドキッ
......!!
TAKA-TOKI...
I DON'T WANT TO GO ALONE.
RELAX, WE'LL BE THERE.
YOU 'D BETTER!
YOU'D BETTER BE THERE!
I'LL BE WAITING FOR YOU!

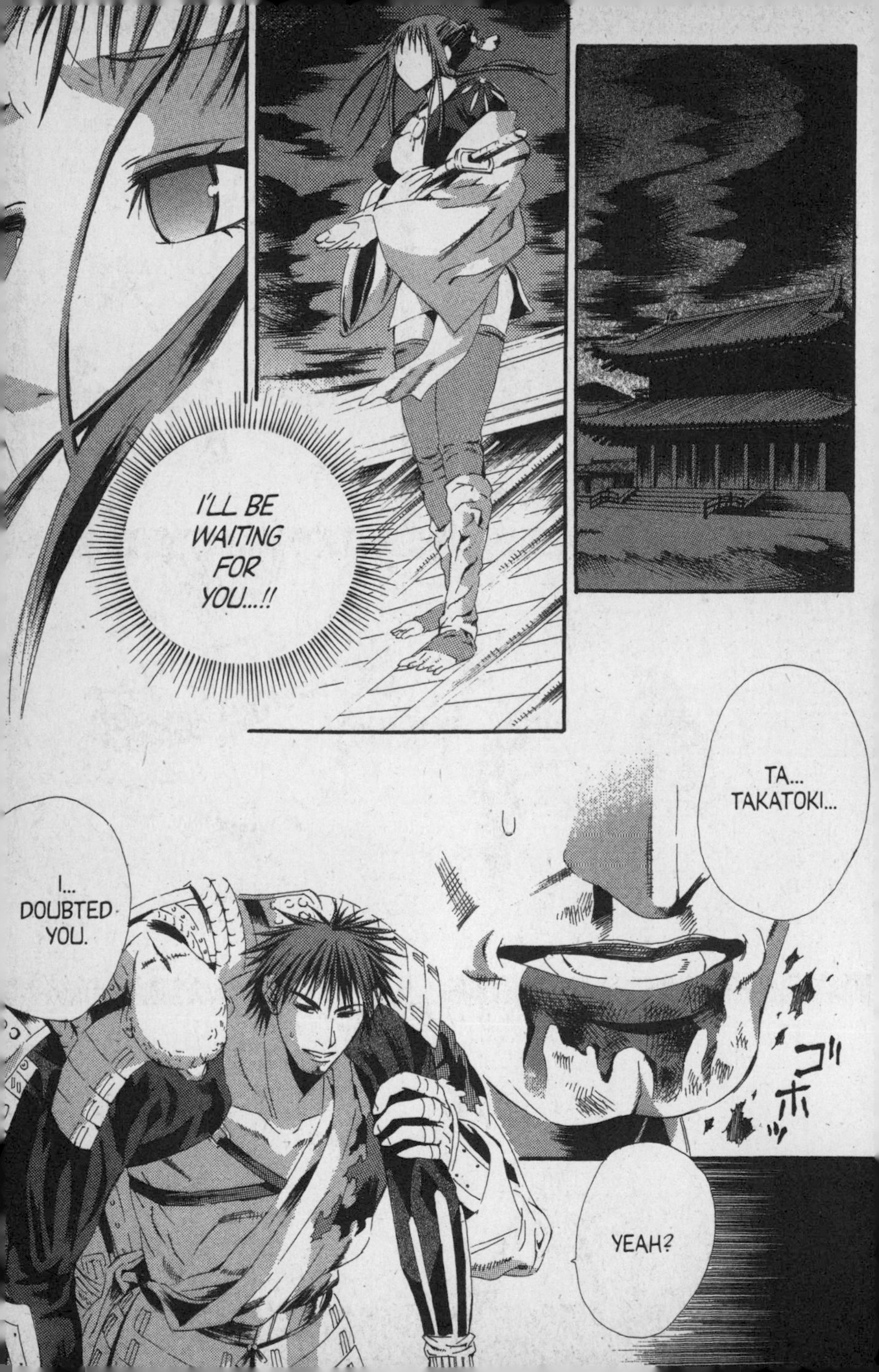
I'LL BE WAITING FOR YOU...!!
TA... TAKATOKI...
ゴボッ
YEAH?
I... DOUBTED YOU.

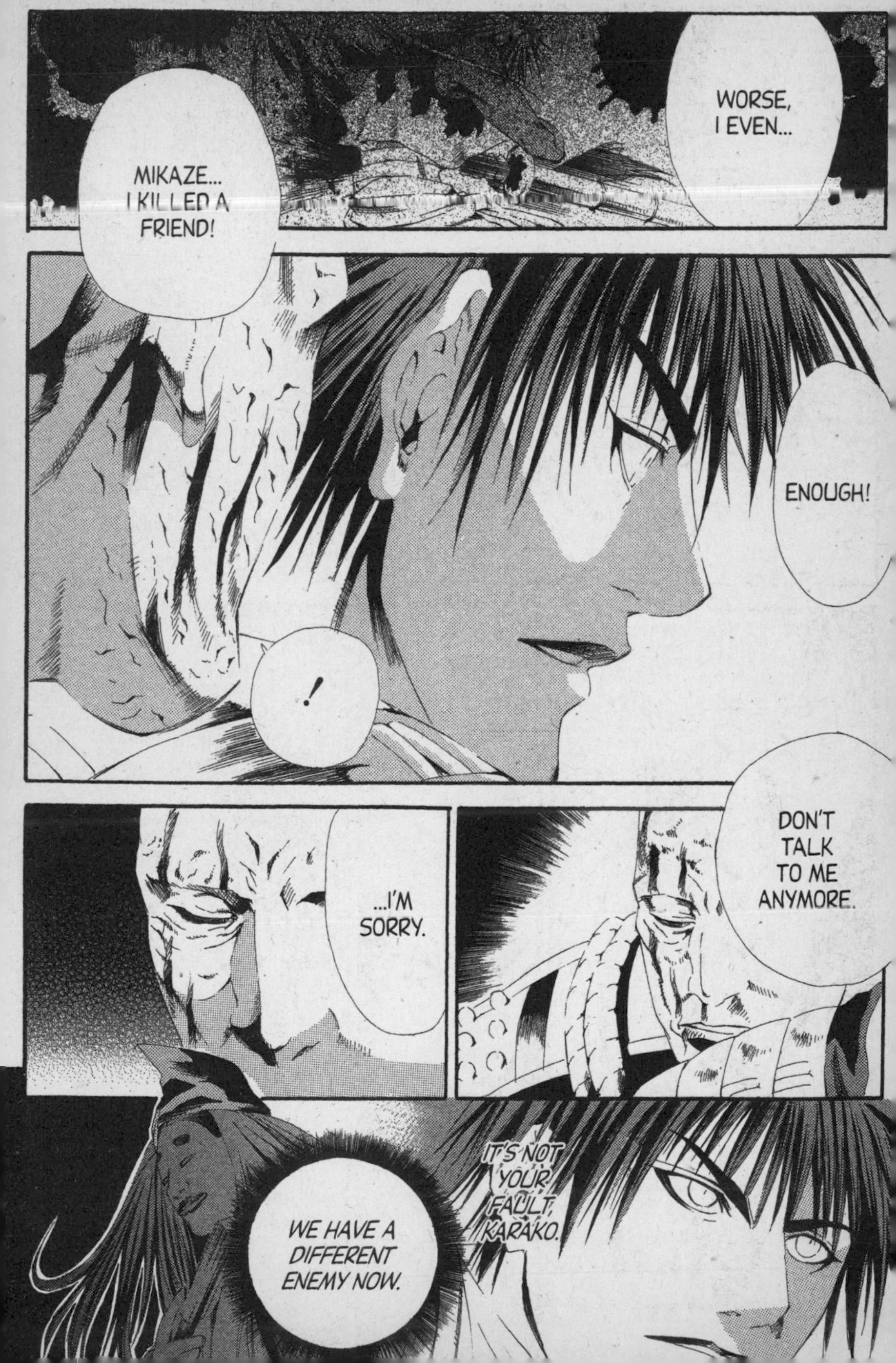
WORSE, I EVEN...
MIKAZE... I KILLED A FRIEND!
ENOUGH!
!
DON'T TALK TO ME ANYMORE.
...I'M SORRY.
IT'S NOT YOUR FAULT, KARAKO.
WE HAVE A DIFFERENT ENEMY NOW.

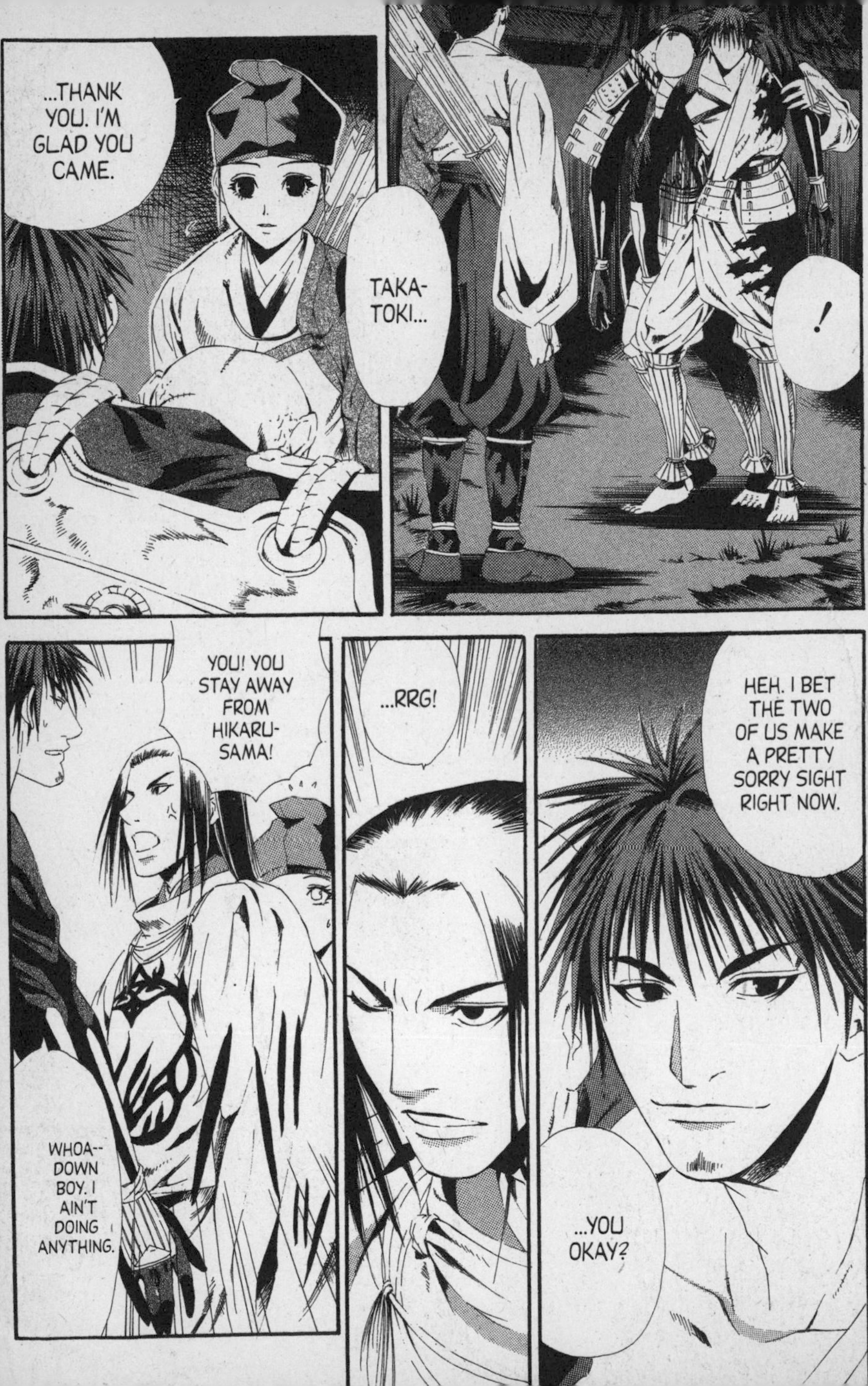
!
TAKA-TOKI...
...THANK YOU. I'M GLAD YOU CAME.
HEH. I BET THE TWO OF US MAKE A PRETTY SORRY SIGHT RIGHT NOW.
...YOU OKAY?
...RRG!
YOU! YOU STAY AWAY FROM HIKARU-SAMA!
WHOA-- DOWN BOY. I AIN'T DOING ANYTHING.

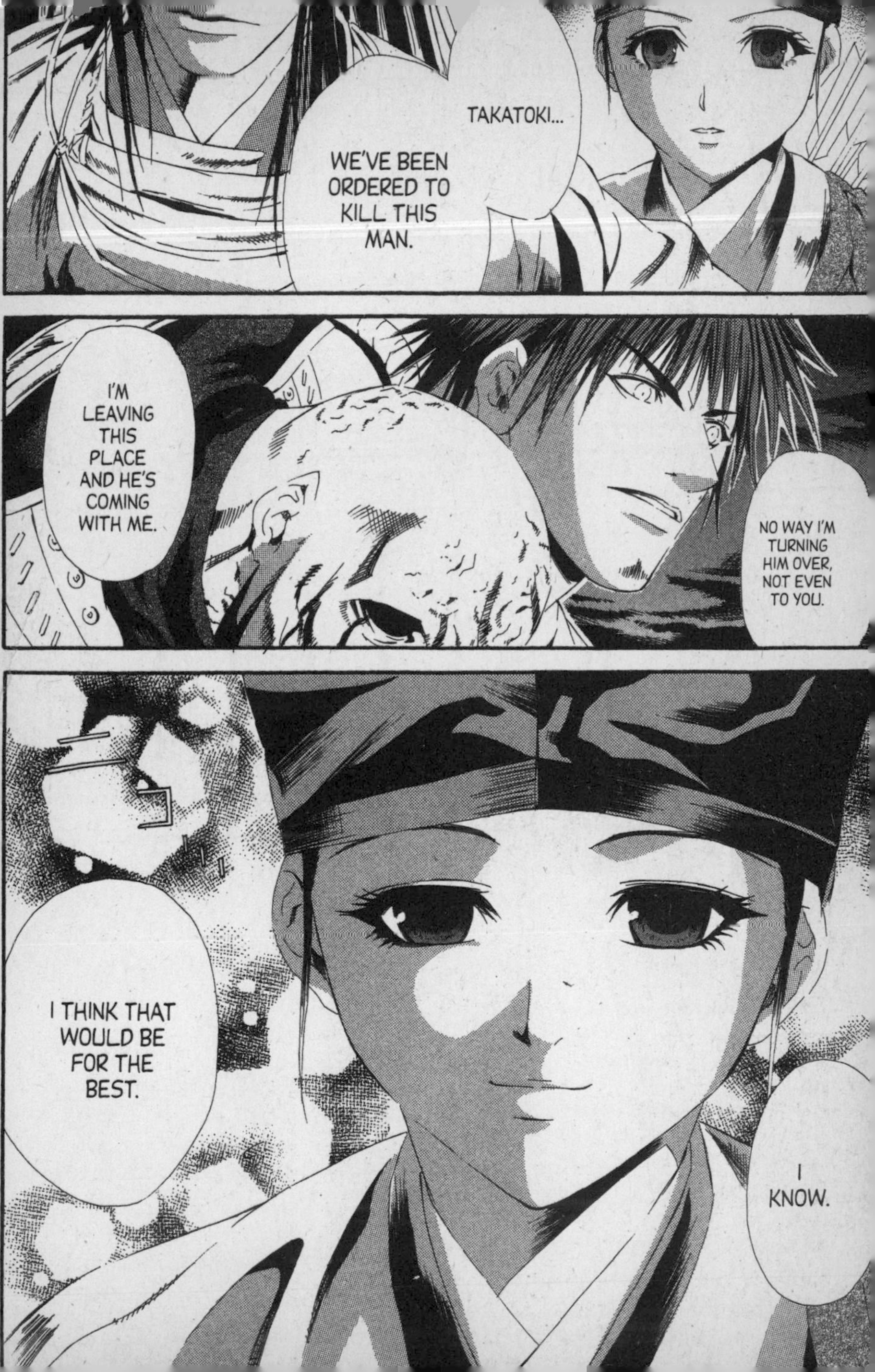
TAKATOKI...
WE'VE BEEN ORDERED TO KILL THIS MAN.
NO WAY I'M TURNING HIM OVER, NOT EVEN TO YOU.
I'M LEAVING THIS PLACE AND HE'S COMING WITH ME.
I KNOW.
I THINK THAT WOULD BE FOR THE BEST.

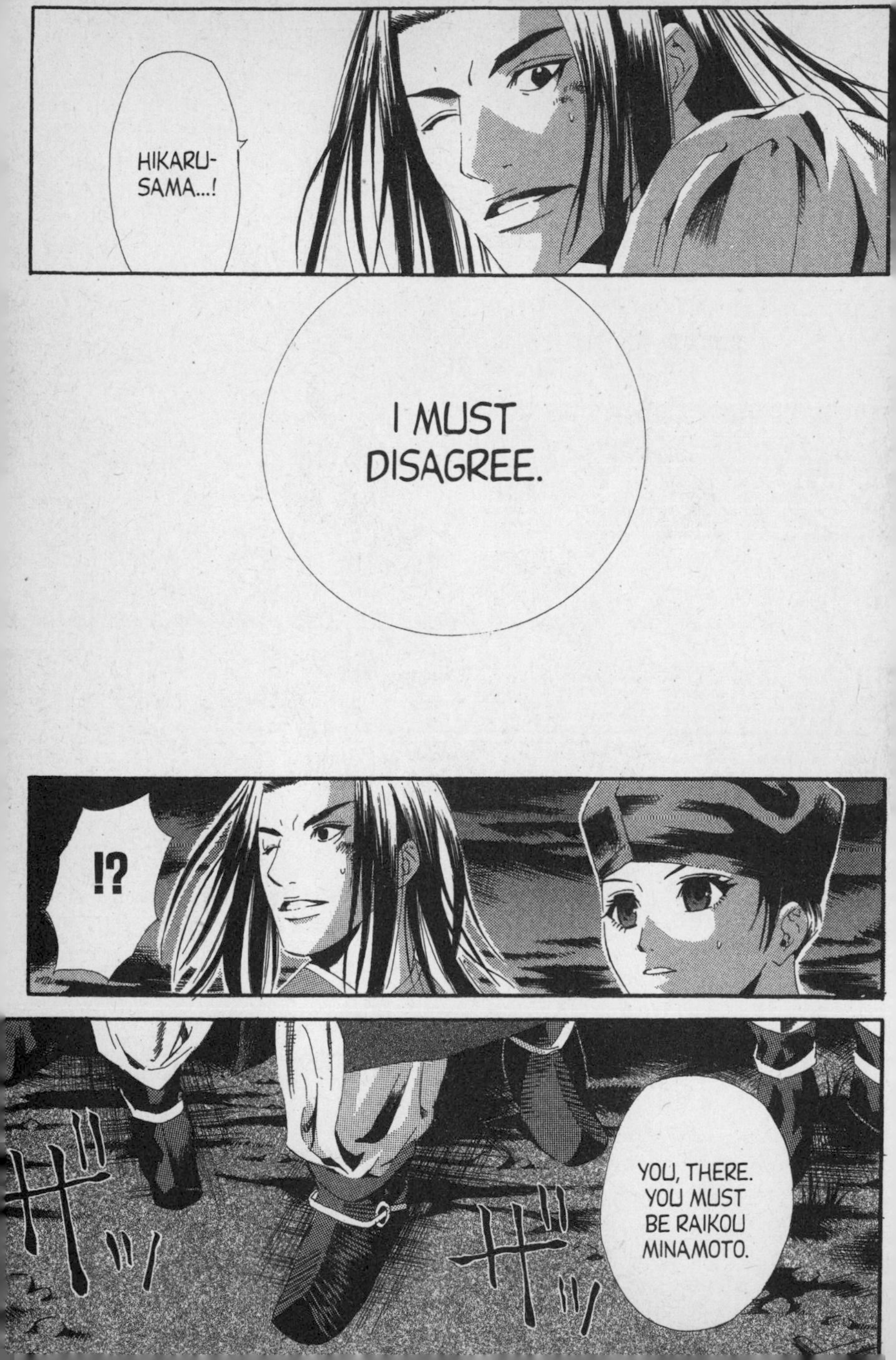
HIKARU-SAMA...!
I MUST DISAGREE.
!?
ザッ
ザッ
YOU, THERE. YOU MUST BE RAIKOU MINAMOTO.

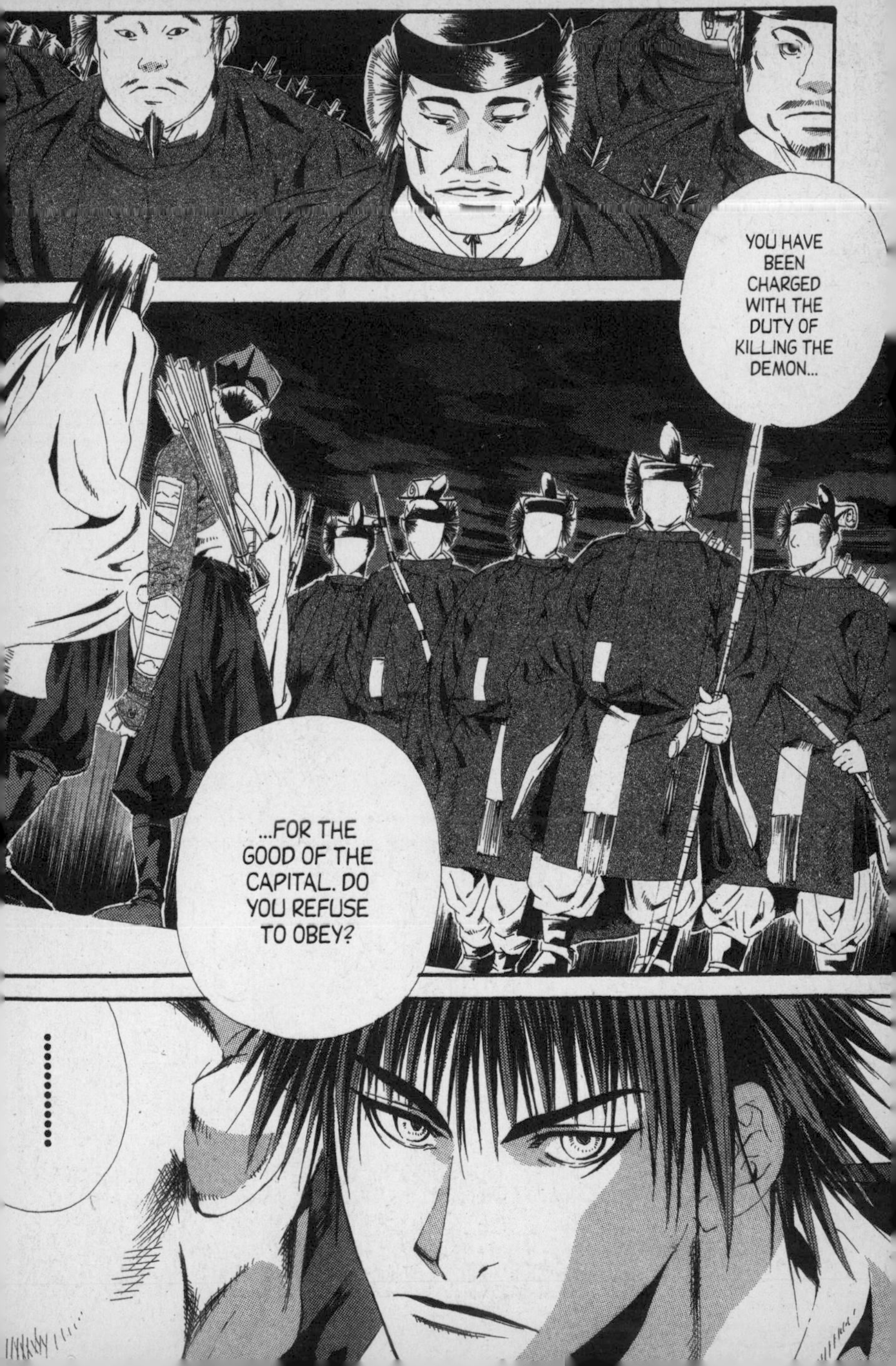
YOU HAVE BEEN CHARGED WITH THE DUTY OF KILLING THE DEMON...
...FOR THE GOOD OF THE CAPITAL. DO YOU REFUSE TO OBEY?
....

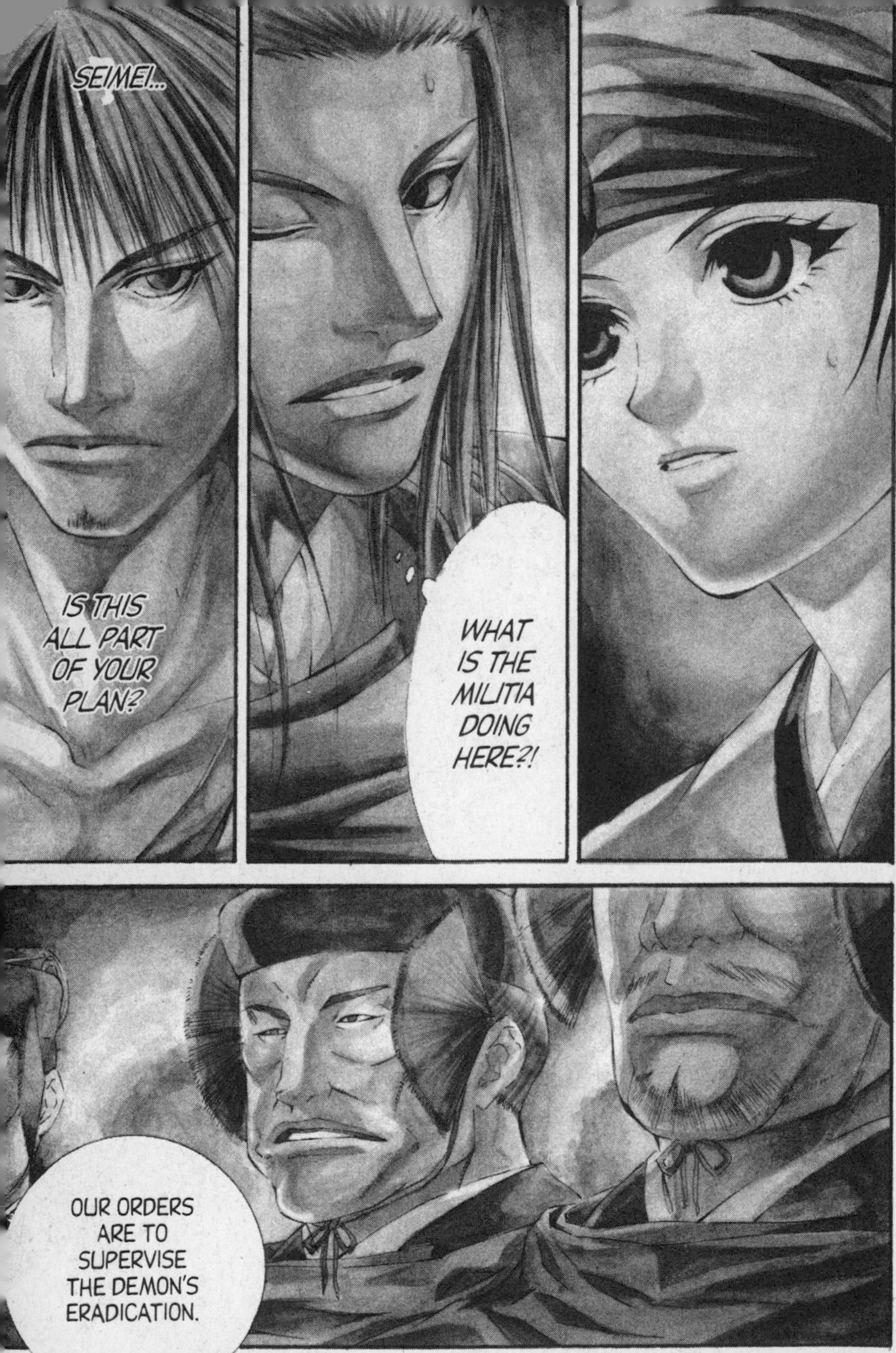
SEIMEI...
IS THIS ALL PART OF YOUR PLAN?
WHAT IS THE MILITIA DOING HERE?!
OUR ORDERS ARE TO SUPERVISE THE DEMON'S ERADICATION.

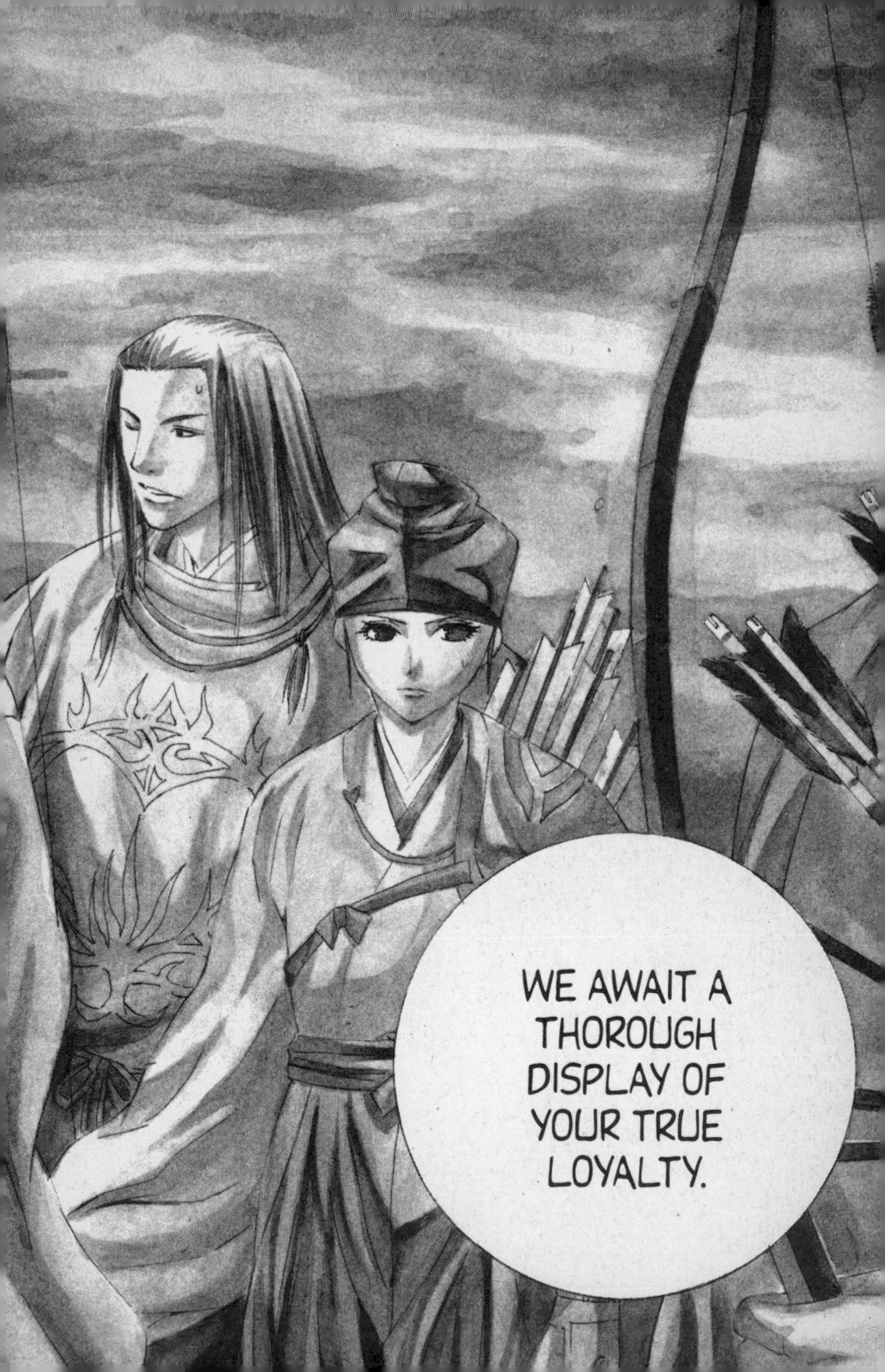
WE AWAIT A THOROUGH DISPLAY OF YOUR TRUE LOYALTY.

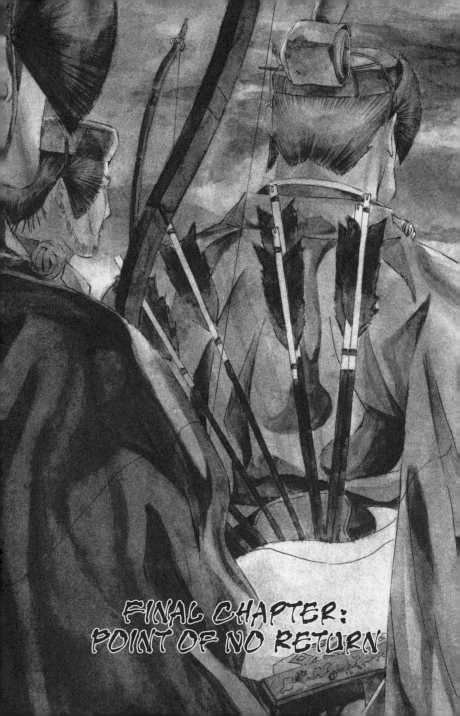

FINAL CHAPTER:
POINT OF NO RETURN

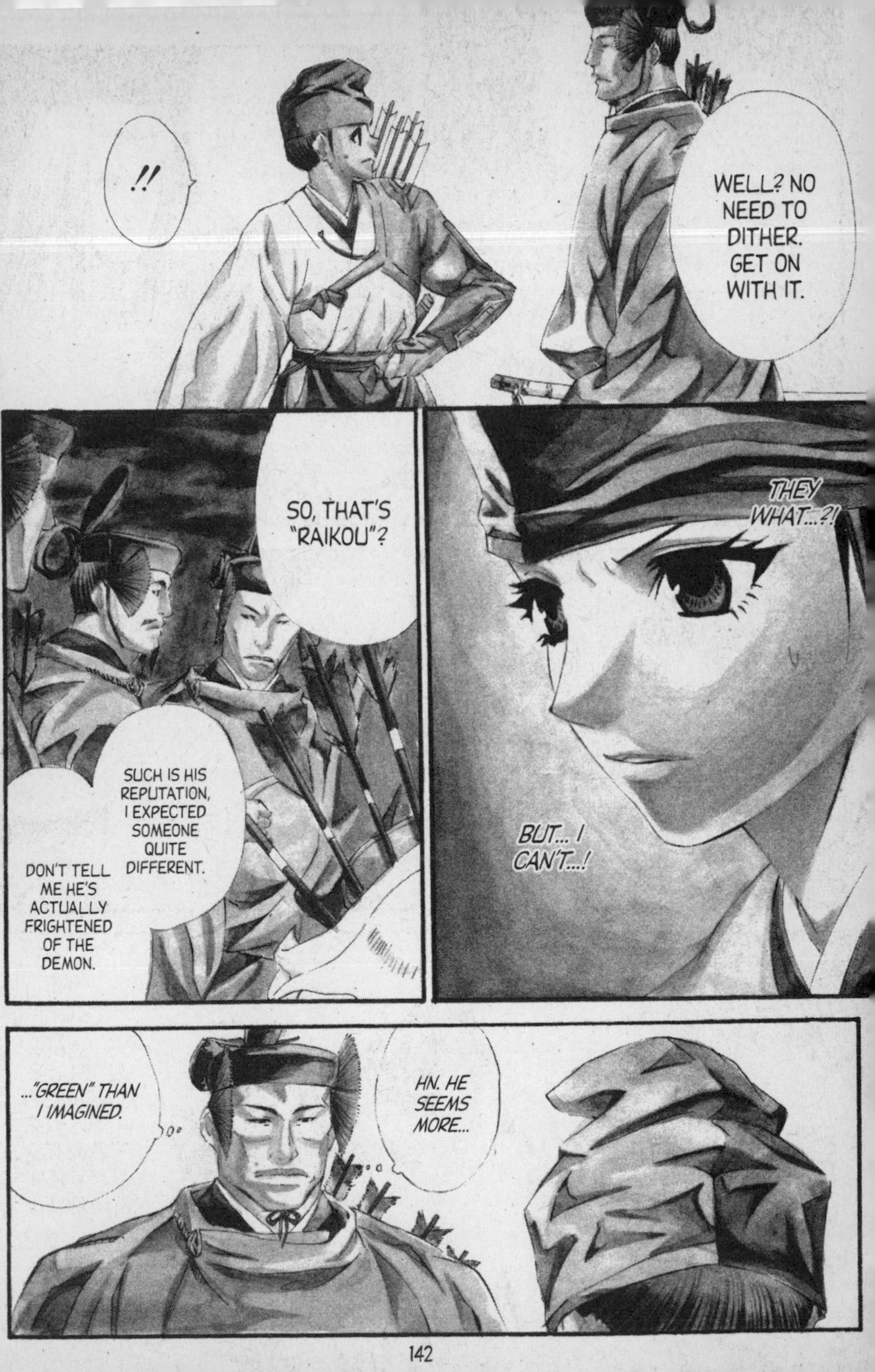
WELL? NO NEED TO DITHER. GET ON WITH IT.
!!
THEY WHAT...?!
BUT... I CAN'T...!
SO, THAT'S "RAIKOU"?
SUCH IS HIS REPUTATION, I EXPECTED SOMEONE QUITE DIFFERENT.
DON'T TELL ME HE'S ACTUALLY FRIGHTENED OF THE DEMON.
HN. HE SEEMS MORE...
..."GREEN" THAN I IMAGINED.

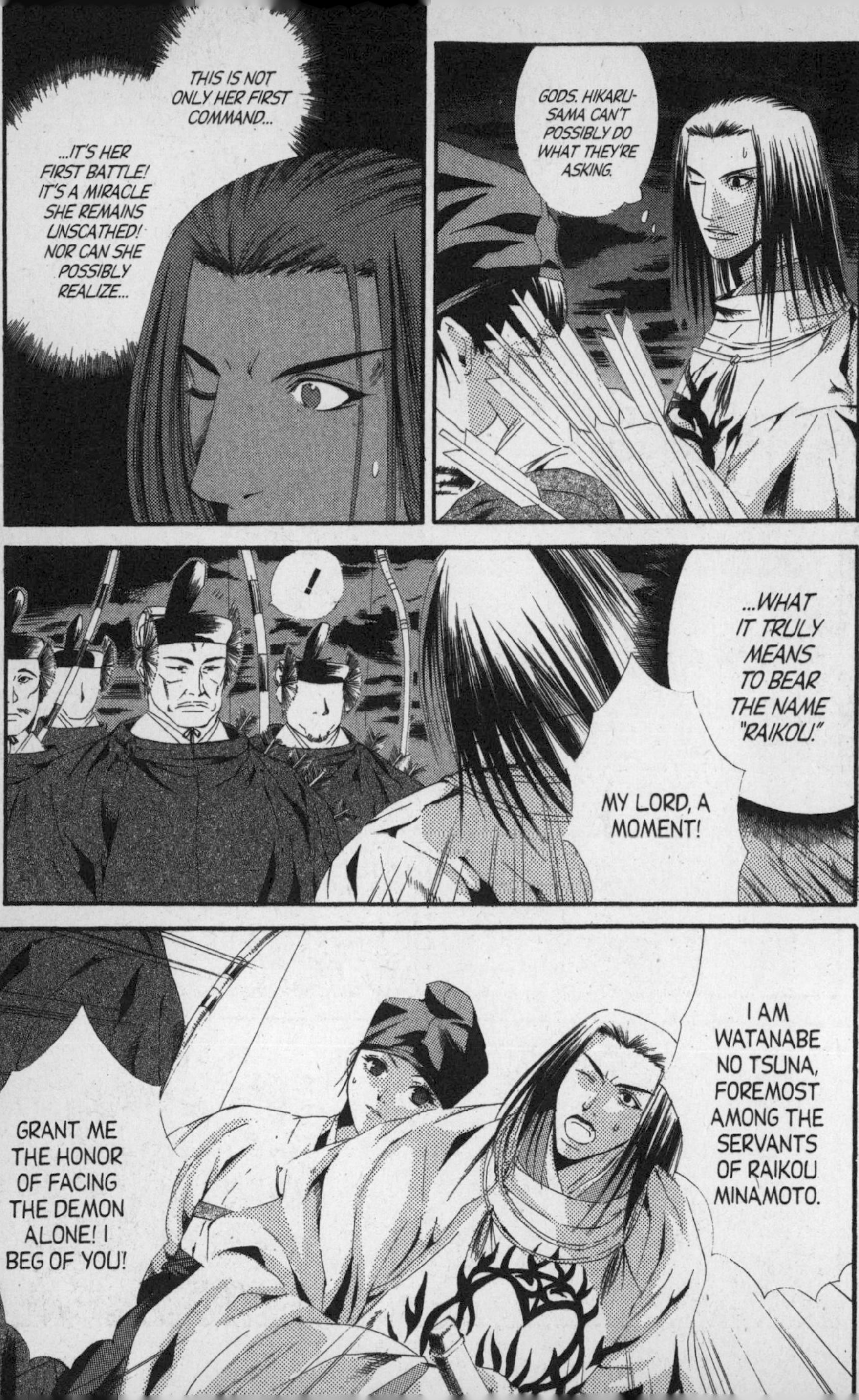
GODS. HIKARU-SAMA CAN'T POSSIBLY DO WHAT THEY'RE ASKING.
THIS IS NOT ONLY HER FIRST COMMAND...
...IT'S HER FIRST BATTLE! IT'S A MIRACLE SHE REMAINS UNSCATHED! NOR CAN SHE POSSIBLY REALIZE...
...WHAT IT TRULY MEANS TO BEAR THE NAME "RAIKOU."
MY LORD, A MOMENT!
!
I AM WATANABE NO TSUNA, FOREMOST AMONG THE SERVANTS OF RAIKOU MINAMOTO.
GRANT ME THE HONOR OF FACING THE DEMON ALONE! I BEG OF YOU!

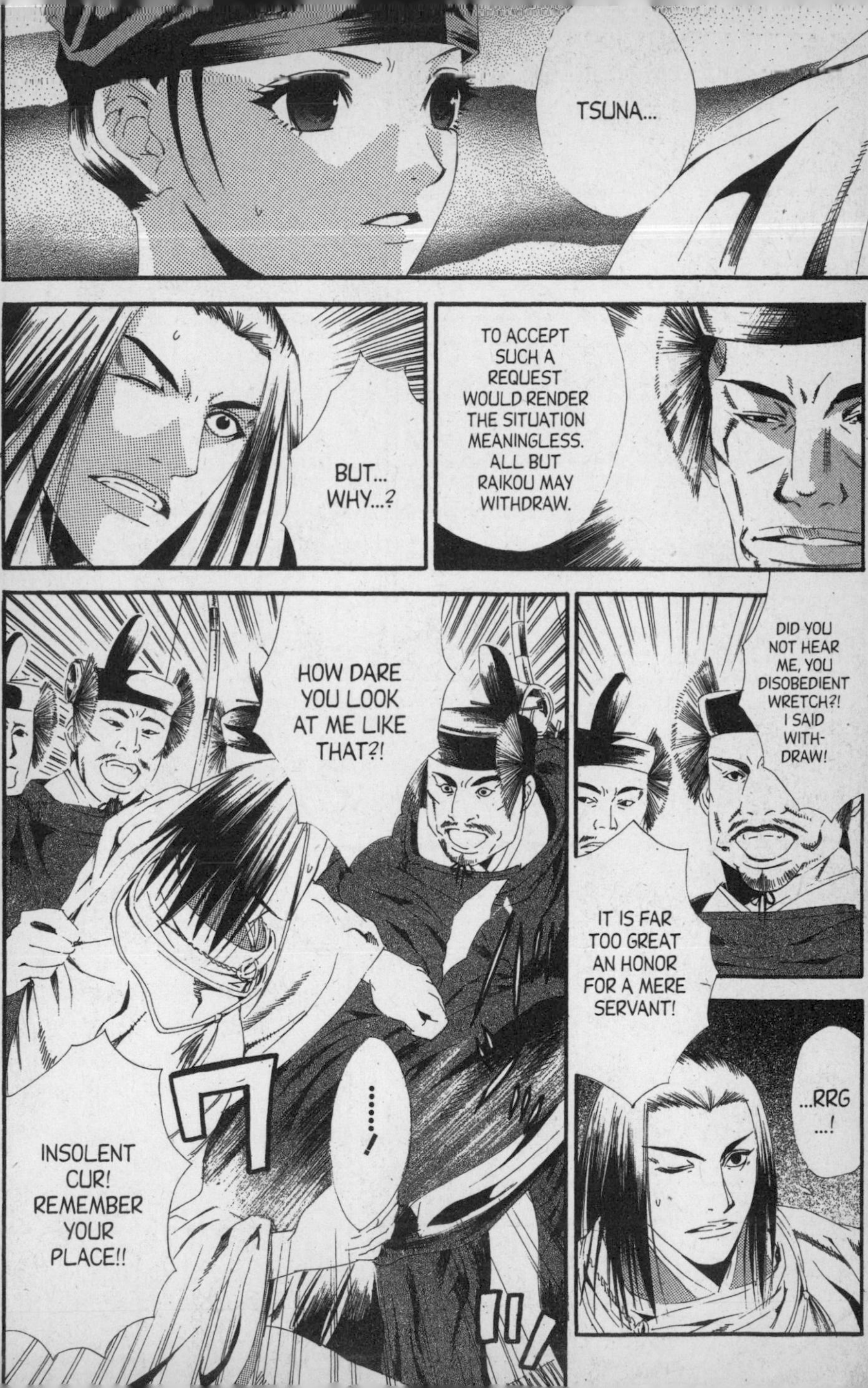

TSUNA...
TO ACCEPT SUCH A REQUEST WOULD RENDER THE SITUATION MEANINGLESS. ALL BUT RAIKOU MAY WITHDRAW.
BUT... WHY...?
DID YOU NOT HEAR ME, YOU DISOBEDIENT WRETCH?! I SAID WITH-DRAW!
IT IS FAR TOO GREAT AN HONOR FOR A MERE SERVANT!
...RRG ...!
HOW DARE YOU LOOK AT ME LIKE THAT?!
......!
INSOLENT CUR! REMEMBER YOUR PLACE!!

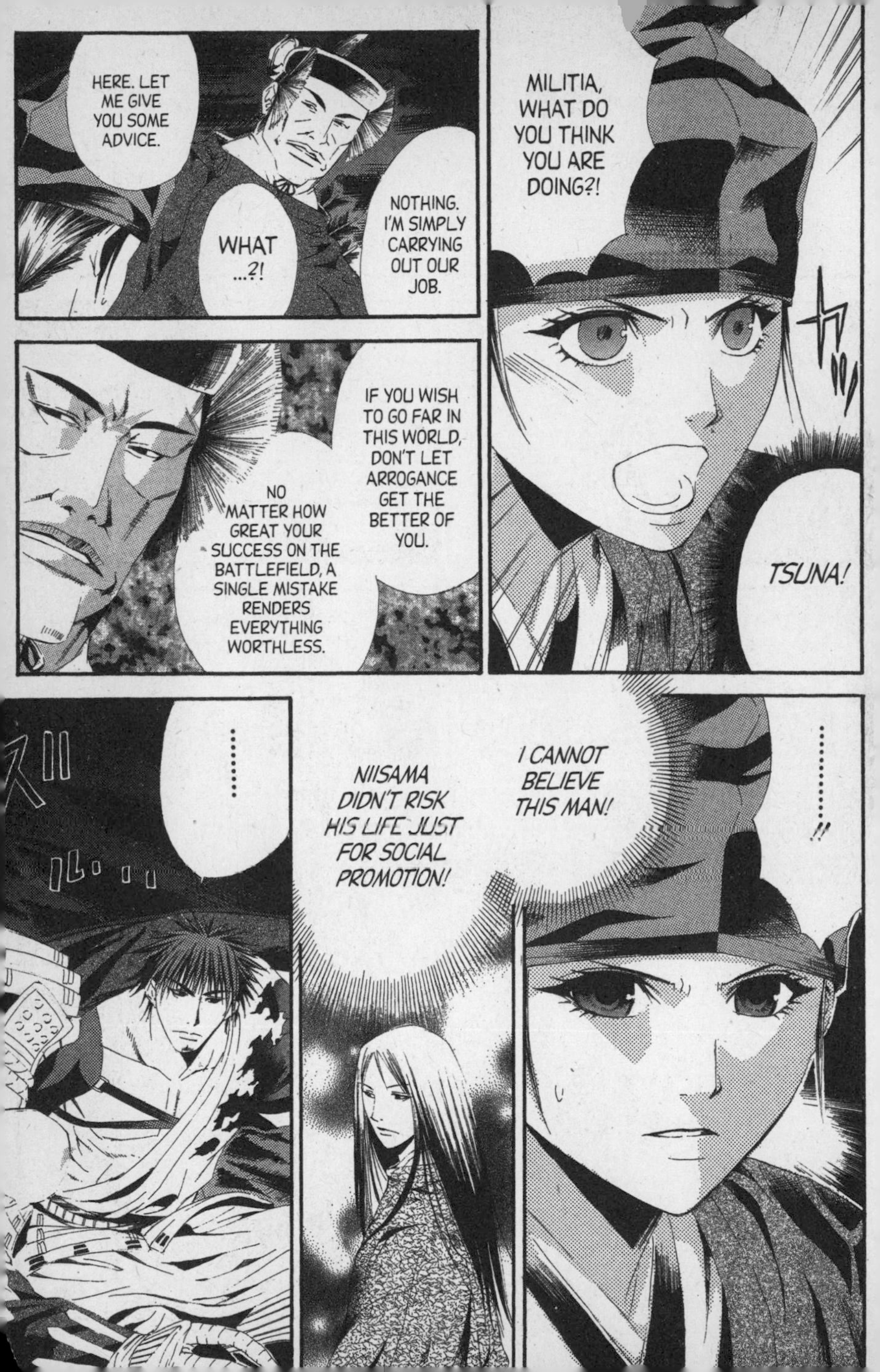
MILITIA, WHAT DO YOU THINK YOU ARE DOING?!
HERE. LET ME GIVE YOU SOME ADVICE.
NOTHING. I'M SIMPLY CARRYING OUT OUR JOB.
WHAT ...?!
TSUNA!
IF YOU WISH TO GO FAR IN THIS WORLD, DON'T LET ARROGANCE GET THE BETTER OF YOU.
NO MATTER HOW GREAT YOUR SUCCESS ON THE BATTLEFIELD, A SINGLE MISTAKE RENDERS EVERYTHING WORTHLESS.
.........!!
I CANNOT BELIEVE THIS MAN!
NIISAMA DIDN'T RISK HIS LIFE JUST FOR SOCIAL PROMOTION!
....

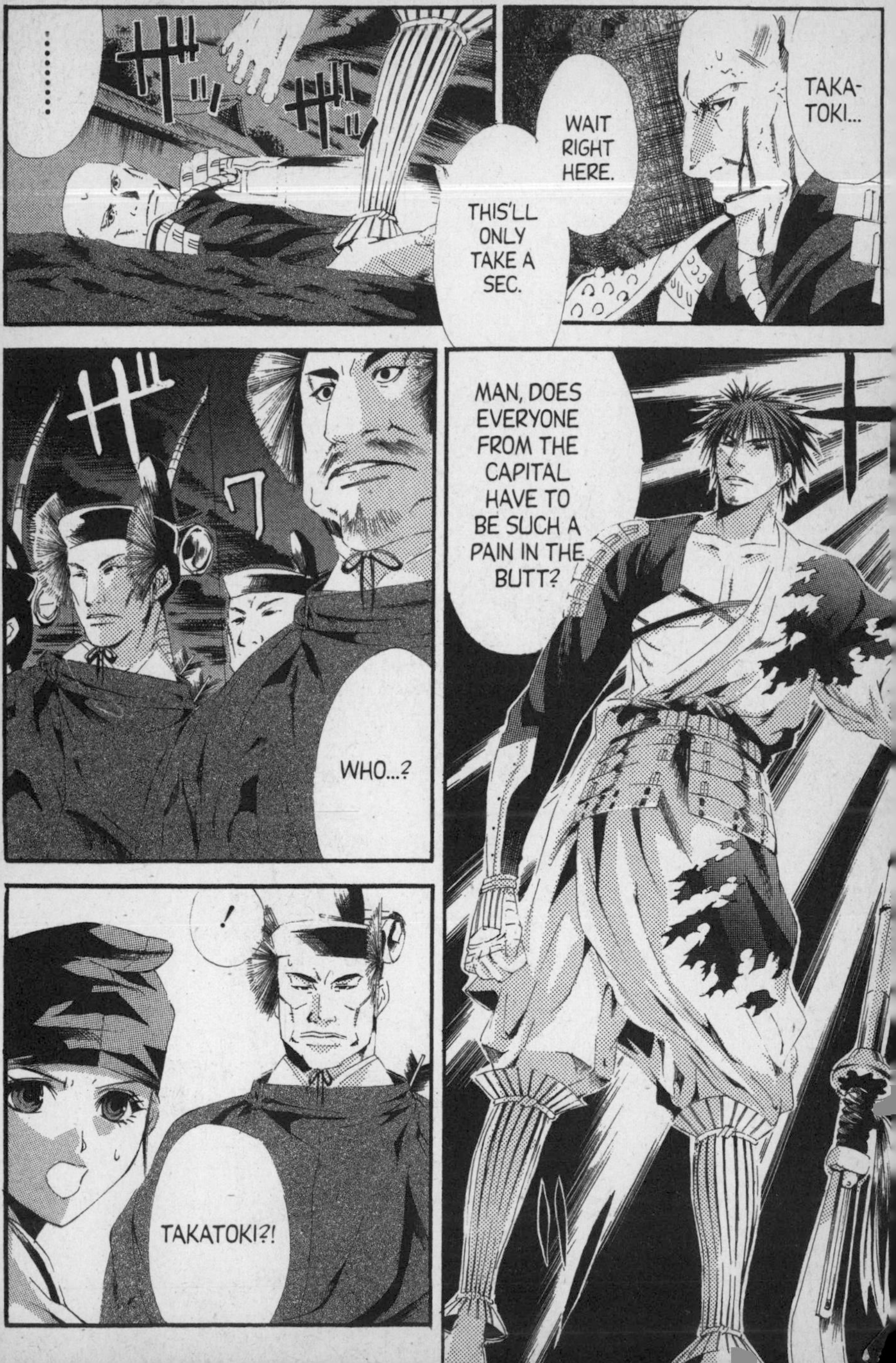
TAKA-TOKI...
WAIT RIGHT HERE.
THIS'LL ONLY TAKE A SEC.
......
MAN, DOES EVERYONE FROM THE CAPITAL HAVE TO BE SUCH A PAIN IN THE BUTT?
WHO...?
!
TAKATOKI?!

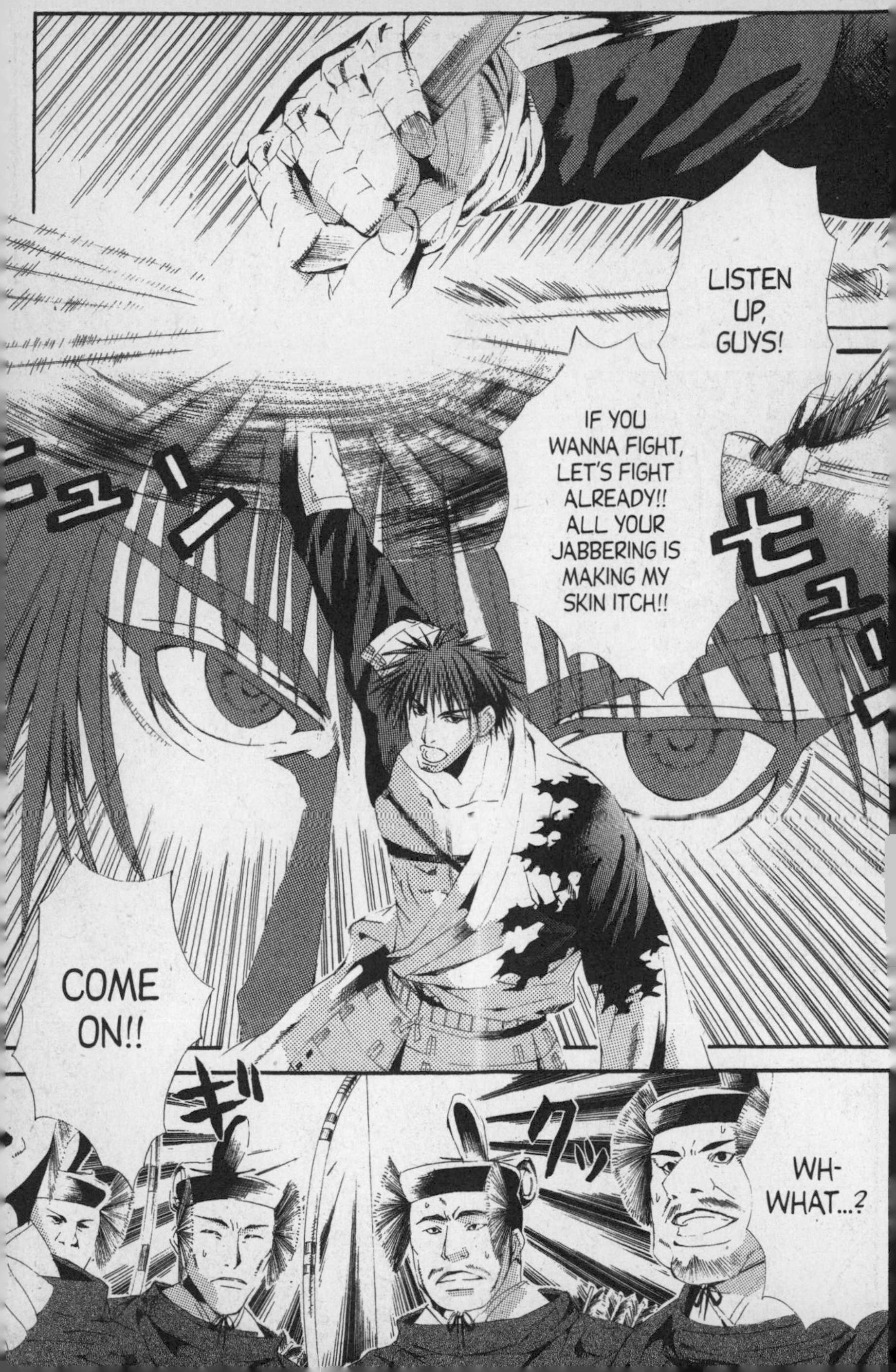
LISTEN UP, GUYS!
IF YOU WANNA FIGHT, LET'S FIGHT ALREADY!! ALL YOUR JABBERING IS MAKING MY SKIN ITCH!!
COME ON!!
WH-WHAT...?

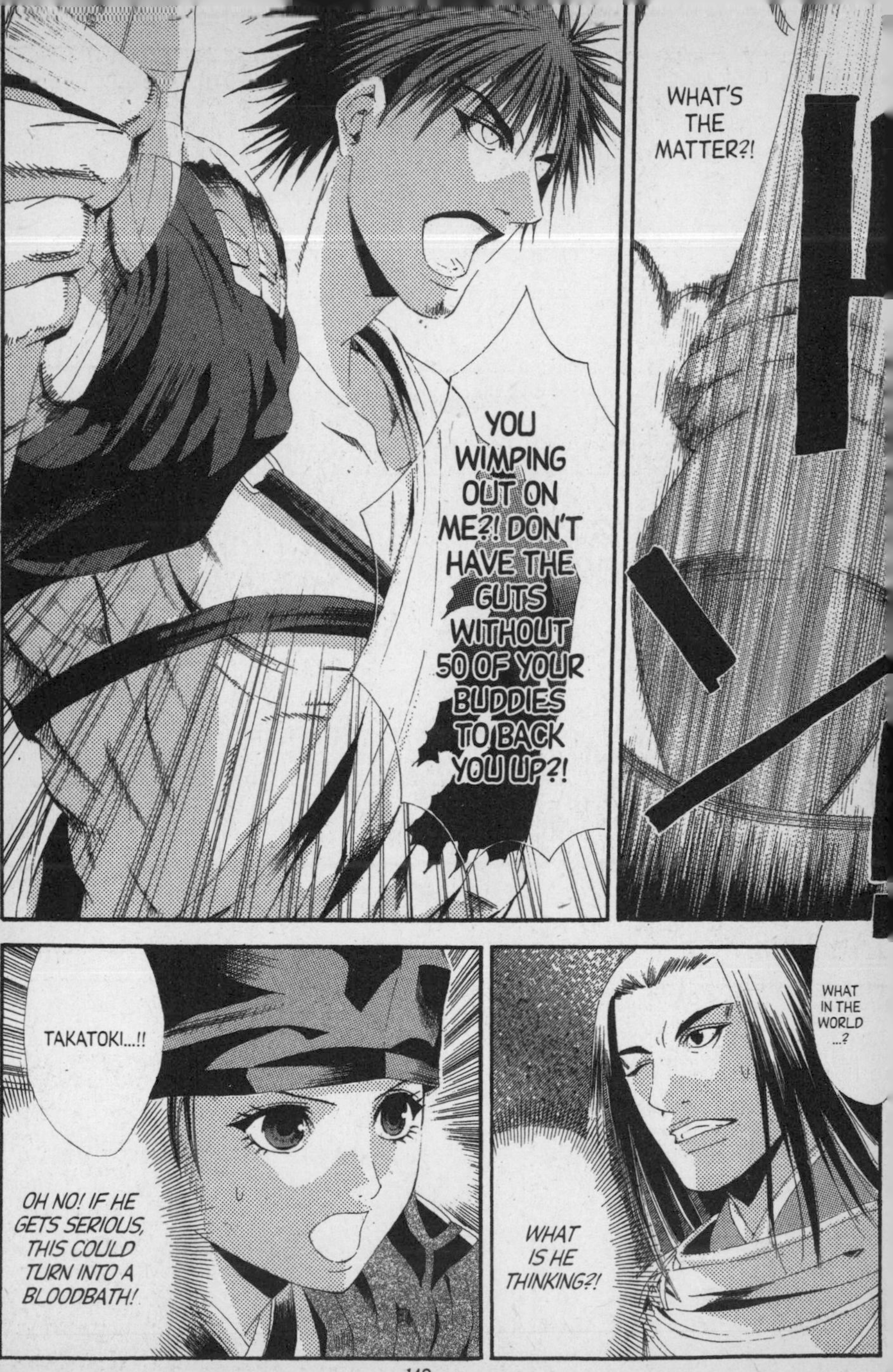
WHAT'S THE MATTER?!
YOU WIMPING OUT ON ME?! DON'T HAVE THE GUTS WITHOUT 50 OF YOUR BUDDIES TO BACK YOU UP?!
WHAT IN THE WORLD ...?
WHAT IS HE THINKING?!
TAKATOKI...!!
OH NO! IF HE GETS SERIOUS, THIS COULD TURN INTO A BLOODBATH!

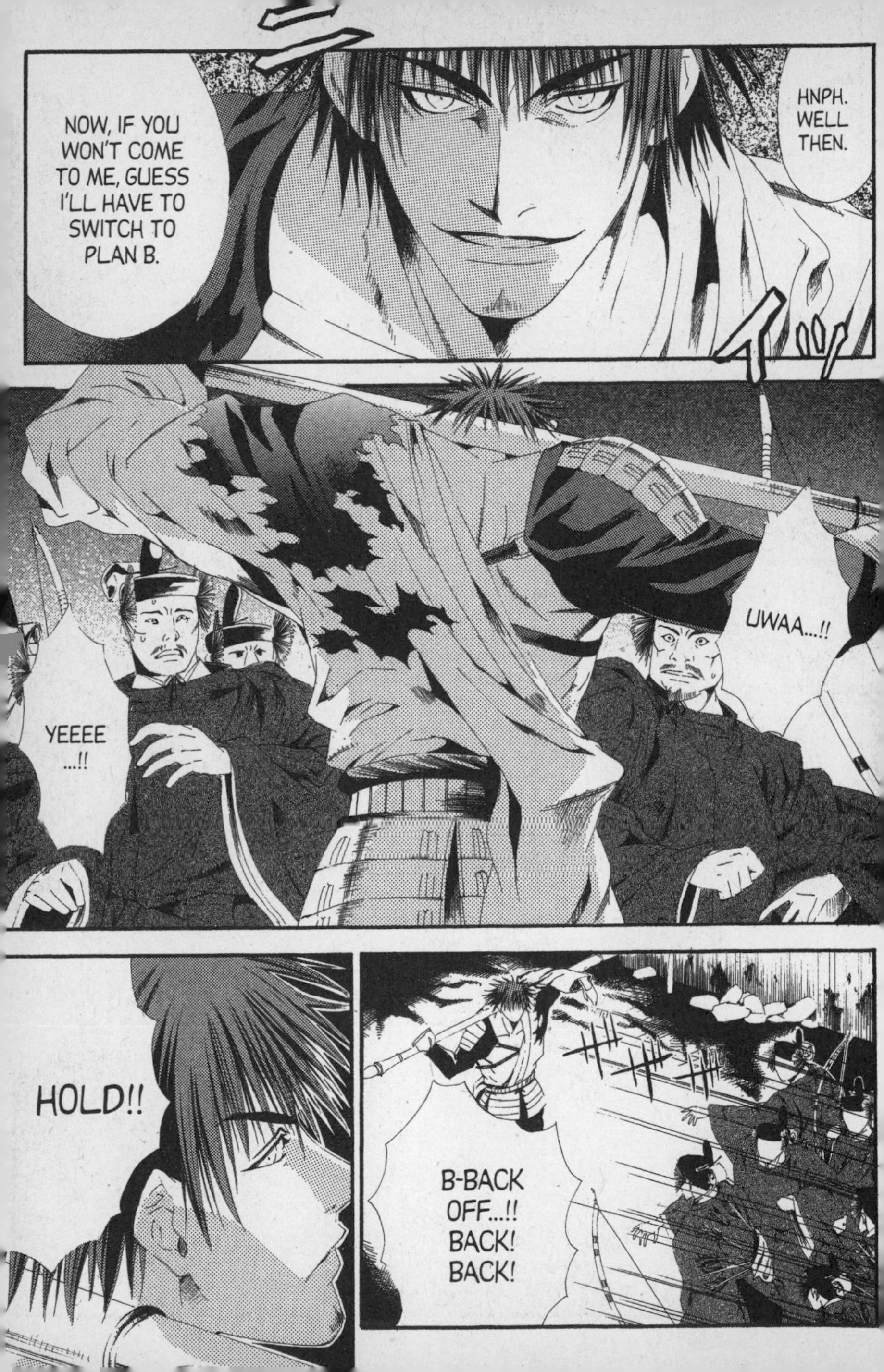
HNPH. WELL THEN.
NOW, IF YOU WON'T COME TO ME, GUESS I'LL HAVE TO SWITCH TO PLAN B.
UWAA...!!
YEEEE ...!!
B-BACK OFF...!! BACK! BACK!
HOLD!!

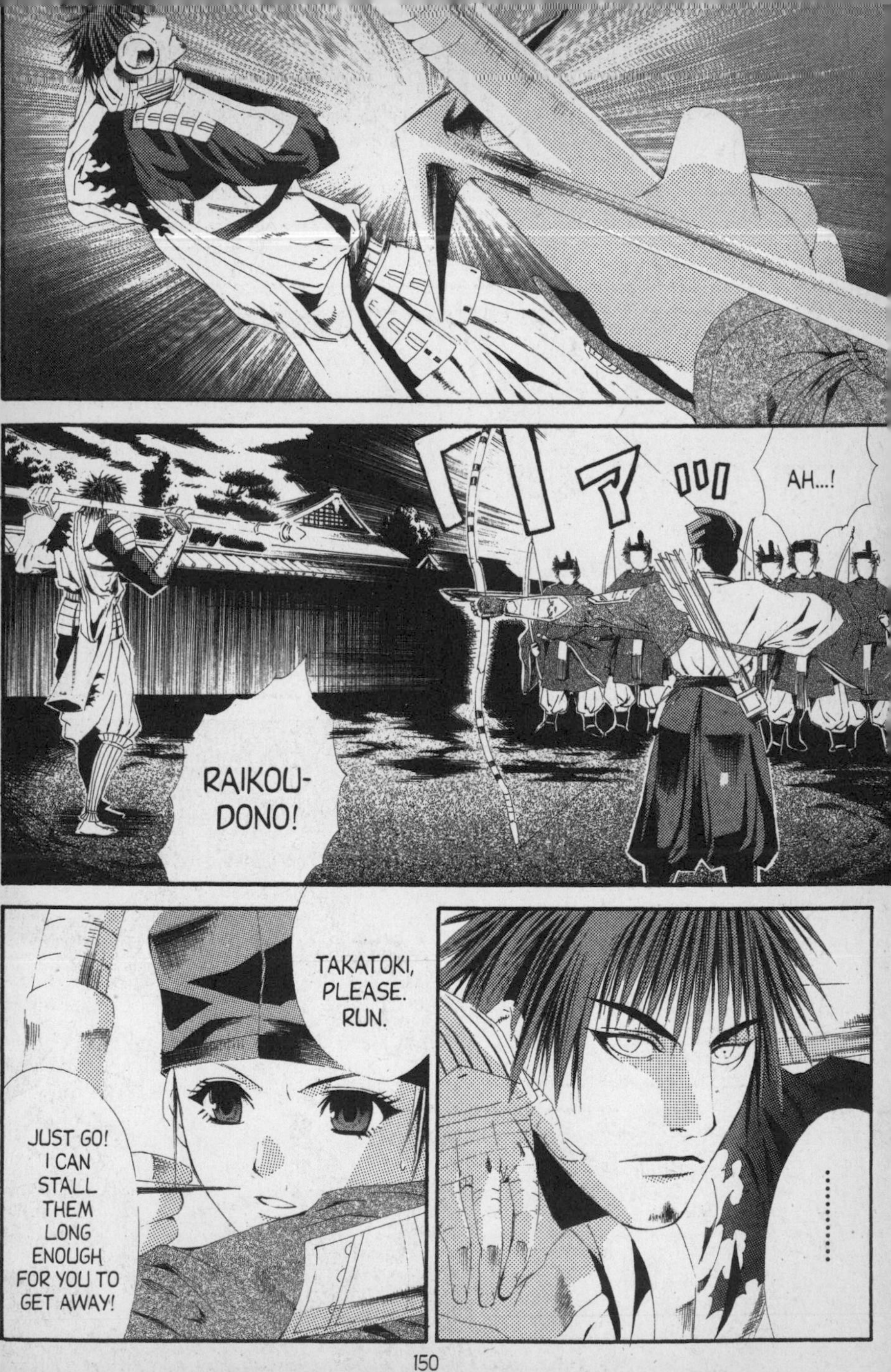
AH...!
RAIKOU-DONO!
TAKATOKI, PLEASE. RUN.
JUST GO! I CAN STALL THEM LONG ENOUGH FOR YOU TO GET AWAY!
......

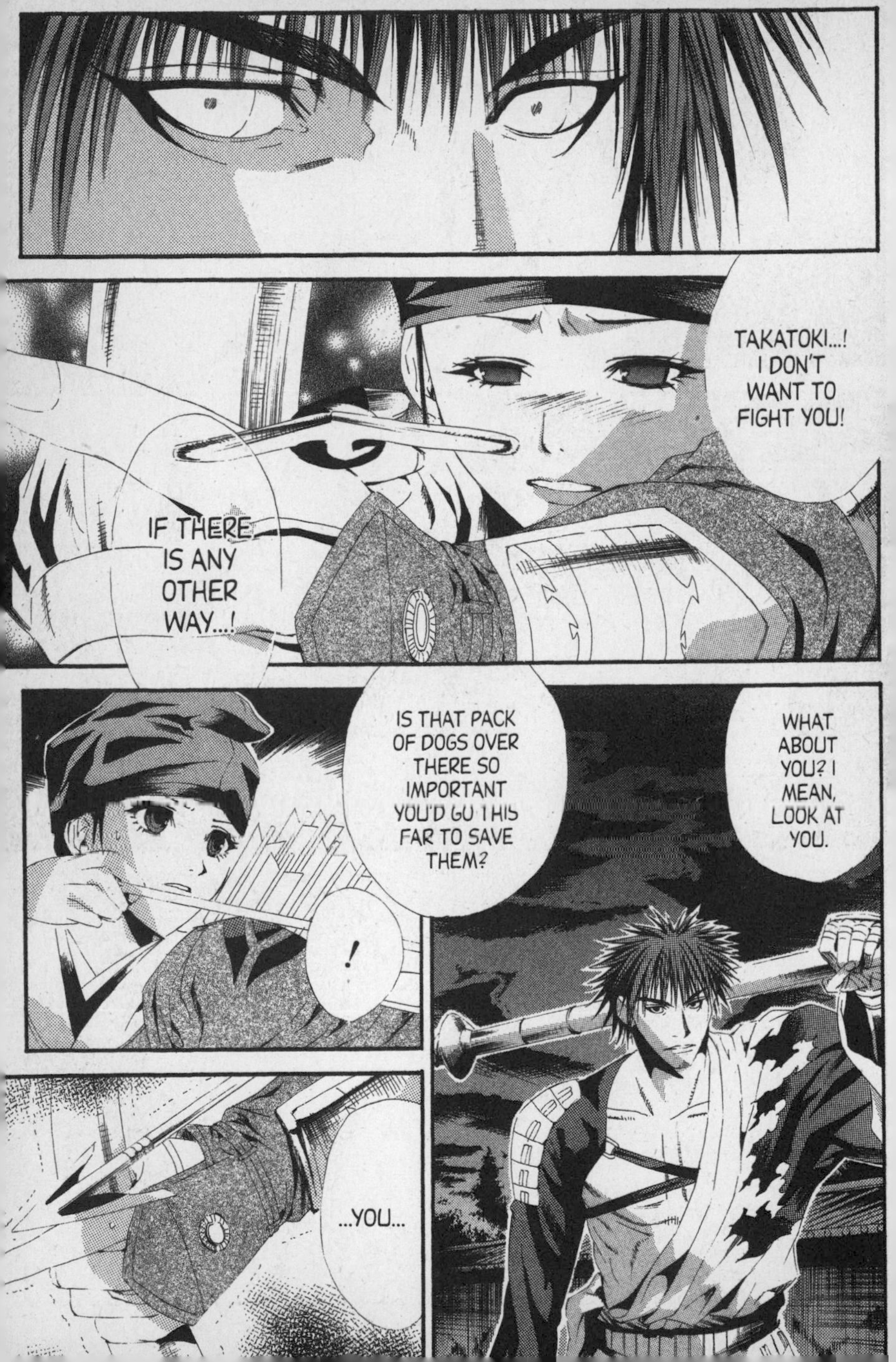
TAKATOKI...! I DON'T WANT TO FIGHT YOU!
IF THERE IS ANY OTHER WAY...!
WHAT ABOUT YOU? I MEAN, LOOK AT YOU.
IS THAT PACK OF DOGS OVER THERE SO IMPORTANT YOU'D GO THIS FAR TO SAVE THEM?
!
...YOU...

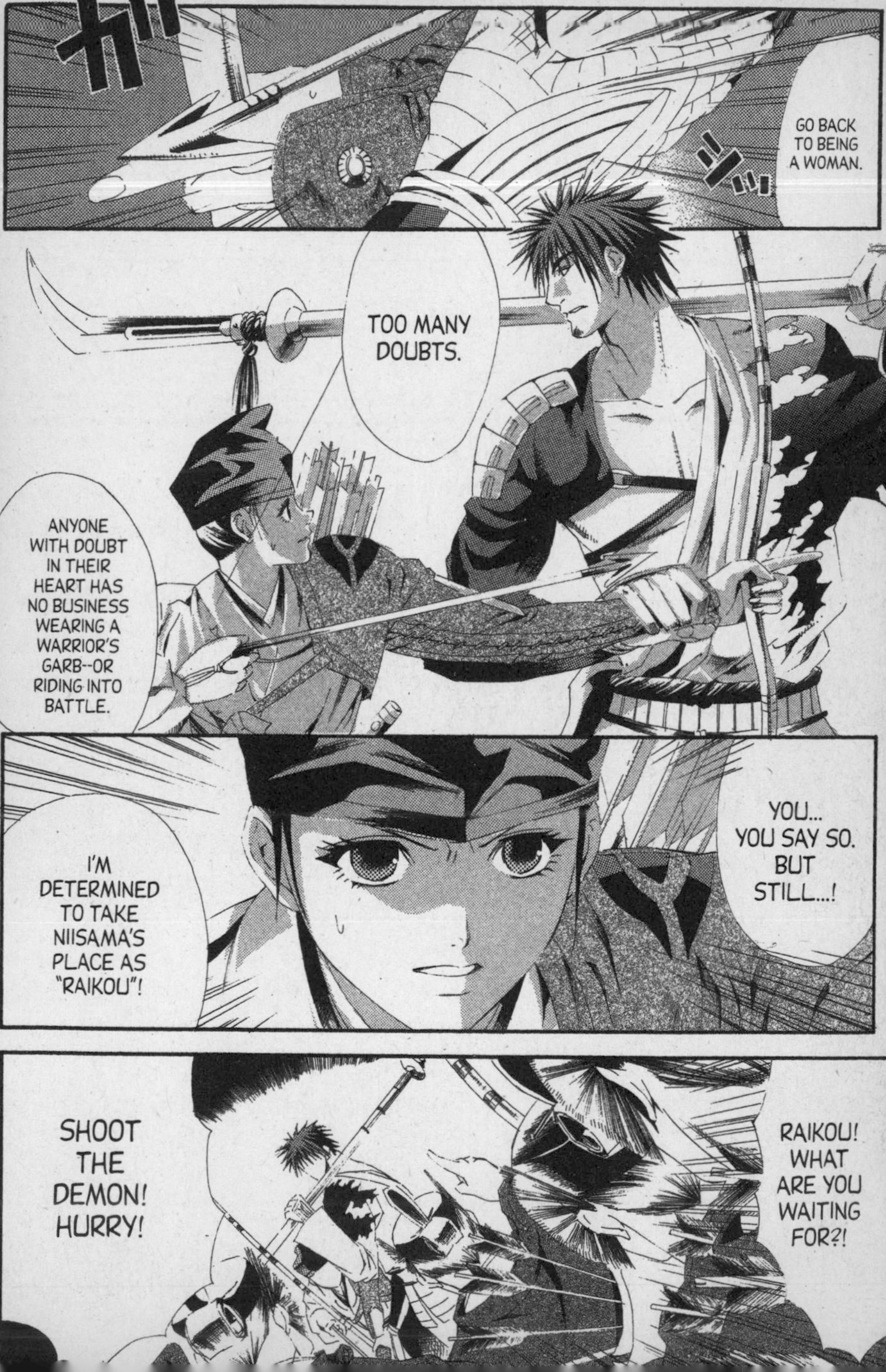
GO BACK TO BEING A WOMAN.
TOO MANY DOUBTS.
ANYONE WITH DOUBT IN THEIR HEART HAS NO BUSINESS WEARING A WARRIOR'S GARB--OR RIDING INTO BATTLE.
YOU... YOU SAY SO. BUT STILL...!
I'M DETERMINED TO TAKE NIISAMA'S PLACE AS "RAIKOU"!
RAIKOU! WHAT ARE YOU WAITING FOR?!
SHOOT THE DEMON! HURRY!

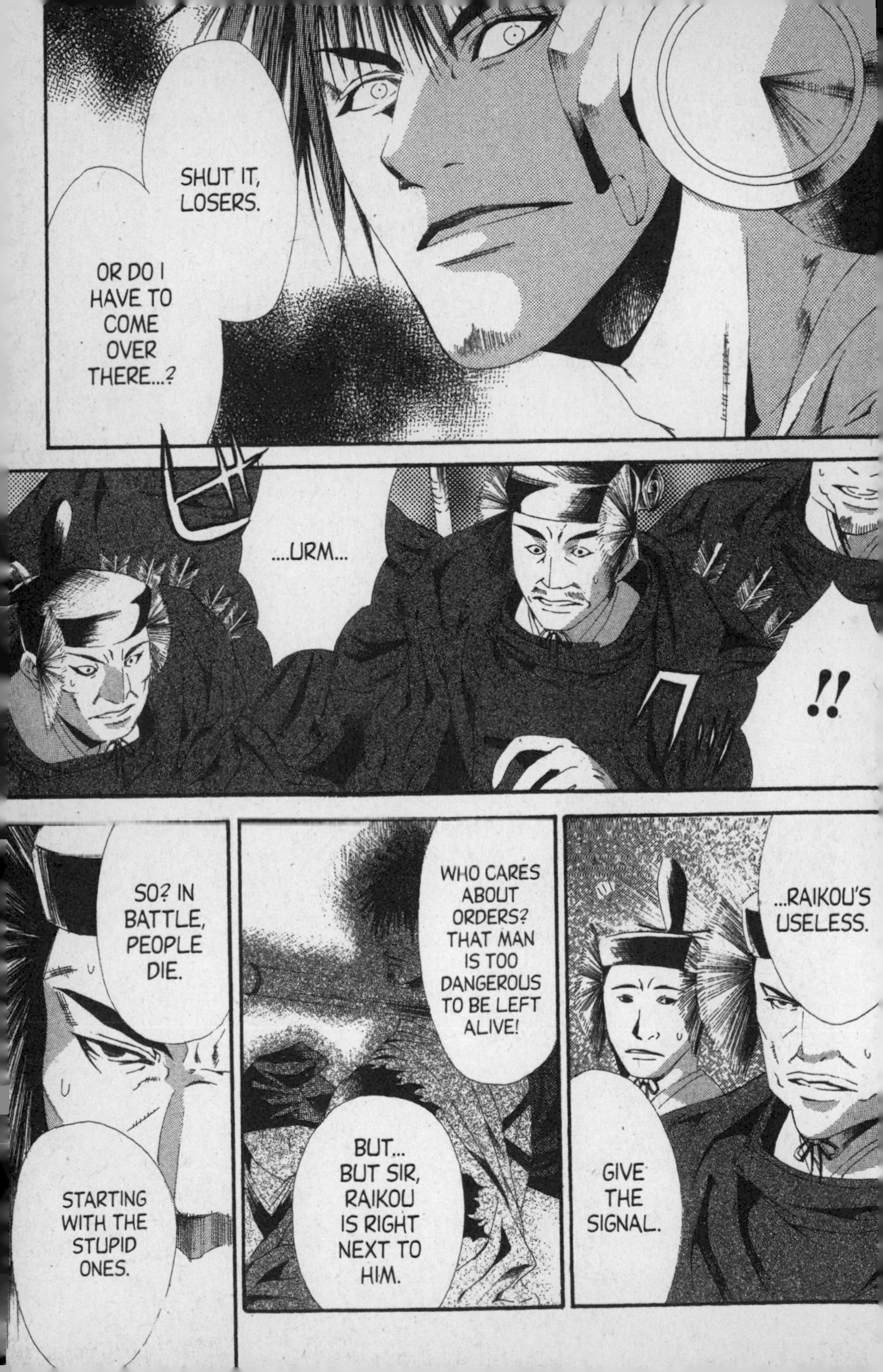

SHUT IT, LOSERS.
OR DO I HAVE TO COME OVER THERE...?
!!
....URM...
...RAIKOU'S USELESS.
GIVE THE SIGNAL.
WHO CARES ABOUT ORDERS? THAT MAN IS TOO DANGEROUS TO BE LEFT ALIVE!
BUT... BUT SIR, RAIKOU IS RIGHT NEXT TO HIM.
SO? IN BATTLE, PEOPLE DIE.
STARTING WITH THE STUPID ONES.

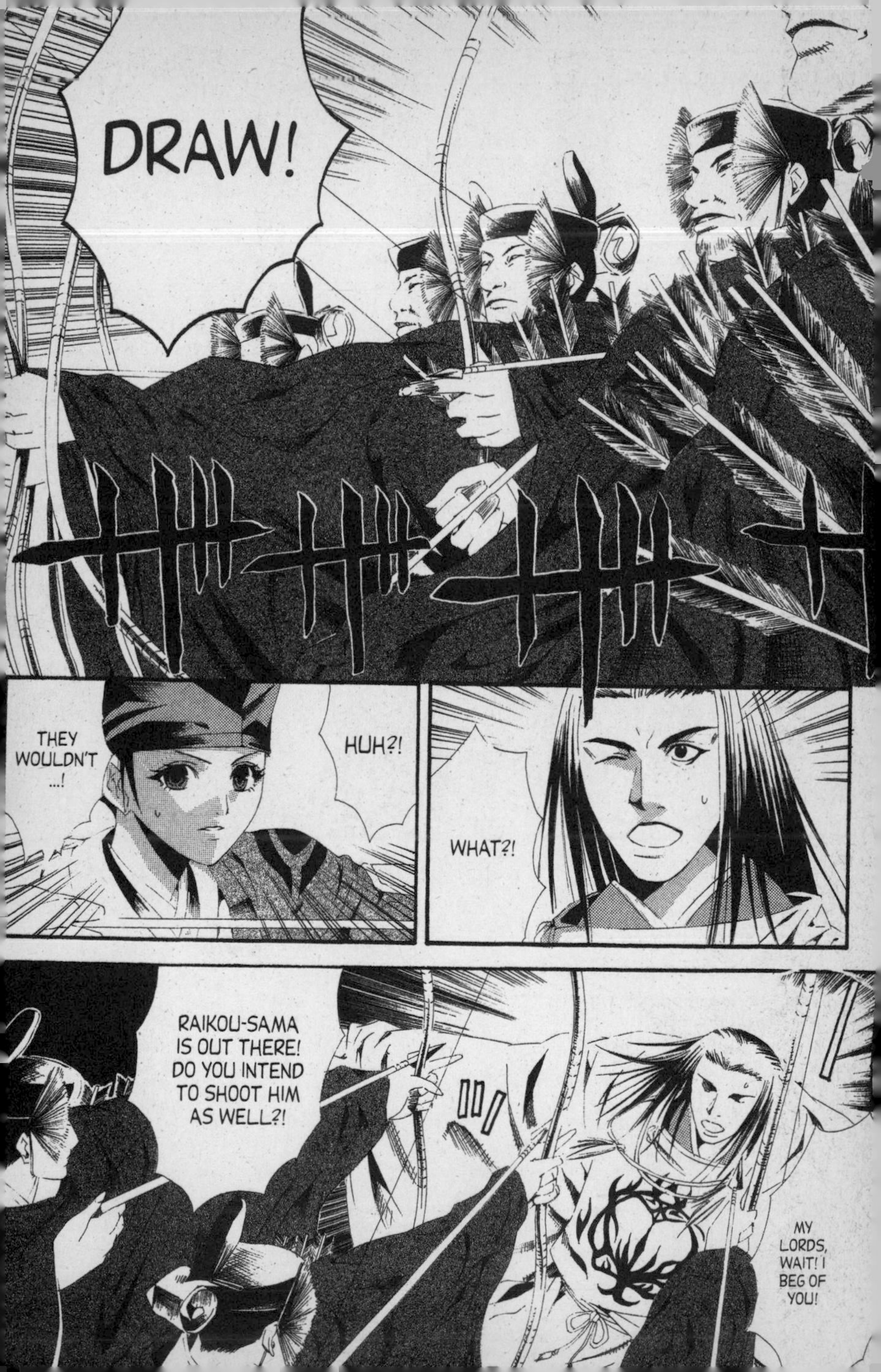
DRAW!
HUH?!
THEY WOULDN'T ...!
WHAT?!
RAIKOU-SAMA IS OUT THERE! DO YOU INTEND TO SHOOT HIM AS WELL?!
MY LORDS, WAIT! I BEG OF YOU!

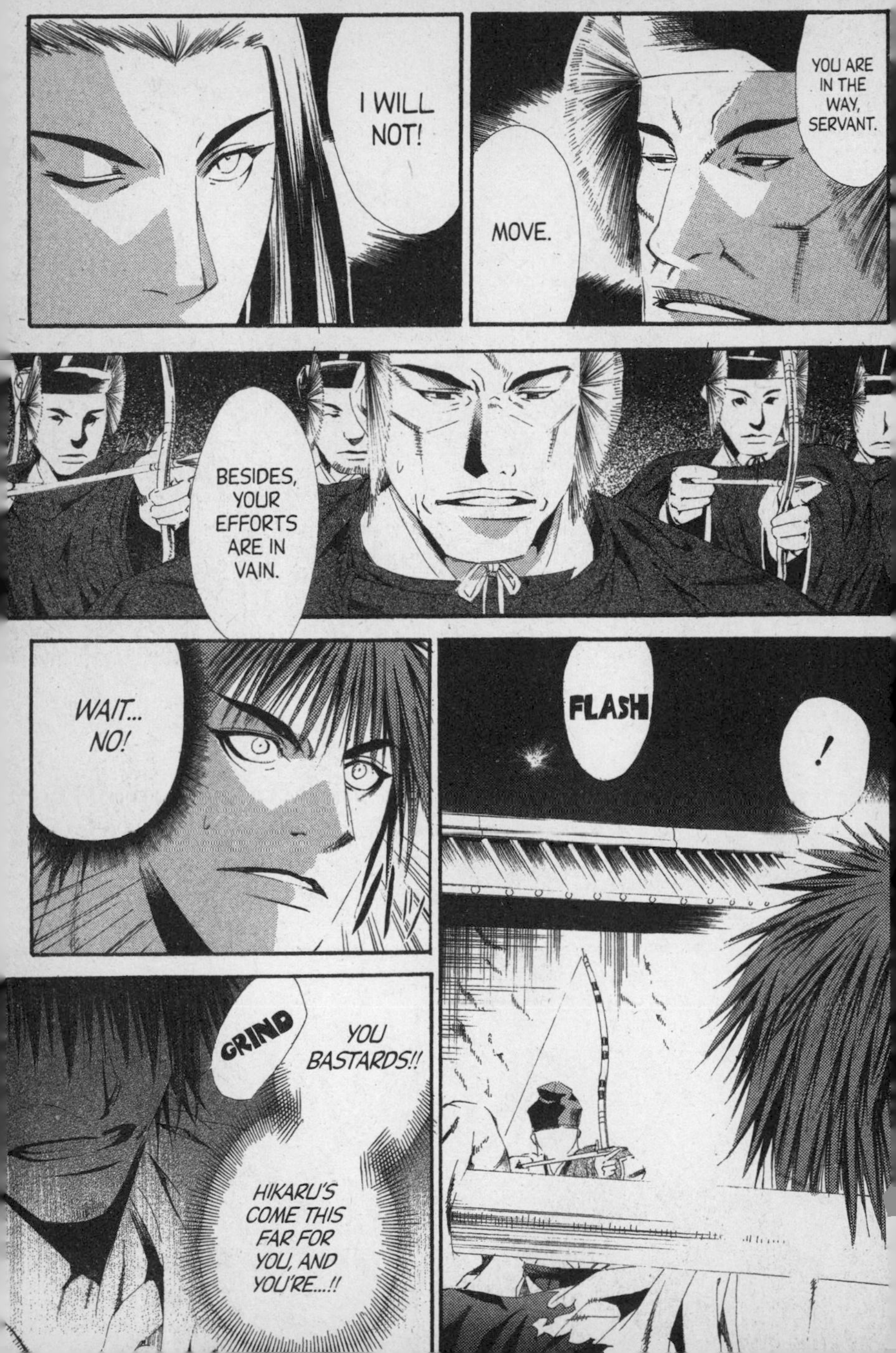
YOU ARE IN THE WAY, SERVANT.
MOVE.
I WILL NOT!
BESIDES, YOUR EFFORTS ARE IN VAIN.
FLASH
!
WAIT... NO!
GRIND
YOU BASTARDS!!
HIKARU'S COME THIS FAR FOR YOU, AND YOU'RE...!!

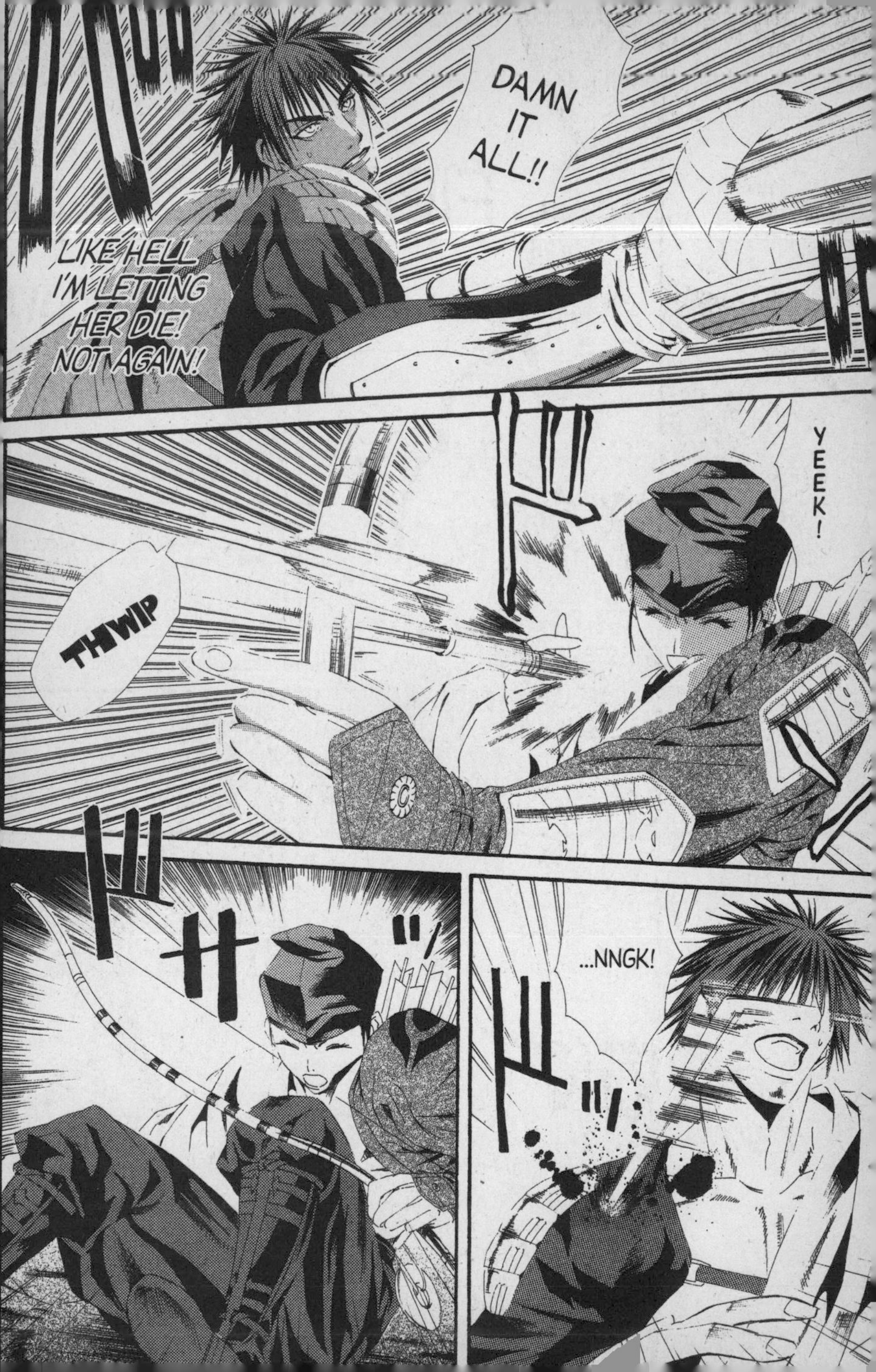
DAMN IT ALL!!
LIKE HELL I'M LETTING HER DIE! NOT AGAIN!
YEEK!
THWIP
...NNGK!

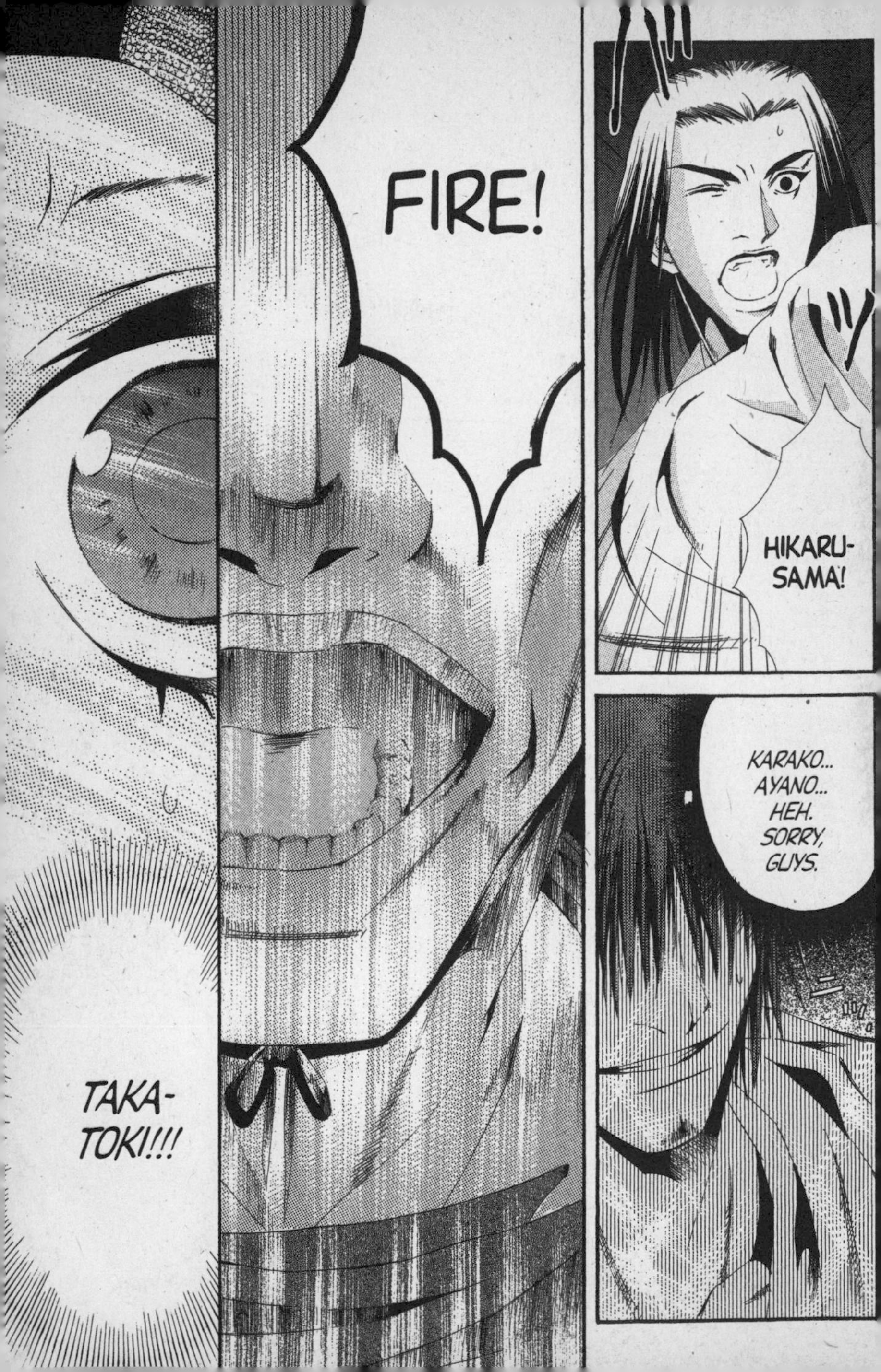
HIKARU-SAMA!
KARAKO... AYANO... HEH. SORRY, GUYS.
FIRE!
TAKA-TOKI!!!

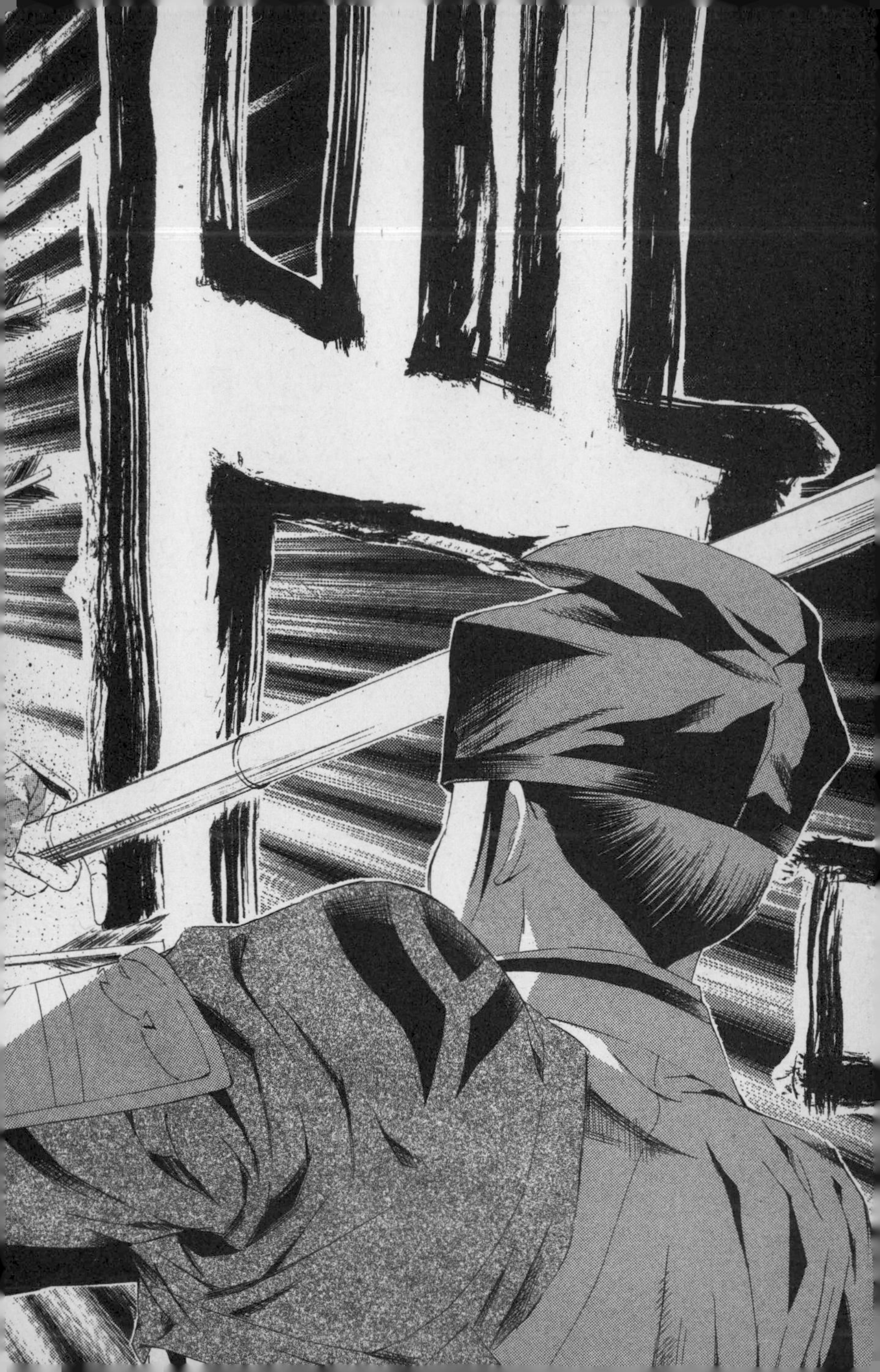

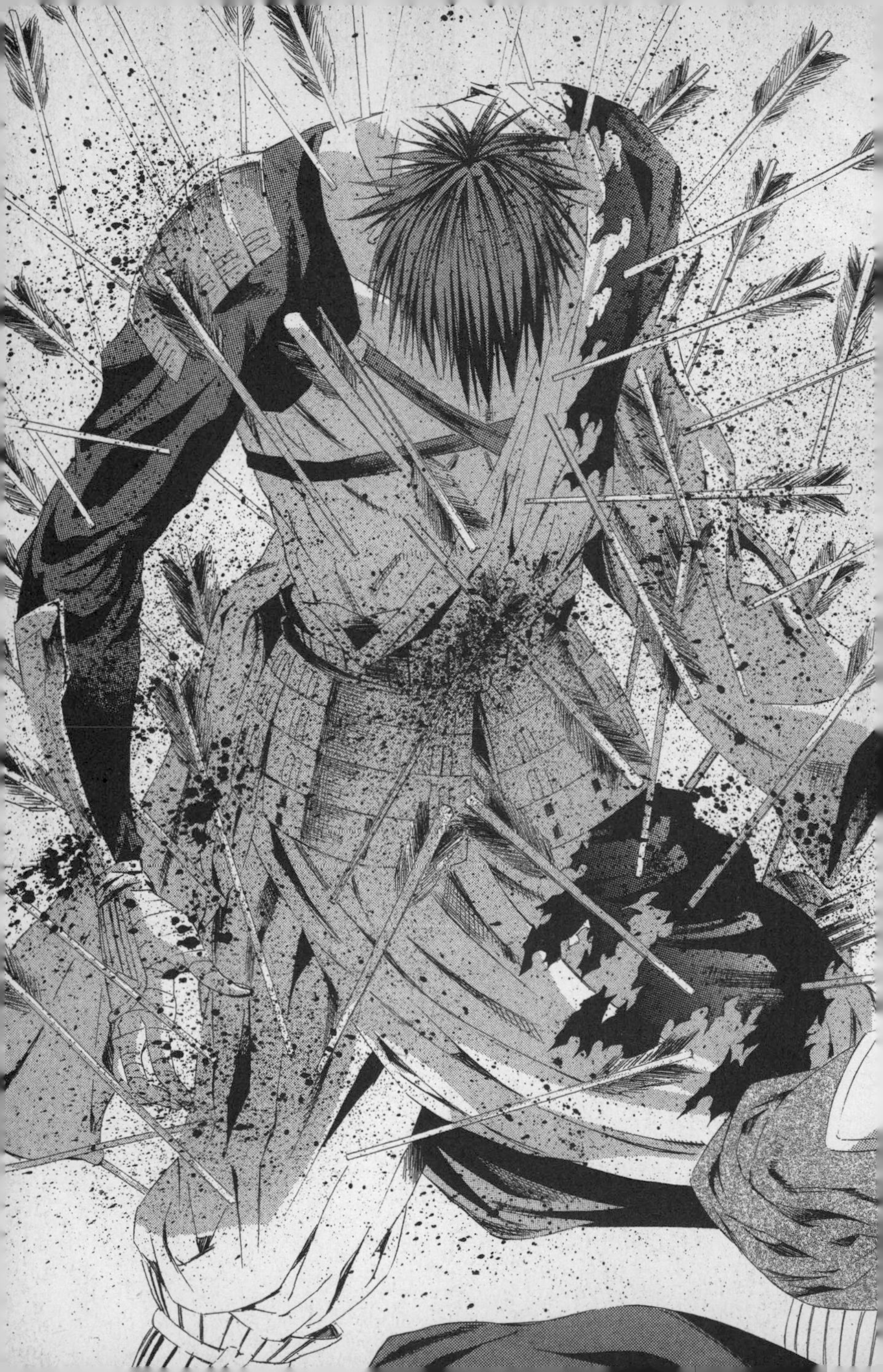

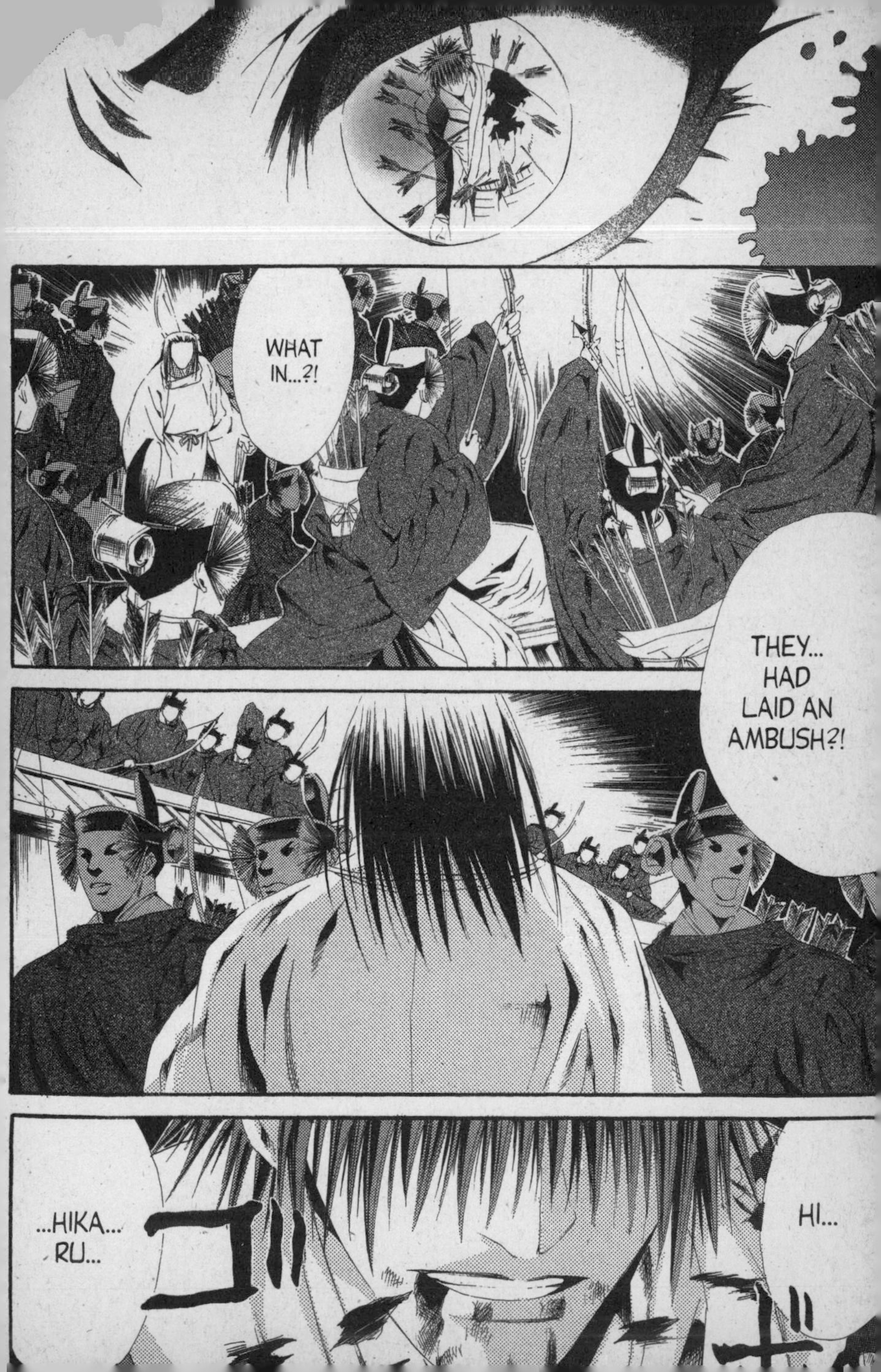
WHAT IN...?!
THEY... HAD LAID AN AMBUSH?!
HI...
...HIKA... RU...

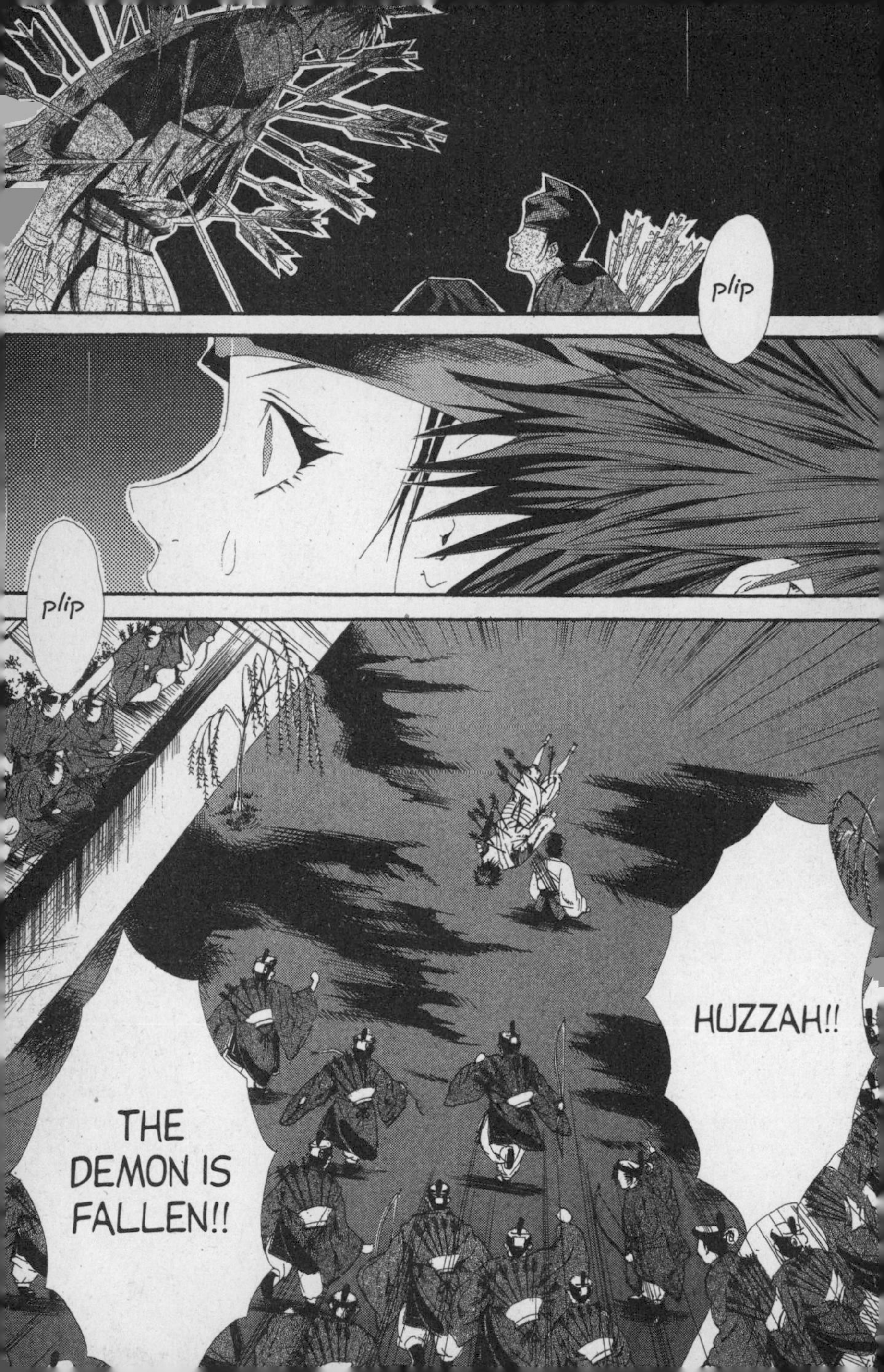
plip
plip
HUZZAH!!
THE DEMON IS FALLEN!!

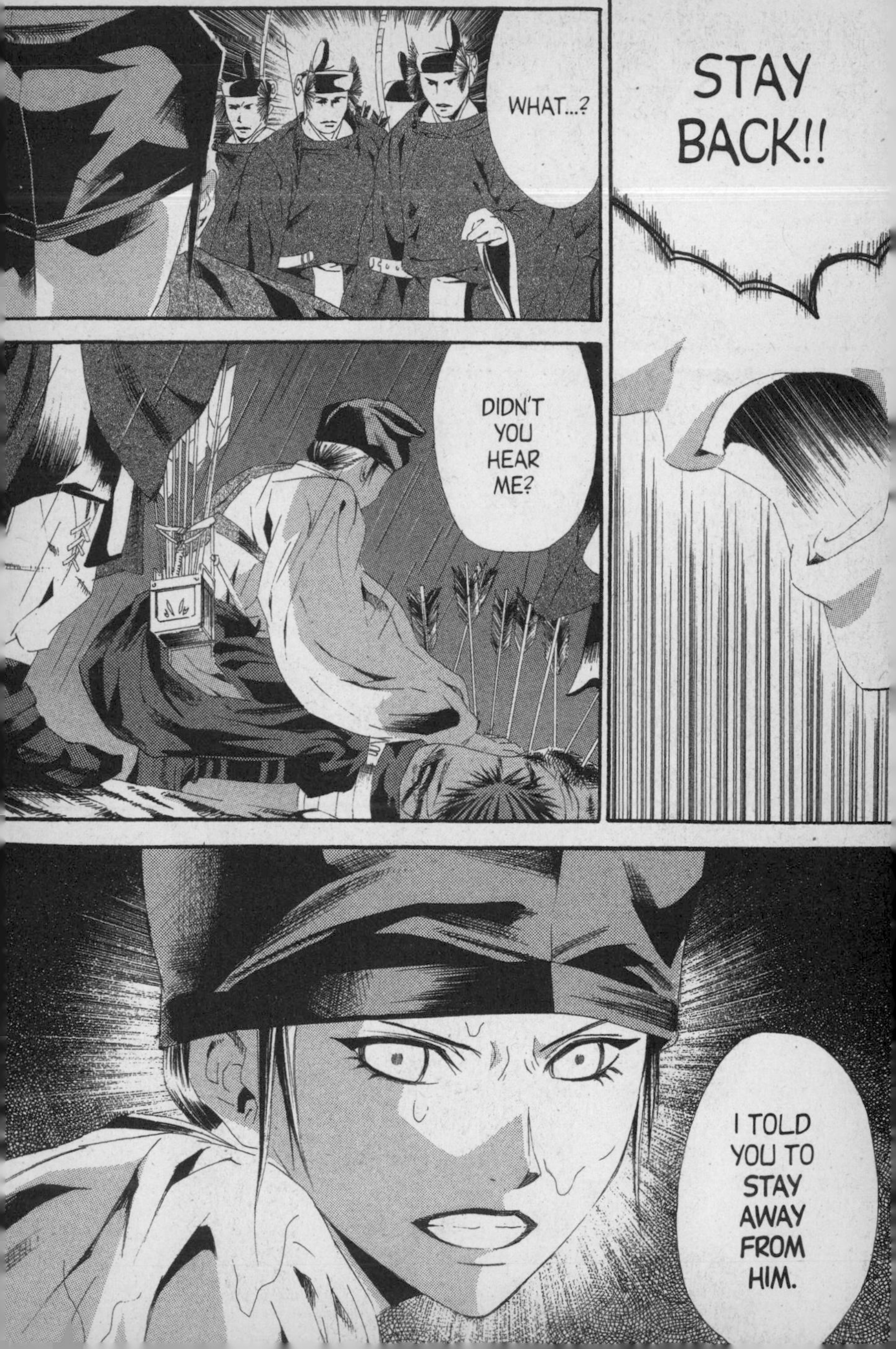
STAY BACK!!
WHAT...?
DIDN'T YOU HEAR ME?
I TOLD YOU TO STAY AWAY FROM HIM.

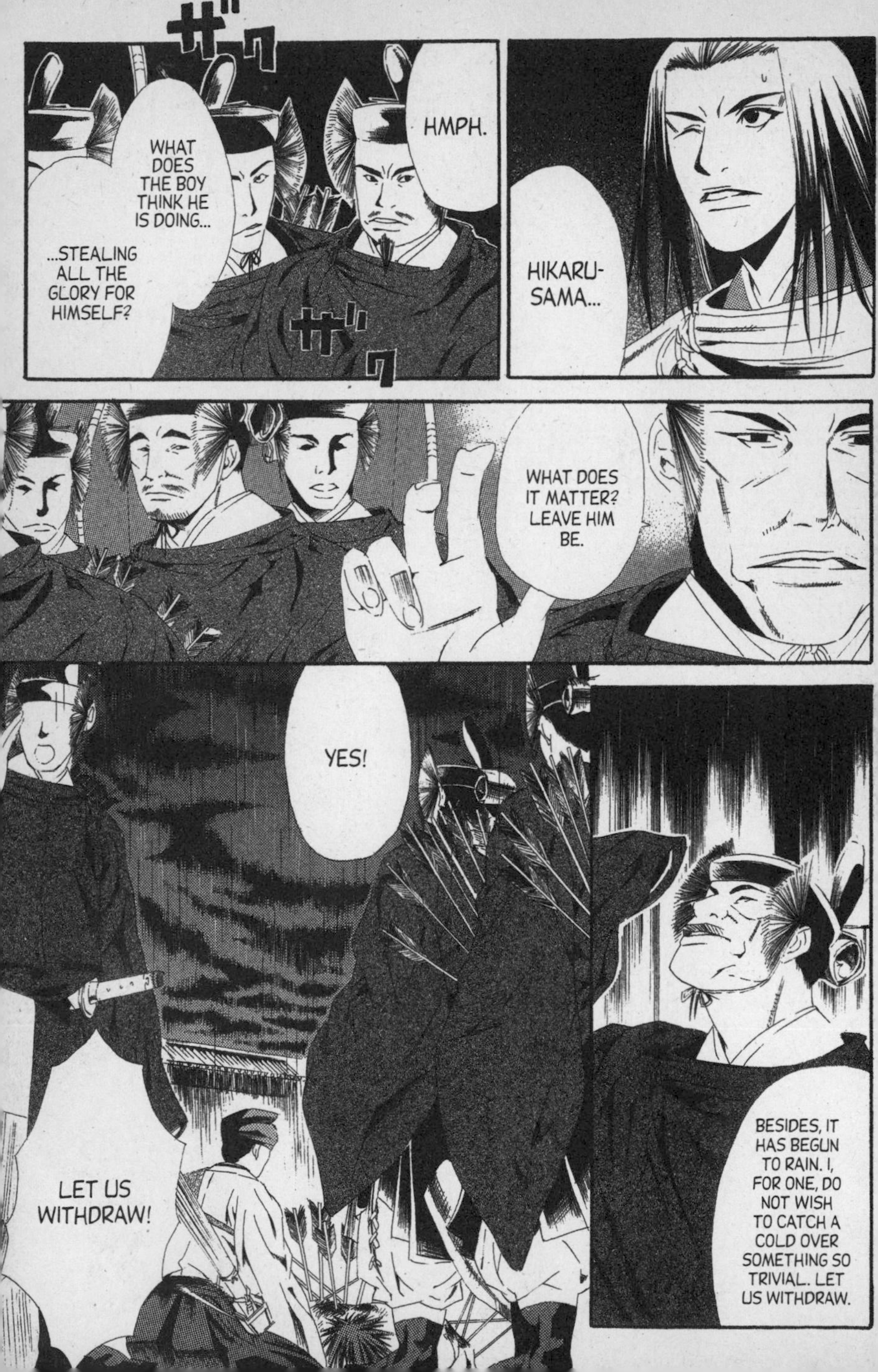
HIKARU-SAMA...
ザワ
HMPH.
WHAT DOES THE BOY THINK HE IS DOING...
...STEALING ALL THE GLORY FOR HIMSELF?
ザワ
WHAT DOES IT MATTER? LEAVE HIM BE.
BESIDES, IT HAS BEGUN TO RAIN. I, FOR ONE, DO NOT WISH TO CATCH A COLD OVER SOMETHING SO TRIVIAL. LET US WITHDRAW.
YES!
LET US WITHDRAW!

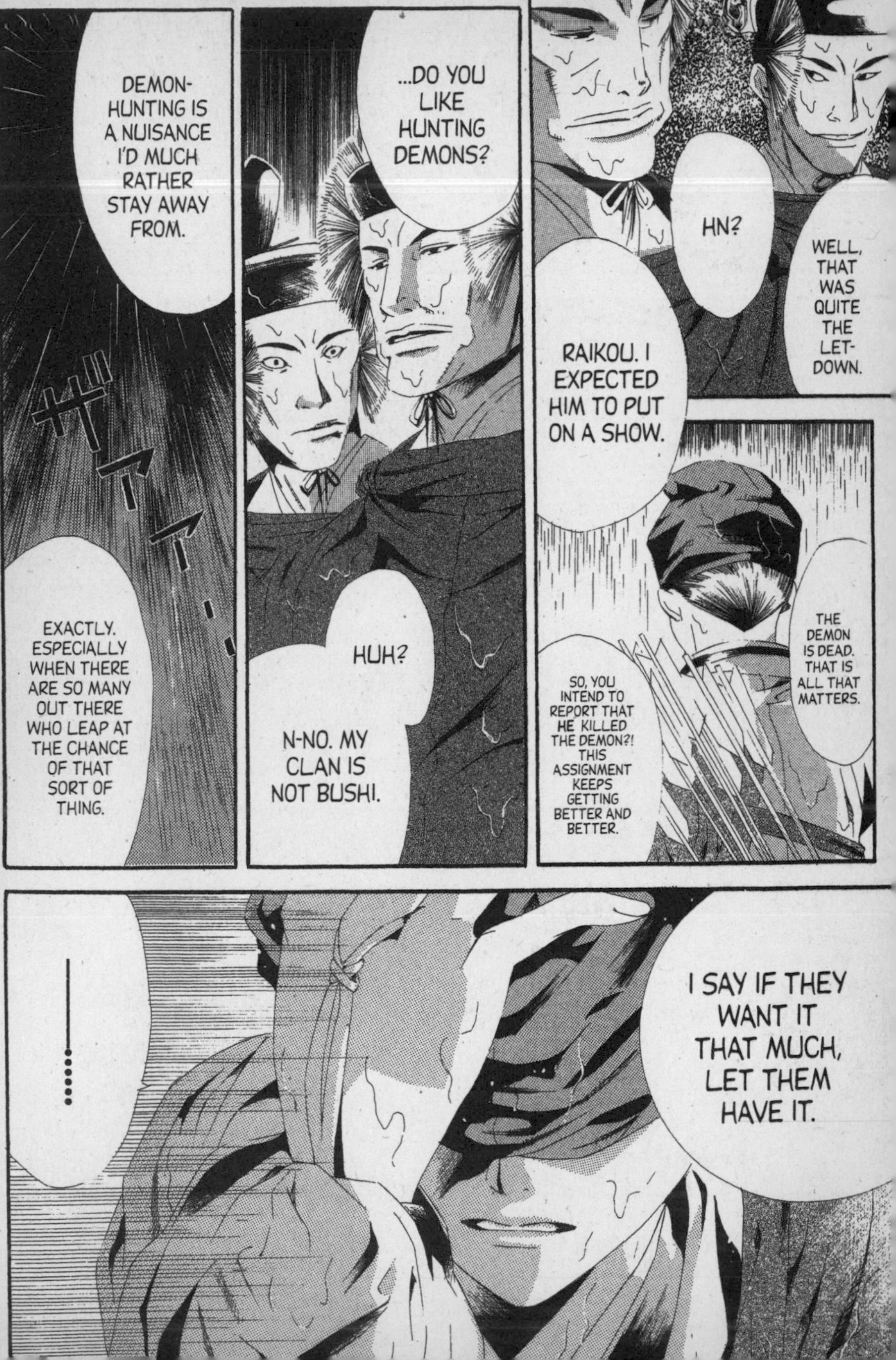
WELL, THAT WAS QUITE THE LET-DOWN.
HN?
RAIKOU. I EXPECTED HIM TO PUT ON A SHOW.
THE DEMON IS DEAD. THAT IS ALL THAT MATTERS.
SO, YOU INTEND TO REPORT THAT HE KILLED THE DEMON?! THIS ASSIGNMENT KEEPS GETTING BETTER AND BETTER.
...DO YOU LIKE HUNTING DEMONS?
HUH?
N-NO. MY CLAN IS NOT BUSHI.
DEMON-HUNTING IS A NUISANCE I'D MUCH RATHER STAY AWAY FROM.
ザァァ…
EXACTLY. ESPECIALLY WHEN THERE ARE SO MANY OUT THERE WHO LEAP AT THE CHANCE OF THAT SORT OF THING.
I SAY IF THEY WANT IT THAT MUCH, LET THEM HAVE IT.
—……

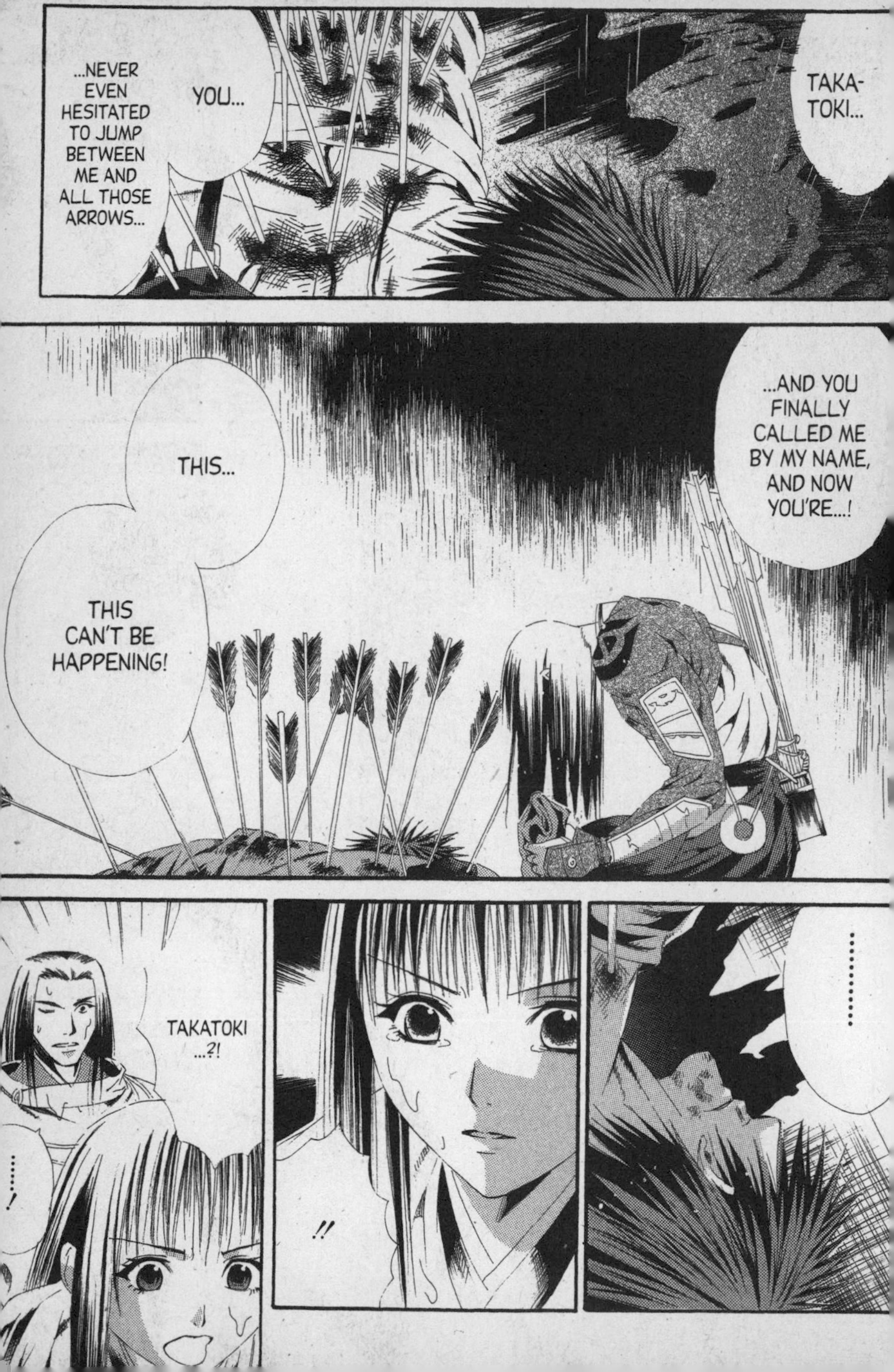
TAKA-
TOKI...
YOU...
...NEVER EVEN HESITATED TO JUMP BETWEEN ME AND ALL THOSE ARROWS...
...AND YOU FINALLY CALLED ME BY MY NAME, AND NOW YOU'RE...!
THIS...
THIS CAN'T BE HAPPENING!
....
!!
TAKATOKI ...?!
......!

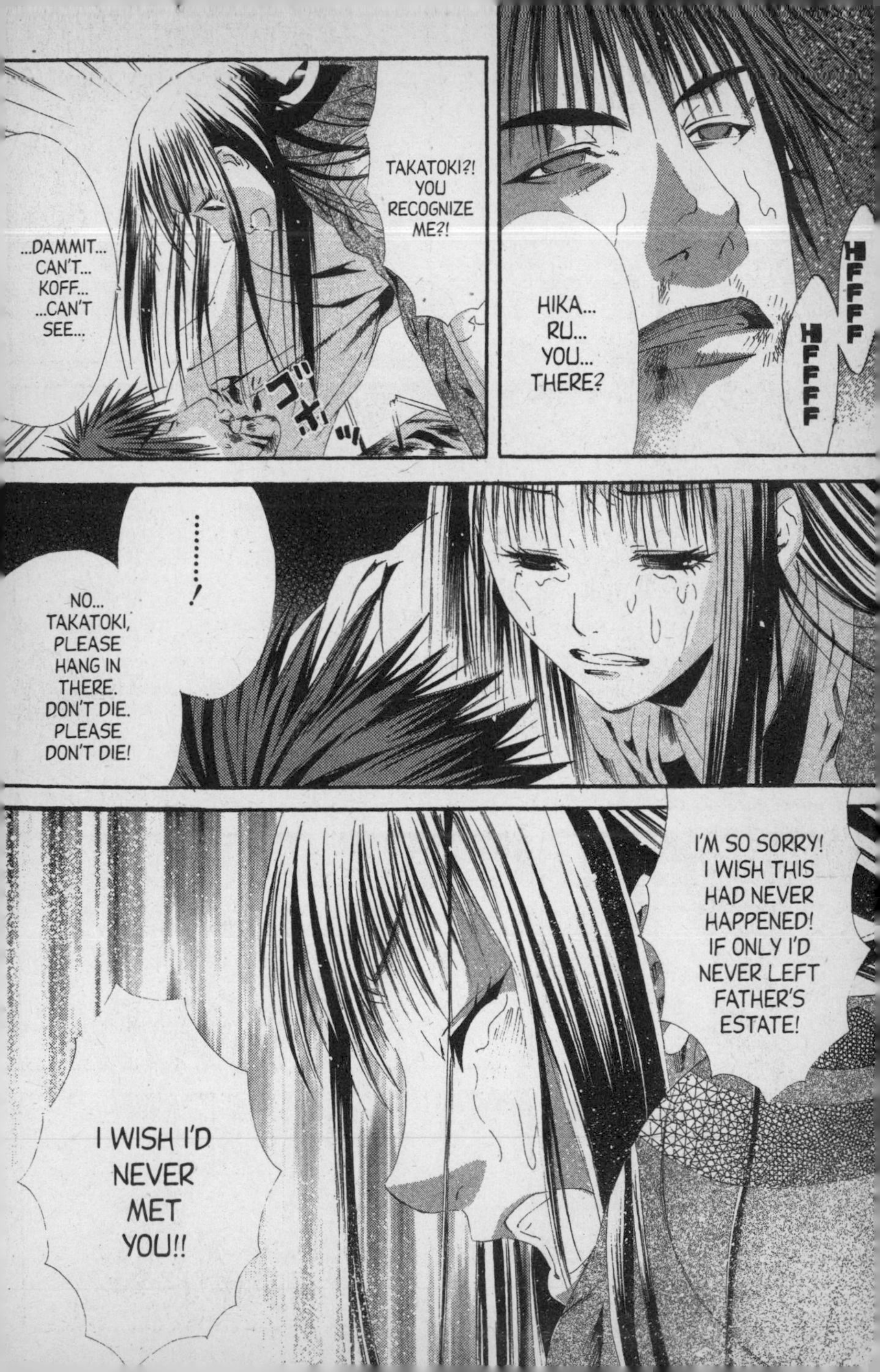
HIKA... RU... YOU... THERE?
HFFFF HFFFF
TAKATOKI?! YOU RECOGNIZE ME?!
...DAMMIT... CAN'T... KOFF... ...CAN'T SEE...
ゴボッ
......!
NO... TAKATOKI, PLEASE HANG IN THERE. DON'T DIE. PLEASE DON'T DIE!
I'M SO SORRY! I WISH THIS HAD NEVER HAPPENED! IF ONLY I'D NEVER LEFT FATHER'S ESTATE!
I WISH I'D NEVER MET YOU!!

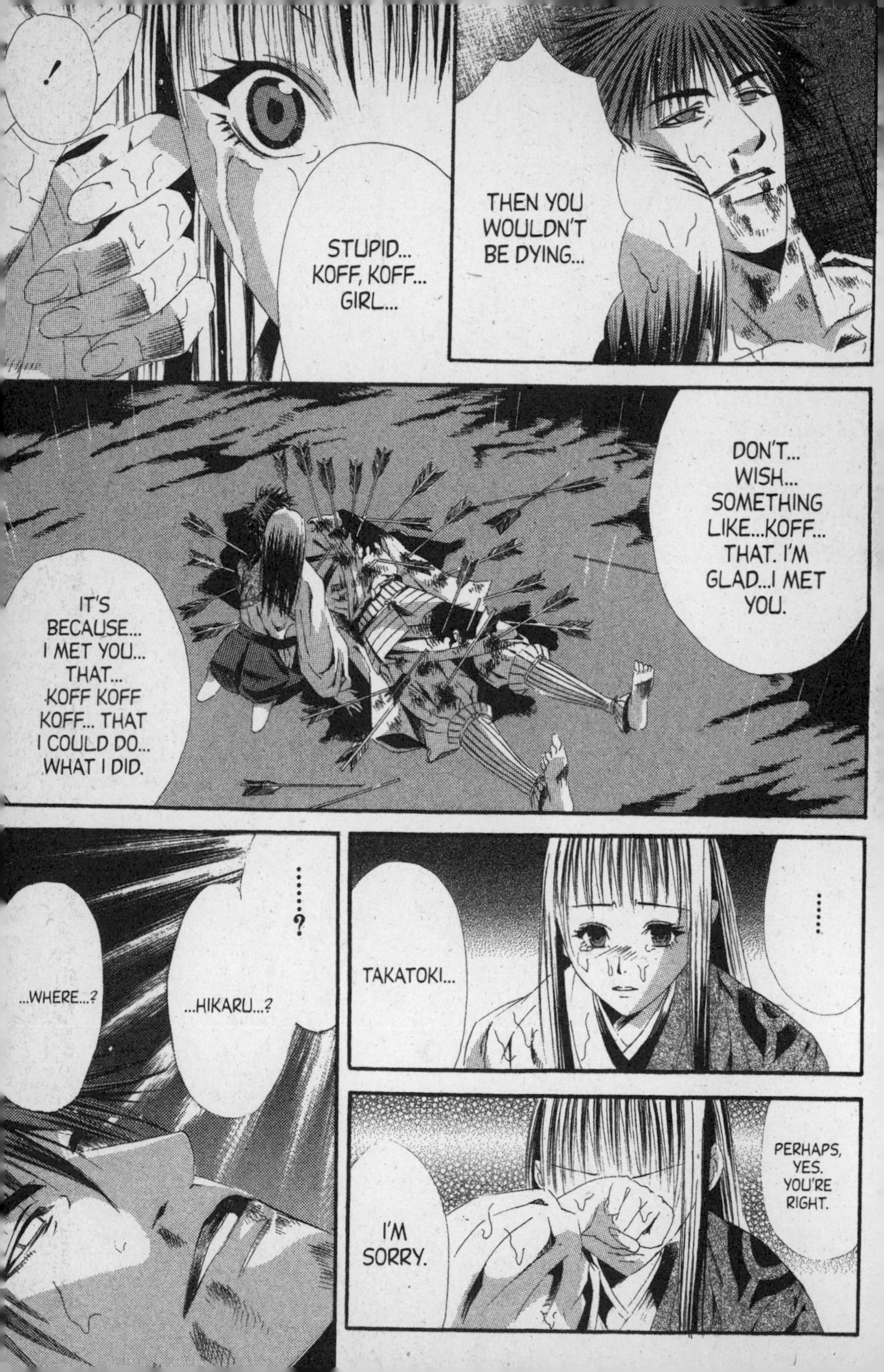
THEN YOU WOULDN'T BE DYING...
!
STUPID... KOFF, KOFF... GIRL...
DON'T... WISH... SOMETHING LIKE...KOFF... THAT. I'M GLAD...I MET YOU.
IT'S BECAUSE... I MET YOU... THAT... KOFF KOFF KOFF... THAT I COULD DO... WHAT I DID.
......
TAKATOKI...
PERHAPS, YES. YOU'RE RIGHT.
I'M SORRY.
......?
...HIKARU...?
...WHERE...?

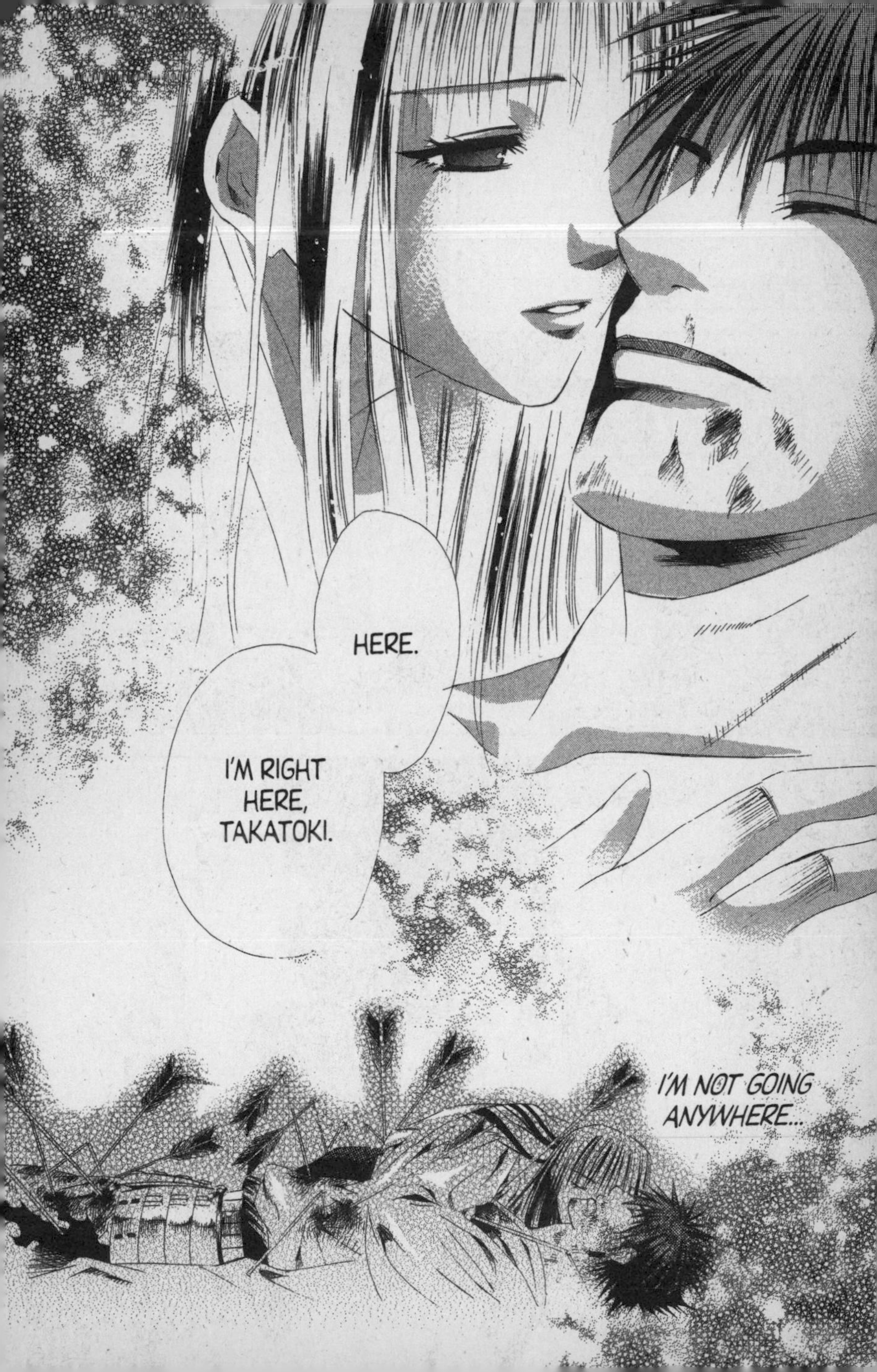
HERE.
I'M RIGHT HERE, TAKATOKI.
I'M NOT GOING ANYWHERE...

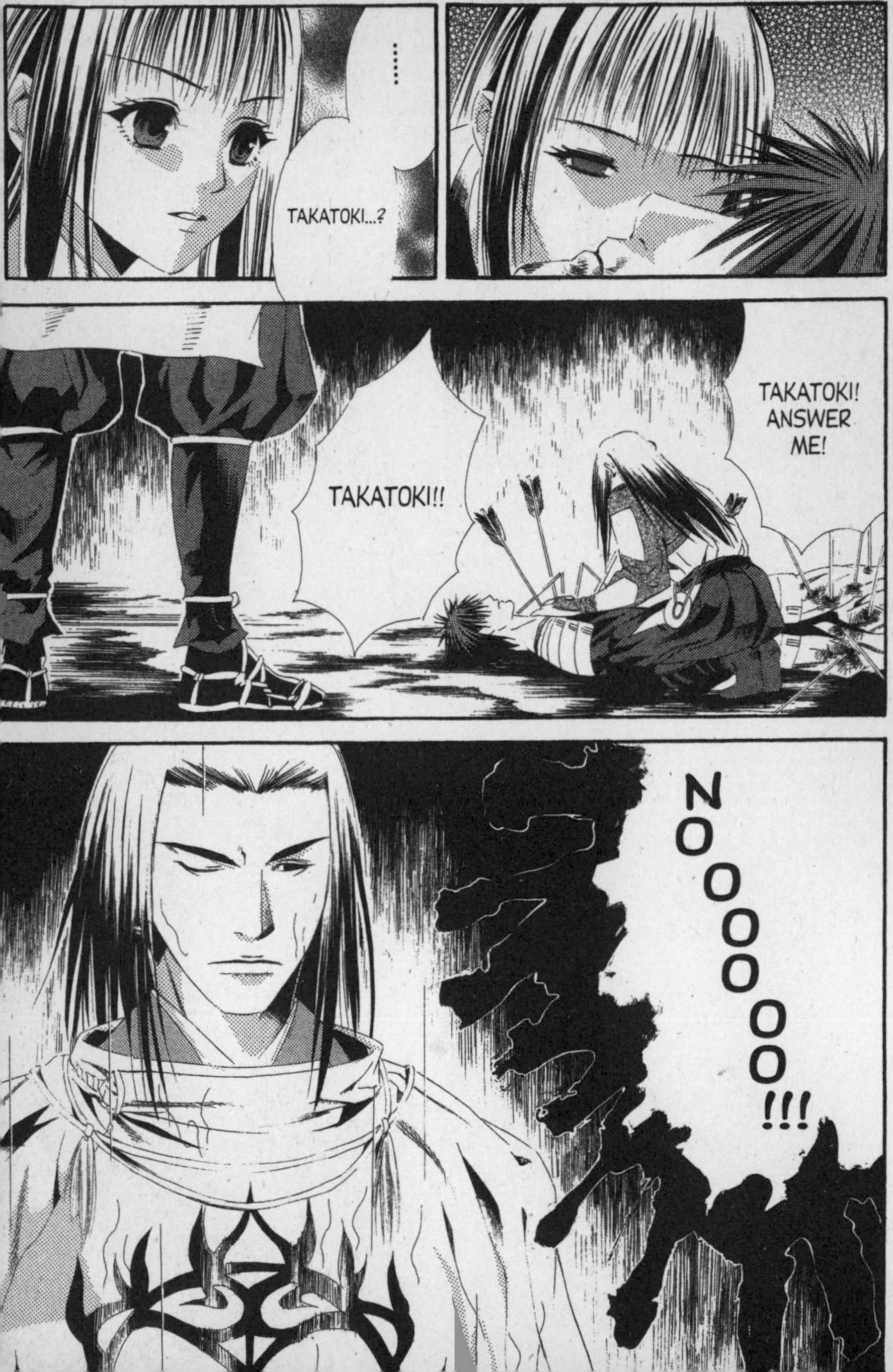
......
TAKATOKI...?
TAKATOKI! ANSWER ME!
TAKATOKI!!
NOOOOOO!!!

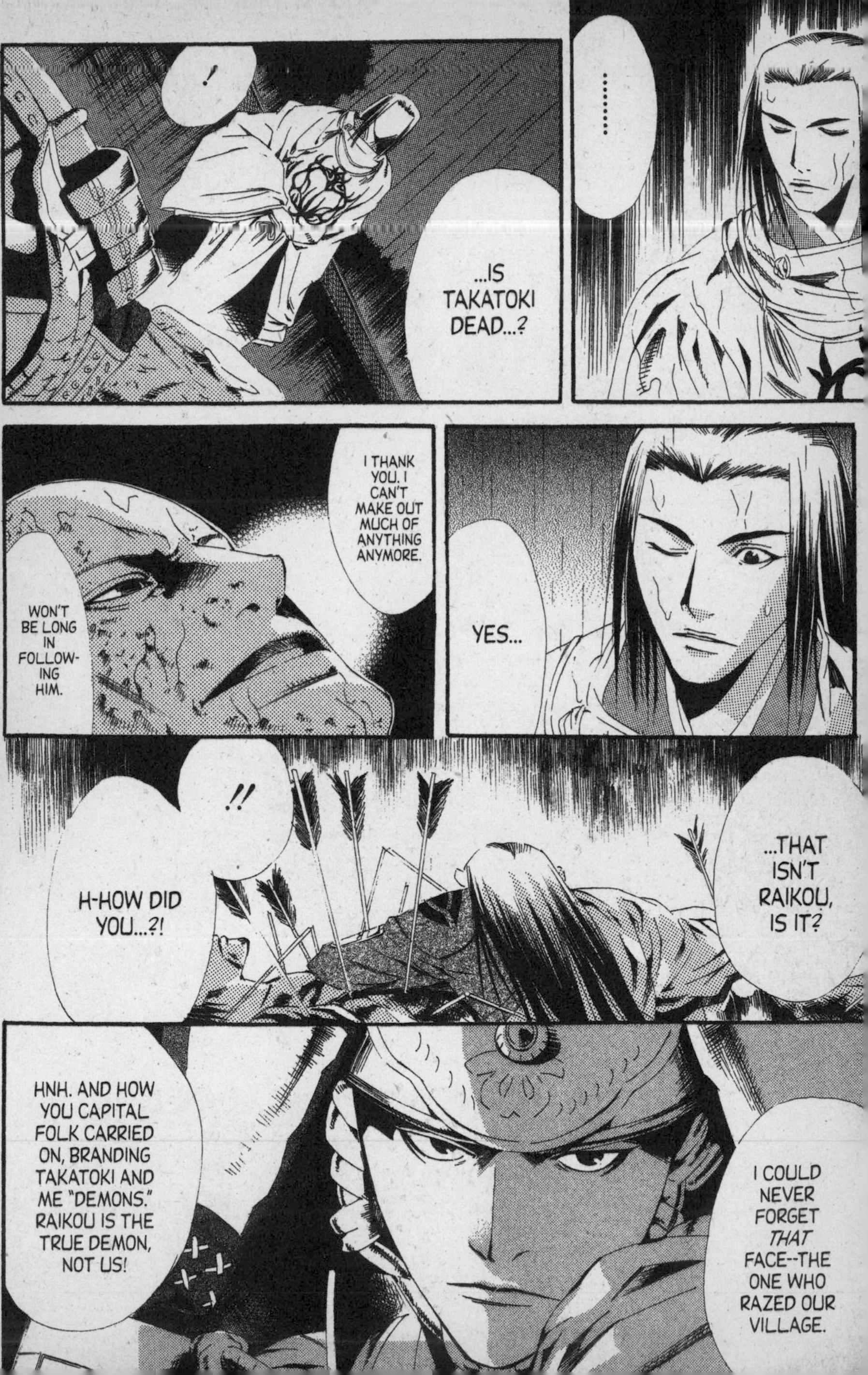
......
...IS TAKATOKI DEAD...?
!
YES...
I THANK YOU. I CAN'T MAKE OUT MUCH OF ANYTHING ANYMORE.
WON'T BE LONG IN FOLLOW-ING HIM.
...THAT ISN'T RAIKOU, IS IT?
!!
H-HOW DID YOU...?!
I COULD NEVER FORGET *THAT* FACE--THE ONE WHO RAZED OUR VILLAGE.
HNH. AND HOW YOU CAPITAL FOLK CARRIED ON, BRANDING TAKATOKI AND ME "DEMONS." RAIKOU IS THE TRUE DEMON, NOT US!

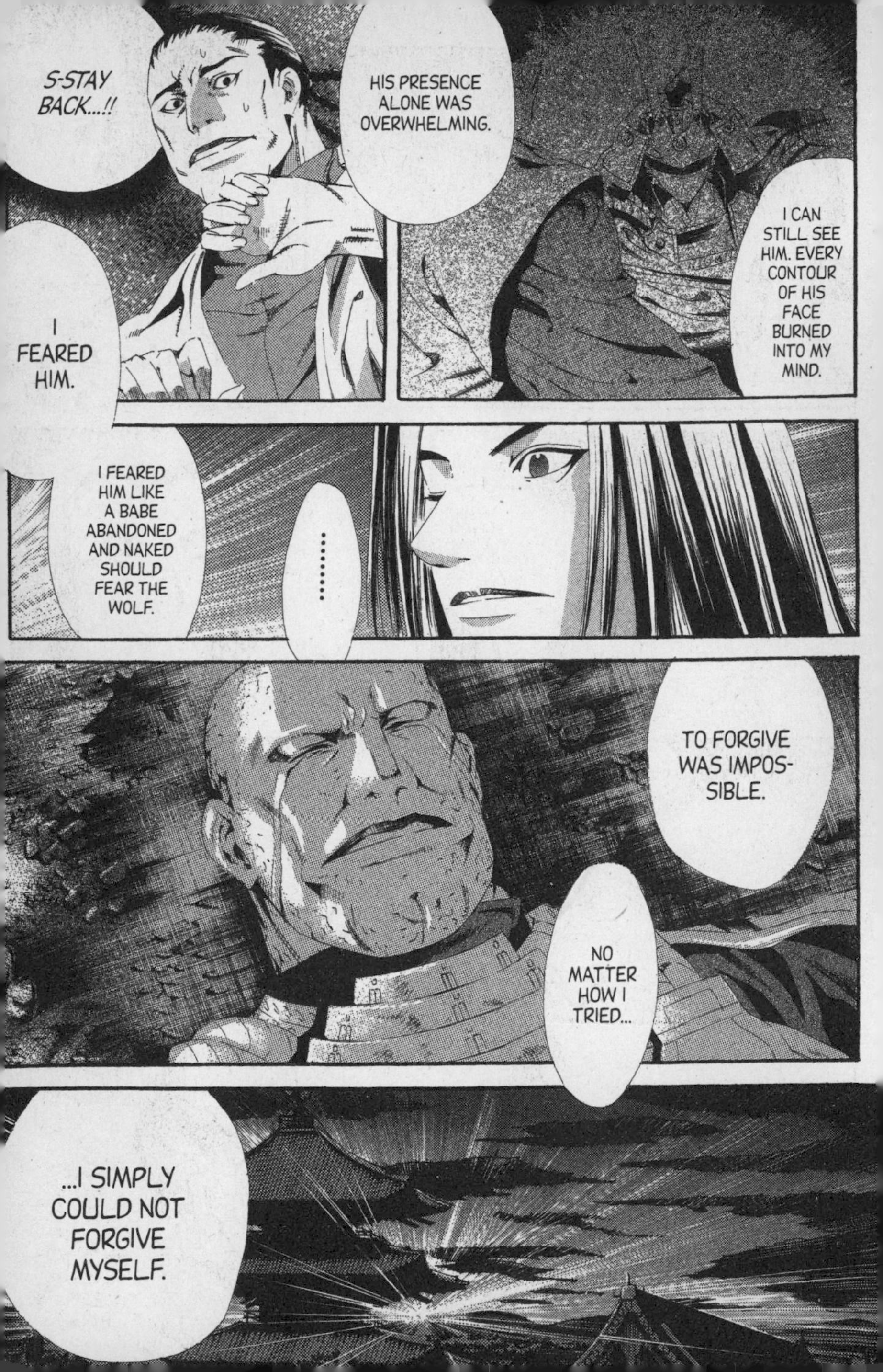

HIS PRESENCE ALONE WAS OVERWHELMING.
I CAN STILL SEE HIM. EVERY CONTOUR OF HIS FACE BURNED INTO MY MIND.
S-STAY BACK...!!
I FEARED HIM.
I FEARED HIM LIKE A BABE ABANDONED AND NAKED SHOULD FEAR THE WOLF.
......
TO FORGIVE WAS IMPOS-SIBLE.
NO MATTER HOW I TRIED...
...I SIMPLY COULD NOT FORGIVE MYSELF.

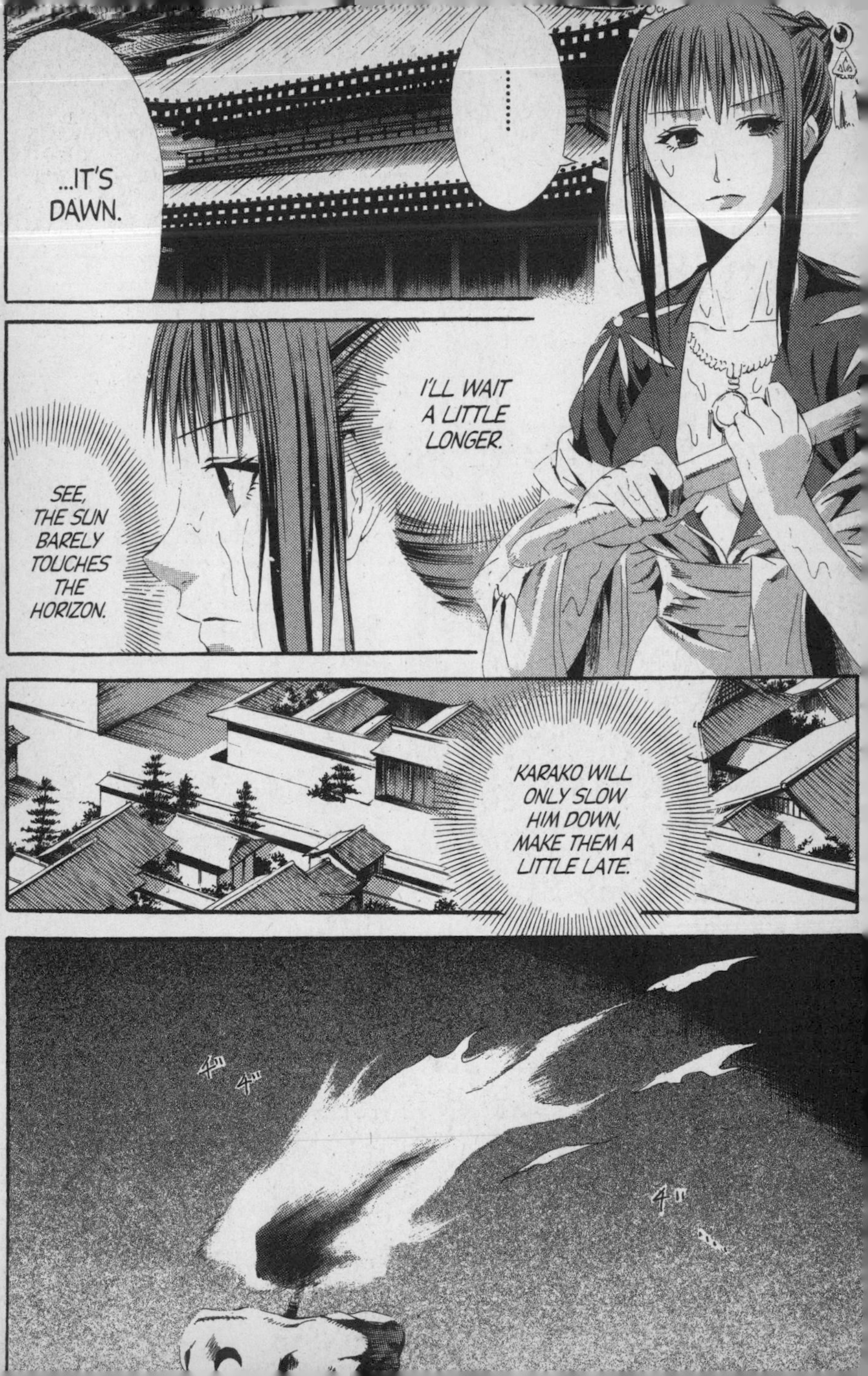

...
...IT'S DAWN.
I'LL WAIT A LITTLE LONGER.
SEE, THE SUN BARELY TOUCHES THE HORIZON.
KARAKO WILL ONLY SLOW HIM DOWN, MAKE THEM A LITTLE LATE.

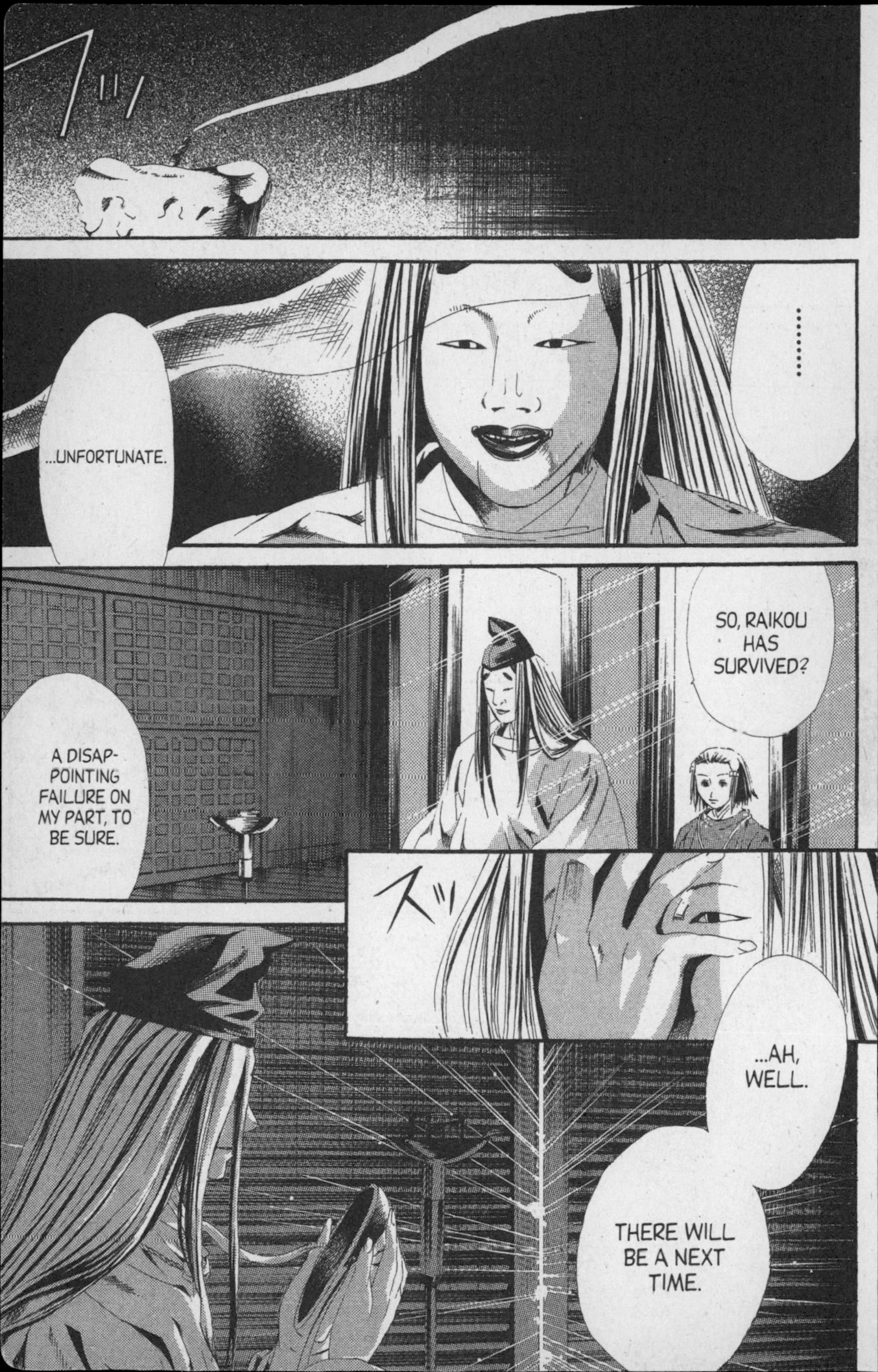
フッ
......
...UNFORTUNATE.
SO, RAIKOU HAS SURVIVED?
A DISAP-POINTING FAILURE ON MY PART, TO BE SURE.
スッ
...AH, WELL.
THERE WILL BE A NEXT TIME.

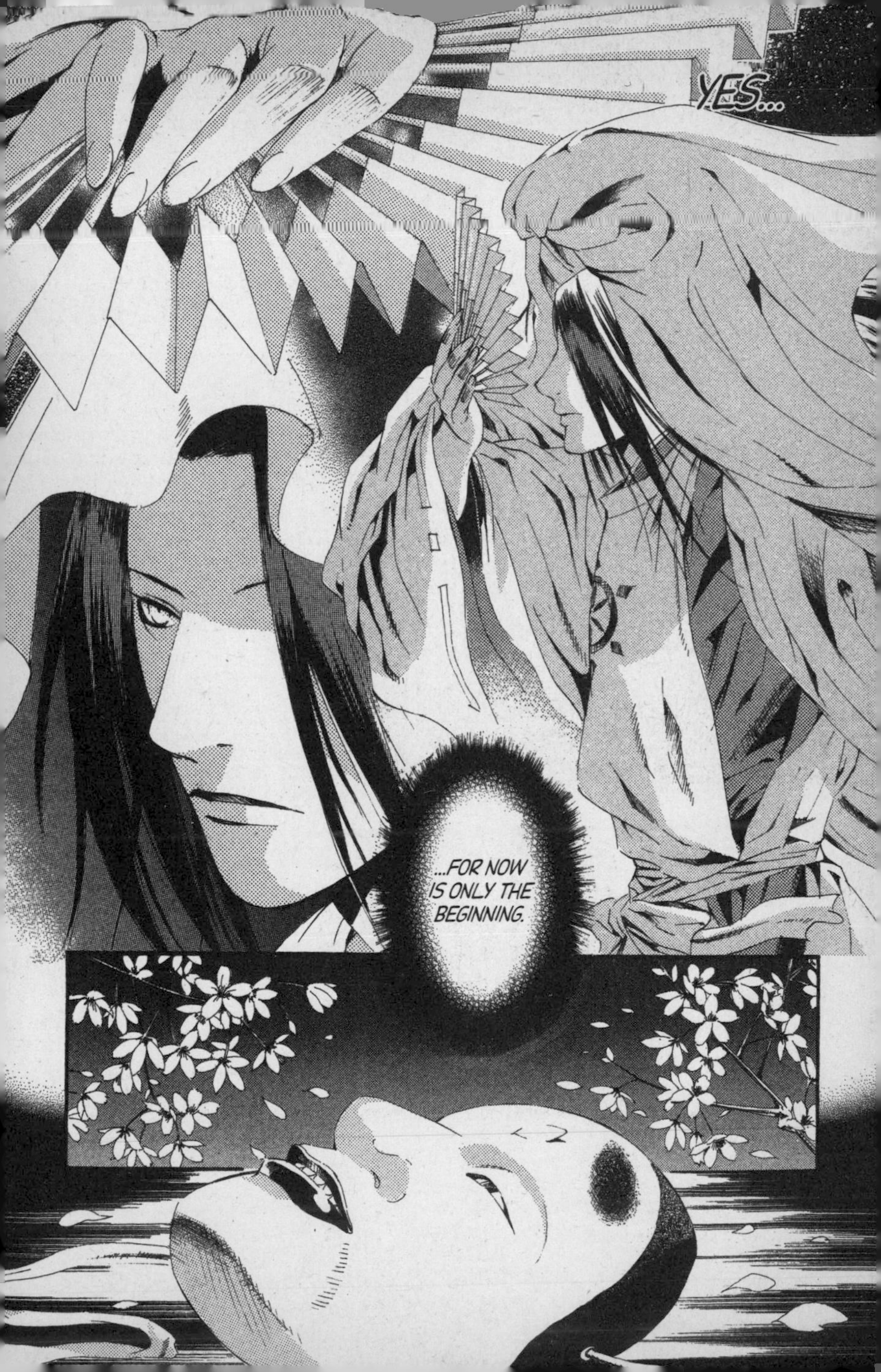
YES...
...FOR NOW IS ONLY THE BEGINNING.

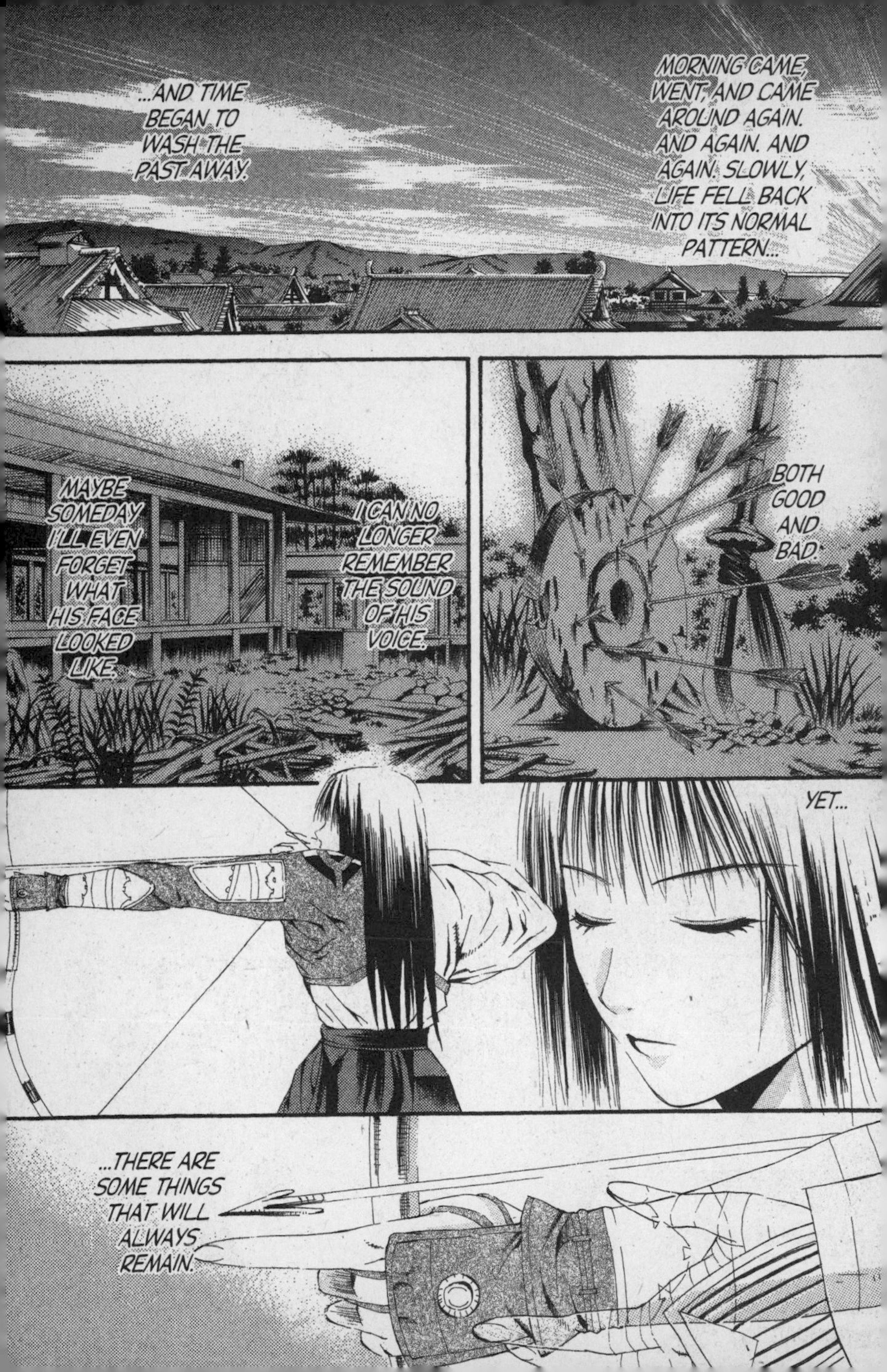
MORNING CAME, WENT, AND CAME AROUND AGAIN. AND AGAIN. AND AGAIN. SLOWLY, LIFE FELL BACK INTO ITS NORMAL PATTERN...
...AND TIME BEGAN TO WASH THE PAST AWAY.
BOTH GOOD AND BAD.
I CAN NO LONGER REMEMBER THE SOUND OF HIS VOICE.
MAYBE SOMEDAY I'LL EVEN FORGET WHAT HIS FACE LOOKED LIKE.
YET...
...THERE ARE SOME THINGS THAT WILL ALWAYS REMAIN.

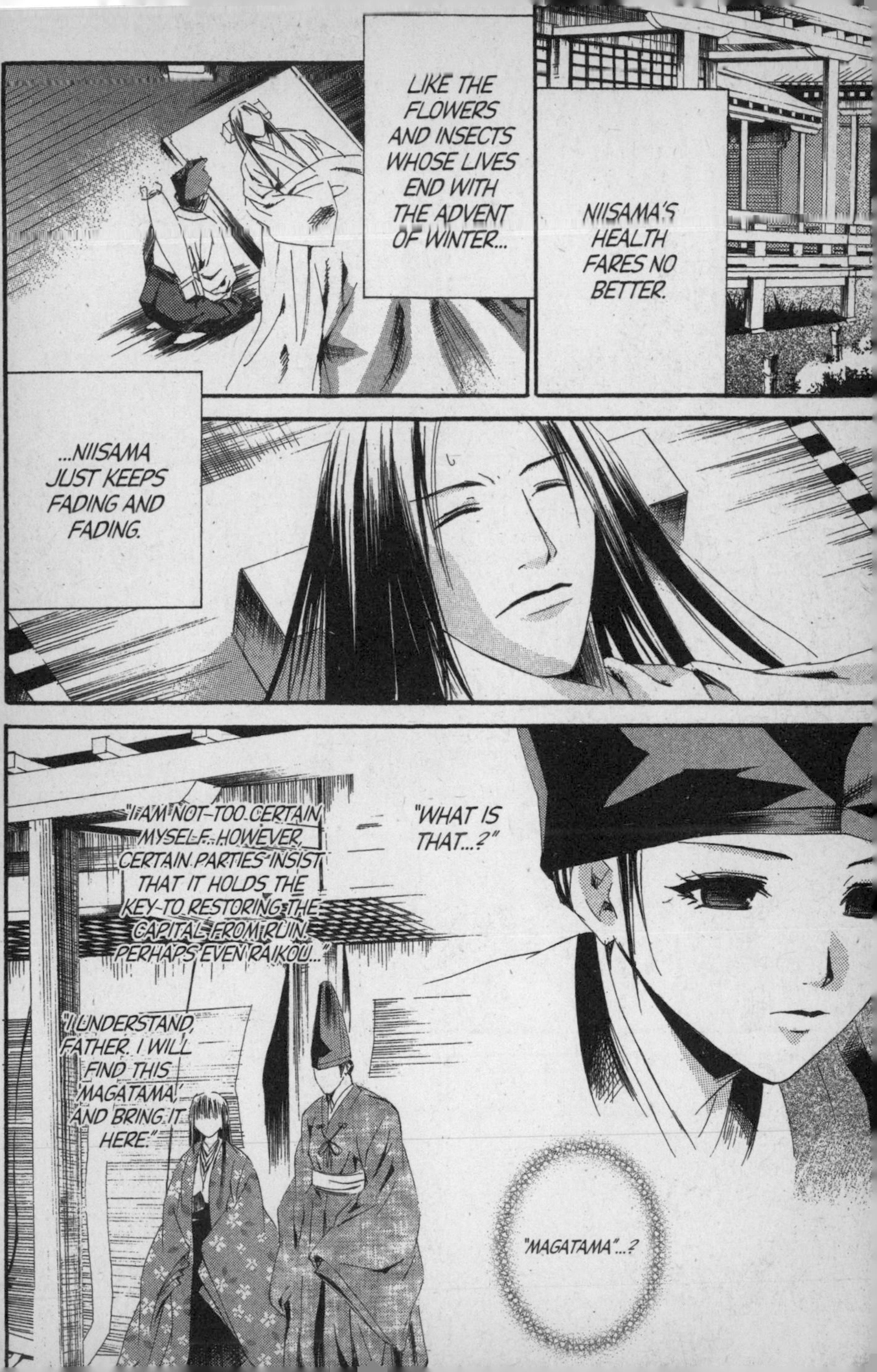
LIKE THE FLOWERS AND INSECTS WHOSE LIVES END WITH THE ADVENT OF WINTER...
NIISAMA'S HEALTH FARES NO BETTER.
...NIISAMA JUST KEEPS FADING AND FADING.
"WHAT IS THAT...?"
"I AM NOT TOO CERTAIN MYSELF. HOWEVER, CERTAIN PARTIES INSIST THAT IT HOLDS THE KEY TO RESTORING THE CAPITAL FROM RUIN. PERHAPS EVEN RAIKOU..."
"I UNDERSTAND, FATHER. I WILL FIND THIS 'MAGATAMA,' AND BRING IT HERE."
"MAGATAMA"...?

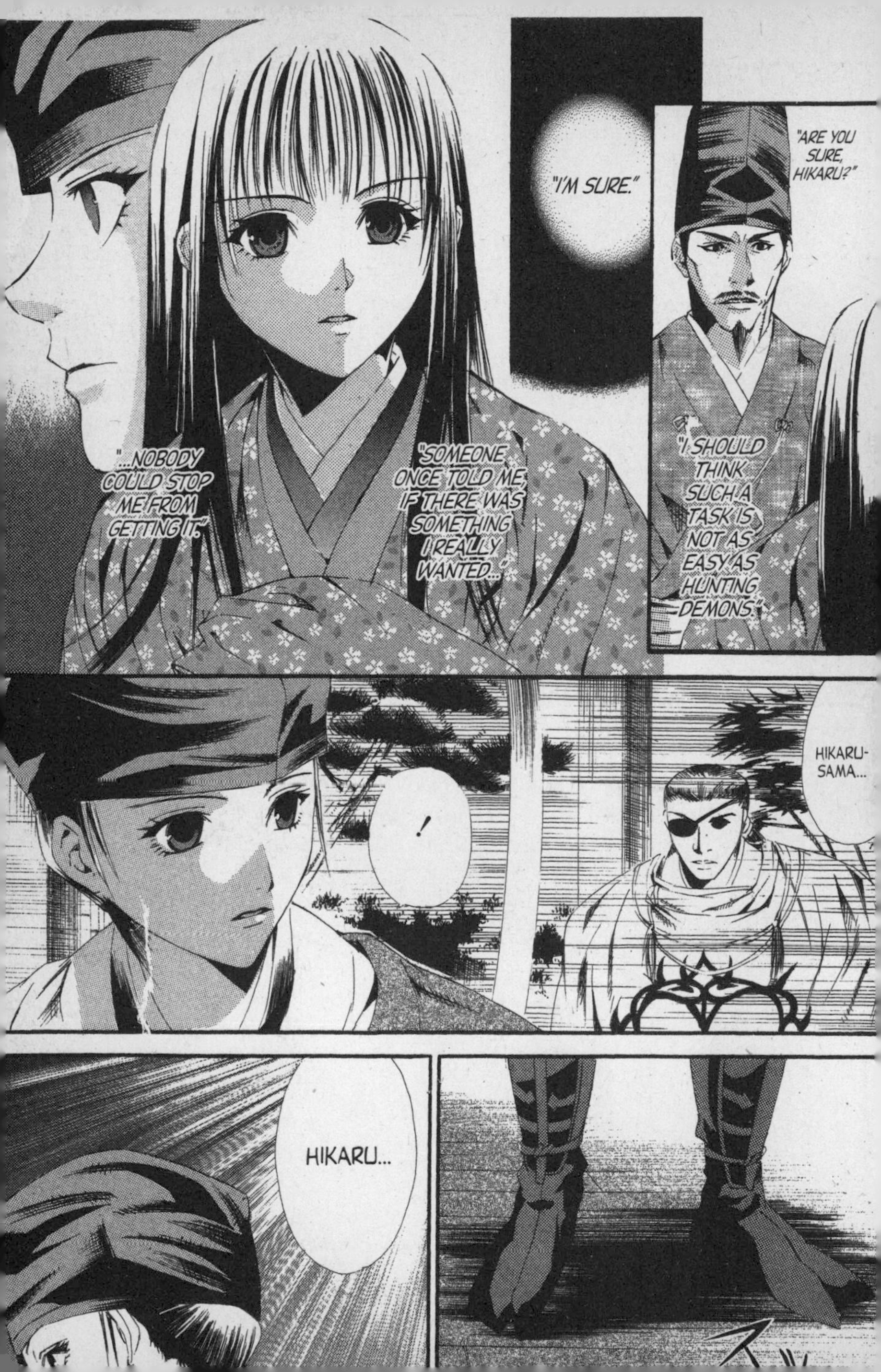
"ARE YOU SURE, HIKARU?"
"I'M SURE."
"I SHOULD THINK SUCH A TASK IS NOT AS EASY AS HUNTING DEMONS."
"SOMEONE ONCE TOLD ME, IF THERE WAS SOMETHING I REALLY WANTED..."
"...NOBODY COULD STOP ME FROM GETTING IT."
HIKARU-SAMA...
!
HIKARU...

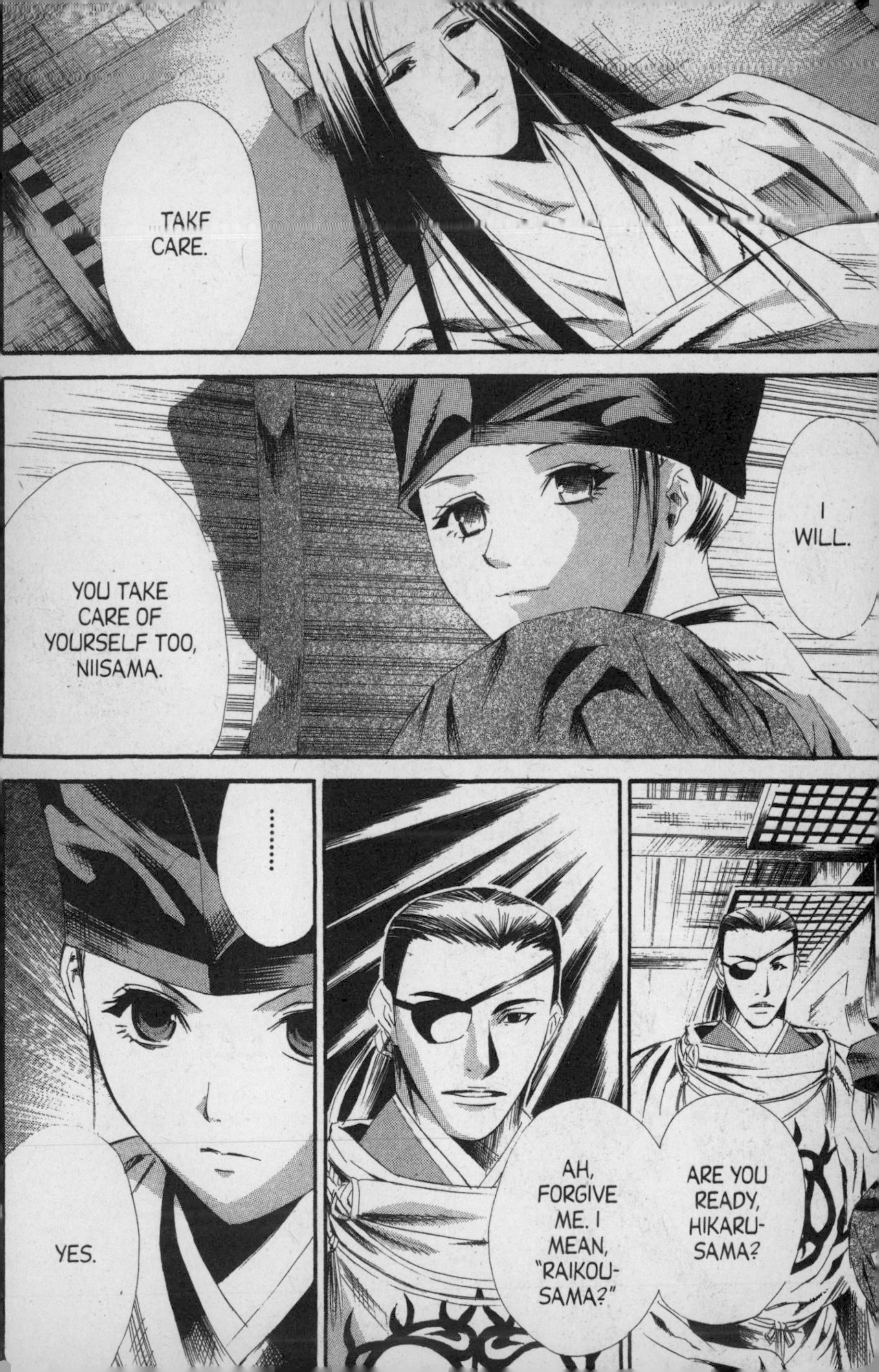
TAKF CARE.
I WILL.
YOU TAKE CARE OF YOURSELF TOO, NIISAMA.
ARE YOU READY, HIKARU-SAMA?
AH, FORGIVE ME. I MEAN, "RAIKOU-SAMA?"
....
YES.

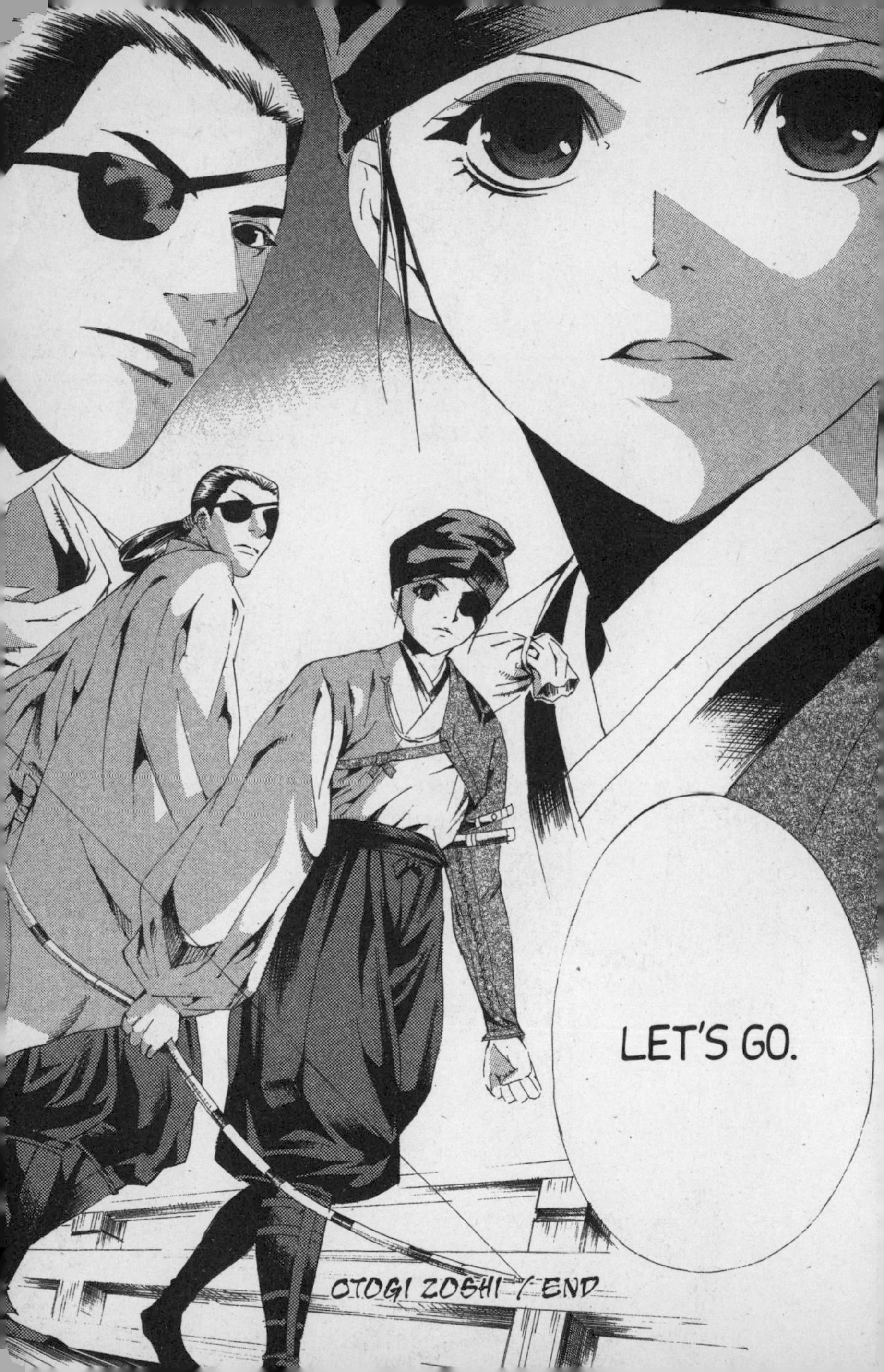
LET'S GO.
OTOGI ZOSHI / END

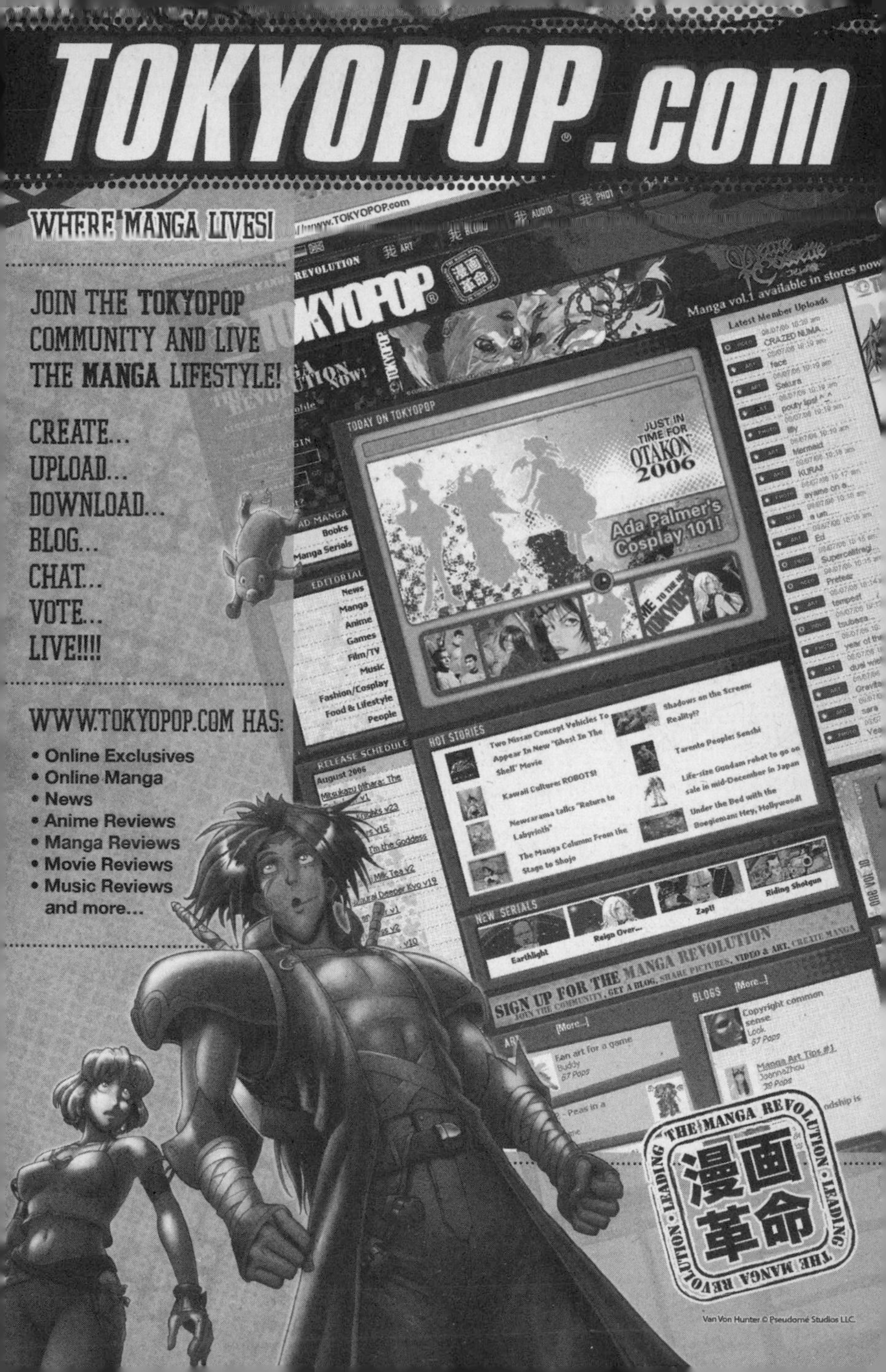
TOKYOPOP®.com
WHERE MANGA LIVES!
JOIN THE TOKYOPOP COMMUNITY AND LIVE THE MANGA LIFESTYLE!
CREATE...
UPLOAD...
DOWNLOAD...
BLOG...
CHAT...
VOTE...
LIVE!!!!
WWW.TOKYOPOP.COM HAS:
• Online Exclusives
• Online Manga
• News
• Anime Reviews
• Manga Reviews
• Movie Reviews
• Music Reviews
and more...
THE MANGA REVOLUTION • LEADING
漫画革命
Van Von Hunter © Pseudomé Studios LLC.

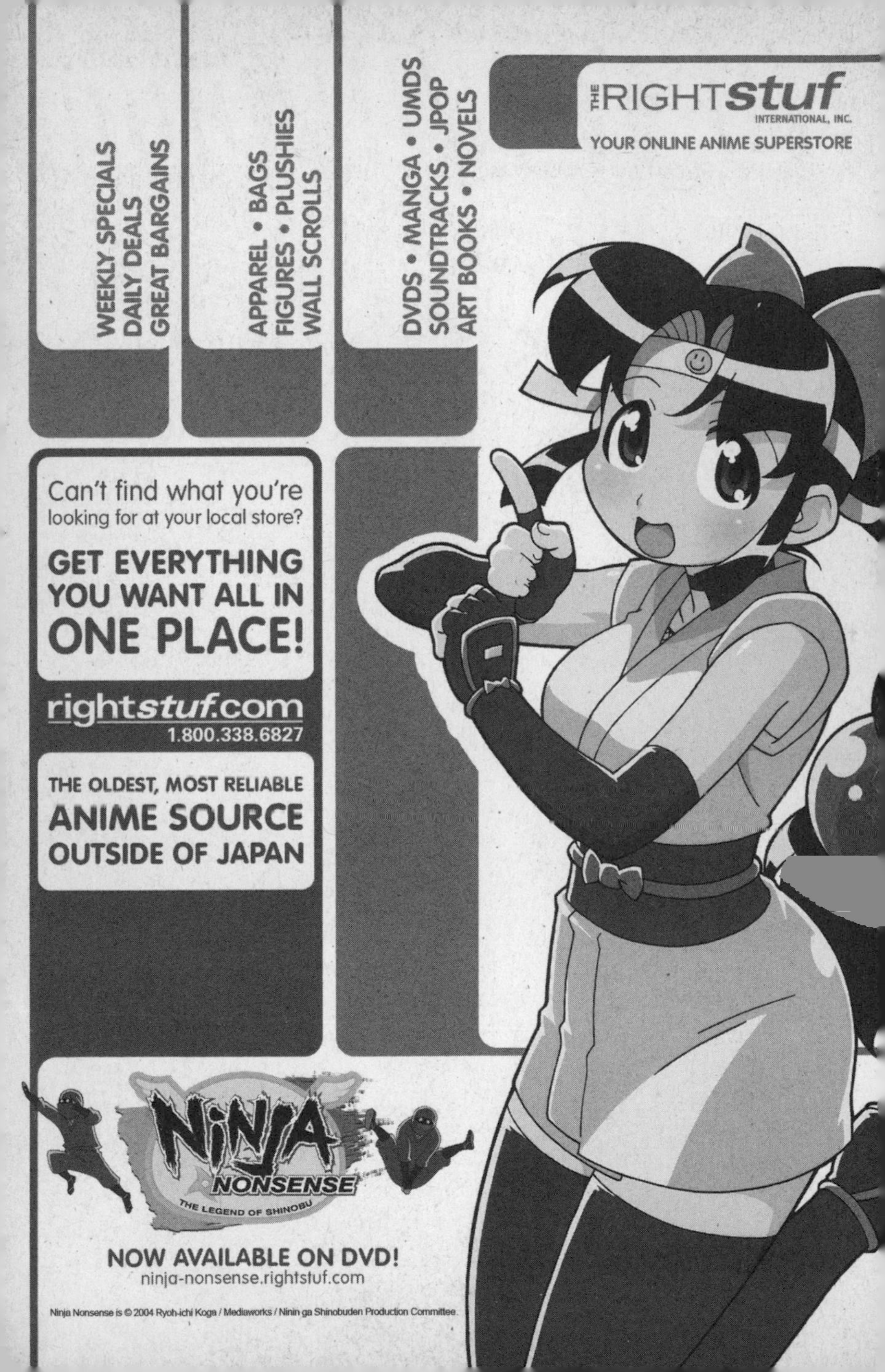

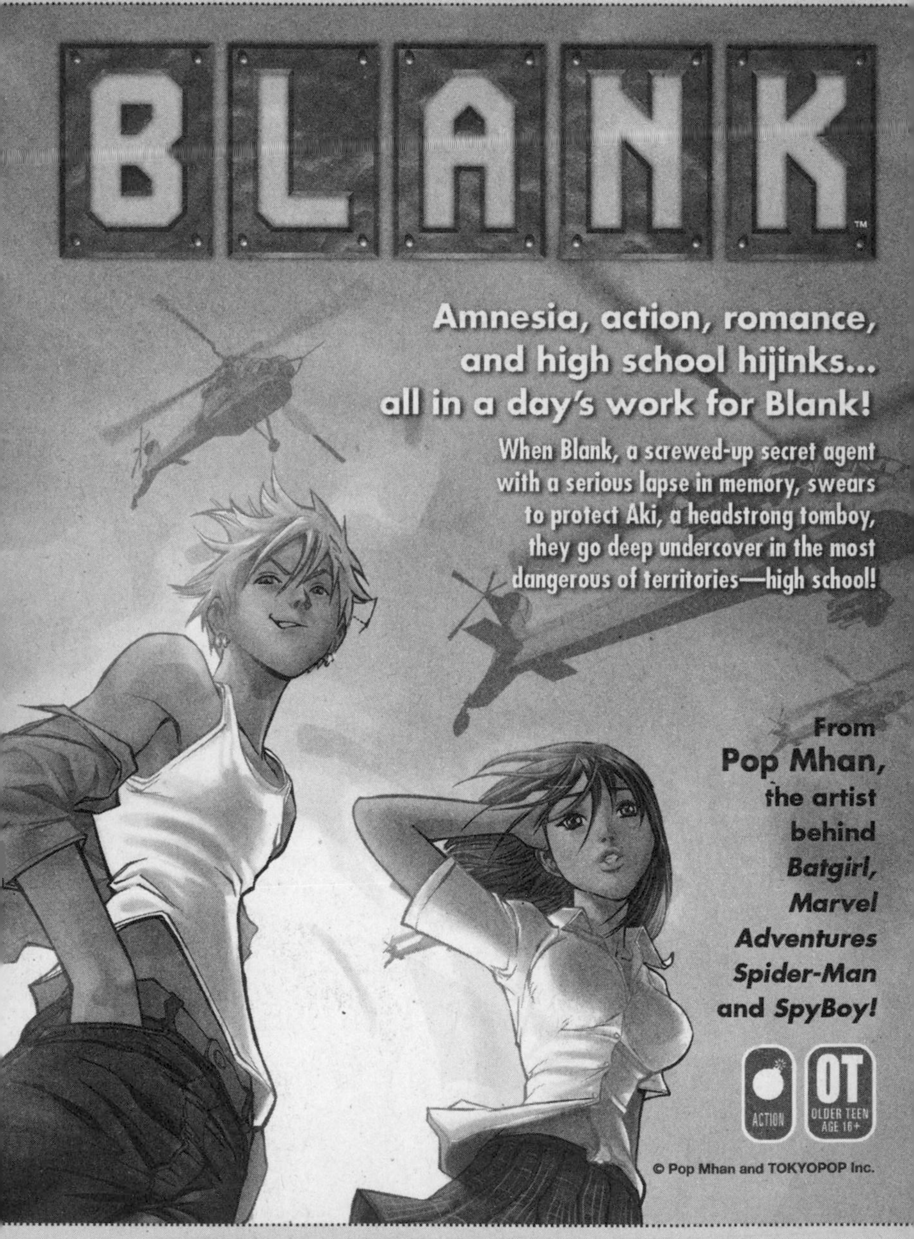
BLANK™
Amnesia, action, romance, and high school hijinks... all in a day's work for Blank!
When Blank, a screwed-up secret agent with a serious lapse in memory, swears to protect Aki, a headstrong tomboy, they go deep undercover in the most dangerous of territories—high school!
From Pop Mhan, the artist behind Batgirl, Marvel Adventures Spider-Man and SpyBoy!
ACTION
OT
OLDER TEEN AGE 16+
© Pop Mhan and TOKYOPOP Inc.